Leonard M. Wankel

S P O R T
AND SOCIAL THEORY

C. Roger Rees, PhD
Adelphi University

Andrew W. Miracle, PhD
Texas Christian University
Editors

Human Kinetics Publishers, Inc.   Champaign, Illinois

Library of Congress Cataloging-in-Publication Data
Main entry under title:

Sport and social theory.

Bibliography: p.
Includes index.
1. Sports—Social aspects—Addresses, essays,
lectures. 2. Socialization—Addresses, essays, lectures.
3. College sports—Addresses, essays, lectures. 4. Group
games—Addresses, essays, lectures. I. Rees, C. Roger.
II. Miracle, Andrew W.
GV706.5.S695 1986   306'.483   85-19758
ISBN 0-87322-041-2

Developmental Editor: Gwen Steigelman, PhD
Production Director: Ernie Noa
Copy Editor: Olga Murphy
Typesetters: Yvonne Winsor and Angie Snyder
Text Layout: Cyndy Barnes
Cover Design: Chu Usadel
Printed by: Edwards Brothers, Inc.

ISBN: 0-87322-041-2

Printed in the United States of America

10 9 8 7 6 5 4 3 2 1

Human Kinetics Publishers, Inc.
Box 5076 Champaign, IL 61820

Contents

Preface

In a penetrating review of the status of sociology of sport, John Loy (Loy, Kenyon, & McPherson, 1980) noted several problems that confronted this emerging subfield. Of great importance was the question of the "critical mass" of research, that is, the view that high quality research in sociology of sport was the exception rather than the rule. Among their suggestions to improve the situation was the contention that research in sociology of sport should be grounded in social theory. This point has been made by others in general criticisms of the field (e.g., McPherson, 1978) and in reviews of substantive areas (e.g., Bend & Petrie, 1977).

This position is reflected in the organizational structure and content of this book, a departure from the usual social problems or issue-oriented approach that typify textbooks in the sociology of sport. We recognize several dangers in our approach. Some scholars may feel that a particular theory has been overlooked, whereas some students may react negatively to the word *theory* and wonder what all the discussion is about.

We hope that the organization of the volume can reduce such problems. Because there is no wrong or right theory, the major theoretical statements in Part 1 are followed by critiques written by scholars who present a different viewpoint (e.g., Kenyon & Ingham, chapters 1 and 2; Dunning & Curtis, chapters 3 and 4). Also, the substantive areas in Part 2 are discussed from several theoretical positions (e.g., small groups, chapters 11 to 14; college athletics, chapters 15 to 18). To help students see the relevance of the theories, we have included summary notes at the end of each part that suggest suitable questions for term papers and class discussion.

Our aim, therefore, is to show the importance of social theory to the development of sociology of sport and to demonstrate its application in several substantive fields within our subdiscipline. Our hope is that this volume will encourage readers to start their search for answers to questions about sociology of sport from some theoretical perspective. This will help to increase the "critical mass" of our subdiscipline and will, we hope, ultimately lead to the wider acceptance of the utility of sociology of sport among sociologists and sport practitioners alike.

A book of readings such as this is obviously the work of many people. We are grateful to the contributors for the time taken to prepare and to revise their chapters and to their commitment to the book's theme. We also would like to acknowledge the following individuals for their special help in motivating and assisting the editors in the preparation of this volume: Aidan Dunleavy, now a research analyst with Lockheed Corporation, who coordinated the Second Annual NASSS Conference in Fort Worth, Texas, where the ideas for this volume were developed; Barry McPherson, past president of NASSS, for his consistent interest and support of this project; Rainer Martens of Human Kinetics for agreeing to publish this volume; and Gwen Steigelman, our editor, for her energy, skill, and persistence. The book would not have been possible without their help and support.

Finally, this book is dedicated to the members of NASSS and all others who aspire to the sociological study of sport.

C. Roger Rees
Andrew W. Miracle
Editors

Theoretical Perspectives

The chapters in this section reflect the current status of social theory with regard to sport. A few scholars are engaged in exciting efforts, and the field as a whole no longer seems to be an incipient one. General agreement is that it is no longer fruitful just to talk about the need for serious theoretical studies of sport. However, that is the only consensus the authors of these chapters might reach.

Kenyon (chapter 1) reviews the existing literature with regard to the significance of social theory in the development of sport sociology. His goal is two-fold: to evaluate past efforts and to determine appropriate expectations for future efforts. That even a report of the literature may be charged with theoretical bias is one of the issues raised by Ingham in chapter 2. Differences in domain assumptions as major as those that separate Kenyon and Ingham can be resolved, but it seems unlikely.

Dunning builds on the work of Elias and provides a theoretical perspective not often expressed in North American sociological circles (chapter 3). Indeed, the Atlantic appears to serve as a significant barrier to intellectual exchange between European and North American social scientists. Although Dunning's work certainly is thought-provoking, it is not without its critics. Curtis (chapter 4) evaluates the underpinnings of Dunning's theoretical foundation and suggests they are flawed.

Pearton (chapter 5) provides an intriguing theoretical discussion of a European phenomenon often cited in North American sport sociology—soccer hooliganism in the United Kingdom. Pearton's analysis, however, indicates that traditional interpretations of hooliganism may be insufficient.

Sutton-Smith (chapter 6) reassesses the relationship between play and sport. Are play and sport polar opposites? Are they culturally distinct or psychologically antithetical? Clearly, this is an important issue that may not be resolved categorically as Fine demonstrates in his response (chapter 7) to Sutton-Smith.

Although each of the chapters in this section may serve to inform, taken as a composite, they offer a rare opportunity. The reader may compare and contrast theoretical perspectives of prominent scholars who often differ diametrically. The challenge is for each individual to explore the underlying assumptions and to articulate the paradigms that the various authors have used in preparing their arguments. Such an effort may not be easy, but it should prove most rewarding for the serious student.

CHAPTER 1

The Significance of Social Theory in the Development of Sport Sociology[1]

Gerald S. Kenyon

In the beginning or shortly thereafter—depending on whether you are of creationist or evolutionist persuasion—meaningful social interaction and socially determined behavior appeared. In due course these increased in number and complexity and eventually came to include what we now call *sport*, one of our more obvious social pastimes. Until recently, common sense provided all there was to know. But, as in the case of other lasting social phenomena, the notion of going beyond common sense became attractive, and we have been in trouble ever since. Nevertheless, there arose the idea that it was time to consider sport from the perspective of the social sciences. After much speculation, together with some more or less systematic observations of various sporting elements, the question of theory predictably emerged. Here we are, still wrestling with the idea—which brings me to this rather pretentious subject, namely, "the significance of social theory in the development of sport sociology."

The topic will be approached with two questions in mind: (a) How significant has it been? and (b) How significant should we expect it to be? By way of a preview, the answer to the first is "Not particularly great," and to the second, "It has its place." Some other conclusions will also be justified, including the following:

1. We should not forget that theory is secular.
2. Theory, whether as an end or a means, will require the following to have greater significance in the sociology of sport: (a) a healthy division of labor, (b) a deliberate effort to accumulate, (c) a greater intellectual independence, and (d) an informed and acknowledged coexistence.

Before going any further, however, some boundary conditions should be stated. The sociology of sport is a more than casual attempt to understand those nontrivial and persisting social phenomena related to or part of sport, where sport is considered in a contest/physical prowess/ enduring-social-context sense. Understanding is a confirmed generalization which either describes the social characteristics of sport or explains how certain of such phenomena come to be.

First, the context for the sociology of sport will be set out; second, the activity within that context will be described by looking at some of the literature of the past 15 to 16 years; and third, the capability or capacity of sport sociology to become more theoretically interesting will be reflected upon.

Context: The Dimensions of Sport Sociology

Like any other discipline or speciality, the sociology of sport has *subject matter*, *object matter*, and something in between called *predicate matter*.

Subject Matter

The subject matter of sport sociology, surely, is all of those sport-related phenomena present within social reality, where social reality has two basic dimensions, namely, a microscopic/macroscopic continuum, and an objective/subjective continuum. These in turn, provide four domains (Ritzer, 1981): macro-objective, macro-subjective, micro-objective, and micro-subjective (Figure 1).

MACROSCOPIC

I. Macro-objective	II. Macro-subjective

OBJECTIVE ─────────────────────┼───────────────── SUBJECTIVE

III. Micro-objective	IV. Micro-subjective

MICROSCOPIC

Figure 1. Major elements of social reality.
Note. From Toward an Integrated Social Paradigm (p. 26) by G. Ritzer, 1981, Boston: Allyn and Bacon. Copyright 1981 by Allyn and Bacon. Adapted by permission.

For example, within the macro-objective domain Ritzer would include society, law, bureaucracy, architecture, technology, and language; in the macro-subjective he would include culture, norms, and values; in the micro-objective he would include patterns of behavior, action, and interaction; and in the micro-subjective domain he would include various facets of the social construction of reality (Ritzer, 1981:26). One can easily envisage one or more aspects of sport touching the various elements of each level of social reality. Any aspect of sport can be situated in such a matrix, and its specific location will have implications for how one approaches the subject matter.

Object Matter

If we have "subject matter," we also have "object matter." The object, namely, the manifest aspirations held for the sociology of sport, has both character and range. The former represents the actual consequences of sport sociology: the descriptions, the explanations, and the predictions. The range, or relevance, is from the specific to the general (Figure 2).

Character of Outcome	Range of Outcome
Descriptions	Specific to General
Explanations	Specific to General
Predictions	Specific to General
(Persuasions)	

Figure 2. Character and range of outcome.

Predicate Matter

Predicate matter, the dynamic element of a statement tying together subject and object, is the means by which the goals of sport sociology are achieved, that is, the pathway between the existential social reality of sport and the descriptions and explanations of that reality. Making progress along this pathway calls for a consideration of both conceptions and operations, each of which has several elements. For example, conceptions include paradigms, theories, models, propositions, and concepts. Operations have two major divisions: (a) formal, such as deductions and inductions; and (b) empirical, such as observations and distillations (Figure 3).

Though not without problems, each of the elements are common enough and need no further elaboration here. However, since this chapter focuses upon theory, more should be said. First, the definition of theory has almost as many variations as there are writers on the subject; sociologists hardly agree (Staples, 1981). Thus we find alleged theory varying from vague persuasions to systematic logic. For purposes here,

Conceptions	Operations
Paradigms	Formal
	deductions
Theories	inductions
general	cumulations
circumscribed	
fragments (elements)	Empirical
	observations
Models	distillations
	cumulations
Propositions	
tested-untested	
confirmed-denied	
Concepts	

Figure 3. Elements in the transformation of social reality to descriptions and explanations.

theories are simply *patterns of reasoning* applied to social reality. To reduce some of the vagueness implied by such a statement, the concept of theory has been approached from three perspectives. In the first, theory is a grand design, hereafter called *general theory*, which is characterized by efforts to incorporate large amounts of social reality. Examples are the classic schools of social theory—symbolic interactionism, structural functionalism, ethnomethodology, and so on. Second, is theory called *circumscribed theory*, or systems of thought characterized by constraints upon subject matter and method. Axiomatic or propositional theory construction best represents what is intended in this paper. The result is what Freese (1981) would call *systematic formal theory*. Third, and what might be considered as "pre-theory," is a category of more limited patterns of reasoning, called *theory elements*. While they are not theories per se, they do contribute to the pool of theoretical materials, that is, carefully formulated propositions containing as few as two elements or concepts.

As in any simple heuristic device, overlaps and inconsistencies often show up; in this case they show up as object-predicate blurs. For example, while an important goal of sport sociology is to produce generalizations, theories as such can be both the means to achieving these (my predicates) and the end result of "theorizing" (my object). So, to repeat, we have subject matter, object matter, and that which ties the two together, which has been somewhat arbitrarily broken down to include general theory, circumscribed theory, and theory elements. Having set the stage, or at least "a" stage, an examination of what has been going on within such a context follows.

Content: What Has Been Going On?

The content of the sociology of sport is, for the most part, its literature. Basically, it is either of two kinds; (a) *substantive* or (b) *comments upon substance*—some do it, and some only talk about it. With regard to the latter, the "Who are we? and Where are we going?" literature borders on the voluminous. For example, one writer (Melnick, 1979) recently produced a bibliography of over 100 entries on the subject. Several additional items have appeared since (Haag, 1979; Matveyev, 1980; Sage, 1979, 1980; Tatano, 1981; and Willimczik, 1980). Most say something about theory and its place in the sociology of sport. Opinions have ranged from "The subfield has achieved considerable theoretical growth" (Snyder & Spreitzer, 1980:19), to, "The bulk of literature on sport has degenerated into little more than the bland application of set sociological typologies, a nit-picking concern over problems of definition, pointless collections of 'social facts,' or crude phenomenological discussions of the 'meaning' of the sporting experience" (Gruneau, 1981:20). However, it is accurate to say that the majority of these contributions contain a lament—in fact it seems to have become fashionable to declare in no uncertain terms—that we pay too little attention to theory.

While no one should argue with the claim that there is more room for theory in the specialty, the extent and nature of this situation is not clear. With a few exceptions, we have not had a systematic analysis of the literature. Before we can fairly assess the significance of theory, we need to appreciate the general characteristics of sport sociology writings; and before we can say much about our object matter, we need to know more about the subject matter as well as how the two are being linked.

To achieve this, at least in part, we have analyzed a body of sport literature consisting of approximately 7,500 contributions,[2] all made since 1965. For some analyses we have taken random samples from each of three time periods, 1965 to 1972, 1973 to 1978, and 1979 to early 1981.[3] Still other analyses have been based on the literature generated by the 10 most productive scholars during each of the three periods. Such data should reveal something about, first, the subject matter that has interested the sport sociologists, which in turn might be instructive in the sense that some topics may lend themselves to particular theoretical approaches better than others; second, the styles of approaches taken to subject matter that emerges; third, the kinds of theoretical materials present and in what context; and fourth, the dominant operations employed.

The Subject Matter: What Interests the Sociologist of Sport?

It could be argued that, at least in part, the extent to which theory emerges in a specialty, and the choice of orientation, is related to subject matter,

that is, how complex it is; how well it has been conceptualized, described, or catalogued; how it is distributed on our objective/subjective and
micro/macro continua, or simply, what has interested the sport
sociologist? With regard to the latter, and without getting into an elaborate
n-way matrix, a simple count of descriptors[4] attached to the citations included in our entire data base reveals that the subjects most frequently
written about (excluding social history) since 1965 are: sport function and
dysfunction, sport involvement, sport and personality, women in sport,
attitudes, socialization, the Olympic Games, motivation, success and
failure in sport, and the coach (Table 1). If these observations are broken
down into the three time periods, some trends emerge, such as increasing interest in women and sport, the Olympics, and inequality. A wan-
ing of interest seems to be occurring in the coach and in small groups
in general. However, writers seem to have been more interested in micro-
than macrophenomena and in objective than subjective phenomena.

Approaches: What Styles Emerge?

As to how researchers have approached the subject matter, one might
expect some reference to previous work. Based on a sample of our data
base ($N = 195$), it would seem that many authors were either writing
in a vacuum or failing to acknowledge others' ideas. More specifically,
almost half had no use for the literature of the social sciences, and almost
one third felt no debt to contributions in sport studies. (Of course some
might wish to conclude that the data suggest that a large amount of fundamental and original work has been underway in the specialty.)

From the standpoint of cumulation, an element in the development of
any field, one in five reports was built directly on the work of others,
while only one-fourth were outgrowths of the author's earlier work. Either
we have been reinventing the inclined plane, and are starting at the bot-
tom at that, or the quality of such work mitigated against its later use,
or some combination of the two.

Conceptions: What Theoretical Material is Present?

Keeping in mind the first of the general questions, namely, "How significant has theory been in the sociology of sport," an analysis of the entire
data base ($N = 7473$) provides a clue to the answer, as seen in Table 1.
The number of citations having a descriptor label of "theoretical" is a
relatively small proportion of the items in the base. The proportion of
writing containing reference to theoretical material has actually been
declining somewhat over the 15-year period. Ironically, there is a lack
of correspondence between popularity of subject matter and use of explicit theory. For example, given the consistently high rankings of "sport
functions-dysfunctions," "complex organizations," "women in sport,"
and "aggression and violence," one could reasonably expect far greater
appearance of functionalist or conflict theories than has appeared in earlier

Table 1. Number of Contributions to the Literature by Subject, Over Three Periods of Time: What Has Interested the Sport Sociologist?

Subject	1965-72		1973-78		1979-early-1981		Total	
	N	Rank	N	Rank	N	Rank	N	Rank
Sport: Functions-Dys-functions	239	2	597	1	170	1	1006	1
Sport Involvement	207	4	534	2	165	2	906	2
Modern Social History	251	1	468	3	153	4	872	3
Personality	213	3	353	5	122	5	688	4
Women	109	6	373	4	160	3	642	5
Attitude	104	7	303	6	90	7	497	6
Socialization	85	9	246	7	79	9	410	7
Olympic Games	81	10	193	9	108	6	382	8
Motivation	67	13	223	8	85	8	375	9
Theoretical	112	5	183	10.5	65	13	360	10
Success-Failure	55	15	183	10.5	76	11	314	11
Coaches	71	12	142	14	49	17.5	262	12
Intercollegiate	49	19	130	16	78	10	257	13
Values	53	16	149	12	46	20.5	248	14
Social Change	39	22	136	15	49	17.5	224	15.5
Aggression	36	23	121	17.5	67	12	224	15.5
Social Structure	90	8	110	20	20	29	220	17
Self	51	17	121	17.5	46	20.5	218	18.5
Economics	50	18	145	13	23	26	218	18.5
Spectators	57	14	103	23	48	19	208	20
Complex Organization	28	25.5	116	19	58	14.5	202	21
Religion	47	20.5	107	21	24	25	178	22
Play	47	20.5	97	24.5	25	24	169	23
Small Groups	74	11	76	28	17	31.5	167	24.5
Social Class	21	29.5	105	22	41	22.5	167	24.5
Violence	18	31	84	26	54	16	156	27
Family	21	29.5	97	24.5	41	22.5	159	26
Equality-Inequality	16	32	73	29	58	14.5	147	28
Ideology	25	28	78	27	21	27.5	124	29
Socio-Demographic	28	25.5	71	31	21	27.5	120	30
Voluntary Associations	30	24	72	30	10	34	112	31
Cohesion	27	27	53	33.5	9	35	89	32
Femininity	12	34	56	32	19	30	87	33
Stratification	15	33	53	33.5	14	33	82	34
Achievement Motivation	8	35	51	35	17	31.5	76	35

Note. Ns reflect descriptor usage, and therefore neither subjects nor counts are mutually exclusive.

analyses. Although a more extensive investigation would be needed, it might be instructive to cross-tabulate major theoretical orientations with choice of subject matter.

General Theory

When theory is present, however, it may be interesting to examine the various persuasions that might be represented (see Table 2). Using a random sample (N = 174) of the literature base, and although necessarily relying on somewhat tenuous and usually implicit indicators, it appears that three-quarters of the contributions suggested no discernable theoretical orientation; but of those remaining, approximately half fell into the "social behavior" category (Ritzer, 1975). Since frequencies were so small, trends over three time periods were difficult to observe. However, where theory is present some suggestion exists that a structural-functionalist orientation is less common in recent years, as might be expected.

Table 2. Frequency of Appearance of Theoretical Orientations in a Sample of Sport Sociology Literature: 1965 to mid-1981.

Theoretical Orientations (Ritzer, 1975 categories)	N	%
Social Facts		
Structural-Functional	9	
Conflict	3	
Systems Theory	0	
Total	12	6.9
Social Definition		
Action Theory	4	
Symbolic Interactionism	1	
Phenomenological Sociology	5	
Total	10	5.7
Social Behavior		
Behavioral Sociology	22	
Exchange Theory	0	
Total	22	12.6
No Discernable Orientation		
Total	130	74.7
Grand Total	174	99.9

A danger exists, of course, in overlooking the possibility that modal approaches may mask the contributions of those most committed, that is, those who publish regularly and establish sizable curricula vitae or those making the more novel or most "important" contributions. It is to the latter, the "frontiersmen," the most theoretically committed, which we now turn.

Since no satisfactory objective criterion exists to select the most important contributors, this paper will describe first the sport sociology literature that reflects the traditional schools of social theories, including: structural-functionalism, conflict theory, systems theory, action theory, symbolic interactionism, phenomenological sociology, behavioral sociology, and exchange theory. While these labels are those of Ritzer (1975), they appear on most lists of theoretical orientations in one form or another.

Structural-Functionalism. During the late 1960s and early 1970s, North American sport sociology was said to be bourgeois, consensus, and "establishment" oriented (Hoch, 1972). Positivist, empiricist, and functional modeling were running rampant. However, an examination of the literature of the time suggests that it might have been rather devoid of social critique, but hardly bursting with explicit structural-functionalism. Again, very little was running at all, let alone rampant. Serious contributions based upon an explicit functionalist approach have been rare, with some exceptions found in the work of Heinila (1967), Milton (1972), Dunning (1973), Stevenson (1974), and two relatively early pieces by Plessner (1952) and Leitgeb (1955). Most writers who make reference to structural-functional theory have done so in a programmatic or analytical sense. In fact in recent years little use has been made of an explicit functionalist approach,[5] perhaps a spin-off of the so-called "crisis" in American sociology of the '60s (Gouldner, 1970).

Conflict Theory. A cursory glance at the literature reveals that social conflict and conflict theory have hardly been absent from sport literature. There have been numerous writings from psychological and psychiatric perspectives and on the microsociological level of sport contests and sport groups. With regard to the latter, we have seen some useful work (e.g., Lenk, 1965; and Watson, 1977a,b). However, it is at the organizational and cultural level, that is, the macrosociological level where considerably more attention can be found, particularly in recent years (e.g., Kiviaho & Mustikkamaa, 1978; Dunning & Sheard, 1976; and Taylor, 1971). Much of the work has been set in a Marxist or neo-Marxist context with papers by Marxist apologists from socialist and nonsocialist countries alike (e.g., Erbach, 1966; Kidd, 1978; Schulz, 1961; and Stolyarov, 1980). Serious analytical work, of and through Marxist sociology applied to sport, has become relatively substantial (e.g., Lenk, 1973; Brohm, 1976; Helmes, 1978; and Sugden, 1980). Work appearing today under the broad spectrum of conflict sociology represents one of the most serious "movements" that we have seen in sport sociology.[6] This opinion has been reinforced by the quality of papers presented and by the ensuing discussion at the 1981 Regional Symposium of the International Committee for the Sociology of Sport in Vancouver, under such titles as: "Sport, Value and Fetishism of Commodities; Central Issues of Alienated Sport" (Beamish), "Class and Community, the Formation and Control of an English Professional Football club" (Korr), and "State Interventionism, The Wage Labour/Capital Relationship and Sport" (Helmes).

Systems Theory and Action Theory. Somewhat surprisingly, neither of these orientations seem to have been popular among sociologists of sport, although in a slightly different context, the former has been said to have a rich potential (Ziegler, 1980).

Symbolic Interactionism. The early contributions of the late Greg Stone notwithstanding, symbolic interactionism has only attracted a modest following. Interest remains alive, however, judging by some recent papers (e.g., Birrell, 1981; Turowetz & Rosenberg, 1978; and Watson & Wells, 1978).

Phenomenological Sociology. Despite the writings of sociologists in general, sociologists of sport have largely eschewed phenomenological approaches, although the occasional programmatic piece has appeared (Whitson, 1976). It would seem that such an approach is of greater interest to the sport philosopher or sport psychologist. In the latter category, the work of Csikszentmihalyi (1975) and his concept of "flow" has been of some interest to the sport sociologist.

Behavioral Sociology. Although not always made explicit, much of the sport literature seems to fit a behaviorist orientation, particularly if we allow social psychological contributions into the pool.

Exchange Theory. Despite a paper or two in the literature, there seems to be little explicit interest here, although as Ritzer (1981) suggests, it is a much more important perspective than behavioral sociology. Again, this is somewhat surprising given the heavy social-psychological approach in much of the sport studies literature.

Circumscribed Theory

The foregoing suggests that general theory has not loomed large in the literature of sport sociology. Another way of looking at the presence of theory in the literature, however, is to examine writings for any hint of formal statements that might be the forerunners to systematic formal theory (Freese, 1981). Approximately one tenth of our sample did contain stated hypotheses or propositions capable of testing. Moreover, precursors to systematic formal theory appear in somewhat greater numbers in the more recent literature.

Theory Elements: As Reflected in the Work
of the Most Prolific of the Sport Sociologists

Using the same data base, the 10 authors with the highest number of contributions to the literature for each of the three time intervals were identified. Their combined writings totaled 188, 162, and 97 for each of the three periods respectively (Table 3). Overall, the proportion of contributions suggesting theoretical content exceeded the proportion without theoretical content during each period, but only if a rather loose definition of "theoretical" is used, namely, any effort to explain phenomena in question using concepts drawn from the social sciences. Writers rarely mentioned traditional "schools" of theory explicitly, or authors usually associated with specific schools. *Empirical* content appeared in fewer than half of the writings (Table 4). Examining the trends over time suggests that in recent years the literature produced by the more prolific writers is becoming less theoretical.[7] Moreover, the proportion of articles with the empirical content peaked during the middle period (1973-78), but dropped precipitously in recent years. Life cycle effects might explain these results, at least in part. However, overlap occurred only for two authors from 1965-72 to 1973-78, and for four authors from 1973-78 to 1979-mid-1981.

While only indirectly, a citation analysis of the most productive writers in the sociology of sport can be indicative of the extent to which their literature relates to that of mainstream social science. One analysis of this nature (Spreitzer, Snyder, & Jordan, 1980) suggested that between 1973 and 1977, the work of "core" authors in the sociology of sport (those having published 10 or more articles during the period, as based upon Loy, McPherson, & Kenyon, 1978a) was being incorporated into the larger discipline, as shown in Table 5.

Table 3. Frequency of Empirical Content in the Work of the 10 Most Prolific Writers in the Sociology of Sport for Each of Three Time Intervals

Empirical Content	1965-72		1973-78		1979-early-1981		Total	
	N	%	N	%	N	%	N	%
Present	64	34.0	74	45.7	30	30.9	168	37.6
Absent	99	52.6	68	42.0	67	69.1	234	52.3
Uncertain	25	13.3	20	12.3	0	0.0	45	10.1
Total	188	99.9	162	100.0	97	100.0	447	100.0

Table 4. Frequency of Theoretical Material in the Work of the 10 Most Prolific Writers in the Sociology of Sport for Each of Three Time Intervals

Content	1965-72		1973-78		1979-early-1981		Total	
	N	%	N	%	N	%	N	%
Theoretical Material	93	49.5	82	50.6	52	53.6	227	50.8
No Theoretical Material	65	34.5	54	33.3	43	44.3	162	36.2
Uncertain	30	16.0	26	16.1	2	2.1	58	13.0
Total	188	100.0	162	100.0	97	100.0	447	100.0

Table 5. Citations of Most Productive Writers in the Sociology of Sport

Journal Type	1973-77	
	N	%
General Sociology	321	52.1
Sport Sociology	50	8.1
Physical Education	76	12.3
Other Academic Disciplines	162	26.3
Interdisciplinary	7	1.2
Total	616	100.0

Note. Compiled from Spreitzer, Snyder, and Jordan (1980), based upon Loy's (1978) "core" of 18 authors.

Operations: Which Dominate?

It would appear that the proportion of data-based writings, whether quantitative or qualitative, has diminished considerably over these three time periods, from well over 50% during the early years to just over 30% at present (mid-1981). The individual is the dominant unit of analysis over the full decade and a half. The number of strictly empirical studies is clearly diminishing from close to 60% in the 1965-72 period to just over 30% in recent years.

Finally, two additional observations: The proportion of literature coming from North American authors seems to be steadily increasing, though crudely observed in this analysis; and there seems to be a slight improvement more recently in the degree to which authors have related their work to the parent discipline.

Capacity: What Can Be Expected From Sport Sociology?

From the foregoing, it is apparent that the significance of theory, no matter how you "cut it," is not great in the sport sociology literature, whether explicitly or implicitly, or whether as general theory or theory in more contained forms. However, rather than succumb to the temptation of further and prolonged self-castigation, what should we expect from a field that has yet "to come in from the cold" (Loy, McPherson, & Kenyon, 1978a); a field that has yet to reach either the "specialty" stage (Mullins, 1973), or the "intellectual autonomy stage" (Selznick, 1959)? Again, the rather formidable barriers of a less-than-critical mass, low academic status, and conflicting ideological orientations (Loy, McPherson, & Kenyon, 1978b) go a long way in explaining our plight. Moreover, if we need to, we can take comfort in the fact that other specialties are in the same boat. For example, those who study the military are still debating whether it should be the sociology of the military or military sociology.[8] Nevertheless, whether or not Godot may some day come, there is no need to sit on our hands while waiting.

Returning to my simple declarative sentence—There is no shortage of subject matter, from subjective to objective, from the micro to the macro— the object of the specialty is still worth pursuing. Moreover, signs show that the richness of our predicates is rising; an increasing number of sport sociologists are comfortable and competent in the world of general theory; in fact it is here where we are seeing some of the better scholarship in the field today. With regard to more circumscribed approaches, despite some efforts, there is room for more initiative here, something that will be further discussed later.

No doubt the field will always witness considerable interest in the formulation and test of theory elements. Although the theory elements represent a quick-and-dirty route to getting into the literature, if done well, they provide new information and contribute to the construction of nonelaborate theoretical schemes. However, to move to a higher level of maturity as a sociological specialty, we might benefit from closer attention to such matters as a healthy division of labor, cumulation, intellectual independence, acknowledged and informed coexistence, and finally, a recognition that at times theory may be a misplaced goal. But first, perhaps we should discard some old saws.

Some Old Saws

Since 1965, and continuing to the present, there has been an abundance of self-analyses and disciplinary polemics. We have heard much of normative versus nonnormative, basic versus applied, theoretical versus empirical, middle range versus general theory, and radical versus traditional world views. No doubt the last word has not been heard on any of these, but dwelling on such issues should not be the substance of the specialty, except for those interested in history or wanting to seriously pursue the sociology of sport sociology. Apart from occasional stock-taking, time and energies should be placed elsewhere.

A Healthy Division of Labor

Sometimes we forget that there really is a distinction between sociology and its practitioners. While confirmed generalizations are the stuff of sociology, it does not necessarily follow that individual sociologists appear on stage during each act. Some are more at home in the abstract world of general systems, while others relish in elaborate multivariate attacks on large data sets. A few seem to have a firm grasp of both. What is necessary is a healthy mix of all types, and more importantly, an awareness of each other's existence. If our ultimate aim is to arrive at explanations, whether in the form of general theories, circumscribed theories, or even theory fragments, I suggest the best payoff will come from collaborative efforts, where the special skills and perspectives of several persons, all with an interest in a specified problem, are brought together routinely—both as challenge agents and contributors to a significant outcome. For example, the research group has been shown to be most effective, if not essential, in the natural and biological sciences. Although circumstances are not entirely alike, and while some team efforts are in evidence in sport sociology, I believe the potential payoffs for advancing the field are great. But it must happen on a regular ongoing basis, and not depend on the occasional meeting together at national and international meetings. Some would say such a proposal is unrealistic given the geographical and critical mass problems of our field. However, using the capabilities of computer conferencing for starters, lack of physical proximity is no longer a barrier. In fact for the first time we have the prospect of "rolling scholarship," whereby a network of 5-20 scholars representing a variety of theoretical persuasions can trade blows with relative ease, or a smaller group with members of more or less common orientation could fine-tune some circumscribed theoretical materials.

Cumulation

Simply put, the field needs more cumulative research. Cumulative is not meant as the often heard (and valid) call for more panel or longitudinal studies. If this is a problem in sociology it is even a greater one in sport sociology, as the data cited earlier attest. The lack of research and scholarships designed to accumulate and integrate findings over a period of time stems in part from the absence of an appropriate critical mass, but also from some of the same powerful mitigating circumstances as those found in the parent field. These include (a) research fashions and fads precipitated by major social issues of the time; (b) the negative aspects of the academic reward system, whereby quick results pay off better than "none-for-now," driving projects to too narrow a scope; (c) the fact that replication often goes unrewarded when competing with novelty; and (d) the increase in theoretical alternatives, which sometimes produces subsequent bandwagon effects—mainstream fashions tend to produce theoretical gadflies in the subfields. In addition a reluctance still exists among sport sociologists to take a serious analytical stance in dealing with the work of others. However, there are exemplars in sociology per se (e.g., the Lazarsfeld studies; the stratification work of Blau & Duncan; and Berger et al.). But most of these efforts have been heavy on the empirical side. In sport sociology some work is beginning to accumulate in such subjects as social differentiation, socialization, centrality, and sport and career. In quantitative terms, however, albeit crude, only 9% of the most published authors in sociology of sport contained self-references, compared to 60% of those in the top sociology journals (Spreitzer, Snyder, & Jordan, 1980). What is needed is an incentive system that would lead to clearly delineated but concentrated programs of research by both individuals and groups, in which such efforts would have the characteristics of focus, meaningfulness, interaction, feedback, revision, testing, and retesting. Also, the gatekeepers of conferences and journals could do more to encourage such work, although the support of granting agencies and academic institutions will be slow in coming.

While empirical studies come to mind when cumulative work is mentioned, what is probably most needed is *cumulative theory*, whereby efforts of individuals and possibly groups are concentrated on the development and critical appraisal of theoretical materials leading to increasing scope and logical efficacy.[9] Here the distinction should be noted between theory use and theory development. Where theory is made explicit in the sociology of sport, it tends to represent the former, that is, theory use.

Intellectual Independence

The question of whether the sociology of sport is in any way separate or outside of sociology per se arises from time to time (Ball & Loy, 1975).

It is assumed here that it is not. But this does not mean that mainstream sociology can or should be considered uncritically when employed for the study of sport.

Given the availability of theoretical alternatives, too often we see un-justifiable amounts of energy devoted to "defense work," that is, the justification of one perspective while criticizing those who would choose another. This is particularly problematic, given the state of the parent discipline. For example, we have on the one hand, Bernstein (1976) describing the decline and fall of so-called "mainstream" social science, perhaps to the point in which it has reached "intellectual paralysis" (Rossi, 1981). On the other hand, we have Collins (1975:1) stating that "we now have a solid framework of a scientific sociology," indeed, "the elements of a powerful explanatory theory," and more recently from a subfield perspective, Hauser (1981:62) stating that sociology as a science is "gaining in ascendency at an accelerated rate."

So what is a poor sport sociologist to do? Well, now is hardly the time to be using current social theory unexamined. But then again there probably never was a time when this should have been done. Thus, a degree of detachment, but not withdrawal, is appropriate. Also, the danger exists of ignoring perfectly legitimate theoretical materials because others presently enjoy greater popularity. In a word, it would be a pity to abandon "mainstream social science" before really giving it a "go." Having alternatives to structural-functionalism, or to any other orientation is one thing, but assuming that it has nothing to offer the sociology of sport is quite another.

The true test of intellectual independence comes when the sport sociologist takes on social theory per se, either in recognition of the need for its modification to incorporate sport phenomena or, via the study of sport, the discovery of a fundamental flaw in the theory itself. When we see more of this we will have achieved intellectual maturity. Mere imitation will not do. For example, making symbolic interactionism or exchange theory fit to sport is almost tautological since sport, after all, is a social phenomenon. Thus, in reflecting upon the sport sociology literature, in general, it would seem that we need more invention and less reinvention. Otherwise we will not be at the frontier, but only filling in behind it.

Acknowledged and Informed Coexistence

If a degree of tolerance is in order among those of different general theoretical persuasions, so it is among those choosing approaches within circumscribed theory or theory elements, though our expectations for each should differ somewhat.

General Theory

Approaching sport from the perspective of classical social theory keeps one in good company, tends to maintain a broad view of the scene, and

permits the use of a large and well-critiqued literature. So when alienation in sport is looked at from a Marxist perspective, or status attainment
is looked at from a Weberian view, we should expect analyses of considerable sophistication. However, a danger lies in the formal or artificial
use of theoretical materials that were produced at different times and
under different circumstances or were less than precise in their application. Inevitably, we have controversy over meaning, among other problems. In fairness, some recent work in the sociology of sport has reflected
a keen sensitivity to history. Nevertheless, the use of general theory for
the analysis and explanation of sport phenomena can produce some interesting accounts of sport not otherwise obvious, which in turn can add
to the storybook of humanity. However, the stories told are also ends
in themselves, a kind of intellectual cultural products. As such, expectations necessarily need to be limited when we demand explanations or
even predictions of discrete events.

Not everyone has been satisfied with what often appears to be vague
persuasion. As Freese (1981:348) has observed, "classically, sociological
theory has developed on the model of a discursive system of theoretical,
empirical, and historical insights produced by deep thinkers, on whose
attributed profundity the staying power of their insights in part have
depended." Or, in commenting on the diversity of theory, "The problem
is that language, conceptions, proposals, interpretations and results of
formal theorizing are so thoroughly labelized. The hallmark of the
literature is its incredible anarchy" (Freese, 1980:189). Nevertheless, we
should not overlook the fact that various schools of social theory have
been fine-tuned to make them coherent systems of thought, often with
empirical referents.

Circumscribed Theory

For those less comfortable with grand designs, we have seen efforts to
make the construction of theory more systematic or "formal," from the
natural language propositions of Zetterberg to the structural equations
of Blalock and systematic formal theory of Freese. These approaches are
largely methodology and not so much connected to specific schools of
theory, although Homans' work and exchange theory employ such
strategies. Thus, classical sociology theories "must now compete with
the model of a formal system of law-like propositions whose staying
power depends on their logical and empirical adequacy as assessed
through formal and quantitative methods" (Freese, 1981:349). So if
systematic formal theory is largely methodological, where does that leave
the sport sociologist? I suggest that it frees them from the dogma of general
theory without having to discard some or many of the ideas contained
within. Problems remain, however, particularly with the creation of adequate operational definitions of the concepts contained in the system of
equations under study. So while the design of research and the treat-

ment of quantitative data have reached high levels of achievement, the "measurement" problem persists and deserves far greater attention than it has received heretofore. By way of one example, the ideas of Harry Webb have been incorporated into a sizable number of studies (probably more than Webb intended). Yet the operational substantiation has been attended to with remarkably little rigor.

Finally, with regard to increasing the sources of circumscribed theories, there is a growing recognition of the importance of "conditionalization" (Walker & Cohen, 1981), whereby the researcher specifies "scope" conditions to preserve the falsifiability of theories without making them universally false.[10]

Theory Elements

As Goffman (1981:4) recently observed: "I have grave doubts about the value of recent grand sociological theories, and even about their circumspect successors—theories of the middle range (It is our easy use of the term "theory" everywhere in sociology, not our having any, that marks us off from those disciplines that do)—So what we need, I feel, is a modest but persistent analyticity: frameworks of the lower range." Although the comprehensiveness of general theory can be reduced and controlled somewhat through systematic formal theorizing, much empirical and logical complexity can remain. Thus there are times when a more fundamental exercise is called for, namely: In what way and to what extent is X a function of Y where X and Y are social concepts and where their relationship might serve as an important element in theory either general or circumscribed? Or, as Homans has put it, we should find a proposition and test it, without worrying about theory. Sooner or later a leap of the imagination "will suggest what general propositions must be invented or borrowed to explain the empirical ones" (Homans, 1980:21). Thus, I suggest that curiosity about simple relationships is a legitimate reason for formulating propositions for empirical tests. Once tested ("Nothing is more precious than a tested proposition" [Homans]), the result may very well be a useful element in theories to come.

In general, we need to acknowledge different orientations toward theory and its construction. The expectations are different, as should be the criteria used to evaluate the results. Acknowledging alternative approaches to one's own goes part way, but understanding the others' is to go a lot farther. Perhaps we should seek greater mutual awareness, not as mere tolerance, or even as an "ecumenical" gesture, but to create a larger reservoir of ideas so that our work goes beyond both dogma and cowardly eclecticism.

Theory as Mistaken Goal

As stated at the outset, sociologists of sport should strive to establish confirmed generalizations that either describe the social characteristics of sport or explain how such phenomena come to be. Theory, of course, can, and very often should, help to achieve these goals. Nevertheless, it is a mistake to suggest that theory is sacred. Distaining "mere descriptions" (Snyder & Spreitzer, 1980) is misplaced and idle, however fashionable it might be. Moreover, theory, particularly of the grand variety, can be an unseeing slave master.

But if dogma is inappropriate, intellectual anarchy is equally so. Rather, I suggest that our objective ought to be simply that of sound scholarship and all that it implies, no matter how old-fashioned that may appear.

Summary and Conclusion

With regard to the significance of theory in the sociology of sport, an analysis of the literature suggested that in explicit terms theory hardly prevails, but in more implicit terms it shows up here and there. If theory is in short supply, to some extent this is understandable, but if we are to achieve a higher level of intellectual maturity, including the greater use of theory—general, circumscribed, and elemental, I suggest that we: (a) acknowledge a division of labor; (b) seek more cumulation, both empirical and theoretical; (c) move further toward intellectual independence; (d) acknowledge alternative perspectives; (e) set first-rate scholarship as our overriding objective; and finally (f) declare a 10-year moratorium on conference sessions addressed to the subject of this chapter.

Notes

1. I am greatly indebted to B. Brown for extensive assistance with the tedious work of sampling, interpreting, and numerically distilling the sport sociology literature; to B. Smith and G. Wheeler for help with searching the SIRLS data base; to J. Curtis, B. McPherson, and N. Theberge for taking the time on very short notice to read and constructively comment upon an earlier version of this paper; to G. Monahan for preparing the manuscript under great pressure of time; and to L. MacDonald for preparing the references.
2. The "population" in question was the appropriate part of the SIRLS data base at the University of Waterloo. More particularly, three random samples of about 65 citations each were drawn from a population of 7,473 records. The latter emerged when the data base was searched by the key words: sport, performance, game, and play. Those not meeting the sport as contest/physical prowess criteria were discarded. About 90% were in the English language, with two-thirds originating in North America.
3. The periods chosen were not entirely arbitrary. So that possible comparisons might be made at another time, they conform to those used in a previous contribution that analyzes the stages of development of sport sociology as a specialty. (Loy, McPherson, & Kenyon, 1978b).
4. Out of obvious necessity, the descriptors were those used in the SIRLS systems and as such were not designed to meet the objectives of this study as such.

5. Interestingly, Ponomarov, from the Soviet Union, in a paper given at the 1978 World Congress of Sociology in Uppsala, built his entire thesis on a functionalist approach.
6. I particularly like the example of scholarly play provided by Ball (1973b) in his analysis of Monopoly and Marx.
7. "Theoretical" and "empirical" are not mutually exclusive categories.
8. A discussion heard at the 76th Annual Meeting of the American Sociological Association, Toronto, August, 1981.
9. An interesting set of "research strategies," which clearly represent a program of research, has been outlined by Gruneau (1981:214-215).
10. "Circumscribed theory" suggests limited in magnitude, such as Merton's theories of the middle range. While not wanting to exclude these, I am more concerned with theory restricted in scope, but not necessarily comprised of a system of formal equations.

Contra the Dominant Paradigm in the Sociology of Sport: A Response to Kenyon

Alan G. Ingham

Let me state at the outset that Gerald Kenyon has been given a thankless task. He, in effect, has been set up as the clay pigeon. I would like to take this opportunity not only to fire a salvo at Kenyon, but also to take some potshots at the scholarship in the field as well.

Obviously Kenyon, like most positivists, did not try to praise philosophy but to bury it. Thus, for now, I want to direct my attention to his concern for a division of labor exemplified in his use of Ritzer's (1981) categories, and then to outline what I would infer from the use of SIRLS descriptors and frequency counts regarding the development of the field.

Inadequacy of the Ritzer Typology

Ritzer (1981) presents us with a four-fold typology concerning the type of theorizing visible in the parent discipline of sociology (see chapter 1, Figure 1). The typology is constructed vis-à-vis the object of sociologists' studies. The four quadrants then are the macro-objective, the micro-objective, the macro-subjective, the micro-subjective. According to this schema, the macro-objective represents the study of society, law, bureaucracy, technology, language, and so on; the macro-subjective represents a concern for culture, norms, and values; the micro-objective represents a focus upon patterns of interaction, action, and behavior; and the micro-subjective involves the social construction of reality. Kenyon does not do much with these categories, so let me try to show you why I believe Ritzer's categories clearly depict a retreat from the classical theory of our European forefathers and thus a trend toward institutionalized specialization within the parent discipline—a product of empiricism and the preference for low-level/middle-level generalizations. The construction of these categories presumably reflects the objects/problems that sociologists have set for themselves. As I have hinted, I would contest that the problem here is not that the categories adequately represent trends in the field, but rather that they deflect attention from what adequate theorizing ought to be like. Thus, as used by Kenyon, they can become a celebration of specialization and object management. The example of bureaucracy shows why specialization and object management produces inadequacy at the "level" of theory.

To treat bureaucracy from the macro-objective perspective suggests (a) that bureaucracy is a large-scale phenomenon, and (b) that bureaucracy is somewhat reified as a social fact. From the macro-objective position, I presume that bureaucracy can be located in a context, and its functions/dysfunctions analyzed. That is, bureaucracy can be understood or apprehended in reference to a generic type of social order. Thus, bureaucracy functions differently under patrimonial, retainership conditions than under rational-legal, impersonal conditions. Hence, the first level of apprehending bureaucracy would be ideal-typically descriptive, and could require the full use of historical materials involving a broad concern for the mode and relations of production and for the institutionalized pattern of domination that exists in a given historical society. Presumably, this is what Ritzer's macro-objective category embraces.

Bureaucracy is more than an administrative apparatus whose functions relate to a generic type of society. Bureaucracy also relates to the structural and cultural changes arising in conjunction with the development of a society. Structurally, bureaucracy in an industrial capitalist society is, as Weber (1946) noted, a power instrument of the first order for those who know how to use it. Thus, to study bureaucacy involves not only the macro-objective but also the micro-objective, for the patterns of behavior, action, and interaction represented by bureaucracy are embedded in patterns of relationships that are anchored in power.

In addition to this, bureaucracy has, as Berger, Berger, and Kellner (1973) remind us, a *style*. Here, I think it is legitimate to argue that bureaucracy is justified not only by recourse to rational-legal modes of social action, but also to the *Zeitgeist* of the profit/performance society that allows for the treatment of people as things. Weber saw bureaucracy as a manifestation par excellence of instrument rationality: in particular, the subsumption of substantive rationality by formal rationality. To understand bureaucracy meaningfully as a style or mode of social action legitimated by rational legal imperatives and the *Zeitgeist* of the *Leistungsgesellschaft* entails macro-subjective analyses. In order to understand that bureaucracy, as a manifestation of formal rationality, poses a threat to substantive rationality means that we must understand how people respond (e.g., resist, accept, pragmatically accommodate) to bureaucracy in the social construction of their life-worlds. Here, we need the micro-subjective.

By now it should be clear that I believe adequate theorizing involves all four perspectives and not the parcelling up of the subject matter like boxes of Kentucky Fried Chicken ready for consumption. The latter management mentality thus represents a retreat from the kind of theorizing that would involve a more holistic concern for the structuralization of structures, conflict, contradiction, power, and human agency. It may be acceptable for systematic, empirical theory to engage in this retreat, but this is a major deficiency of the systematic, empirical, nomological style of "theory" that Kenyon seems to be advocating as an instrument for sociology of sport's future development.

Description in Sociology of Sport

Let me deal now with SIRLS by way of its descriptors. The lament for theory that is contained in functionalist critiques can easily be justified here. That is, on the basis of a perusal of the descriptors, we can see how blissfully ignorant of theory sport sociologists have been. In a very technical sense, we have broken up our subject matter into higher particularistic, manageable packages. Although Kenyon admits that the descriptor/study counts in Table 1 (see chapter 1) are not mutually exclusive, this statement is beguiling. As a fair student of the literature in the sociology of sport, my experience has been that the papers do tend to isolate a problem and to handle it as if it were in a vacuum. Let me give two examples: (a) gender role socialization, and (b) social stratification.

Gender Role Socialization

Gender role socialization contains three possible descriptors. When discussed in sport sociology (e.g., the female in sport), the concern becomes considerably reduced. Usually it focuses around either the so-called masculinization problem or the "schizophrenia" problem. In the former, we are concerned only with moral stigmatization; in the latter, we are concerned only with the moral conflict involved in being a woman and an athlete. The social system is a priori reified here. Thus, we are not dealing with the ongoing restructuration of life-chances qua options vis-á-vis the openness/closure of mobility chances that inhere within a generic type of class society and the status groups that provide for vertical cleavages within that class system. By posing the problem as one of personality or one of moral dilemma, we miss the opportunity to understand how women might use sport in a conjunctural and/or organic movement to change the system of recruitment and reward so as to move toward the, as yet, unrealized promises of liberal democracy.

Social Stratification

Something similar can be said about conventional analyses of sport and social stratification. Although social class and social stratification presumably overlap as descriptors in SIRLS, they do not in the work of most North American sociologists. The reason they appear to overlap is because concepts such as social class, social status, and social stratification are used interchangeably and in a theoretically unreflexive fashion. Certainly, the vast majority of societies are stratified, but what is the basis for this stratification? Is it status, is it class, or is it party? Do these dimensions of stratification intersect and, if so, how? In contemporary America, it is fairly obvious that race (as a status group) and class (as a production relation) intersect as is revealed in the high-unemployment rates of black youth. Also, it is fairly obvious that race (as a status group) and party (as a political formation) intersect to the degree that blacks were disenfranchised and, today, are still grossly underrepresented in the political process. What about women as a status group? They are vertically represented throughout the stratification system. If they were not, classes could not biologically reproduce themselves.

Kenyon might argue that some form of multivariate analysis can handle this problem—plug race, gender, and socioeconomic status in as variables and perform some cross-tabulations. This approach tells us nothing about the class in itself/for itself problem or the status group in itself/for itself problem. Nor does it tell us much about what Frank Parkin (1979) has called the boundary problem. What it does do, is conflate class, status, and party into a purely distributive focus on the division of labor. Thus it blocks off analysis concerning status groups and classes as objective formations within the social relations of liberal democracy. The net result is that our analyses of social stratification are divorced from the understanding of social stratification and its axial forces. My claim is that the empirical generalizations Kenyon seeks and that are part and parcel of mainstream, empirical functionalism will do nothing to rectify the situation.

The Development of the Sociology of Sport

"Normal" Scientific Approaches

Finally, let me say something about the critiques of functionalism that, for Kenyon, represent some kind of internecine warfare we can do without if the sociology of sport is to reach scientific maturity. The well-thought-through critiques, of which there are few, do not state that functionalism is useless; they generally state that functionalism has been found to be deficient. Moreover, when geared to North American sociology, it seems that the critiques are aimed not at functionalism per se, but rather at the idea that many North American sport sociologists are functionalists and do not know it. Thus, the well-thought-through critiques are as much about what Kuhn (1970) would call the assumptions of "normal" science and how "paradigm" shifts can occur as they are about Gouldnerish polemics (Gouldner, 1970) against the pitfalls of positivism, functionalism, and structural functionalism. In this regard, the debate is about what scientific maturity really means and the ways in which we can reach it, if at all. The critiques are anchored in a mistrust of what we might call the search for criteria that can demarcate between science (implicitly assumed to be the only genuine knowledge) and nonscience (see Benton, 1977:6). As Benton points out, in Locke's day the principal targets for exclusion were theology and speculative metaphysics; today they are psychoanalysis and historical materialism. Thus, the well-thought-through critiques are grounded in a concern for such exclusionary practices of the so-called normal scientific community and not purely for the methodology of functionalism.

Alternative Approaches

As a journal reviewer, I receive submissions that typify how so-called normal science can constrain the imagination of researchers. Most submitted articles are blissfully ignorant of alternative approaches to the study of sport. Thus, the conclusion that can be drawn is that via their own socialization into sport sociology, a paradigm bias has been reinforced and internalized to such an extent that the bias is not seen as a bias, but as the obvious, sensible, reasonable, scientific approach (see Coulson & Riddell, 1980:8). The exclusion of alternative approaches results, then, from unreflexive self-censorship. Where other traditions are embraced, they are incorporated into the mainstream by the imposition of methods and procedures that have normal canons of legitimacy. For example, the *Zeitgeist* orientation of cultural idealism to, say, the achievement society is readily absorbed into empirical studies of *n-Ach*. On occasion, I have been asked "How can we operationalize alienation?" Surely, the development of the sociology of sport can hardly be expected if there is no reflexive rationalization within the community of scholars. Kenyon's concern for a division of labor cannot be the answer, for under conditions of self-censorship, alternative styles of theorizing and knowledge production lose their distinctiveness as critiques, as they become absorbed by the bias of the mainstream.

Conclusion

In conclusion, like many reviewers of the state of the art—whether the art be sociology or the sociology of sport—Kenyon has allowed certain untenable distinctions to remain as definers of the forms of the sociological imagination, for example, order-conflict, quantitative-qualitative, general theory-hyperfactualism, *erklären-verstehen*, and so on. This approach is too simplistic. For example, Durkheim is usually seen as a conservative order-type theorist. Yet, this is patently false. He was a liberal republican in a conservative France. He was concerned with conflict as much as with consensus qua moral integration; indeed, the latter presupposes a concern for the former. Marx is usually viewed as a conflict theorist, yet in Marxism we find evolutionism, eschatology, functionalism, and so on.

These examples are raised only to show that no discipline can be predefined. A discipline develops in terms of the problems that are set; its "progress" can be continuous or discontinuous, incremental, or revolutionary. A discipline can hardly progress at all if the dead labor of past scholarly generations is viewed as adjunct to the business at hand. We can hardly stand on the shoulders of giants if we do not know what they were about and why. We can hardly remove bias if we do not know its history and that of the alternatives posed. Only a specious disjunction exists between systematic theory and the history and philosophy of theory. The former arose within the latter as one of its variants and, for many, not *the* variant at that. Thus, the progress of sport sociology cannot be measured by how soon it will become scientific and systematic. Such a yardstick reinforces a bias. Nor can the community of scholars be counted on to be the best judge of progress. In this regard, there is no clear restriction on the concept of community—it can be as broad or as narrow as its definers wish it to be. We cannot, by advocating the cognitive supremacy of an approach, generate external standards to judge the respective merits of rival paradigm candidates (see Benton, 1977:9). As Weber (1946) said, with regard to values, science cannot tell us what we ought to believe; we must make a choice—so too with theory. By now it should be clear that my choice and that of Kenyon are different. To use an analogy of Giddens (1976:13), in catching the train of progress, Kenyon and I are not only not waiting on the same platform, we are probably not even in the same station.

The Sociology of Sport
In Europe and the United States:
Critical Observations
from an "Eliasian" Perspective

Eric Dunning

Although its title suggests a wide-ranging review of the relative merits of European and American approaches to the sociological study of sport, the focus of this paper is, in fact, rather narrow. More particularly, it is a discussion of some of the work on sport that I have carried out from an "Eliasian" or, more properly, a "figurational" or "figurational-developmental" perspective (Elias, 1978b; Goudsblom, 1977; Gleichmann, Goudsblom, & Korte, 1977). As I hope to show, such a perspective has a synthesizing potential that may contribute to the resolution of some of the difficulties currently evident in the sociology of sport and, indeed, in sociology more generally. Because, however, it is little known in the American sociological world, I have decided to devote this chapter to clarifying what it entails. That is, this chapter is concerned with just a small part of European work in the sociology of sport. It is divided into three parts: (a) The first involves an abstract discussion of the Eliasian perspective together with an attempt to locate it on the sociological map; (b) the second involves a critical examination from an Eliasian perspective of selected American work in the sociology of sport; and (c) the third attempts to provide a more concrete illustration of what the Eliasian approach entails by means of a figurational-developmental analysis of the problem of violence in sport. To be more concrete, my first task is to provide an exposition of the figurational-developmental approach to sociology and to locate such an approach on the sociological map.

The Figurational-Developmental Synthesis of Norbert Elias

Like Marxism and Weberianism, the figurational-developmental approach to sociology is a synthesis initially developed by a particular individual. Norbert Elias, the individual in question, was born in 1898 and began his sociological career in the 1930s at the University of Frankfurt where he was Karl Mannheim's Assistant in the Department of Sociology (Gleichmann et al., 1977:37–97). Then as now, the Frankfurt Sociology Department was separate from Adorno and Horkheimer's more famous Institute for Social Research, that is, the institutional base of the so-called "Frankfurt School." I mention this only to locate the initial emergence of Elias's developing synthesis in a specific place and, more importantly, at a specific conjuncture in the attempt to resolve what Germans call the *Methodenstreit*—the "fight over method"—that is, the ongoing struggle in which various schools have disputed over the years in an attempt to determine which concepts and methods are most appropriate for the scientific study of human beings.

Elias himself sees his work as an attempt to resolve the dualisms that have recurrently plagued sociology and related disciplines, forming the main axes of tension in the Methodenstreit. I am referring, of course, to the tendency conceptually to reduce the study of human beings to one or another side in a set of partly overlapping dichotomies. This tendency has led, time and again, to the formation of antagonistic schools that fight more or less explicitly over issues such as *materialism* versus *idealism, rationalism* versus *empiricism, naturalism* versus *anti-naturalism, agency* versus *structure, voluntarism* versus *determinism*, and many others. Such schools tend to become firmly committed to different but equally one- or two-dimensional views of the multidimensional social world. Elias's contention is that the resolution of the dualisms that underlie them is necessary at the present stage of sociological development in order to facilitate further growth, that is, the development of theories that have a better "fit" to what can be factually observed and that will help to combat the tendency toward fragmentation into conflicting schools—a recurrent tendency in the development of our subject.

Figure 1 provides a more complete list of the dualisms that Elias has set out to resolve. They are divided under the headings of (a) *epistemological* dualisms, that is the dualisms that arise from contrasting views of how people gain knowledge; (b) *ontological* dualisms, that is, dualisms connected with different perspectives on the social world as part of reality; and (c) dualisms connected with the *division of scientific labor* or, more properly, the social organization of science.

A tendency exists for positions taken with regard to these dualisms to overlap both between and within these main categories. Moreover, the

Epistemological Dualisms

anti-naturalism	versus	naturalism
involvement	versus	detachment (value-bias vs. value-freedom or ethical neutrality)
subjectivity	versus	objectivity
nominalism	versus	realism (reductionism vs. reification)
empiricism	versus	rationalism
induction	versus	deduction
analysis	versus	synthesis (atomism vs. holism)
quantitative methods	versus	qualitative methods
absolutism	versus	relativism

Ontological Dualisms

nature	versus	society
material	versus	ideal
individual	versus	society
agency (action)	versus	structure
change (process)	versus	structure
dynamics	versus	statics
voluntarism	versus	determinism (freedom vs. constraint)
harmony	versus	conflict
consensus	versus	force
order	versus	disorder (structure vs. chaos)

Dualisms Connected with the Division of Scientific Labor

sociology	versus	biology
sociology	versus	psychology
sociology	versus	history

Figure 1. Dualisms that recurrently plague sociology.

positions of specific schools can be based on a mixture of dichotomies from both the right-hand and the left-hand columns. For example, it is possible to be simultaneously a nominalist and a rationalist, to see societies as part of nature, to stress both agency and conflict, and to see sociology as an ahistorical subject that is independent of biology but dependent on psychology. However, it is Elias's position that concerns us here. The Eliasian synthesis is an attempt to steer the human sciences between the "Scylla" of one-dimensional problem—solutions represented on the left-hand side of the list—and the "Charybdis" of one-dimensional problem—solutions represented on the right-hand side. More specifically, the aim is to contribute to the development of a more object-adequate theoretical-empirical synthesis, to a picture of people and the societies they form that, to paraphrase Ranke, depicts them "as they really are" and not as they are supposed to be, according to the *diktat* or fantasies of political ideologists, philosophical theorists, theologians, or laymen. A subsidiary aim is to contribute to the development of a scientific methodology that is adequate for dealing with the human-social level of natural integration. In order to achieve these aims, it is necessary, according to Elias, to develop a conceptual apparatus and a terminology that are more closely attuned to the dynamic and relational character of human societies than has so far been achieved. Let me become a little more concrete and discuss one or two aspects of Elias's complex paradigm.

The Naturalism–Anti-Naturalism Dichotomy

Elias's (1974:21–42) position on the naturalism—anti-naturalism dichotomy argues that human beings and their societies are part of nature. However, nature is not a seamless web but a differentiated structure comprised of a series of emergent levels. These levels are interrelated yet relatively autonomous. They vary, first, in terms of the degree of structuredness of the elements they comprise, and, second, in terms of the speed at which these elements and the patterns that they form evolve. There are basically three such levels: (a) the inorganic level, (b) the organic level, and (c) the human-social level. All are amenable to scientific study, but the methods appropriate for one are not necessarily appropriate for the others. Thus, the human-social level is relatively autonomous. This level emerged from the inorganic and organic levels. Hence, it continues to be subject to processes at these levels but, at the same time, has a number of unique, emergent properties (e.g., languages, moral rules, states, strikes, marriages, economies, economic crises, sports, and wars). According to Elias, these unique, emergent properties of the human-social level of natural integration manifest regularities of their own that cannot be explained reductively, that is in terms of the methods, concepts, and models derived from the study of phenomena at the inorganic and organic levels.

However, this tends not to be recognized by philosophers. Popper, for example, a philosopher still highly regarded in some sociological circles, argues that only explanations in terms of "general" or "universal laws" deserve scientific status (Popper, 1957). Elias subjects this view to multiple attack, arguing that the concept of universal laws emerged at an early stage in the development of science, more specifically when classical physics was only just in the process of disengaging itself from theological and metaphysical conceptions (Elias, 1974:23). Like them, he argues, it is an attempt to discover something unchanging and eternal behind observable change but lacks object-adequacy because, in order to explain a change, reference has to be made to some *prior change*, not to some static and eternal "first cause." However, recognition of this is not to claim, according to Elias, that the concept of laws lack object-adequacy in some total sense. On the contrary, lawlike explanations, he maintains, are relatively object-adequate regarding loosely structured, slowly evolving phenomena such as gases but lack object-adequacy as far as more highly structured, rapidly evolving phenomena such as organisms and societies are concerned. Here models of structure and/or process have to take precedence over lawlike generalizations. Examples are the double-helix model of DNA, Darwin's theory of evolution, Marx's theory of the capitalist mode of production, and Elias's own theory of the "civilizing process" (Elias, 1974:40).

According to Elias, the relative lack of object-adequacy of the concept of universal laws at the human-social level stems basically from the relative speed at which the development of societies, a type of highly integrated phenomenon, takes place. As such, the concept represents a blockage to knowledge at that level. A related blockage derives from certain features of language. Thus, we tend to express constant movement or constant change in ways that imply an isolated object existing in a state of rest, and then to add a verb to express the fact that this isolated object moves or changes. For example, we say "the wind is blowing," as if the wind were actually a thing at rest that, at a given point in time, begins to blow. That is, we speak as if the wind were separate from its blowing, as if a wind could exist that did not blow (Elias, 1978b:112).

In sociology, the conceptual separation of *structure* and *change*, *structure* and *process*, and *structure* and *action* are examples of this tendency. For example, we say that the structure of sport in British society changed between 1750 and 1850, as if "it" did not change before or after those dates, and as if "its" structure were somehow seprate from "its" change. Such dichotomic and reifying forms of conceptualization imply the notion that actionless, changeless, nonprocessual structures could exist. This notion flies in the fact of what one can actually observe at all the different levels of natural integration, including, most obviously, the human-social level. Elias refers to this tendency as *Zustandsreduktion*, a German term that literally means "state-reduction," that is the conceptual reduction of observable processes to steady-states, although Mennell and Morrissey have translated it, not unreasonably, as "process reduction" (Elias, 1978b:112).

Figurations

Closely related to this, according to Elias, is the conceptual tendency to separate the "objects" of thought, including people, from the relationships in which they are involved (Elias, 1978b:13). Between them, these two conceptual tendencies—*state* or *process-reduction* and the separation of objects from relationships—have unfortunate consequences for sociology. More particularly, they contribute to a doubly inadequate mode of conceptualization, namely, a tendency to conceptualize the "objects" of sociological thought as static, on the one hand, and as uninvolved in relationships, on the other. In order to contribute to a resolution of what he regards as the pervasive tendency to reify and conceptually separate individuals and societies, while simultaneously reducing both to isolated objects in a state of rest, Elias coined the related concepts of *figurations* (Elias, 1978b:15) and *homines aperti,* or "open men" (Elias, 1978b:125, 135). The former refers to a web of interdependent human beings who are bonded to each other on several levels and in diverse ways. The latter refers to the open, processual, inherently "other-directed" character of the interdependent individuals who comprise these figurations.[1] The two terms do not refer to independently existing objects but denote different, though inseparable, levels of the human world. Figurations are not just congeries of individual atoms, however; the actions of a plurality of separate people intermesh to form an interwoven structure with a number of emergent properties such as power-ratios, axes of tension, class and stratification systems, wars, and economic crises. Because, according to Elias, power is a fundamental property of any figuration, I shall single out his discussion of that issue for special mention. I shall then consider his concept of the "immanent dynamics of figurations."

Power
Elias has developed a thoroughgoing relational concept of power that gets away from the tendency to reify it, to treat it as a "thing" that some possess in an absolute sense and of which others are absolutely deprived (Elias, 1978b:74). His concept, moreover, is based on a firm recognition of the polymorphous, many-sided character of power. As such, it can serve as a corrective to the pervasive tendency to reduce power to one or another unidimensional conception, for example, the Marxist reduction of it to the ownership and control of the means of production and the construction on that basis of a lawlike theory. Power, as Elias puts it,

> is a structural characteristic...of *all* human relationships....We depend on others; others depend on us. Insofar as we are more dependent on others than they are on us, they have power over us, whether we have become dependent on them by their use of naked force or by our need to be loved, our need for money, healing, status, a career, or simply for excitement. (Elias, 1978b:74, 93)

As long as one party to a relationship has a function and, hence, a value for another, he or she is not powerless, however great the discrepancy may be in the power-ratio between them.

Immanent Dynamics of Figurations
From what I have said so far, one can see that the figurational-developmental perspective rejects the more common, *analytical* approach according to which the social totality is broken down into a set of *factors, variables,* or *spheres* for example, the political factor, the education variable,

the economic sphere, and so forth, and in which the attempt is then made to assess the relative causal weights of these factors, variables, or spheres in the social process or some aspect of it. What is implied, however, it is not so much a *total rejection* of factor theorizing, as a call for a shift in the balance in sociology between analysis and synthesis in favor of the latter. That means a greater concern than has been evident in most sociological theories so far for the structural location of particular factors in wider totalities and for the structure of such totalities *per se*. In effect, what is being called for is greater sensitivity to the fact that, just as the structure of the DNA molecule as worked out by Crick and Watson is a function, not simply of its particular constituents and their quantities, but of their arrangement as a *double helix*, so the structure of human social totalities, for example, their bonding as tribal, city-state, or nation-state units, is a function, not only of their particular constituents and the relative quantities of these, but of the manner in which these constituents are bonded or arranged. Moreover, in social totalities, in contrast with their physicochemical counterparts, there is a greater tendency for the quality of constituents to vary as functions of the totality of which they form part.

It follows from this that one cannot make universal generalizations about the primacy in social dynamics of the economic sphere or the mode of production, for example, at least not universal generalizations of a non-tautological character that go beyond people's need to eat. That is because the economic sphere and the mode of production are manifestly not the same in all types of social totalities. They differ, for example, in their degrees of institutional separation from the political and religious spheres, that is, in their relative autonomy. They also differ in terms of the part played in them by express violence or force. That is less significant for present purposes, however, than the fact that, even though it attacks unidimensional theories, the Eliasian synthesis cannot be held to be a form of vacuous interactionism, a position that asserts that, in human societies, "everything is as important as everything else."

Nothing could be further from the truth because what the Eliasian position actually asserts is that the question of relative importance has to be defined structurally and relationally, for example, in terms of the strategic significance of particular institutions for controlling resources and handling recurrent problems. Because these resources, problems, and institutions are developmentally specific, it is impossible to make meaningful universal generalizations about them. As an example, the state is a strategic institution in industrial societies, but in specific types of tribal societies it does not even exist. Furthermore, in industrial societies, the struggle to control the state is a key part of the social process but, especially given the location of state-societies in an international network, the state enjoys a degree of autonomy in relation to the society's economy or mode of production. Elias is critical of the tendency in Marxist theory, for example, to treat particular societies as if they existed on their own and developed solely according to their own endogenous dynamics. In particular, he argues that looking at intersocietal relationships leads one to see that all human societies form "attack-and-defense" units, and that this is one of the bases for the emergence of the state (Elias, 1978b:138-139).

Elias also argues that the struggle to control the state is different in times of peace and war, relative domestic social harmony and revolution, and national or international boom and slump, suggesting that the power chances of different groups are favored under these differing conditions. Nevertheless, according to Elias, one can say that together with a struggle to control industrial, financial, and educational institutions—and in less developed state-societies, religious institutions, too—the struggle to control the state forms an ongoing feature of the dynamics of all state-societies. It is directed, guided, or channelled, as it were, by the skeletal structure or anatomy of the society, that is, principally by (a) its division of labor or, in Eliasian terms, the length and structure of its interdependency chains;[2] (b) the form taken by the state and the degree to which it has penetrated other institutions; (c) whether it has a barter or a money economy and, if the latter, whether and how far that economy is integrated into an intersocietal framework; and (d) the structurally determined balance of power between its constituent groups. This balance is fundamentally affected by the degree to which interdependency chains facilitate the exercise of reciprocal controls within and between groups, and by the degree to which the position of groups in the division of labor facilitates communication and organization among their members and gives them access to strategically significant knowledge and key institutions such as the state.

The term *the immanent dynamics of figuration,* refers to the ongoing process that obtains most of its momentum from such struggles. This process is channelled by the social structure but simultaneously transforms it. In the long term, it has a blind or unplanned character largely because it is the unintended outcome of the intentional social actions of innumerable unintentionally interdependent groups and individuals (Elias, 1978a). However, though unplanned, it has a determinable structure that ought to form a—if not *the*—central object of sociological investigation. The development of modern sport has taken—and is taking—place within the long-term, unplanned social process that led to the emergence of urban-industrial-nation-states (Dunning & Sheard, 1979). Sport occupies an increasingly important place within the structure of such societies and in the relationships between them. As such, the sociological study of sport ought to form an important part of the discipline as a whole. Its importance is certainly recognized within the Eliasian paradigm. Indeed, it is probably not going too far to say that the figurational-developmental perspective is the only major sociological paradigm to have spontaneously developed a theoretical-empirical approach to sport. At least it is true to say that its founder is the only sociologist with a claim to major status who has contributed significantly to the field.

An Eliasian Critique of Selected American Approaches to the Sociology of Sport

A point has now been reached where I can attempt an Eliasian critique of American approaches to the sociology of sport. The space available in this chapter means that, again, I have to be very selective. More specifically, I have chosen (a) to look critically at some of the metatheoretical and methodological assumptions on which *Sport and Social Systems* by Loy et al. (1978b) is based and (b) to develop some critical observations on substantive aspects of the thesis propounded by Allen Guttmann (1978) in *From Ritual to Record*. The former exemplifies certain general tendencies and assumptions typical of American approaches to the sociology of sport. Indeed, they seem to be typical of American sociology more generally. I have chosen the latter because, although it seems on the surface to be based on a position similar to the Eliasian perspective, particularly given its comparative and historical emphasis, it nevertheless reaches conclusions that are suspect from an Eliasian point of view. Although my discussion will be almost wholly critical, I do not intend this to be understood as an entirely negative judgment on the work of Loy, McPherson, and Kenyon, and Guttmann. On the contrary, what they have written is challenging and important, and hence worthy of serious critical debate.

Critical Remarks on the Metatheoretical and Methodological Foundations of Sport and Social Systems

Although it was published as late as 1978, *Sport and Social Systems* is reminiscent in many ways of sociology more than a decade ago when empiricism and functionalism reigned supreme and when American hegemony over the sociological world remained relatively undisturbed. This means that the usefulness of Loy, McPherson, and Kenyon's paradigm is strictly limited by, from an Eliasian standpoint, a number of restrictive epistemological and theoretical assumptions. Let me attempt to demonstrate how that is so.

Definitional Deficiencies

Central in this connection are a number of deficiencies in their basic definitions, for instance, of *sociology* and *social systems*. More specifically, these tend, from an Eliasian standpoint, to contain a number of false and misleading dichotomies. Take, for example, their following definitions of the subject:

Broadly conceived, the focus of sociological enquiry is the study of
human behavior as influenced by social organization... (S)ociology
is the scientific study of the structure and composition, functioning
and change of social systems and their relation to human behavior.
(Loy et al., 1978b:27)

Because social organization consists of human behavior, the first of these
definitions is either tautological, or it reifies the concept of social organization. The second repeats this error and is, at the same time, confused
because structure and composition, functioning and change are not and
cannot be separate. Nor can the functioning and change of social systems
be properly conceptualized independently of human behavior. Probably
more crucial than either of these conceptual inadequacies, however, is
the arbitrary and, above all, consensual and harmonistic character of Loy,
McPherson, and Kenyon's concept of a social system. They write:

The concept of a social system is not employed (here) in the particular
Parsonian sense of the term, but rather...in the generic sense...to refer
to all social units...that are characterized by persons engaged in patterned social interaction by means of and according to shared normative expectations. (Loy et al., 1978:v, vi)

Or, as they define it later on, relying partly on Wiseman and, in my
view, unwisely perpetuating the false dichotomization of the empirical
and the conceptual:

Empirically considered, a social system consists of a set of ''(1) individuals who are (2) interacting with others on the basis of a minimal
degree of complementary expectations by means of, and according
to (3) a shared system of beliefs, standards, and means of communication''....Conceptually considered, a social system is composed of
(1) a normative subsystem called culture, (2) a *structural* subsystem
termed social structure, and (3) a *behavioral* subsystem of persons in
social interaction (Loy et al., 1978b:29)

The arbitrariness in this passage is manifold. It consists, partly, in the
unexplained separation of the empirical from the conceptual, a separation that seems to imply that empirical observation would be possible
without concepts, and that conceptualization would be possible without
data. Equally arbitrary, however, is the conceptual separation of norms,
structures, and behavior, a conceptualization that invites the belief that
structures could somehow exist independently of norms, persons, and
behavior, or that behavior could occur independently of structures, norms,
and persons. Applied to actual analysis, the result of such distinctions
would be, at best, to produce a Ptolemaic complexity. Further than that,

the conceptual separation of structure and culture is reminiscent of the hoary old philosophers' dichotomy between the material and the ideal, and equally untenable as far as human societies are concerned because they are simultaneously both and not reducible to one or the other. That is, human societies form part of the material world of nature, but one of their distinguishing characteristics is that they are constituted by thinking, idea-forming human beings.

Harmonistic Bias

Probably that is less significant than the authors' harmonistic definition of social systems in terms of shared beliefs and standards, or shared and/or complementary normative expectations. A number of reasons explain why such a conceptualization is inadequate. For example, it is consensualist in the sense that it fails to take account of the normative *conflicts* and *divergencies* that are observable in all stratified societies. It also ignores the part played by *force* and *constraint* in the social integration of such societies. Of course, Loy, McPherson, and Kenyon would probably not want to hide or deny the use of force or the occurrence of conflict in social systems. Simply such phenomena are inconsistent with their basic definitions.[3]

Perhaps the general American tendency to conceive of social structures harmonistically and in normative terms is partly connected with a failure to appreciate properly a crucial distinction from an Eliasian standpoint, namely, the distinction between the moral and the scientific concepts of order. This complex and difficult issue is probably best introduced by reference to Elias's own words. He writes:

> Rule-governed human relationships cannot be understood if there is a tacit assumption that norms or rules are universally present from the outset as an unvarying property of human relationships. This assumption bars the way to asking and observing how and in what circumstances contests which are played out without rules transform themselves into relationships *with* set rules. Wars and other kinds of human relationships with few or no rules are proof enough that this is not merely a hypothetical problem.... According to a strong sociological tradition, norms are identified with structure...(and structure is identified with order). But even a situation that appears to be the height of disorder to the people involved in it forms part of a social order. There is no reason why historical 'disorders'—wars, revolutions, rebellions, massacres, and power struggles of every kind— cannot be explained. To do that is in fact one of the tasks of sociology. It would be impossible to explain normless conflicts if they had no structure and, in that sense, no order. The distinction between 'order' and 'disorder,' so significant for the people involved, is sociologically speaking without significance. *Among men, as in nature, no absolute chaos is possible.*

(T)he word 'order' is not being used here in the sense in which
it is used when people speak of 'law and order' or, in adjectival form,
of an 'orderly' as opposed to a 'disorderly' person. One is talking
about an order in the same sense that one talks of a natural order,
in which decay and destruction as structured processes have their
place alongside growth and synthesis, death and disintegration
alongside birth and integration. For the people involved, these
manifestations seem, with good cause, to be contradictory and irreconcilable. As objects of *study*, they are indivisible and of equal importance. (Elias, 1978b:75, 76)

As Elias uses it, the concept of order stems from the tradition of the
natural sciences where it is used to describe observable regularities irrespective of whether they are good, bad, or indifferent from a human
point of view. By contrast, the concept of order as used by Loy, McPherson, and Kenyon and other American sociologists who share their view,
remains at least partly locked in a philosophical tradition, as, for example, in the case of Talcott Parsons (1951), where the unregulated and
disorderly anarchy of the "Hobbesian jungle" is contrasted with the
orderly and harmonious character of a norm-governed social system.

Let me get back to the underlying assumptions of *Sport and Social Systems*. Two more recurrent tendencies in the approach of Loy, McPherson, and Kenyon are (a) a tendency toward *teleological* conceptualization,
as when they write, "Abstractly viewed,... *values* constitute the goals of
social systems" (Loy et al., 1978b:30); and (b) *reification*, as when they
argue, "The *social structure* of a social system consists of patterned interaction among a set of social positions" (Loy et al., 1978b:31). The former
statement is teleological because, while individual human beings can have
goals, social systems cannot. The latter involves reification because, while
individual human beings can interact, social positions cannot.

Eclecticism

Such inadequacies, however, are insignificant relative to the eclecticism
or theoretical agnosticism that Loy, McPherson, and Kenyon explicitly
espouse. Thus, they describe sociology as "a multimethod and a multiple paradigm science," (Loy et al., 1978b:49) and go on to cite Ritzer who
argues that, "no aspect of social reality can be adequately explained
without drawing on insights from all of the paradigms" (Loy et al.,
1978b:51). Such eclecticism is, in fact, a further indication of the harmonistic bias in Loy, McPherson, and Kenyon's approach. That is so first
because it fails to take account of the inconsistencies, incompatibilities,
and divergencies of the different paradigms, and second because it ignores
the degree to which the growth of knowledge is aided by the competition and clash of paradigms. From an Eliasian standpoint what is needed
in sociology at the present juncture is not eclecticism of the "let a hundred
flowers bloom" variety. In that way lies perpetuation of the current chaos.

Rather, syntheses are required, of the kind attempted by Anthony Giddens (1976) and, in my view, more successfully realized by Norbert Elias, above all because of the grounded, theoretical-empirical character of his work.

Quantitative Methods

Also problematic from an Eliasian perspective in the approach of Loy, McPherson, and Kenyon is their stress on quantitative methods and their related view of explanation as consisting fundamentally of the search for laws. As I suggested earlier, laws and lawlike generalizations are more appropriate to lower-level sciences than sociology where, if Elias is right, models of structure and process ought to reign supreme. One might also say that, whereas it is relatively strong on *figures*, Loy, McPherson, and Kenyon's approach to sociology is relatively weak on *figurations*. That is, they stress measurement and precision at the expense of revealing the interdependency structures that form such a basic, integral part of the human-social world. Their approach also involves a specific type of static bias, namely, a tendency toward what Elias calls *Zustandsreduktion*, that is, to reduce observable processes conceptually to steady states. They attempt to disavow this and to disarm the critic by claiming that their text is "seemingly static in nature" but "*dynamic* in the sense that emphasis is placed on the analysis of psychosocial processes such as leadership, discrimination, socialization, communication, conflict, and cooperation" (Loy et al., 1978b:vi). Such an emphasis, of course, is welcome, but it does not allow them to escape the charge of static bias because the emphasis in their text remains *synchronic*: They eschew *diachronic* or *historical* analysis. Moreover, one is left with the impression from much of what they write that they believe either that sport has always existed in its present form and is destined to continue to do so, or that it is possible to explain sport or any other social phenomenon by means of synchronic studies alone. My impression is that the latter is closer to their view: that is, they eschew diachronic analysis because they regard history as unscientific.

Such a position is radically at variance with the Eliasian perspective with its stress on long-term processes, an emphasis closely attuned to the observably changeful and processual character of the societies in which we live. From an Eliasian standpoint, human societies vary in the rates at which they change, but even their relative unchangefulness, where it exists, has to be explained in processual, dynamic terms. In short, the division between sociology and history expressed in the Loy, McPherson, and Kenyon position has its roots in a division of scientific labor radically at variance with human societies, the phenomenon with which both are concerned.

The work of Allen Guttmann, an American scholar whose work is explicitly historical and comparative appears at first glance to have more in common with the perspective of the "Eliasian school."

Critical Remarks on *From Ritual to Record*

Despite its comparative and historical orientation, Guttmann's analysis seems to remain typically American, particularly in its failure to appreciate some of the deeper, underlying structural pressures that have molded, and are molding, modern sport. Coupled with this is the fact that his analysis arguably remains evaluative in one or two crucial respects. Nowhere are these two problems more apparent than in his treatment of spectators and spectator sport.

Spectators and Top-Level Sport

"Watching a physical contest," Guttmann writes, "is not really very much like engaging in a physical contest" (Guttmann, 1978:8). Of course, that is partly but not entirely true. There are *similarities* and not just differences between sport-participation and sport-spectatorship as types of social actions. An important similarity is emotional arousal, that is, the generation of excitement (Elias & Dunning, 1969, 1970).

The existence of such similarities and the differences pointed to by Guttmann are of less significance sociologically than the fact that, where they are present at a sport-event, spectators form, together with the players, part of a *single figuration*. That is, although they have a degree of scope for relatively autonomous action, players and spectators are *interdependent* groupings. The former may be dependent on the latter for their wages and for ego-boosting prestige, while the latter are dependent on the former for emotional arousal and the opportunity to identify with one or more hero-figures or with the social unit that the team they support represents. This is not to claim that the interdependence of players and spectators is symmetrical and identical. It is wrong, however, to make the latter peripheral to the action. Players and spectators may not be a *universal* ingredient of sport, but they are *crucial* to top-level and professional sport, an important part of an overall social figuration that can only be properly understood as such, as a figuration. Moreover, top-level and professional sport play a crucial defining role in modern sport more generally, not just as an arbitrary addition. In any case, there are not many sport events that are not watched by at least some spectators, if only by casual passers-by.

This failure to conceptualize adequately the centrality of spectators to modern sport is not a trivial matter but one that arguably vitiates Guttmann's analysis of the main distinguishing characteristics of modern sport more generally. He argues there are seven such characteristics: secularism, equality, specialization, rationalization, bureaucratic organization, quantification, and the quest for records (Guttmann, 1978:16). In most respects, this analysis is revealing and to the point. However, the idea that "secularism" is a basic characteristic that distinguishes modern/sport from its ancestors is an oversimplification facilitated by the ambiguity of the term *religious*. Thus, whereas top-level, representative sporting events in the modern world may not be centrally theological in character in the sense that they are connected with the worship of a divinity or divinities, they are essentially religious in the Durkheimian sense of the term (Durkheim, 1976). That is, although they are nontheological and in that sense secular, such events are religious ceremonies in the sense that they form a medium and focus for collective identification. Perhaps it is not too far-fetched to suggest that sport is coming to form *the* religion, or one of the principal religions, of societies that are growing increasingly secular in the sense that, although this is not a simple unilinear or irreversible trend, theological beliefs are becoming less salient and all-pervasive within them (Dunning, 1979; Coles, 1975). Sport, of course, is a humanistic religion in which people worship other human beings, their achievements, and the groups to which they belong rather than anthropomorphic projections of themselves. Nevertheless, it has all or most of the characteristics of a religion, unless one insists on restricting the meaning of that term to practices associated with theological beliefs.

The "Idealist" Elements in Guttmann's Analysis of Sport

Guttmann offers an "idealist" explanation of the development of modern sport. That he offers such an explanation is not, I think, surprising for a scholar who explicitly adheres to what he calls a "Weberian" perspective, although it is based in some respects more on a common misinterpretation of Weber than on an understanding to which the majority of Weberian scholars would accede. I agree with Guttmann when he writes that "an advantage of the Weberian interpretation is that it does not reduce explanation to the economic determinism which is Marxism's everpresent beast in the jungle" (Guttmann, 1978:81). That is essentially correct because, without some form of economic determinism, Marxism ceases to be distinctive and merges into one or another of the paradigms that Marxists are wont to lump together under the label, bourgeois sociology.

In my view, however, the Weberian perspective is equally problematic, not because it is necessarily idealist as is often thought to be the case. What Weber (1956:183) sought to do was not to replace a materialist explanation by an idealist one but to correct the balance between the two. Nevertheless, Weber's perspective remains problematic because it fails to get far enough away from single-factor determinism, that is, from the notion that human societies are divisible into separate levels and spheres (e.g., the material and the ideal, the polity and the economy one of which can be said to be the *prime mover* in the development of all the others. In Guttmann's case, the prime mover that replaces material or economic determination is ideas. He writes that

The emergence of modern sports represents neither the triumph of capitalism nor the rise of Protestantism but rather the slow development of an empirical, experimental, mathematical *Weltanschauung*. England's early leadership has less to do with the Protestant Ethic and the spirit of capitalism than with the intellectual revolution symbolized by the names of Isaac Newton and John Locke and institutionalized in the Royal Society, founded during the Restoration, in 1662, for the advancement of science. (Guttmann, 1978:85)

In the present context there is no need to develop a detailed critique of this argument. Just to note its idealist character is sufficient. If there had been a direct causal connection between the scientific revolution and the rise of modern sport, at least insofar as the stages in this process were concerned which occurred when England was in the lead, then modern sport-forms would surely have begun to emerge in the 17th century and not, as in the case of cricket, horse-racing, and fox hunting, in the 18th century, or, as in the case of soccer, rugby, tennis, athletics, and boxing, in the 19th century. At the very least, these facts suggest that there is an unexamined, unexplicated time-lag in Guttmann's explanation. In fact, of course, it is more reasonable to assume that a *constellation* of developments contributed to the emergence of modern sports. The scientific revolution was undoubtedly one of them, especially as a determinant of some of the technological features of modern sport and the stress on precise measurement found in some of its branches, such as swimming and athletics.

It is wrong however, to extract such developments from their wider context and to view them, as Allen Guttmann does, as *the* prime mover of the process overall. It is especially wrong to view any such prime mover as an uncaused cause, that is, in this case, to treat the scientific revolution as unproblematic. Above all, it is wrong simply to assert rather than to demonstrate its priority over the prime movers stressed by others such as the Protestant ethic and the spirit of capitalism, or the incipient development of the capitalist mode of production. Indeed, from an Eliasian standpoint, associated with but underlying all these developments and channelling them structurally, as I have attempted in my earlier work to show, are deeper, figurational transformations such as the lengthening of interdependency chains and the processes of state-formation and functional democratization (Dunning, 1979; Dunning & Sheard, 1979).

Expression and Control of Violence in Sport

I shall make just one more comment on the work of Allen Guttmann. In his otherwise excellent discussion of violence in sport, he reaches the conclusion that

In plain terms, it is likely that the disadvantaged members of every society tend to express their frustrations in direct forms of deviance while the advantaged make greater use of the Saturnalia-like opportunities of the institutionalized "time-out." (Guttmann, 1978:135)

I agree with Guttmann's conclusion that there are significant class differences regarding the expression and control of violence. I disagree with the idea that these can be explained entirely as differential responses to frustration. I am not suggesting that the frustration-aggression hypothesis he uses is totally wrong. Simply this hypothesis is inadequate in specific respects, particularly to the degree that it is bound up with a negative evaluation of violence. Hence, it is difficult to account either for the fact that people can enjoy violence or that violence can be positively sanctioned. In fact, it is reasonable to suppose that class and other social differences regarding the expression and control of violence depend, not only on differential frustrations and different responses to deprivation, but also, and at least equally importantly, on the different norms or standards that tend to be generated in different social structural settings. These, according to the context, promote violence as well as condemn it. I shall conclude this chapter by attempting to demonstrate, by means of a figurational analysis of the problem of violence in sport, how that is so.

Social Bonding and Violence in Sport

It is widely believed that we are living today in one of the most violent periods in history. Indeed, it is probably fair to say that the fear that Western societies are currently undergoing a process of decivilization—with regard to physical violence if not in other respects—is deeply imprinted in the contemporary *Zeitgeist*, a dominant belief of our time.

A significant part of this belief is the widespread feeling that violence is currently increasing in and around sport. Andrew Yiannakis and his colleagues, McIntyre, Melnick and Hart (1976:200), for example, write that: "There can be little doubt that both crowd and player violence in sport are increasing at an alarming rate." Kurt Weis (1976), the German sociologist, agrees with such a diagnosis. More specifically, he argues that the putative trend toward growing violence on the sport field and among sport spectators represents at least a partial disconfirmation of Elias's theory of the civilizing process. It is with this issue—the relevance of this putative trend for Elias's theory—that I shall concern myself in the rest of this chapter. For reasons that will emerge, I disagree, first, with the view that contemporary sport and contemporary society are, unambiguously and in some simple sense, growing more violent. As you will see, my view of the problem coincides in some respects with that of Graham and Gurr (1969) when they concluded that, although violence increased in the United States during the 1960s, the 1960s as a decade were considerably less violent than, for example, the America of the post-Reconstruction era. Second, I disagree with Kurt Weis's view that the supposed trend toward increasing violence in and around sport represents a partial disconfirmation of Elias. At the same time, however, I want to argue that the issue of violence in contemporary sport and contemporary society raises a number of problems that it will only be possible to tackle adequately by advancing the relevant aspects of the theory of the civilizing process beyond the level reached by Elias himself. That is the goal I have set myself in this part of the chapter. More specifically, I want to develop three main points:

1. I want to advance beyond Elias by developing a typology that distinguishes analytically between the different forms and dimensions of violence observable in sport and elsewhere.
2. I want to argue, along with Elias that, in the industrially most advanced societies of Western Europe, a long-term civilizing transformation has taken place both in society at large and in sport. I shall move beyond Elias by conceptualizing this transformation as a change in the balance between some of the forms of violence distinguished in the typology.
3. I want to suggest that the changing pattern of empirically observed violence is, in large measure, attributable to a change in the forms of social bonding.

    My argument in this connection will be reminiscent in some ways of that developed by Charles Tilly (1969) when he argued that primitive and reactionary violence spring from a communal base, while modern forms of violence spring from a base that is associational in character. More specifically, like Tilly, I shall use in this connection a reworking of the *Gemeinschaft-Gesellschaft*/Mechanical Solidarity-Organic Solidarity distinction developed originally by Tönnies (1887/1957) and Durkheim (1964), and later elaborated by writers such as Redfield (1960) and Parsons (1951). However, in reworking it, I shall attempt to transform into an Eliasian, that is, dynamic and relational, conceptual tool. Let me become more specific. My first task is to lay the foundations for a typology of violence.

Toward a Typology of Human Violence

The types of violence engaged in by human beings, in sport and elsewhere, are diverse and very complex. It seems reasonable, however, to suppose that a degree of purchase on the problem can be obtained by drawing distinctions between its separable forms and dimensions. It seems to in that there are at least eight distinctions, namely

1. whether the violence is actual or symbolic, that is, whether it takes the form of a direct physical assault or simply involves verbal and/or nonverbal gestures;
2. whether or not a weapon or weapons are used;

3. where weapons are used, whether or not the assailants come directly into contact;
4. whether the violence is intentional or the accidental consequence of an action-sequence that was not intentionally violent at the outset;
5. whether one is dealing with violence that is initiated without provocation or with a retaliatory response to an intentionally or unintentionally violent act;
6. whether the violence take a mock or play form, or whether it is serious or real. This dimension might also be captured by means of the distinction between *ritual* and *nonritual* violence. It has to be noted, however, that ritual and play can both have a highly violent content; ritual and violence are not mutually exclusive categories (Marsh, Rosser, & Harré, 1978);
7. whether the violence is legitimate in the sense of being in accordance with a set of socially prescribed rules, or whether it is illegitimate in the sense of involving the contravention of accepted social standards; and
8. Whether it takes a *rational* (instrumental) or an *affective* (expressive) form. This distinction hinges on whether violence is rationally chosen as a means for securing the achievement of a given goal, or whether it is engaged in as an emotionally satisfying and pleasurable end in itself. Of course, retaliatory violence undertaken immediately in response to a violent attack is also liable to have a high effect content, that of anger as opposed to, or as well as, that of pleasure. However, retaliatory violence can also be engaged in more instrumentally as part of a longer term campaign of revenge.

The different forms and dimensions of violence observable in sport and other contexts overlap and can be transformed into one another. Thus, verbal and nonverbal gesturing often precede hand-to-hand fighting in war situations and find their sporting counterparts in professional wrestling, for example, and ceremonial battle dances such as that of the Maori rugby team. Similarly, a fast bowler in cricket may bowl a bouncer with the intention of merely intimidating a batsman but may strike him accidentally with the ball. Or, an act of instrumental violence in rugby, soccer, or American football, perhaps engaged in on the instruction of a manager or coach with the aim of neutralizing a key opponent or "taking him out of the game," may provoke retaliation, leading to a fight in which the emotional level rises.

It is common, indeed, to think of the different forms and dimensions of violence as mutually exclusive dichotomies—as simple either-or affairs—but it is more in keeping with observable reality to conceptualize them as poles on a series of continua. Because, moreover, one is usually confronted empirically with situations that involve an admixture between two or more dimensions, or in which one type is transformed into another, the most adequate way of thinking about the problem is by conceptualizing violence as varying around a complex of interdependent and overlapping polarities. Thus, because human rationality and emotions are inseparable aspects of a single whole, violence is never entirely rational or entirely affective, but *more or less* rational or *more or less* affective. That is, it is a question of balances and degrees. Let me become more empirical and apply this mode of conceptualization to some of the problems of violence in sport. I shall start by considering some general issues and then proceed to make some observations about the development of modern sport.

Sport and Violence in Developmental Perspective

Although all sports are inherently competitive, I shall concern myself here solely with those such as rugby, soccer, American football, and boxing where the competition takes the form of mock combat between individuals or teams. That is because an essential element of sports of this kind consists in the ritualized expression of violence and, just as the real battles that take place in war can involve a ritual component, so the mock battles that take place on a sport field can involve elements of, or be transformed into, nonritual violence. This may occur when people participate too seriously in a sport with the consequence that the tension-level is raised to a point where the incidence of hostile rivalry is increased and the rules and conventions designed to limit violence are suspended. The people involved start to fight one another in earnest, that is, with the aim of inflicting physical damage and pain. However, the standards governing violence-expression and violence-control are not the same in all societies. And, in particular societies, they differ between groups and historical periods. In fact, I want to argue that a central aspect of the development of modern sport has been what Elias would call a "civilizing process." Centrally involved in this regard has been a long-term shift from violence in its more affective forms toward violence in its more rational forms; or, more properly, a shift in the balance between these two polarities. Let me illustrate what this means by reference to the development of rugby football.[4]

Modern rugby is descended from a type of folk-game in which particular matches were played by variable, formally unrestricted numbers of people, sometimes considerably in excess of 1,000. The boundaries of the playing area were only loosely defined and limited by custom. Games were played both over open countryside and through the streets of towns. The rules were oral and specific to particular localities but, despite such local variation, the folk antecedents of modern rugby shared at least one common feature: they were all play-struggles that involved the customary toleration of a level of physical violence considerably higher than is normatively permitted in rugby and comparable games today.

By contrast, modern rugby exemplifies a civilized game-form in at least four senses that were lacking in the ancestral forms. In this respect it is typical of modern combat sports more generally. More specifically, modern rugby is civilized by

1. a complex set of formally instituted written rules that demand strict control over the use of physical force and that prohibit it in certain forms, such as, stiff-arm tackling and *hacking* (kicking an opposing player off his feet);
2. intra-game sanctions clearly defined, that is, penalties, which can be brought to bear on offenders and, as the ultimate sanction for serious and persistent rule-violation, the possibility of excluding offenders from the game;
3. the institutionalization of a specific role that stands, as it were, outside and above the game and whose task is to control it, that is, the role of the referee; and
4. a nationally centralized rule-making and rule-enforcing body, the Rugby Football Union.

This civilization of rugby football occurred as part of a continuous long-term social process. Two significant moments in it were (a) the institution, at Rugby School in 1845, of the first written rules; These attempted, among other things, to place restrictions on the use of hacking and other forms of physical force, and to prohibit altogether the use of *navvies*, the iron-tipped boots which had formed a socially valued part of the game at Rugby and some of the other mid-19th century schools; and (b) the formation in 1871 of the Rugby Football Union. The RFU was formed partly as a result of a public controversy over what was perceived as the excessive violence of the game, and one of its first acts was to place, for the first time, an absolute taboo on hacking. What happened at each of these moments was that the standards of violence-control applied in the game advanced in the sense, first, of demanding from players the exercise of a stricter and more comprehensive measure of self-control over the use of physical force, and, second, of attempting to secure compliance with this demand by means of externally imposed sanctions.

To speak of rugby football as having undergone a civilizing process is not to deny the fact that, relative to most other modern combat sports, it remains a rough game. Features such as the *ruck*,[5] for example, provide the opportunity for kicking and *raking* players who are lying on the ground, (scraping their faces with metal-studded boots) while the close-packed *scrum*,[6] which is difficult for the referee to control, offers opportunities for such forms of illegitimate violence as punching, eye-gouging, and biting.

Nor is the contention that rugby has undergone a limited civilizing development inconsistent with the fact that, in specific respects, it has probably grown more violent in recent years. It has certainly grown more competitive, as is shown by the introduction at all levels of cups and leagues. That is, a game where until 1971 matches were organized predominantly on a friendly basis with nothing at stake beyond the results of particular matches, now has a plethora of competitions where teams compete regularly for an extrinsic, long-term goal, that is, for the honor of winning a trophy as well as for winning each particular match. Growing competitiveness means that the importance of victory has increased, and this elevation of the success-goal has involved a further erosion of the old amateur ethos; for instance, it has diminished considerably the significance of the idea that taking part is more important than winning. Simultaneously it has probably increased the tendency of players to play roughly within the rules and to use illegitimate violence in pursuit of success. In short, it seems *a priori* likely that the use of rational, or instrumental violence in the game has recently increased.

To assert this is not to claim that in the past the violence of the game was entirely noninstrumental and affective, but rather that the balance in it between rational and affective violence has changed in favor of the former. That is because the structure of modern rugby, together with the relatively civilized personality structure of the people who play it, means that pleasure in playing now has to be derived far more from the expression of skill with the ball, in combining with teammates, and from more or less strictly controlled and muted forms of physical force, and far less from the physical intimidation and infliction of pain on opponents than used to be the case in its folk-antecedents and in the mid-19th century public schools when hacking and the use of navvies remained central and legitimate tactics.

The social and personality structures that have given rise to this modern game-form, however, have simultaneously increased the incidence of instrumental violence. Players who are able to gain satisfaction from the comparatively mild forms of physical force that are permitted in the modern game and who do not usually take pleasure in inflicting pain on others, are constrained to use violence, both legitimately and illegitimately, and in an instrumental fashion. They do not gain pleasurable satisfaction from such violence per se. It is engaged in not as an end in itself, but as a means to achieving a long-term goal—winning a league or cup. As such, it is, on balance, rational and planned in character rather than spontaneous, a deliberate tactic which, in its illegitimate forms, is probably introduced most frequently in game situations where it is most difficult to detect and control.

How is this apparently paradoxical development, that is, that a game has grown less violent in certain respects and simultaneously more violent in others, to be explained? My hypothesis, first, is that rugby is typical of all or most other sports in this respect, and, second, that this transformation is principally a consequence of a long-term shift in the pattern of social bonding, of the manner in which the members of a society are related to one another. To illustrate what this means I shall have to discuss some general sociological issues. Let me briefly summarize those aspects of Elias's theory of the civilizing process that are relevant for present purposes.

Violence and the Transformation of Social Bonds

In his seminal work, *Über den Prozess der Zivilisation*, Elias (1978a) sets out to demonstrate that a civilizing process has occurred in the societies of Western Europe since the Middle Ages. He explains this process principally by reference to (a) the establishment in these societies of a state monopoly on the right to use physical force, that is, a process of internal pacification under the aegis of the developing state; and (b) the correlative lengthening of interdependency chains, expressed more crudely, to a growth in the division of labor. The consequences of this twin transformation were first evident on the upper classes. They were subjected to growing social constraint simultaneously from two directions, more particularly from above and from below. That is, to increasingly effective state control and to pressure from a widening range of lower groups as, with the growing division of labor, their dependency on such groups increased. The result was that they were compelled to exercise greater control over themselves. Then, as state-formation and the lengthening of interdependency chains continued, particularly as the modern, urban-industrial type of society began to emerge, the effects of this civilizing process began gradually to percolate down the social scale. Its principal consequence has been a more or less constant growth in the social pressure on people to exercise self-control.

Central to this civilizing transformation has been a change in the pattern of social bonding. For want of better terms, this aspect of the process can be described as one in the course of which segmental bonds came gradually to be replaced by functional bonds. The significance of the inherited ties of family and residence grew gradually less important, while that of achieved ties determined by the division of labor grew gradually more important. Bonds of the former type are segmental in the sense that they tend to divide a society into blocks or segments that internally are relatively homogeneous and that maintain sharp boundaries vis-à-vis outsiders. Bonds of the latter type are functional in the sense that they grow out of the interdependency of divided occupational functions. Segmental bonding is conducive to a high rate of violence in social relations. Such violence tends to have a high emotional or affective content. Functional bonding is conducive to a relatively high degree of individual and social control over violence, together with a tendency toward the use of violence of a more rational, instrumental kind. Let me, very briefly and schematically, explore why that is so.

Segmental Bonding

The structure of a society where segmental bonding is the dominant type is conducive to physical violence in a number of mutually reinforcing ways. That is the case in all spheres of social relations, including sports and games. Expressed in terms of a cybernetics analogy, one could say that the various elements of such a social structure form a positive feedback cycle that escalates the tendency to resort to violence at all levels. The weakness of the state, for example, means that such a society is prey to outside attacks. The fact that there are few interpenetrating ties with other societies and that in-group ties are very strong, with a corresponding tendency for out-groups to be viewed with hostility, increases the frequency of war. A premium is thus placed on military roles and that, in its turn, leads to the consolidation of a predominantly warrior ruling class, a class trained for fighting and whose members, because of their socialization, derive positive satisfaction from it.

Internal relations in such a society work in the same direction. Fighting is endemic, largely because in-groups are defined very narrowly with the consequence that even ostensibly similar groups from the same locality are defined as outsiders. So intense are the feelings of pride and group attachment generated within particular kin and local segments that conflict and rivalry are virtually inevitable when the members of two or more of them meet. The norms of aggressive masculinity, which grow out of the fact that fighting is endemic in such a society, coupled with the lack of social pressure to exercise self-control, mean that conflict between them leads easily to fighting. Indeed, fighting, both within and between such groups, is necessary for the establishment and maintenance of reputations in terms of their standards of aggressive masculinity. The best fighters tend to emerge as leaders, and all the members of such groups have to fight in order to feel and prove to others that they are men.

The fighting norms of such segmentally bonded groups are analogous to the vendetta systems still found in many Mediterranean countries. An individual who is challenged or feels himself or herself slighted by one or more members of an outsider group feels that his or her group's honor and not simply his or her own is at stake. Correspondingly, he or she is liable to seek revenge, not simply by retaliation against that or those particular members but against *any* member of the offending group. On both sides, furthermore, there is a tendency for others to come to the aid of the initiators of the conflict. In that way, fights between individuals tend to escalate into feuds between groups, often long-lasting ones, thus providing a clear indication of the very great degree of identification under such social circumstances of individuals with the groups to which they belong.

The endemic violence characteristic of societies of this type, together with the fact that their structure consolidates the power of a warrior ruling class and generates an emphasis on male aggressiveness and strength, is conducive to the general dominance of men over women. In its turn, male-dominance leads to a high degree of separateness in the lives of the sexes and, with it, to families of the mother-centered type. The relative absence of the father from the family, coupled with the large family size typical in societies of this type, means that children are not subjected to close, continuous, or effective adult supervision. This lack of effective adult supervision, in its turn, has two principal consequences: (a) Because physical strength tends to be stressed in relations among children who are not subjected to effective adult control, the violence of such communities is increased; (b) lack of supervision is conducive to the formation of gangs who persist into early adult life and who, because of the narrowly defined group allegiances characteristic of segmental bonding, come persistently into conflict with other local gangs. The sports of such communities—for example, the folk antecedents of modern rugby—are ritualized expressions of the gang warfare typically generated under such conditions. The sports are an institutionalized test of the relative strengths of particular communities that grows out of, and exists side by side with, the perpetual and more serious struggles between local groups.

Functional Bonding

A society based on functional bonding is, in most respects, diametrically opposite to one where segmental bonding is dominant. Like the latter, such a society is subject to a positive feedback cycle but, in this case, the cycle performs, on balance, a civilizing function: That is, it serves mainly to limit the level of violence in social relations. However, the structure of such a society simultaneously generates intense competitive pressures and a tendency for rational means to be used in goal-achievement. In its turn, this combination generates a tendency for illegitimate violence and other forms of rule-violation to be used rationally in specific social contexts, such as in highly competitive combat-sports. Let me elaborate on this.

A key structural feature of a society where functional bonding is the dominant type is the fact that the state has established a monopoly on the right to use physical force. To the degree that its monopoly is stable and effective, the division of labor is permitted to grow, and that, reciprocally, augments the power of the state, because, for example, central control becomes increasingly necessary as the social structure grows more complex.

Both the state monopoly on physical violence and the growing division of labor exert a civilizing effect. The former exerts such an effect directly because the state is able to prevent citizens from openly carrying arms and to punish them for using violence illegitimately. The latter exerts such an effect indirectly because the division of labor generates what Elias calls *reciprocal* or *multipolar* controls. That is, bonds of interdependence allow the parties to a division of labor to exert a degree of control over one another mutually. In this sense, the division of labor exerts an equalizing or democratizing effect. Such an effect is civilizing for at least two reasons: (a) because the reciprocal controls generated by interdependence are conducive to greater restraint in interpersonal behavior, and (b) because a complex system of interdependencies would be subject to severe strain or even break down altogether if all or even some personnel failed to exercise a high degree of self-control.

A society of this type is highly competitive because a complex division of labor also generates a tendency for roles to be allocated on the basis of achievement rather than ascription. The division of labor diminishes the part played by heredity in occupational placement and augments that of competition. This intensification of competition leads to a general increase in rivalry and aggressiveness in social relations. It cannot be expressed in the form of openly violent behavior because the state effectively claims a monopoly on the right to use physical force. The dominant standards generated in such a society work in the same direction by decreeing that violence is wrong and, to the extent that such standards are internalized in the course of socialization, men and women come to have what Elias (1978a) calls a high threshold of repugnance with regard to engaging in and witnessing violent acts.

While the dominant tendency in such a society is toward a comparatively high level of effective control over violence, competitive pressure, coupled with the fact that long chains of interdependence and the correlative pattern of socialization constrain people to use rational means for achieving their goals, means that there is a parallel, and by no means, insignificant, tendency toward the instrumental use of violence by ordinary citizens in specific social contexts; this is most notable in sport and also in crime and, to a lesser extent, in the socialization and education of children. However, only the use of instrumental violence in sport need concern us here.

The first thing to note in this connection is the fact that, in a society based on functional bonding, combat sports such as rugby, soccer, and boxing form a social enclave where specific forms of violence are socially defined as legitimate. Such sports are ritualized and civilized play-fights where the use of physical force is hemmed in by rules and conventions, and controlled, immediately, by specific officials such as referees and, at a higher level, by the committees and tribunals set up by national and international ruling bodies. To the extent that the competitive pressure in such sports increases, either because their practitioners are competing for extrinsic rewards such as financial remuneration or the honor of winning a cup or league, or because they are subject to pressure to win from the local or national groups whom they represent, there will be a tendency for the significance of victory to be raised and, correspondingly, for players to break the rules as a deliberate tactic. As part of this, there will be a tendency for them to use violence illegitimately in situations where they perceive the likelihood of detection to be low and where they take a calculated risk that the penalties incurred upon detection will not detract significantly from the achievement of their own or their team's long-term goals.

Of course, the tendency toward the use of instrumental violence in modern sport is counteracted (a) by the fact that sportsmen are socialized into the dominant values of a society that condemns physical violence; and (b) by the fact that because they are potential victims as well as potential aggressors, they have personal interest in controlling the level of violence. The picture is further complicated by the fact that acts of instrumental violence are liable to call forth retaliation, either in the form of a spontaneous emotional outburst or as a delayed and calculated act of revenge. In short, the increasing resort to rational violence that is generated in modern sport by competitive pressure, on the one hand, is counteracted by general values and sport-specific norms. On the other hand, because it is liable to provoke retaliation, it serves simultaneously to increase the general level of violence in sport. Such a factual increase is highlighted and perceptually magnified in at least two ways: First, by the technology and practice of modern mass communications, for example, the frequent use of the zoom lense and the action-replay; and Second, by the adherence of socially dominant groups to civilized values, a fact which is conducive to the definition of even relatively minor acts of violence as close to Armageddon.

Thus, the civilizing process, in the course of which there has occurred a long-term shift in the balance between affective and rational violence, has simultaneously led to the perceptual magnification of the rate and seriousness of the latter. It seems reasonable to suppose that such a perceptual magnification and the moral panic to which it has given rise, in Britain and also in the United States, could have seriously decivilizing consequences. If we are not very careful, we could shortly find ourselves on the brink of decivilizing return, of greater or lesser magnitude and duration, to some kind of dark age both in sport and society at large. Indeed, there are a growing number of signs in Britain and elsewhere that we have passed over the brink already.

Notes

1. The term *other-directed* is not used here in the sense introduced by David Riesman in *The Lonely Crowd*.
2. The concept of *interdependency chains* refers to the bonds that exist between human beings linked through a system of functional differentiation. Such bonds can exist between, as well as within, societies. The concept is similar to the more usual concepts of *division of labor* and *role differentiation* but lacks the economistic connotations of the former and the formalistic emphasis of the latter. Also, it is used in a nonharmonistic sense and without a connotation of equality; that is, interdependencies tend to involve a conflictual element and they can vary along a *symmetry-asymmetry* continuum. Finally, the term *chains* carries a connotation of the *constraining* character of social bonds.
3. Similarly, consensualist and harmonistic assumptions appear in Snyder and Spreitzer (1978). They claim that "sociologists are more concerned with how a social system works...that is, in the norms, roles, and structures that *hold something together*" (1978:7). There is, of course, no doubt about the existence of binding norms, roles, and structures. The point is rather that, in what is perhaps in their case best called a *residual consensualism*, there is no counterbalancing emphasis on the fact that there are norms, roles, and structures that are *divisive* and *pull things apart*. Snyder and Spreitzer's approach to social change is similarly problematic. Thus they write that, "social change is almost always threatening to some people" (1978:8). This statement again seems reflexive of a cultural background shot through with consensualist assumptions because they evidently did not feel the need to point out that social status or stability can be at least as threatening as social change.
4. This analysis is taken from that in Dunning and Sheard (1979).
5. The *ruck*, technically a form of *loose-scrum*, is a game-situation where players scramble for the ball and where those lying on the ground are liable to be kicked. See Dunning and Sheard (1979:290–302) for a discussion of this and other aspects of the Rugby Union game.
6. The *scrum* technically the *set-scrum*, is awarded when the ball is thrown, knocked, or passed forward. It is a game-formation where seven players from each side form two interlocking rows and push against each other. The ball is thrown into the tunnel formed between each group of seven. See Dunning and Sheard (1979:300).

CHAPTER 4

Isn't it Difficult to Support Some of the Notions of "The Civilizing Process"? A Response to Dunning

James Curtis

I welcomed the invitation to read and comment upon Eric Dunning's chapter, "The Sociology of Sport in Europe and the United States: Critical Observations from an 'Eliasian' Perspective." Dunning's various works in the sociology of sport have never been anything but informative, interesting, and thought-provoking. I expected the same from this latest work as well. I was, of course, not disappointed; it was all of these things. This said, I will soon give emphasis to the negative for a while. I do this to follow through on my duties of making some brief critical comments on Dunning's analyses. I trust that it is understood that my critique was carried out only because the time involved in this has been much more than compensated for by the ideas that I gleaned from Dunning's effort.

Let me begin with a few words on the importance of the works by Elias from which Dunning builds.

Seconding the Motion that Elias' Work Should be Consulted

Considering the three sections of Dunning's chapter, the first part, on what the Eliasian perspective is all about, and the third part, on an application of this perspective to violence in sport, were the most important and the most informative. These sections prompted me to read carefully for the first time Elias' *The Civilizing Process* (1978a) and *What is Sociology?* (1978b). I must, admit I had only a page-flipper's acquaintance with these pieces until then. This reading was rewarding, and I am in Dunning's debt for the prompting.

Let me describe, briefly, what I found in these works. In *The Civilizing Process* I discovered macrosociology and social history par excellence. This book is full of details and insights on how the upper classes lived in different periods. It gives a sweeping portrayal of changes that seem to have taken place in the manners of people since the Middle Ages. In medieval times, Elias says, people faced few constraints on acting out affect, whether in the form of aggression, sex, hunger, or what have you, and irrespective of the social situation, at play, in the bedroom, or at the table, in private places, or in public places. The process of civilization involves a progressively tighter set of controls on impulses and emotions. This occurred with the passage of time. Norms of restraints were developed. These were first imposed upon inferiors by superiors, via various social control processes. With time and social acceptance, the norms of restraint became more powerful because they came to be standards that were internalized by people. The restraint came to be more a matter of self-respect and self-approval. Social control has always been present, but this came to be less important as self-restraint became more prominent.

This interpretation of history is not all that novel perhaps (see, for example, Freud's work). However, there has been nothing written which even begins to approximate the sweep of history (since medieval times) and the painstaking detail involved in Elias' attempt to support his interpretation. Elias' evidence is largely from various books on etiquette. From these he draws a dynamic portrait of historical change in norms, patterns of social relations, and social character.

Elias' *What is Sociology?* gives a concise portrayal of his approach to sociological analysis. Elias invites sociologists to reconsider the way they think about society. Elias says that "he deviates from the familiar paths and in doing so endeavours to help the reader to think through anew the basic problems of society" (1978b:7). The volume is replete with exhortations concerning the proper sociological view and the errors in other views, as in Dunning's paper. Beyond this, however, the material that Elias delivers is often very familiar sociology. For example, he emphasizes the distinction between "processes of integration and differentiation" (1978b:144) and between "international development" and "intranational development" (1978b:167) and says that we should "recognize all of them as structural aspects of the overall process" (1978b:172). Also emphasized is the point that we should study "figurations," or webs of interdependent people (1978b:15). According to Reinhard Bendix's Forword to *What is Sociology?*, the basic subject matter of Elias' sociology is best summarized in this quote:

In the interweaving of innumerable individual interests and intentions—be they compatible, or opposed and inimical—something eventually emerges that, as it turns out, has neither been planned nor intended by any single individual. And yet it has been brought about by the intentions and actions of many individuals. And this is actually the whole secret of social weaving—of its compellingness, its regularity, its structure, it processual nature, and its development, this is the secret of the sociogenesis and social dynamics. (Elias, 1978b:211)

The comments to the contrary by Elias and Dunning notwithstanding, I doubt that many sociologists will find this approach and subject matter to be very new or absent from their own thoughts on society. Elias does, however, suggest some new terms for social phenomena and sets of phenomena known previously under other labels. For example, what are *figurations* except people in structures (or networks or systems) with these structures limited to interdependent relationships? *What is Sociology?* is often old wine in a new bottle, but a nice, clear bottle. Much of it is fairly standard fare in sociology when it comes down to it, whether we are speaking of European or American sociology.

What is Sociology? is well worth pursuing because it is clear, to the point, and well integrated. It is also important because it is a good short statement of Elias' views on social phenomena and sociology. Elias is now gaining the recognition that he deserves for the detailed work of *The Civilizing Process.* Many readers of this book will have an appetite for more from the author. *What is Sociology?* will help to satisfy these readers. However, this volume has little of the sustained analysis of *The Civilizing Process.*

I support Dunning's recommendation that we carefully attend to Elias's work.

Has There Been a Linear Civilizing Process With Respect to Aggression and Violence?

As interesting and insightful as Elias' analyses are, his theory has a flaw. His assumption of more or less unilinear evolution is very questionable. For example, he says that ontogeny repeats phylogeny, that societies go through a process of development similar to that of humans, from infants through childhood and adulthood. Surely, we must reject this view. One problem is that the process of civilization is not as irreversible as biological maturation.

Elias argues that "the direction of the main movement...is the same for all kinds of behavior...control grows even stricter. The instinct is slowly but progressively suppressed from the public life" (1978a:287–288). Does not the record of aggression and violence in this century put the lie to this linear view, at least with respect to the increased internalization of controls on violence? While reading *The Civilizing Process,* I could not help thinking of all the contrary evidence ("yes, but..." events) from the past few years: the slaughter of Jews in Nazi Germany; the devastation laid on people in Dresden; the annihilation provided the people of Hiroshima; the destruction of life and property in the bombing of Tokyo; and the massacres at My Lai and in other places in Vietnam, to name but a very few. How do we reconcile these events with the notion that people are moving toward a pinnacle in self-restraint of aggression?

One response to this question might be that the civilizing movement has not gone very far yet. I would agree with this. Indeed, I cannot see how it can be conclusively argued that there has been a steady vertical incline of any slope at all with respect to the self-restraint of aggression. I agree that people tend to express aggression and do violence in somewhat different ways now, largely because of changes in social control procedures, including opportunity structures. However, I see no clear evidence that, *controlling* for the types of social control procedures, there is greater self-restraint around aggression today than in earlier times. This type of evidence is required for a compelling comparison of how "civilized" people are now versus in earlier centuries. Here I am defining civilized more narrowly than in the approaches of Elias and Dunning. Civilized becomes a matter of internalization of values and self-restraint on aggression, and not some nonspecific mixture of these processes along with differences in social control structures, as in the analyses of Elias and Dunning. The problem with their analyses is that they speak of civilizing in the sense of internalized values and self-restraint and in the sense of social control procedures (e.g., rules, rule enforcement, latitude for breaking rules, etc.), without maintaining clear distinctions between the two. However, in their data, the development of more effective social control procedures is the major indicator of the civilizing process.

Information on social control procedures may tell us little about the civilized values internalized by people. We can see this problem more clearly if we consider applying the Eliasian emphasis on control procedures in comparative cross-cultural analysis of the national values of contemporary cases. We would find the procedure wanting here. For example, for years Canada has shown far lower per capita figures for law enforcement personnel (and lawyers) than the United States. Does this suggest that Americans (who, incidentally, also have shown a far higher murder rate than Canadians) are somewhat more civilized than Canadians in terms of internalized values? Of course not. The opposite conclusion would be as reasonable: Because Americans require more control agents, they may be a people with *less* self-restraint of aggression compared to Canadians. Actually, each conclusion is not very reasonable. Information on control agents, or any other aspect of control procedures, does not allow us to say anything conclusive about internalized values. This is true of information on rules of all sorts, unless these rules are internalized norms. Elias and Dunning provide little data on the latter.

The approach that I am recommending calls for a conceptual distinction between internalized values and self-restraint, on the one hand, and social control procedures on the other, which makes the character of their relationship problematic. We can speak of *either* of these as possibly following a civilizing process. However, we should make the precise relationship between the two an empirical question. Elias and Dunning, without sufficient supporting evidence, imply that there is a close, near-one-to-one relationship between the character of rules and self-restraint; there has been civilizing of both. My hypothesis is that there have been marked changes in control procedures over time (in the direction described by Elias and Dunning), but that these have not at all been matched by changes in internalization of values against aggression. Events such as those to which I have called attention suggest this. When opportunities allow this, people seem to find it easy to aggress. It is difficult to make a case for any steady improvements in self-restraint over time.

The greater implementation of norms of restraint on aggression through history by those in power does not make the case for historical changes to greater self-restraint by these select few either. The implementation of these rules can have had little to do with the greater internalization of civilized values by the power holders. I will resist listing various alternative interpretations based on the vested interests of the elite. Some of the same explanations can be applied to why procedures of control, once implemented would be maintained and enhanced over time.

My suggestion does *not* imply a nonrelationship between social control and self-restraint. They can affect each other. But, when? How? and In what way? Until we can make a better case for a close relationship in the case of the civilizing of aggression, why not *limit* the referent for this concept to changes in social control procedures?

Another response that might be given to my question about recent world events is this: These events are just minor recent perturbations in the overall pattern of progressive control and self-restraint of aggression. The problem with this response is that it makes it difficult to imagine what would have to happen for the theory of unilinear change to be called into question. Would it take preparation and planning for the elimination of one society by members of another? This has occurred in different quarters of the world. Would it take the implementation of that destruction in nuclear war? If so, let us just hope that the theory fits well with social reality. Let us forget hypothesis-testing here.

We might also hear the response that the recent events listed above are different from earlier violent events because they involve higher levels of, using Dunning's terms, "instrumental violence" or "rational violence." This proposition is debatable. However, accepting the point for a moment, how does it make sense to say that people involved in the killing and destruction in these examples are a little more civilized in terms of self-restraint than was the case for people participating in such events earlier in history because the former were more instrumentally oriented and did their killing with less affective orientation? I find it difficult to accept this reasoning. Cold, calculated killing shows no more self-restraint of aggression than affective killing. I will have more to say on this later.

Another possible response to my question might be that subscribers to Elias' theory would need to see higher levels of commonplace, every-day violence currently before they would question the theory. Still, a visit to the routine street violence of almost any city in the world will show us plenty of it. Whether there is more now than in earlier times is an open question, one for which we have few data. This is especially the case if, in keeping with the definition suggested previously we ask if aggressive behavior is less frequent or more frequent than in earlier times *controlling for control procedures*.

To be fair, Elias wrote *The Civilizing Process* before the occurrence of the events cited above. However, he wrote a new introduction to the book recently, after the events and there have been many other such events. Yet, Elias apparently felt no need to qualify his trend analysis for aggression and violence in the new introduction. This is puzzling.

Some scholars romanticize the past and see very clearly the dark sides of the present. I believe that faithful subscribers to the linear view of the civilizing process applied to self-restraint of aggression must do the opposite. They must attend to the dark sides of the past and not attend to some somber details of the present and recent past.

All that can be reasonably said is that aggression and violence have undergone changes in organizational processes over time: For example, there is now more state-control of these; there is more of an international component to them; and there has been the development of much more efficient death-delivering technology.

Are Sportspeople Becoming More Civilized?

Dunning builds from Elias' theory and goes beyond it when he considers the question of aggression and violence in sport. He distinguishes between different types of dimensions of violence. Then he finds that there has been a long-term civilizing transformation in sport because there has been a change in the balance between forms of violence; modern sport has more of the *rational* (vs. *affective*) form of violence. This change is attributed to the development of more *associational* (vs. *communal*) bonding in modern society and sport. Dunning illustrates his arguments with materials from rugby.

I have no quarrel with Dunning's distinctions. I have a couple of questions on the implications of the distinctions on his analysis. One question parallels one of my concerns with Elias' analyses. Dunning, too, extends his analysis of social trends to personality structures. Are we not left with a curious definition of more civilized sportspeople as personalities, if we say that their violence, while becoming more prevalent overall, is more rational and association-based? The problem that I have with this argument is made clearer when examples are, again, taken from warfare and murder rather than from combative sport. I suggest that we do this because the violence is more clearly seen as very consequential in these examples. The case of sport confuses things because, in this setting, rational violence sometimes implies less hurtful action toward others than does affective violence. I would suggest that this is one of the reasons why the Dunning analysis seems so reasonable on first blush.

Of course, rational violence is more civilized than affective violence! The former is less aggressive, less harmful than the latter! But, is it more civilized? Let us set the consequences of the acts of violence at death. Would we agree that the killing in current wars that are more instrumental in their orientation bespeaks a more civilized set of internalized values than killing in earlier wars? Suppose that a people began a major war, nuclear or nonnuclear, tomorrow, and this was done more out of instrumentality (e.g., to get some valuable territory or other resources) than out of affect. Would they merit the term *more civilized* compared with another people who started a war on the same scale because of hatred and anger? It seems to me that each act of aggression, whatever vocabulary or motives, did not portray internalized restraint on aggression.

Let us take another example. It is not at all clear how the cold, calculating murderer who commits the act because of perceived utilities (e.g., to get some life insurance money) is characterized by greater internalization of standards of restraint on aggression compared with the person who murders in a fit of rage. Indeed, one of the major differences between the two is that the former thought things through and still could not restrain the aggressive impulse, whereas the latter did not think things through as much. There is a parallel problem in the argument that sport with a larger component of rational violence versus affective violence bespeaks players who have internalized more civilized values. Expressing aggression in either kind of violence shows a lack of self-restraint.

Why not restrict the notion of civilizing in these analyses of sport? Why not apply it only to changes in the social control processes, until we know more about changes, if any, in self-restraint? For the moment, its application as a characterization of internalized values is questionable.

Although sport may, indeed, be coming to be more characterized by rational versus affective forms of violence, for a strong demonstration of this, we would need a panoramic examination of sport over time including studies of as many forms of sport as possible: those recently developed, those developed years ago, and those that have come and gone; those highly organized and those less organized; those combative and those less combative; those highly competitive and those less competitive. This holistic research approach is, of course, consistent with Elias' views on how to do sociological analyses. Again, I do not mean to suggest that Dunning should have found time to do this for his chapter in this text. Of course, he has provided some valuable additional analyses elsewhere in his work. However, the broad research task remains to be completed.

I would emphasize, before concluding this section, that Dunning closes by saying that it is possible that a dark age of sport may be coming. I gather from this that he rejects Elias' linear evolutionary view, for sport at least. Or, is this to be understood as a short blip in the process of social development of sport?

Demonstrating that American Studies in the Sociology of Sport are Less Eliasian

I have three concerns regarding the second part of Dunning's chapter, where the Eliasian approach is illustrated by showing how it contrasts with the approaches in American works in the sociology of sport. I will mention one of these here and the other two will be presented in the next two sections.

Dunning argues that American studies in the sociology of sport are less Eliasian than European studies in the sociology of sport. I suspect that this is true. However, a clear demonstration of the difference between these literatures would require comparisons of samples of the works from each, an effort well beyond Dunning's discussion of two American studies and some of his own work. Again, it is, of course, too much to ask that Dunning should have done this for the purposes of his present work.

The Perspectives of European and American Sociology

Dunning suggests that European sociology, in general, is more Eliasian than American sociology in general. I believe that this is the case, although I would like to see more evidence from comparative studies. It is probably also true that each of these sociologies involves different commitments to one or the other side of some of the polarities listed by Dunning. Each of the two sociologies is characterized by a different type of realism, by one individualist, the other societal. As Kurt Wolff has put it,

American sociology places [reality] on the individual withdrawing it from society. We may refer to this by saying that American sociology represents individual realism (and social nominalism).... European sociology places it on society or history, withdrawing it from the individual. It represents social realism (individual nominalism).... As Ernest Mannheim points out, it is only in what has been called "individual realism," that is, when the individual becomes the ultimate term of reference...that questions of motivation can have meaning for the analysis of social action. Sociological concepts formed on the level of the group are impervious to psychology. Thus we can formulate a further contrast: American sociology is characterized by psychological realism (social nominalism); European sociology, by social realism (psychological nominalism). (Wolff, 1959:581)

To the extent that this is an accurate portrayal, both European and American sociology fall short of the holistic perspective preferred by Elias. However, one gets the feeling from his work that to err in the direction of individual realism is a greater sin than to err in the direction of social realism.

It has been hypothesized that the differences described by Wolff are responsible, for example, for the different ways in which the sociology of knowledge and the sociology of sociology developed in Europe and America (Wolff, 1959; Curtis & Petras, 1970). It has also been suggested that French Canadian sociology differs from English Canadian sociology in these ways, with French Canadian sociology characterized more by social realism than English Canadian sociology because the former has it deepest intellectual roots in European sociology whereas the latter has drawn more heavily on American sociology (cf. Curtis, Connor, & Harp, 1970; Vallee & Whyte, 1968)

A Final Caution

In his second section Dunning chides Loy, McPherson and Kenyon (1978b), the North American authors of *Sport and Social Systems*, for drawing conceptual distinctions between norms, structures, and behavior in such a way that it "invites the belief that structures could somehow exist independently of norms, persons, and behavior, or that behavior could occur independently of structures, norms, and persons" (see chapter 3, p. 38). I did not get the same impression from their material. I did not see a stronger invitation in their work than in Dunning's distinctions between rules, affect, personality structure, people, and violence in his description of rugby. The mere drawing of analytic distinctions, here and by Loy, McPherson, and Kenyon, does not imply the independent existence of the referents in the distinctions. My guess is that the North American authors would vehemently deny that they subscribe to the position attributed to them by Dunning. They might agree that their work is more characterized by individual (psychological) realism than by social realism.

Violence in Sport and the Special Case of Soccer Hooliganism in the United Kingdom

Robert Pearton

It is widely believed that we are living in an age of unprecented violence. The 1,733 homicides in New York City in 1979 illustrate the awesome fact that for males between the ages of 15 to 44 who live there, murder is the leading cause of death. In the United States a homicide occurs every 24 minutes of each day. Michener (1976) reports that in 1976, over 9,000 reported rapings and 100 murders in American schools occurred during the school day.

In the United Kingdom, crime rates have increased sharply since the early 1960s with a 250% increase in violent crime over the 20-year period. Violence is also increasing in sport. Yiannakis, McIntrye, Melnick, and Hart (1976:216) write, "There can be little doubt that both crowd and player violence in sport are increasing at an alarming rate." Professional ice-hockey has attracted the first successful prosecution in the courts for conduct within the playing area after an incident in which a deliberate stick-inflicted wound caused a player injuries requiring 25 stitches and surgery on his eye socket. In the third week of the NFL 1976 season, one third of quarterbacks failed to complete their matches, and by midseason, six of them were out for the rest of the season. The increased incidence of violent episodes in American prosport have led to the introduction of the 1980 congressional Violence Bill (H.R. 7903). In the English prosoccer league, serious fouls increased 75% between 1960 and 1970. In the 1979-80 season, the Referees Association for the first time had to insure its members against loss of earnings through assault. In 1978 the International Cricket Conference met in London to consider ways to regulate bodyline bowling after a series of incidents which culminated in the near death of a batsman in an international match. Now players go out to bat padded and visored like American footballers—a particularly dramatic development in a noncontact game popularly associated with tea intervals for cucumber sandwiches.

Sport Violence: A Useful Social Function?

These are merely examples of trends, and one could cite countless others (cf. Atyeo's [1979] *Blood and Guts*). But does the trend amount to a social problem as well as a sport problem? It is popularly argued that sport serves as an outlet for violence generated or built up in other ways. Does sport violence serve useful social functions in the manner that the former excesses of the Roman arena were held to do? At least our modern gladiators volunteer, and are well rewarded financially and in terms of social status. This popular hypothesis, which I shall briefly examine, is increasingly being questioned by three social trends:

1. The apparent growth of both societal and sport violence.
2. The evidence that our modern gladiators are being emulated at lower levels of competitive sport as high status models of sport violence.
3. The belief that sport and violent behavior off the field of play are related because of a growing problem of spectator violence both at and around sport contests.

In their book, *Every Kid Can Win*, Orlick and Botterill (1975) list numerous incidents of both players and spectators hospitalized at organized children's sport contests following acts of violence. Such incidents are increasing. In the United Kingdom, schoolboy soccer players copy professional fouls and are sometimes encouraged by sport teachers. It is in this context that educators are concerned. Not only do such behaviors endanger the many positive personal and social benefits of competitive sport, but they may also transfer to other situations rather than act as a safety valve. Contrary to the popular belief in England that the battle of Waterloo may have been won on the playing fields of Eton, it is increasingly speculated that more battles were started than won there.

This is the conclusion reached by Richard Sipes in his article "War, Sports and Aggression" (1973) in which he uses a cross-cultural analysis to demonstrate that violent competitive sports show a direct relationship with war and other institutionalized forms of violent behavior. In the United Kingdom, soccer hooliganism has attracted far greater public and media attention than other more violent youth countercultures, or folk-devils. Edwards and Rackages (1977:16) in a paper entitled "The Dynamics of Violence in American Sports" give numerous examples of increases in, to use their words, "Unquestionably the most feared type of sport-related violence—non-routinized spontaneous spectator violence."

The media in both British and American societies have led campaigns for tougher sanctions (popular in Britain are traditional remedies: birch 'em, cane them, bring back conscription). In other ways the media message on violence is very different, and it reveals the high degree of ambivalence towards violence in our societies. Advertising for both films and certain sports frequently extol the violent characteristics of the action, and we are offered more and more gratuitous violence and appear to delight in it. The sports media is heavy with war-like analogies to describe competitive sport. Thus, teams prepare for campaigns, attacks blitz defenses, wingers raid, and defenders fight rearguard actions.

Violence is not only a significant feature of history, but one which has been institutionalized and legitimated in different ways at both national and international levels. Thus, that it is a recurrent cultural theme is not surprising. However, how can its recent increase and (in the particular context of this chapter) the alarm which attends violence in and around sport be explained? There is not a simple answer, but a consideration of a number of factors may contribute to our understanding. To this point, sociological contributions to this understanding have been limited. This is partly the result of a more general neglect of sport among sociologists who have often conceptualized it in terms of its surface features as play, outside real life, and therefore trivial. It is also partly because of the popularity of drive-discharge models which posit aggression as part of our genetic make-up. Thus, despite the fact that violence is, at very least, observably social in its manifestations, the scientific study of violence has been from biological and/or individualistic perspectives.

One of the problems for the sociologist is the methodological one of studying violent behavior in real life settings, a problem made more difficult by the limitations imposed by certain sociological paradigms. Recent sociological interest in sport violence in the United Kingdom has been stimulated by the elevation of soccer hooliganism to the status of social problem. It has generated some alternative approaches to those which currently dominate sport sociology.

A concern with sport violence, as well as with violence more generally, is sociologically relevant. In part, this concern may be seen as part of a heightened level of general sensitivity toward certain aspects of violence and more particularly to the infiltration of such behavior into areas of social life considered sacrosanct. Sport, it has long been claimed, "does us good," both personally and societally. This "does good" value pervades sport at every level, from sport education programs to the central ideology of Olympism, portraying sport as a harbinger of peace and understanding. However, sport it would appear is not doing everyone good.

A great deal of confusion surrounds the concepts of violence and aggression. Violent behavior varies in both intensity and type, and a typology of violence in sport would include a number of conceptually discreet yet behaviorally overlapping dimensions. Is such behavior accidental or intentional, legitimate or illegal, real or symbolic, instrumental or affective?

Aggression, Violence, and Sport

The present analysis focuses on defining aggression as behavior which harms or injures another, including psychological harm, and defines violence more narrowly as the physical dimension of aggression. These definitions exclude two aspects of behavior which cause a great deal of confusion in the sport literature, namely, high level of goal-striving, or motivation, and physical contact.

Aggressiveness is popularized as a positive human quality, an important characteristic of humankind's control of the environment. But we must distinguish between aggressiveness and aggression because a high level of success orientation is not, per se, evidence of harm to others. Much of our ambivalence with respect to sport violence may be attributed to the confusion between the two, particularly because the search for the personality profile of successful athletes (a dominant interest in sport psychology) consistently suggests that aggression is a requirement of the top-level performer.

Even if the personality variable being measured was indexing harm or injury, nothing causal from the relationship could be inferred; in fact, it is a measure of competitiveness. A number of researchers do suggest a link between sport violence and personality dispositions. The importance of personality variables is not being refuted; rather such studies take insufficient account of both different types of violence and situational variables, including the rules and strategies of the game.

Neither is physical contact per se aggressive. This is not a clear-cut distinction, particularly in such physical contact sports as American football, in which legitimate physical contact yields a high incidence of serious injuries; however, unlike boxing, the intention of the game, as defined by its rules, is not physical injury. The dividing line becomes even more blurred when, as the result of increased pressure for success, illegitimate contact becomes a built-in part of the game strategy and escapes appropriate sanction. This is, of course, the current issue of violence among players: Are the rules of sport, rules which suspend the realities of the everyday world, sufficient to control real world transgressions? According to the Sport Violence Bill placed before the U.S. Congress in July 1980 (H.R. 7903), the answer lies in the courts—the law courts, and not the ball courts.

Theories on Violent Behavior

Sport as a Safety-Valve

Hence the most popular theory of the link between sports and violence is challenged: the belief that in serving as the last real enclave of ritual violence, sport acts as a personal and social safety-valve. A longer term perspective suggests that in many ways, modern societies are less violent than in earlier stages in their development; we have become more civilized. Norbert Elias (1978a) in his book, *The Civilizing Process*, argues that there has been a long-term shift in the patterns of violence expression and control in modern industrial societies. This shift has led to a lessening in the desire to attack others, a raising of the threshold of repugnance with respect to displays of physical violence, and an internalization of a taboo on interpersonal violence as part of long-term socialization processes. Sport may be seen as a barometer of such a process.

In England, 100 years ago, one of the most popular spectator events to which crowds of over 100,000 flocked were "hanging matches." According to Kellow Chesney, the only difference between these matches and the sport events of the time was that in the former case nobody bet on the result. The antecedents of our modern contact sports were much bloodier, as accounts of preindustrial folk games suggest. Prize-fighting provides the best example, but football was typified by the combined brutality of the use of *navvies* (iron-toed boots with projecting nails) and rules that permitted hacking opponents above the knee.

Many sports have undergone a civilizing process in which some of the bloodier aspects have been eliminated, and others emphasizing skill, strategy, and dexterity have become established. Pete Rozelle, former NFL commissioner, suggested that rule changes in football have had the same sensitizing intention. "I think all our rule changes during the recent years would indicate that we share the . . . . view on undue violence in sports" (*Chicago Tribune*, October 8, 1980 sec. 4:14). Sport is itself part of the civilizing process and yet a channel for violence-control.

Ethological Studies

How can this be? The most popular theory among laymen and sportsmen rests on the belief that violence in humans is an instinct. It has its origins in the psychoanalytic theories of Freud, but found popular expression through accounts of animal behavior of the ethologists Lorenz (1963) and Eibl-Eibesfieldt (1971). Briefly, the ethological argument is this: Extensive animal studies indicate that aggression is an instinct which serves species survival by selective breeding, territorial spacing, and the establishment of social rank orders. Because humankind evolved from lower animals, then instigation to aggress must also be an instinct in humans.

In animals, the preservative function is further affected by built-in instinctive inhibitory mechanisms such that intraspecific injury is rare. In humans however, the instinct has "gone wild." Evolutionary selective processes have not only nurtured instigation as an instinct, they have, through the development of tools (particularly weapons) led to the ineffectiveness of human inhibitors.

The human being, therefore, has become the "killer-ape," a regular and habitual conspecific mass-murderer. Instinctive aggression has hydraulic characteristics: It builds up like steam in a boiler and will eventually explode without "demonstrable external stimulation" (Ardrey, 1966). Freud's juxtaposition of life and death instincts was similarly hydraulic in positing aggression as a constantly flowing impulse toward destruction and self-destruction. Both Freud and Lorenz claim that failure to express aggression in action is unhealthy and stress the importance of socially prescribed safety-valves like sport.

There have been numerous criticisms of both the Freudian and the ethological theses on the basis of empirical observation, both of animals and of humans. While we must accept that we are born with the capacity to behave violently, there is no evidence that a spontaneous aggressive impulse exists in humankind or in most animals. Research on animals in natural settings suggests that most defensive aggression consists of threatening postures which are only called forth in the presence of appropriate external stimuli. Aggression among animals in captivity (Lorenz's animals) is related to the breakdown of animal social order and particularly to crowding.

Regarding violence in humans, the evidence is of enormous diversity in different cultures. It is possible that aggression in humans is also related to crowding, that we live in a "human zoo," and this might explain recent increases in violence. Certainly, the statistics advanced by Goldstein (1975) and others are suggestive because they indicate greater levels of violence in urban than suburban or rural areas; however, there are too many exceptions to such a monocausal explanation, particularly from cross-cultural variations in serious crime rates in both countries and cities of similar densities. Violence, it would seem, is not due to crowding per se but to the social, psychological, cultural, and economic conditions of which it can be a manifestation, that is, to deficiencies in social life.

Why then, are these theories so popular? For a number of reasons that are elaborately detailed in Eric Fromm's book, *The Anatomy of Human Destructiveness* (1977). Foremost is that a belief that humankind is doomed by its genes absolves us of a sense of responsibility for our actions and rationalizes our sense of impotence in the age of the neutron bomb. However, in rejecting instinct theories we need not reject the thesis that sport may serve as a safety-valve because the most influential theory of aggression among psychologists reaches similar conclusions.

Frustration-Aggression Hypotheses

The frustration-aggression hypothesis emphasizes the role of acquired drives in violent behavior. Originally, the theory claimed that aggression was always the consequence of frustration (interference with a personal objective) and that frustration will always result in the desire to aggress. This desire to aggress need not be manifested in overt aggressive behavior because it is essentially an internal mechanism. Moreover, the likelihood of punishment serves to inhibit aggression toward the source of frustration. However, the aggression is not destroyed; rather it is displaced, delayed, or disguised. For example, your boss gives you a rough day, so you go home and beat the kids because aggressing against your boss is inhibited by the chance that you might lose your job. The early theorists termed this *displacement*, a change in the object of aggression. Having aggressed against the source of frustration either directly or indirectly, the person experiences a reduction in the drive to aggress.

The frustration-aggression hypotheses have been much critized and subsequently have been modified in a number of ways. While advocates of the theory regard frustration as the necessary antecedent of aggression, research has shown that attack, physical pain, or noxious stimulation can also lead to aggression, because in a similar way to frustration, these increase arousal. Because frustration is not the sole antecedent of aggression but merely one in a list, the original theory loses much of its power. However, despite the fact that little research has been done in sources of frustration, researchers still feel safe in invoking its existence, arguing that "he must have been frustrated because he behaved aggressively."

Catharsis Principle

While the frustration-aggression hypothesis assumes that aggression is the consequence of certain environmental conditions, it shares with the ethological and psychoanalytic perspectives the view that aggression is general and inevitable. For Lorenz and Freud, the instigation to aggress is instinctive. For Dollard and his associates (1939), it is seen as a drive which, once aroused, must have an outlet. All three theories predict that an act of aggression serves to reduce the drive. *This is the principle of catharsis*. Furthermore, it is held that through displacement, aggressive behavior may be channelled, diverted, and controlled. Thus, the importance of sport, it is claimed, is that it is cathartic. By a process akin to empathy or osmosis, the safety valve may work for spectators as well as participants, so the capacities for sport are considerable. Lorenz, for example, regarded the capacities for sport as the last great hope for the salvation of mankind.

In its original form, catharsis refers to drive-reduction as the consequence of an aggressive act, and displacement refers to object displacement as the display of aggressive behavior against something or someone other than the source of frustration. What is being claimed for sport, generally, is something very different—that physical contact or some other dimensions of sport serve as catharsis to aggression, not only for the participant but for spectators as well! This is the argument proposed by the psychologist Marsh and his colleagues (1978) regarding watching soccer from which he draws the distinction between real and ritual violence. Central to the argument is the proposition that watching sport represents opportunities for the enactment of ritual or "good" aggression, *aggro* (Marsh, 1975). While there is a great deal of rowdyism, most of the fan activities in the arena involve symbolic forms of aggression: chants, jeers, derogatory songs, and ritual encroachments on opposing fans' territory, or forms of physical contact which are ritual in the sense that they do little physical harm and are mutually recognized by those concerned as components of the "rules of disorder." Such ritual activities take the place of "bad" violence and, according to Marsh (1978), should not be over-controlled if they are to work effectively in a cathartic way. This notion is captured by this example of graffiti on the London subway: "A bit of aggro never did any harm."

But, doesn't sport have an inevitable capacity to frustrate because winning presupposes losing? Losing may be an especially important source of frustration when it happens as the result of bad luck or incompetent refereeing. This question is particularly relevant with regard to top levels of performance where winning becomes increasingly important for extrinsic reasons and strongly represents the societal values of competition and success. For example, the professional foul was developed in British soccer as a result of the decision to abolish maximum wage legislation. More generally, this aspect of sport may help account for some differences between British and American societies in terms of both the nature and the rates of player violence; represent fundamental differences in sport ideology: that of America encapsulated by the dictums of Vince Lombardi, and of Britain, evidenced by the wide-spread belief that "if a game's worth playing, it's worth playing badly."

A number of studies invoke the frustration/aggression hypothesis to account for player violence (Coakley, 1978; Lefebvre & Passer, 1974). Martens (1975) and Volkamer (1974) also subscribe to the theory, particularly with regard to sport where the outcome is of greater significance than the process. Hughes and Coakley (1978) suggest that the social organization of sport teams builds up frustration in players through deprivation, and deprivation equals physical aggression. Two points may be made with regard to some of these studies.

First, they invoke an explanation for violent play which can, in fact, be explained without recourse to such a theoretical model. Volkamer, for example, explains violence in soccer via frustration/aggression. Fouls are higher when (a) a team is losing; (b) a team is playing away from home; (c) a team occupies a low league position; (d) the score is low; and (e) a high-ranking team meets a low-ranking team. All but the last relationship can in fact be explained with reference to the tactics and rules of soccer. Losing teams play more defensive soccer than winning teams, and it is a common strategy to play defensively in away games. Low scoring emphasizes defensive soccer (e.g., Italian soccer). Fouling may be related to defensiveness, but while 75% of fouls in the United Kingdom's professional leagues are committed by defenders, in the penalty area (the most vital area of defense) fouls by the offense outnumber those by the defenders 20:1 because the sanction for a defensive foul in the penalty area, a penalty kick, almost always results in a goal for the opponents. Similar explanations to Volkamer's have been advanced for ice hockey violence, and it is worth asking whether the sanctions against violence within ice hockey are effective. Cullen and Cullen (1975) and Vaz (1978) indicate that the violation of contact rules in ice-hockey is a strategy legitimized by coaches and players and endorsed by officials. Thus Vaz suggests that violent acts are "occupationally essential skills for aspiring players" (Vaz, 1978:212). Russell (1974:825) argues, "it is an accepted strategem to slow down the play of the opposition with hard body checking—instrumental aggression occasionally drawing a penalty." Evidently player violence attracts smaller penalties than verbal abuse of officials.

Second, a major limitation of the explanatory power of the frustration-aggression hypothesis is its assumption that arousal is part of the process, an emotional readiness to aggress. It is in this context that one may differentiate between emotional (or affective) and instrumental violence. Clearly, in practice, they overlap and can be transformed into one another; however, much of our current concern *relates to rationally chosen violence as an intentional behavior, rather than angry or emotionally satisfying violence as an end in itself.* While this contention relates to player behavior and not spectator behavior, it is important in the context of the alternative theme of human violence—social learning.

Social Learning Theory

Social learning theory, (Bandura & Walters, 1963), proposes that aggressive responses, like any other social behavior, are learned through observing and imitating others, particularly others of high status. Learning violence is part of a socialization process in which parents and peers are the most important models, but which includes other pervasive long-term and often subtle factors: the use of weapons as toys, an emphasis in history teaching upon the significance of institutionalized aggression in achieving society's goals, and trends in the media. Social learning theory does not embrace the principle of catharsis as drive reduction because aggressive acts and displays serve to normalize, heighten, and reinforce violent behavior. Some aspects of sport have this potential, particularly where rule violation meets with success and approval.

Much of the research on violence in society has been designed to subject the drive-discharge and social learning theories to empirical test. Most of it has focused upon the effects of media violence on viewers, and Gold-

stein summarizes the findings: "The evidence for a reduction, or catharsis of aggression following the observation of violence is far outweighed
by the scores of studies reporting that the observation of violence serves
to stimulate aggression" (1975:36). Not surprisingly, studies on watching
sports balance out with similar conclusions—not surprisingly because the
majority of them are similar in experimental structure, utilizing filmed
episodes of sports in laboratory settings. A typical experiment involves
two conditions: Subjects are shown either a violent boxing/football match
or an exciting track meet. Following this, subjects take part in an apparently unrelated experiment on learning in which they are asked to act as
a teacher and give electric shocks to a learner each time a mistake is made.
Typically, those who watch the violent episode administer more intense,
or longer shocks than those who watch the track meet. Thus, it is assumed
that watching aggression leads to increased aggression. Such interpretations must be treated cautiously, particularly regarding their generalizabil-
ity to nonlaboratory situations.

   Field studies which have tested the drive discharge, frustration-
aggression, and social learning theories in sport settings (Goldstein &
Arms, 1971) avoid some of the limitations of laboratory experimentation
but reach similar conclusions; that is, witnessing vigorous physical combat games increases spectators, readiness to aggress through a decrease
in inhibitions against aggression, regardless of whether people support
the winning or the losing team. However, even though artificial experimental laboratory situations are avoided, such findings must still be
interpreted with caution.

   First, the experimental design focuses upon individual responses to a
verbal questionnaire. Whether or not such attitudes are a reliable indicator
of actual behavior is problematic. While violent acts in sport may include
many verbal and other symbolic dimensions of aggression, there is a
distinction. Marsh's (1978) analysis of the rules of disorder, for example,
is based upon this distinction between what Marsh called ritual, or "bad
violence," and nonritual or "good violence." Moreover, heightened
arousal is likely to last for a relatively short period of time, although
repeated exposure may have a long-term effect on violence levels as social
learning theory would predict.

Collective Sport Violence

For reasons I have suggested, the sociological literature on collective sport
violence is limited. Empirical studies have been mainly correlational and
have focused upon the structural characteristics of the immediate sport
setting. Theories of crowd behavior have been advanced to support correlational studies that link spectator behavior to specific features of the
sport situation such as the physical setting. DeWar's (1980) study of fights
at professional baseball matches and Harrington's (1968) study of soccer
hooliganism both support the notion that fights result from the con-

vergence of lower socioeconomic categories. Both Merton's (1957) theory of social structure and anomie and, particularly, Smelser's (1963) theory of collective behavior have been utilized as appropriate theoretical models.

Edwards and Rackages (1977) employ Smelser's theory to explain spectator violence in terms of cultural strain and boundary system maintenance. Briefly, the argument is that spectator sports serve the societal functions of pattern maintenance and social control by legitimating and integrating fans with wider cultural values. In a social system characterized by both competition for scarce resources and the legitimation of certain institutionalized forms of violence, sports, generally, and accepted levels of player violence, specifically, allow for tension release through vicarious identification. However, at times of cultural strain and instability (which create anxiety concerning the norms and values of wider society, particularly in the context of intergroup antagonism), the competing values of different groups, structured along ethnic, religious, or geographical lines, may override more general cultural norms and values (particularly in the context of economic and political competition) and "may transform on the field episodes of either violent or nonviolent sport into .... violent collective behavior by spectators themselves" (Edwads & Rackages, 1977:23). Moreover, severe systematic strains may be transmuted into widespread collective behavior precipitated in the anonymity of the sports setting, thus leading to deindividualization: the result—intragroup conflict ranging from rowdyism to full-scale riot.

There have been few empirical tests of Smelser's theory, although the belief that events on the field of play may precipitate off field crime is a popular one to which social learning theory would subscribe. M.D. Smith's (1973) analysis of soccer crowd riots supports this view, with refereeing decisions rather than player behavior as the most frequent situational precipitants. Further empirical study along these lines has not been forthcoming, and a number of limiting factors are inherent in this approach. The assumption that violent behavior is irrational obscures the fact that, sociologically, most violence is normal. It is a general and recurrent feature of social life that occurs within normal social processes. This is negated by the application of approaches that view violence as a departure from recurrent social activity and that abstracts violent behavior from the contexts that give it meaning.

Definitions of both violence and violence control may vary considerably within societies and in different social environments. Hence, one of the limitations of Marsh's analysis of the rules of disorder is the assumption that people's perceptions of good violence, bad violence, and the dividing line between them is the same for everybody. Violence as a concept refers only to identical social phemonena if one disregards the social context to which it is applied. *In this sense, violence itself is not a suitable topic for sociological analysis. Central to the task of the sociologist in the quest for "connectedness" is that immediate facts have to be related to other aspects of social life*. As Elias (1978a) powerfully argues, human interdependence is characterized by change. The concept of the civilizing process and its apparent contradiction by recent events both in society, generally, and in sport, specifically, attest to the importance of viewing violence as part of wider dynamic processes, rather than from theoretical perspectives that regard the static nature of society as normal rather than its changing nature.

Young Soccer Fans in the United Kingdom

The following analysis represents an attempt to discover and understand the meanings people attribute to social activity in the social context in which such activity occurs. The analysis utilizes a variety of methods, chiefly those of participant observation and documentary analysis to create a profile of the social milieu of young soccer fans in the United Kingdom. The analysis stems from an ongoing interest in problems of youth conflict and earlier research interests in vandalism. Finally, an attempt will be made to place this appreciative approach in a theoretical context by relating it to Elias's theory of the civilizing process as it has been elaborated upon and developed by Eric Dunning (1983).

Support from the Working Class

Although soccer is the national game, it derives the bulk of its support from sections of the working class. Because most professional clubs are located in working class areas of the larger industrial towns, the majority of players are working class. Soccer grew in popularity as a counter to the routines of work and the drabness of life in areas lacking recreational opportunities. Soccer's popularity, however, is more fundamental than just as a counter to work, for it represents important aspects of working class life. As it is traditionally played, it reasserts qualities and values important in working class culture: individual skill, physical toughness, manly aggressiveness, confrontation, give-and-take, and group cooperation. Through soccer there is the possibility for success and acclaim for those who have never experienced it and who have learned they could only win through collective action.

Thus, supporting a soccer team has never meant merely watching a match. Being at a match is part of a dynamic process among players, supporters, and opponents. It is intensely social and with respect to the majority, it seems particularly inappropriate to explain soccer support as catharsis to aggression. What emerges from such an analysis is a picture of soccer as an arouser that provides an opportunity for tension build-up and for becoming excited. This was Aristotle's concept of catharsis: a two-way process in which it is just as important to lift people from the dismal depths as to bring them down from the dangerous heights. People need excitement, and support can be an important provider. Some sports or sport occurrences have greater potential than others to be cathartic in this way. Supporting a soccer team may be an important part of this process. But why does it lead to the mob violence which has become the British sport disease? Why isn't soccer providing harmless excitement? There is no reason to believe that it isn't for most supporters, because soccer hooligans do not typify supporters.

Any response to such questions as raised here will have to account for the extent to which soccer represents important values and for the fact that soccer hooliganism is not new. Through an analysis of newspaper reports and court transcripts, a research colleague has uncovered several hundred accounts of mob violence at soccer matches as far back as the 1880s. Seemingly, physical violence has always been associated with professional soccer. Its apparent increase in recent years must be analyzed in the context of social changes of a broad cultural nature. In the past 30 years, economic and social improvements have had widespread consequences. Until recently, these were significantly in the area of improved (and improving) living standards and more leisure opportunities. However, for many working class youths, prospects and opportunities have not kept pace with such general expectations and remain as limited as ever. These youths are more sensitized to their relative deprivation, partly as the result of the increased permeability of the boundaries that existed around traditional (amorphous) working class communities, and partly through the media message. Television, for example, is scripted in the language of the middle-class consumer society. Many people, in fact, switch off to reality of a different kind—that of financial struggle and of limited opportunities.

Many groups have opportunities to behave in ways which for other people or in other contexts would be regarded as unacceptable. Such activities, which Gaskell and Pearton (1979) have termed *risque shifts* include overdrinking, office parties, sports tours, and foreign holidays. These give a pleasurable lift from the routines of everyday life. However, the working class youth living at home has few such opportunities: The soccer match is one. Corrigan (1977), who used participant observation techniques in a northern English town, noted in his book, *The Dialectics of Doing Nothing*, the importance of supporting the local team. It is not just a matter of going to a match. Soccer and the team are important ongoing aspects of such working-class youth cultures.

Highly Committed Support

Why is the nature of this support so committed? In part, it is a reaction to changes within soccer, to attempts by sports entrepreneurs to make soccer attractive to a wider, more affluent clientele, with more expensive seats, bars, and restaurants. The players themselves, certainly the stars, have shed their working-class images and have come part of show-biz razzamatazz. Thus, the highly committed nature of support is a reaction against attempts to make soccer merely a part of the entertainment industry. It is also the consequence of societal changes of a more general nature: the emergence of youth cultures emphasizing "separateness" from adults, stressing escape from authority, and preferring being with peers in their leisure activities. Although support for the team may be traditional, the manner of support is less so; it is more committed—part of the quest for excitement and involvement restated by youths on their own terms.

Why is violence the result? Marsh (1978) suggests it isn't (although his analysis relates only to activities inside arenas). But he does touch upon the problematic nature of meanings in social life. Activities which appear mindless and gratuitous to the distanced observer do not appear so to the participants. Such activities may be replete with meanings which can only be understood in the context of a system of norms and values which can differ in important ways from more widely accepted ones.

The Civilizing Process and Increasing Violence Paradox

To attempt an account of the paradox which is presented by the apparent recent growth in sports violence in the context of long-term civilizing influence upon sport, Elias's theory of the civilizing process and its recent elaboration by Dunning (1980) in a paper entitled "Social Bonding and the Socio-Genesis of Violence," must be summarized. A more detailed explanation is in chapter 3, Dunning's contribution to this volume; however, a brief review may be helpful at this time.

The decline in modern people's propensity directly to engage in and enjoy violent acts is part of a long-term complex process derived from two interrelated aspects of social development in Western European societies: (a) the establishment of a state monopoly on the means of violence, and (b) a lengthening of the chains (or figurations, to use Elias's term) of human interdependencies resulting from increased specialization and division of labor. Over time, through long-term processes of socialization, the consequences have been a more or less constant increase in social pressure upon people to exercise self-control in the use of violence through both external sanctions and the internalization of violence controls in the individual conscience. Part of this long-term process has been a change in the dominant forms of social bonding (or interaction) from those in which the *ascriptive* ties of family and locality gradually grew less typical, while those characterized by the *achieved* ties brought about by specialization and division of labor developed. Dunning uses the term *segmental bonding* to refer to the former and *functional bonding* to refer to the latter as forms of interdependence. Segmental bonding, as an ideal type, is characterized by the following structural factors: they are local in nature, subject to weak central authority, and have strong kinship identification. Other segmental bonding correlates include work homogeneity, conjugal role separation, male dominance, low levels of emotional control, and high levels of affective violence, both in child socialization and in interlocality or interkin rivalry. Such groups are characterized by folkforms of sport as ritualized extensions of fighting between local gangs.

The predecessors of our modern games were certainly violent, as a number of researchers, for example Atyeo (1979), have suggested. As an ideal type, functional bonding is characterized by structurally opposed correlates; nationally integrated communities with strong central controls, a wide range of occupations, high levels of mobility, and group identification based upon achieved affective bonds. Such figurations are also characterized by strong social pressures to exercise control and self-control over physical violence and by a low threshold of repugnance regarding violence and pain. These factors are part of socialization practices which emphasize low-conjugal role separation, perceptions of masculinity based upon skills and strategies rather than physical toughness, and sport forms that serve as ritual play fights with strong pressure to control affective violence.

The Shift in Bonding

What is being proposed here is a long-term shift from segmental to functional forms of bonding, not the *replacement* of the former by the latter. In many ways they coexist and overlap. The importance of the distinction is that each type produces a different emphasis upon violence and violence control. In the former, "in groups" are narrowly defined, norms of aggressive masculinity lead to fighting, and physical strength is stressed in the relationships between children; consequent upon these influences is the formation of gangs which may persist into adult life. "The sports of such communities are ritualized expressions of gang warfare typically generated under such conditions...an institutionalized test of the relative strength of particular communities" (Dunning, 1983:129). Societies characterized by functional bonding are subject to restraints upon the level in social relations. The state can punish illegitimate violence, but the division of labor also produces greater restraints in interpersonal relations.

However, modern societies are highly competitive, and because such competition is based upon achievement rather than ascription, it generates intense rivalries. These cannot be expressed openly in violence because that is subject to state sanction and to the internalized taboo on violent behavior. There is strong pressure, therefore, to use violence *instrumentally* in specific social contexts—in sport, for example. In this respect, sport has thus become a social enclave in which the use of physical force is legitimate although rule-bound and controlled.

Increases in Participant Violence

Why then are levels of participant violence in sport on the increase? The answer is because such increases represent the growth of instrumental forms of violence in our societies. It is likely that violence will continue to grow in sport for a number of reasons, namely:

1. As the competitive pressures in society increase, they will be represented in sport as one of the few areas for their legitimate expression. (To say this is to say nothing of the merits or shortcomings of this development. It may be regarded as either an alarming example of social learning influences at work or, alternatively, as an example of the potential of sport as catharsis, depending on one's fundamental perspectives. It does certainly require one to consider the wider social implications of sport violence in addition to the implications for sport.)

2. Acts of instrumental violence are likely to call forth retaliation, either as a spontaneous angry outburst or as a calculated act of revenge. The existence of a violence multiplier in contact sports is clearly illustrated in the article by Furlong (1980) in the New York Times.

3. Sport at top levels is itself subject to increasing competitive pressures which call forth instrumental violence. As indicated earlier, there are enormous strains at top levels upon the integrity of legitimate means, and sport-specific norms of instrumental violence result.

In this sense, sport has undergone a transition from "play" to "display," increasing the level of extrinsic rewards and the importance of winning. As Merton says, "When winning takes over from winning-under-the-rules, a premium is implicitly set on the use of illegitimate but technically efficient means" (Goldstein, 1975:51). The commercial pressures which create such strains are enormous. Atyeo (1979:376) suggests, "Our hard-edged visions are being constantly reinforced by an ever-flowing superstructure of promoters, owners, coaches, players, and media mouth pieces who live off the proceeds of those visions and who all quote from the sportsman's bible that to win is everything."

But how is spectator violence generated? Dunning argues that while there has been a long-term trend toward functional forms of bonding in Britain, specific areas of social life are still characterized by many of the structural correlates of the segmental form of bonding that characerized earlier social systems. He further argues that this is still generally true of national bonds so that international sports contests are potential areas of conflict. He makes a similar case for the communities that serve as the traditional carriers of working class norms and values.

Dunning proposes that incidents of physical violence are, and have been, centrally connected with norms of physical toughness and the ability to fight. They are thus different in degree from those masculinity norms currently prevalent in society and condemned by socially dominant groups. They are, in fact, characteristic of earlier masculinity norms and are well in evidence in aspects of soccer hooliganism. They are characterized by the enjoyment of fighting among and between rough sections of the working-class; thus such fighting involves *intra* rather than *inter* class conflict. It is also evident that they point to a very high degree of identification by hooligans with the groups to which they belong, that is, rough working class communities. A number of sociological researchers suggest that such communities are characterized by the same kinds of social attributes typified by preindustrial forms of social bonding. However, they now exist as "islands" in a sea of functional bonding correlates. They are subject to linking controls from (a) state agencies like the police, and (b) functionally bonded and powerful groups, who condemn their activities (e.g., the media).

Conclusions

The thrust of the analysis here is that soccer hooliganism represents forms of affective violence of the kind against which taboos have been developed. The analysis is societally specific. Soccer hooliganism, thus described, is unlikely to become a problem in the United States. As Roadburg (1980) indicates, soccer spectating has very different societal and structural dimensions in the United States. However, I think the distinction between affective and instrumental violence is an important one, and the sociological orientation outlined briefly in this chapter may have relevance for the analysis of sport violence in the United States.

The Idealization of Play: The Relationship Between Play and Sport

Brian Sutton-Smith

To make even a small attempt to focus upon a problem that concerned Gregory P. Stone throughout his remarkable career as a sport sociologist of the first rank is an honor for me. Skeptic and humanist that he was, he showed concern throughout his scholarly works for the interrelationships of play and sport. One might say that he hoped that sport would never get quite so bad that it would cease to be played. The preservation of the spirit of play in the activity of sport was one of his sustaining themes. This chapter deals with this particular theme.

Both play and sport are *protean phenomena*. Innumerable and heterogeneous kinds of activities are covered by each of these words. Apparently, however, to keep these two polyglot terms in a kind of dialectical opposition serves our American cultural purposes. Each is a source of the most varied metaphors. One might also argue that they constitute a kind of *living and enactive metaphor*—a protoplasmic metaphoric life if you will— from which we draw such analogies as we need to initiate and sustain our thinking about everyday society (Lakoff & Johnson, 1980). We cannot neatly define the character of the boundaries between the two terms nor explicate all the usages to which we put this contrariness within our cultural heartland. Some sense of breadth of this living dialectic is suggested by the set of correlated terms in Figure 1 where each of the

This chapter was written in honor of Gregory P. Stone and was originally presented as the Gregory Stone Memorial Lecture at the Second Annual Conference of the North American Society for the Sociology of Sport, Fort Worth, TX, November 12–15, 1981.

associated items loads more of its variance (though never exclusively) on one rather than the other: play or sports.

PLAY	SPORTS
female	male
private	public
gemeinschaft	*gesellschaft*
family	state
tribal-oral	civilized-literate
ascriptive	achieving
spontaneous	organized
equity	legality

Figure 1. Correlated terms in play and sport.

Play as Idealized

Examined in this chapter is the way in which the term of *play* has come to be treated in an idealized and romanticized way and then used as criterion for evaluating sport in this century. I will explain some reasons for this, attempt some analysis of its validity, and then suggest some alternatives.

One prefatory note is that the dictionary continues to preserve either an older theory of play, or, perhaps, even a partly hidden modern realization that this idealization is itself a kind of deception. If play is what the dictionary says, then perhaps we are all being had.

To find play denigrated, we need go no further than *Webster's Twentieth Century Dictionary* (1961:1377) where its usages imply that *play* stands for "heedless behavior" as in

playing fast and loose
playing around
being a playfellow, a play actor, or a play maker

The player is also apparently somewhat *not to be taken seriously*:

He played at this work
he did it only in play
he played the fool
he made love only playfully

The player is not *even trustworthy*:

He plays both ends against the middle
plays tricks
plays on words
plays hob
plays havoc
plays one against the other
makes plays for the opposite sex
plays second fiddle
plays into your hands
plays upon your feelings
plays up to you
plays his cards well

Erving Goffman (1959) clearly writes about this player: The personality who sees life as a theatre and manipulates his front stage and back stage relationships in accord with that grounding. Finally, the player who *sees life as a gamble*:

He takes his chances
finds the odds against him
has an ace up his sleeve
is holding all the aces
sees it as a toss-up
knows how to play his cards right
will win big
or is a real loser, but
where is he when the chips are down
perhaps he has an ace in the hole
or he is bluffing
or is playing it close to the vest
should he up the ante
sweeten the pot
stand pat
or wait for the luck of the draw.   (Lakoff & Johnson, 1980:51)

Against the unscrupulousness, unreliability, and triviality of the player represented in these dictionary metaphors, we must weigh this century's efforts to tell us, on the contrary, that in childhood at least, "play is serious business," "a child's play is his work." In the past decade a crescendo of works presumed to demonstrate that play is linked to problem solving, to creativity, to imagination, to the consolidation of cognitive operations, to flexibility, to innovation, and so on. Now advocates of a make-believe industry argue that teaching children how to make believe helps them with their schooling, reduces their aggression, and heightens their persistence. Scholars even write books on *How to Play with Children*, a state of advocacy quite unheard of in earlier Golden Ages (Sutton-Smith & Sutton-Smith, 1974).

More to the point for this treatise is that in much recent sport literature, whether sport is damned as *A Prison of Measured Time* (Brohm, 1978), or lauded as *The Joy of Sports* (Novak, 1975), or carefully assessed throughout cultural history as in *From Ritual to Record: The Nature of Modern Sport* (Guttmann, 1978), it is taken for granted that play itself is a kind of freedom, a kind of ideal sphere outside the constraints of necessity.

In terms of the sociology of sports tradition, this idealization of play begins with Huizinga's *Homo Ludens* (1955), where play is defined as being free:

consciously outside of ordinary life
having no material interest or profit
having a separate place
having rules
being uncertain
being fun

This set of terms is repeated in the majority of texts on sport and treated with high seriousness, comparisons being made between the existence of these qualities in play and in sport (Loy, McPherson, & Kenyon, 1978b). Nor are sport sociologists alone in this. Play psychologists of the contemporary kind eagerly define play as *voluntary activity*, characterized by *intrinsic motivation* and by *positive affect*. These terms have much the same meanings as those used by the sport minded. They have just been decontextualized and inserted in the psychologists homunculus as if they are individual rather than cultural phenomena (Rubin, Fein, & Vandenberg, 1983:693–774).

In a way, sport sociologists can blame the play theorists for this state of affairs (if they so wish) because a succession of very powerful thinkers has proceeded with this idealization of play. Beginning with the evolutionary and developmental theses of the late 19th century, but continuing through Freud, Piaget, and more recently Bateson, play was given a central place in children's growth, adjustment, cognition, and communication. Each major developmental theory has given it a central role. Play reaches its final apotheosis, however, in the writings of phenomenologists as, for example, in James S. Hans' recent work entitled *The Play of the World* (1981) in which we are told that "play is the most meaningful of human activities, the one which continually produces the world in which man lives." Hans says,

I have for some time been working on a theory of meaning and value that would both deny the relativism so rampant in the world today and at the same time refuse to uphold a static or idealistic system of values that would be immediately refuted by everything going on around us....Only gradually did it become clear to me that play was the word which best held together all of the theories subsidiary elements. (1981:vi)

My first contention is that in our century, play has come to be idealized. I trust that I have presented, even if only in a schematic way, my basis for thinking that this has occurred. Actually I suspect, but wouldn't want to have to try to document, that play has picked up some of that *romanticism* that in its historical course has lighted at different times and different places on noble savages, utopian politics, folklore, mother love, young children, works of art, and, more recently, the sexual orgasm.

Why Play is Idealized

Social Status

Status reasons, psychosexual reasons, social science reasons, and nostalgic reasons (and others beyond my grasp) exist for this idealization. Probably the strongest reason for play idealization, and one given by Dunning (1979) and others in connection with their criticisms of Huizinga, is that this definition of play is based on elitist presuppositions. Huizinga's requirement that play must be disinterested in material outcome or profit is a doctrine for gentlemen with independent incomes. Given the original role of "gentlemen" in the games of England and the tenacity of the "amateurism issue" in the Olympics, possibly our reverence for freedom in the concept of play has such social status origins.

In recent years several new historical works strongly suggest that two kinds of play theories with upper status origins apply to the play of children. Thus, if we combine the analyses of Dominick Cavallo (1981) in *Muscles and Morals: Organized Playgrounds and Urban Reform, 1880–1920*, Gary Goodman's (1979) *Choosing Sides: Playground and Street Life on the Lower East Side*, and Bernard Mergen's (1980) *Play and Playthings of American Children*, we can identify a play theory for the poor and a play theory for the rich. This play theory for the poor formulated by the playground theorists of the 1890s and early 1900s says that if the larrikins and urchins who are teeming on the streets are brought into playgrounds and taught team sports, they will be transformed into good Americans. Although Dewey, Baldwin, Hall, and Thorndike all disagree on how to conceptualize child growth, they do agree that team sports are the answer to the contemporary problems of immigrant and delinquent masses of street children. Their *theory of play, however, is that it should be an organized and a collective process, and that it will have character training value.* They do not emphasize the freedom of the "folk play" or "scrub play" or "street play" of the immigrant children (status is a part of this early notion of play; freedom is not.) However, their thesis about team sports and their playground movement are one of the century's phenomenal success stories. Their "sports" movement has had a great deal to do with the idealization of play, although it just as clearly has not contributed greatly to the notion of freedom as play's essence.

The association of play and freedom seems to have had its origins in a play theory for the rich. This theory developed in academia in association with university nursery schools and with wealthy child patients. What it all had in common from Schiller of 1800 to Csikszentmihayli in 1977 was that play was defined as a voluntary and usually solitary activity of the individual, resulting in increased mastery, creativity, or flow. The individualistic philosophical bias in all this becomes explicit in the play therapies of psychoanalysis generally applied to the disturbed children of wealthy parents. Here we are told that through his or her solitary and imaginative play, the individual comes to master basic anxieties. In addition, psychoanalysis gives a new importance to the individual's imagination, although at first this is largely still seen as a "projective" expression of other more important conflicts. In time, that imagination comes to be seen as the source of individual creative activity both in psychoanalytic theory and in cognitive-developmental theory.

In 1968, Sara Smilansky showed that in Israel, disadvantaged children do not know how to play imaginatively, and she proposed to teach them to do so. A few years later in 1973, Jerome Singer in a series of research projects in the United States showed that those children who are more imaginative do better at school, are more joyful, are less aggressive, and so on. Later, Singer and his wife wrote a book called *Partners in Play* (1978) in order to show early childhood educators how to teach deprived children to play imaginatively. These and other authors contest that such play increases children's creativity and flexibility. Beginning with the work of Lieberman in the mid-60s, an increasing number of researchers demonstrate such relationships (Lieberman, 1979).

Whereas team games and playgrounds were once advocated for the *depraved*, exercises in imagination are now being advanced as essential for the *deprived*! Once again a natural propensity in those of upper status is being "organized" for those who lack this competence. Whereas "character" and loyalty were important requirements in the leadership training of the 19th century, creative ability is the new and critical ability that must be fostered in the present day world. Not surprisingly, the individualistic and symbolic character required for such leadership reflects itself in the psychological theories of play. From the present point of view, these are theories about how it is desirable that the children of the economically advantaged should prepare themselves for the flexible management of the information culture in which they live. Freedom of choice in an entrepreneurial civilization is essential to any concept of executive leadership. Freedom, then, becomes a central variable in theories of play applied to advantaged or disadvantaged children.

In sum, profound, if ethnocentric reasons, both in our economics and our social prestige explain why we hang onto the notion that optionality or freedom are core meanings of play. Despite Huizinga's elitist view, his philosophical idealism, his nostalgia for more primitive times, his ignorance of anthropology and psychodynamics, he is the first figure in our times to so clearly symbolize our need to think of our leisure freedom as the very heart of our identity. He makes play central to our civilization and thus symbolizes our deepest need to feel that much which is largely meaningless and alienating about its industrial and mass character, actually can be denied in our most free and happiest moments: and that in our playfulness, indeed, we recreate our history.

The Rhetoric of the Sexes

Play is idealized not only for social prestige reasons but also as a part of the new rhetoric of the sexes. This battle between the sexes begins with the one-sidedness of play and games as male preserves. Arguments say that the whole domain of leisure is a male preserve, that women traditionally did not have much access to what men generally called leisure (taverns, sports, fishing, etc.). Women certainly have had little access to active sports.

Now women investigators add that male students of leisure have overemphasized its organized and rule-structured aspects. They have missed the subtle and ever-present ephemeral and verbal play found in much tribal culture, in much street talk, and in women's everyday lives. From this point of view, Huizinga falters, not because of his emphasis upon freedom, but because of his emphasis that play must take place in a *separate place* and must be *bound by rules*. On the contrary, certainly among oral societies (not literate ones) and, perhaps among women, playfulness is an evanescent bantering thing, light and quick in its coming and going. Play is not the structured thing that men have made of it in modern and complex civilizations. Play is not as easily trapped as has been averred. To follow this point of view, some women scholars tend to favor the concept of play over that of sports. The former seems to contain for them more of these connotations of spontaneity and nonviolence that have been associated with their family lives, whereas sport contains those connotations of structure, organization, and violence associated with the larger society (Schwartzman, 1978).

Another cluster of associations, even more central than this one, further burdens the play/sport distinctions with the encumbrances of female and male identities. William Kessen (1979) made the case that the 19th century separation of the domain of work from the domain of the home, irretrievably separated the sexes and downgraded the role of women. Women became the caretakers of children, and along with children they were sentimentalized and disregarded. The fuzzy cluster that includes women and children also includes noble savages, folklore, children's play, children's innocence, women's delicacy, triviality, nurturance, and collaboration. Theoretically, the noble savages escaped the indictment with Boas's *The Primitive Mind* (1963/1911). Perhaps, women escaped it with Kate Millet's *Sexual Politics* in 1970. Children still have to be liberated from the idea that they are preoperational, emotional, rhythmic, and primitive.

From all of this emerges a well-established subcultural bias toward the view that play as contrasted with sport has more to do with collaborative activity, with the family, with personal resources, and with inner identity. Heavily structured and competitive, sport, which has little scope for these things, is an alien and undesirable thing constantly fought in a variety of ways. One way is to found new movements like those in *The New Games Book* (Fluegelman, 1976), which emphasizes play and games for whole families with the major stress on cooperation as distinct from competitiveness. When competitiveness is involved, it is subordinated to the good feeling of the group, which is the ultimate determiner of the worth of the game. In Bernard DeKoven's book, *The Well-Played Game* (1978), anyone can stop the course of the game if they are unsatisfied with its direction. The tremendous public and media antagonism to sport for children derives from this kind of source. Rainer Martens (1981), Director of the Office of Youth Sports at the University of Illinois, has recently documented how his statements on youth sports are frequently distorted in the press.

> Recently I spent 90 minutes with a prominent reporter discussing children's sports...for 80 of those minutes we discussed the positive aspects, for 10 minutes the problems. He wrote only about the problems. When I endorsed a need for limits on kids' sports activity, citing the example of some ten-year-old boys who played more than 90 hockey games in a single season, a reporter quoted me as saying: "All organized sports for youngsters below the age of sixteen should be eliminated." After a speech I gave at the Boys Club of America, I was quoted in a national newswire story as saying: "Increasing numbers of kids are turned off, burned out, and hung up after participating in sports." What I actually said was that journalists are making this statement—inaccurately. The media has grossly overexposed the negatives in children's sports, leaving many parents dubious about the value of such competition. However, my own experience, as an athlete, as a coach, and now as a sports psychologist and Director of the Office of Youth Sports at the University of Illinois, has been, and continues to be, considerably more positive. And the finding of

carefully conducted research by many sports scientists supports my beliefs. (p. 58-59)

We are faced then with a dichotomy of values between home versus society, family versus state, *gemeinschaft* versus *gesellschaft*, wherein play is said to represent one of these polarities and sport is said to represent the other. Yet, apparently some 3 million parents are involved in volunteer coaching of children's sports in the United States. The children are not simply in the hands of a few maniacal coaches as we are often led to believe and as the recent film *Two Ball Games*, contrasting sandlot and Little League baseball, certainly implies (Sutton-Smith, 1980). For example, many feel that children's sport now plays an essential socialization role that was once provided by the street games that are no longer as readily available. In addition, analyses suggest that despite the competitiveness of sport, what occurs for the masses of sport players are often those very qualities of close companionship, shared identity, and nurturant care that are often associated with female traditional activities (J. Gross, 1981). In addition, playful bantering activity and joking are more often associated with sporting activity than with other kinds of activity for those who participate. All this adds up to a view that sport is also a highly androgenous activity. Clearly, I am not attempting to take sides here, but am only indicating play's subsumption to sex-role rhetoric. Thus, we are again faced with the prospect that the rhetoric of current dichotomizations of play and sport in "feminine" and "masculine" terms obscure more than they clarify.

Socialization

A third and emerging reason for the idealization of play is its increasing use within the metaphysics of social science and, in particular, child psychology. Modern child psychologists have fought hard to give play a socializing function. Even when they acknowledge that the activity of children's play is often less than ideal, they have sought to incorporate the phenomenon within their general view that child psychology can predict how children develop and can, therefore, make positive recommendations about child training. To this end, they assert that much of childrens' play activity has to do with the socialization of aggression and sexuality: processes that the child cannot learn as well from formal educational agencies. Here is a variety of what on other grounds may be regarded as nefarious, disruptive, hedonistic, or political activities, given a translation that makes them acceptable. I suppose here I am pointing a finger at the need of modern psychologists to claim that they can predict and, therefore, can control the course of growth. To know what underlies all this is difficult, perhaps a kind of arrogance of science or even a lingering puritanism, but they seem able to abolish much of play's established irreverence in the name of socialization (Knapp & Knapp, 1976; Opie & Opie, 1959).

Romanticism

Our need to idealize play may be part of a larger historical romantic tradition whereby child life becomes idealized and idyllic as a projection of the presocialized consciousness. The writings of novelists about childhood are often interpreted in this nostalgic light (Covenay, 1967). In Freud or Vandenberg (1964), these nostalgic strivings are interpreted in terms of culturally unconscious desires to recreate in our adult lives feelings that we did not achieve or have lost from our childhood. The idealization of play in these terms becomes a cry either for the lost freedoms of childhood, or a cry for freedoms that we feel we deserved but never achieved. Those of us who are most active in the struggle for child scholarship may be those most afflicted by this need to rejuvenate ourselves through such cultural projections. We may, at the same time, be those who have found a cultural way to master this internal struggle.

As you can see I have made various speculative attempts to suggest some of the reasons for the idealizations of play. Certainly, there is no finality in any of this. However, when such important matters as social status, psychosexual identity, scientific esteem, and personal conflicts are involved, arguments about play and sport take on intensity and the play-sport distinction becomes a vehicle for rhetoric rather than science.

Should Play be Idealized?

The empirical question is whether play deserves such idealization. Is play really as it has been described? The problem at this point is that we are creatures of the same culture that idealizes it, and we cannot take a vantage point fully outside that culture. Although we can seek a relativity from anthropology (Schwartzman, 1978) or from animal studies (Fagen, 1980), are those studies free of Western presuppositions? This is Schwartzman's argument and is easily applied to Fagen's very psychologistic view of animals.

Even though there are limitations to our analysis, some data cause us at least to question our idealized versions of play. The major anthropological argument against play as voluntary is the nonuniversality of this criterion throughout much of the anthropological materials. There we often find people at play in sacred games that are attended by all members of the appropriate age and sex categories. For some players these games, sometimes associated with important rituals, funeral or fertility, can be terminal. Again, if we look at the varieties of animal play in different species with their own age and sex schedules as well as their ecological stimuli, the concepts of freedom or voluntariness hardly seems critical.

Playgrounds

Work with children's play suggests that even with respect to children's playground play, freedom may not be a critical concept. Thus one writer, referring to her play in the 1930s, writes that she doesn't recollect it for freedom and happiness but rather for its perils, its hurt feelings, and rough sobs. "If you didn't know the rhyme or tune of a song you were taunted and derided. To be accepted into the...(group)...you had to know these chants and like children the whole world over, conformity was the ticket." (Pierce, 1979:1–2). Again, in my work (1981, chapter 6) on the history of the playground in New Zealand, similarly, we come to terms with the fact that freedom may not be the most essential concept. Thus, in the 19th century,

> In addition to the roughness to be found in many of the boys traditional games, there were many other ways in which they could show a bellicose spirit. In most schools, for example, there seems to have been a regular fighting pit, either in the school or in the paddock next door. There are many records of schools having a special fighting arena to which boys retired, out of sight, when the pressure became too great for the civil war of childhood. (1981:76)

Here are some of my interviewee's statements:

> We had an arena surrounded by black logs and blackberry bushes. (From Nelson, 1895)
>
> There were hawthorn hedges round a gravel pit. (From Palmerston, 1900)
>
> Two boys were punished for fighting in the school ground. They were encouraged by about thirty others who shared in the dividend at a somewhat lower rate of payment. Often the fights were arranged for the entertainment of the older boys. They were arranged by the school bullies. (Nelson, 1895)
>
> You even had to fight your boy friends if it was arranged for you. (Waikouaiti, 1895)
>
> Small boys were induced to fight for sport. (Waipu, 1880)
>
> There was nothing organized for us so we organized fighting. (Dunedin, 1875)
>
> Fighting was arranged in a paddock. If one flunked it, he was crowned. The victor patted him three times on the back and spat over his head—usually aiming too low. I never remember seeing any boy

consent to crowning even when threatened. Sometimes he was held. Otherwise, it was the ultimate humiliation which no one could stand and retain his self respect. (Petone, 1900)

She learned further during the course of an incredulous investigation that every boy—had to fight twice a week to retain respectability. Opponents were selected by a committee and the fights took place on Wednesdays and Fridays. It was "too, too much" but perhaps not surprising when one looked at the fathers. (Kaikohe, 1890)

Group differences also became a basis for group quarrels. Some took place at school.

The personal and the arranged individual fighting were dwarfed by the mass fighting of the Reds and Blues. Can you imagine twenty Reds pitted against twenty Blues, making use with straps with buckles on them, with waddies, with six-foot manuka sticks, confronting one another in real battle array and at a signal, and with the use of rallying calls, entering the fray determined to overcome and rout the enemy? Blood flowed, heads and bodies suffered, until one or other side was overcome through sheer exhaustion and casualties! This section fighting assumed such ugly proportions that authority, in the shape of the Headmaster, stepped in and prohibited it. (Queenstown, 1880)

The individual and gang fighting of the day was often very harsh, and the younger and less virile members of the playground were terrorized by those stronger than themselves. The harshness did not stop there, however. In many places there were also initiation ceremonies. Ducking the tap was the most widespread of these customs. Others had a more unique flavor. Of these "king of the golden sword" was probably the most interesting.

The new boy was made to face the fence with his hands behind his back. There was a long ceremony about his crowning and entry into the school and then finally the golden sword (which had been dipped into the latrine) was pulled through his fingers. (Mt. Cook, 1890, Taita, 1900, Clyde Quay, 1900)

Another initiation rite was "Pee wee some more yet." The initiate was blindfolded and ordered to pee-wee some more yet into another boy's cap. The cap turned out to be his own. (Mt. Cook, 1890)

In these ceremonies the forbidden parts of the body were involved a number of times. For example,

We would take the boys' and sometimes the girls' trousers down and then spit on their privates. (Hutt, 1900)

One very interesting initiation ceremony was to take the new boys down to the stables and wait till a horse was urinating and then spin him under the stream. (Petrone, 1900)

He had to eat a half a tin of pipis. (Rangitoto, 1900)

We peed in his cap. (Thomas, 1900)

He was invited to a tug of war with his cap. The cap was held in the teeth of the initiate and the teeth of one of the big boys. Hands were supposed to be behind backs. While the struggle was in progress, the big boy urinated over the initiate who would not see the operation because of the hat, but had learned about it only gradually and with surprise. (Takaka, 1870)

These various examples talk about children's play. Obviously, I have chosen some of the more brutal, the more furtive, and the more inversive of the play of those days. I suggest that there is little more freedom in most of this than in most of the play in tribal cultures where all are expected to be involved. My point is that voluntariness, intrinsic motivation, or freedom of choice are not essential concepts to any universal definition of play.

This general position is supported by a review of the most comprehensive book on children's play in England, *The Lore and Language of Schoolchildren* (1959) by Iona and Peter Opie as well as the most recent work of an ethnographic sort on the British playground by Andy Sluckin, *Growing Up in the Playground* (1981). This is true also of the most comprehensive work on American children's play, *One Potato, Two Potato* (1976) by Mary and Herbert Knapp.

Voluntariness is not quite the universal characteristic that we need for a definition of play. Indeed, there is an amusing contradiction in *Homo Ludens* (Huizinga, 1955) between his idealized bloody and terminal contests of chapter 3, which are, in his terms, "fought out in deadly earnest" and "fought to the death" (p. 48), and his lamentations about modern professional sport, which, in his final chapter, he accuses of being insufficiently spontaneous and careless and not like "the play of children."

Nursery Play

Perhaps, we might more easily support the idealized notions of play by an examination of the literature on nursery school play. Here unlike the anthropological, animal, and playground literatures, it becomes increasingly difficult to know what is being studied. In general, in the relevant literature, any voluntary behavior clearly is not play. Unfortunately, of the nonplay free behavior of children, only *exploration* has been very systematically studied. Piaget (1961) has, in addition, talked about the *constructive imagination* as another kind of intelligent activity counterbalanced between accommodation and assimilation. However, he does not call it play. A great proportion of what little children do in any situation, therefore, is simply intelligent activity of the analytic (exploratory) or synthetic (constructive) kind. Possibly, such intelligent activities are free, intrinsic, and positive, but if they are not play that does not help.

In addition, it has been estimated that children spend about 60% of their time observing others (White, 1975). How much of this is observation and how much is idling (vague daydreaming) is not known. We do need to remember that "the big five" of adult leisure across all classes and groups are television, alcohol, tobacco, gambling, and sex. A certain passivity with respect to life is certainly the characteristic of the first three. Our children may be no better. Recent writings on the earlier years also describe the great deal of negotiational activity that must go on as little children argue about their different play frames and either gain or fail to gain access to those of others. In fact, some writers collapse the meaning of play into this kind of political action. Playing, as Garvey (1977) puts it, is saying.

Solitary Play

Finally, we come to solitary playful activity. Unfortunately, we know very little about this at either the adult or child level, but this kind of activity is what those who idealize play attend to in some intuitive way. Much of solitary activity, however, is not play: *Dreams* of the night and dreams as recollected in the morning and those *reveries* that accompany most of our waking activity reprocess our lives in a variety of ways over which we have little conscious control.

Presumably, *fantasies* are a mixture of reverie and wishful control. Here we imagine things the way we would like them to be. Solitary play may be different from this, or it may simply be the child's acted out version of fantasy, because he or she does not have the internal processing to do it in the way an adult can. Seeing that we all control this solitary kind of material to a great extent and, presumably, make it good for ourselves, is, perhaps, some sustenance for our notion that play is voluntary, intrinsic, and positive.

The previous arguments suggest, however, that there is very little relevance in applying this wishful fantasy and solitary activity to any evaluation of active social play. They are simply too different for comparison. In fact, this kind of wishful play can go on in the midst of any other action, whether it be officially termed work or play. Play defined this way is not opposed to work or sport—it is simply omnipresent.

In sum, I have suggested that play is idealized, have given reasons why that is so and reasons why it should not be so. The most difficult thing now is to identify play in a way that is more secure and more scientifically useful to us in our consideration of the relationships between play and sport.

Will the Real Play Please Stand Up

Play can be involuntary, extrinsically motivated, be possessed by negative affect, interstitial and ephemeral and have no clear rules. Of course, as Huizinga says, it can also be the reverse of all these, but the point is that our understanding is not especially advanced by this particular group of terms.

Although I have been working on the subject of play off and on since 1960, I must confess that it is a most abstruse subject matter to me. However, I view play as a kind of cultural antithetical material carefully masked from our full understanding by a series of communication phenomena. These carefully guard its transitions in and out of everyday life.

The Negative

First, with respect to *the negative*, if we follow Bateson on the play of animals, their inability to state a negative forces them to modify their positives, so that their playful intent is unmistakable. They want to indicate that they intend to bite but not to kill. Consequently, they minimize or exaggerate their acts so that there can be no mistake. Similarly, in human behavior we find these same principles at work, whereby our *schematizations* (miniaturizations and exaggerations) of phenomena indicate that this kind of "play" phenomena is of a different order: that we are playing mothers, not being mothers. More important, even when we verbalize that we are only playing, we still state ourselves in negative terms in play by "saying the opposite of what we mean in order to get across the proposition that we mean the opposite of what we say" (Bateson, 1972:141).

Bateson relates this latter role reversibility to the fact that in play we deal with primary process material, which like animal behavior, also has no access to negatives. Can we, indeed, establish that role reversal is fundamental to social play? In play we pretend to be people that we are not. We allow ourselves actions that are not a part of our everyday lives (we scream, we run, we sing, we chant, we skip, we punch with gloves, or we kick footballs). Furthermore, we engage in reciprocal role reversal systems where we take turns at shifts in power and action: We go on attack and then on defense. First, we are the winners, then the losers. We establish order, then we bring it into disorder. Having established disorder, we return to order. Having accepted, we reject: having chased, we escape; having approached, we avoid; and so on. A case can certainly be made that not only does play reverse some aspects of everyday reality, but this is a phenomenon in which reversals within the play itself are a focal concern.

Why is this so? Freudians suggest that inflicted as we are with primary process struggling against the forces of socialization, there is ever such a need to find ways of sublimating this material in nonharmful ways. Cultural symbolists like Simmel (Wolff, 1950), V. Turner (1974), Babcock (1978), and Murphy (1971) add that similar tension between conventional structure and unconventional antistructure also exists on the cultural level. They argue that necessary enculturation instigates tensions to the contrary that make their own demands for fulfillment, which crop out in community festivals, in rites of reversal, in bachanalianism, and so on. They suggest that these irruptions are not simply accidents or deviances but are, in general, fundamental to the maintenance of the whole community structure. They create subcultures that make the dominant cultural system tolerable to all concerned. At the Mardi Gras, the low can be made high. In West Indies cricket, the economically disenfranchised natives can take a temporary position of superiority (James, 1963). In Welsh or New Zealand rugby the ordinary and forgotten folk can exalt in their international superiority at a game formerly the preserve of the upper classes.

Some strength to this argument that play and sport function to deal with cultural or psychological antithetical material is given by the careful way in which these phenomena are packaged or signalled. Considerable research recently on the ways and means of signalling, negotiating, maintaining pretense, and gaining access have all been shown to be of considerable importance at all age levels in the maintenance of play. These may not be rules of play in the old-fashioned sense, but they are clearly systems of communication that are meant to guarantee that all concerned know that this is play or this is sport, not the everyday realm. Adults manage both to support and to ignore the playful state of affairs of children by statements, for example, that it is "only play" or "just kid stuff." More frequently, they adopt a studied disattention. Most adults find children's playgrounds distasteful places to be and do not like to be near them or have to supervise them; nevertheless, by and large, they let them be. We need to know much more about the characteristics of what might be termed the "playese" by which we allow and disattend these arenas of the infantile negative. In adulthood, the boundaries are more clearly institutionalized as far as sports are concerned. In everyday adult behavior we tend to mask our playfulness when it occasionally appears by humor. We are only joking we say, for example, if caught at some immodest mimicry of the opposite sex.

Masks of Play

In much of adult play and sport, we actually conceal our revealed ambivalences by *masking metaphors*. (Sutton-Smith & Kelly-Byrne, 1984). We tend to select from the play or the sport those facets that most clearly support our notions of an ideal self. Thus, at games we emphasize the toughness or skill that we have displayed, a toughness, incidentally, that is antithetical to what we are permitted to show most of the time in everyday relations. We do not emphasize our tenderness: the enjoyment that comes from being acceptable to the group of other players. A built-in duality exists within games in which some parts of the games are sanctioned for use as metaphors for the meaning of the whole game, whereas other parts are not so sanctioned. Thus, the culturally ideologically acceptable terms like winning, skill, guts, stoush, and mash are usable as metaphors for the game; their opposites, dependency, caring, and trust, are not.

Correct or not, these are just more arguments for the careful masking of the function of these plays and sports. In social play we share with others many of our superficial or deeper ambivalences about the life we lead.

Play Systematics

Having emphasized the negative and antithetical or ambivalent character of the phenomena, however, I need now to emphasize that we are not talking about a rebellion or a dissolution of society. What we have here is clearly a subsystem under careful control. Although during childhood and adulthood play can always be irruptive and potentially disruptive, most of the time it is nothing of the sort. Play is usually carefully contained within present boundaries. The systems of framing, of "playese," and of masking, all have their intention that the phenomena should link up with the rest of society in normative ways. We are all aware that a tendency for sports as they become institutionalized is to become idealized and to take on rituals of the flag, for example, thus making them safe for society. In general, however, what most recycles the negative elements back into society is their function in creating small societies of players. When the players are in dyads, then friendships and, perhaps, intimacies occur. In larger grops this sharing of cultural secrets is more superficial but nevertheless in much the same way conjoins the members in mutual enjoyment. They become committed to each other and develop loyalties that can go beyond their involvement in the particular play or sport.

I have not placed any particular emphasis on the qualities of arousal or of flow that some have seen as central to play. Nor have I stressed the importance of the sense of being in control, of autonomy, and so forth, also mentioned by many theorists. Although permitted access to antithetical emotions brings a special kind of delight and passion, we need to envisage this in cultural and systematic terms, not as attributes of the individual alone as these descriptions imply.

The way in which play and sport are parts of relationships has been emphasized with patterned ways in and out of their subsystems. Play and sport are antithetical, and the great extent to which they incorporate as well as antithesize society has been neglected. They are its paradigm as well as its parody; they are its orthodoxy as well as its heresy. We only play at those things that our culture and we care about such as power, love, and achievement. I have argued at great length elsewhere that play and games are best metaphorized as dialectical in structure, being a peculiar synthesis of elements that would be incompatible in the everyday realm. The winning and losing are made compatible by the game, whereas they are often not in the everyday (Sutton-Smith, 1979).

Possibly, play, as an incorporated heresy, actually gives service to the imagination, to creativity, and to the social construction of reality as the various idealizers have argued. Perhaps, its underground warfare vitalizes and irrigates the world of the possible. We cannot blithely assume that play has nothing at all to do with the rest of our creative lives without a more differentiated view of the phenomenon itself. The "play of the world" is not to be purchased by the kind of vagueness that currently characterizes this field.

Play and Sport

Play and sport are of the same order of culture. Both are initially antithetical subsystems of the larger society, both clearly signal and are cleverly masked, both reveal underlying ambivalences, both are structurally dialectical and both involve varieties of reversals.

Play and sport probably differ in their degree of access to private versus public emotion, in their informality or their institutionalization, in their potential randomness versus their relative conservatism. Play is more likely to be irruptive, disruptive, more private, and of less widespread social consequence.

Finally, the idealization of play or sport, which has become the substance of most theories of play, is simply one more mask, one more rhetorical device serving the arguments of those who need this or that prestige, this or that attitude to sex or to family, this or that science, this or that nostalgic childhood. Perhaps, what this idealization fails to admit is that the heresy is the nature of both sport and play, and that incorporated heresy is fundamental to the world in which we live.

For the sport sociologist, the useful *moral* of this story is that although sport may on occasions be bad (exploitation, drugs, national prestige, television, injury, hazards, relevance to college, neglect of women, glorification of violence), to talk of sport as destroying the spirit of play is somewhat absurd. Both play and sport lie in the same bed of ambivalent passion. Whether Greg Stone would have enjoyed this thought or not, he would certainly have liked its trickiness.

CHAPTER 7

A Response to Sutton-Smith's "Idealization of Play"

Gary Alan Fine

Almost 13 years ago to the week, Gregory Stone served as a discussant for a paper by Brian Sutton-Smith at the first Sociology of Sport conference held by the Big-Ten schools in Madison, Wisconsin. I am tempted to echo the opening of Stone's remarks at that time and let my comments go at that: "I'm tremendously impressed and excited by Professor Sutton-Smith's paper. I have really nothing in the way of criticism" (Stone, 1969:148). Then, as was his wont, he took Sutton-Smith's paper on "The Two Cultures of Games" (1969) and tied the discussion of the differences between achievement-oriented and ascriptive cultures to a wide range of phenomena, including why children no longer play tricks on Halloween, David Riesman's concept of inner- and other-directed people, baseball, sex-role socialization, and Turkish linguistics.

It seems fitting that Brian Sutton-Smith should have been honored as the first invited speaker for the Gregory P. Stone Memorial Lecture in the Sociology of Sport. The significance of that choice derives from more than the fact that they are both outstanding scholars in this area; they both have several other traits in common.

First, both men are "terminally interdisciplinary." Are we to classify Brian Sutton-Smith as a sociologist, psychologist, educational researcher, historian, anthropologist, or folklorist? Perhaps, we can add area studies as well for his work in New Zealand social history and culture. Greg Stone, as we all know, also had a wide range of interests ranging from sociology to classics, linguistics, philosophy, and history—to name but a few of the areas where he had some expertise. Both Stone and Sutton-Smith set their task to examine human behavior without regard to disciplinary boundaries. The world for them was one, not segmented by academic turfs.

Second, both men, as those who know them are aware, are playful, game-loving, and sporting people. I shall not attempt to disentangle these highly multivalent terms further. However, both incorporate play into their personalities—they both take their seriousness playfully and their play seriously.

Finally, in their work I see a basic similiarity—a similarity that gives both men their importance in the sociology of sport. Neither is content to accept the commonplace assumptions about sport, the clichés of our field. Both men are profoundly subversive of the traditional ideologies of sport, games, and play. This is true whether it is Sutton-Smith's contention that sport, games, and play are not universal in all their forms, or Stone's contention that orientations to sport and games are contingent on social class.

What is most distinguishing about both is their profound antisentimentalism. Both seem to take a scholarly satisfaction in ripping off the veil of these seemingly pleasant but trivial activities. Sutton-Smith has termed the effect of sentimentalizing children's play "the triviality barrier"; in his chapter he indicates that play is not as "nice" as it might appear. Play can be nasty, and we should not attempt to transform this nastiness to niceness. Stone in his justly classic article, "American Sports: Play and Dis-play" (1955), now over a quarter of a century old, points to tensions inherent in American sports: economic, political, and social. This is a theme to which Sutton-Smith returns in his work.

We must recognize that those fundamental aspects we frequently take for granted in our examination of play and sport may not be valid. Voluntarism has traditionally been a central characteristic of play, but this may be a false claim, as Sutton-Smith points out. Here, we may be getting into some confusion as to what we mean by voluntarism. Traditionally, in the literature on play, the concept has been used to refer to institutional constraints on social actors. In other words, the person is not forced by that strange and omnipotent master (society) and its organizational handmaidens (schools, for one) to play in particular fashion. Thus, work and schooling are in an institutional sense nonvoluntary, and play is somewhat different from this—in that its constraints are not organizational or structural.

Yet, is play truly voluntary? As Sutton-Smith indicates, there can be such intense social pressure brought to bear on potential players that it may not be valid to claim that play is free. Play can be forced, although the force typically derives from a different source than that which requires work.

One word summarizes the focal point of this address: *rhetoric*. The relevant point is that play and sport can be whatever people want them to be, and that what they want them to be may depend on political and status considerations. As sociologists of sport we may have spent too much time on definitional work, assuming that firm boundaries for these concepts could be arrived at, or that they would be helpful if they could be determined. Sutton-Smith's approach is to suggest that definitions and characterizations are tools that are used in sociopolitical struggles. Play and sport, from this perspective, are not terms with clean boundaries; rather, they are symbols that can be manipulated in order to create socially relevant meanings. This viewpoint suggests that the *uses* of sport and play, and the *uses* of the *concepts* of sport and play, should be our foci for discussion.

I found Sutton-Smith's discussion of the class-based perspectives on the so-called need for more sport, play, and, recently, fantasy for disadvantaged children particularly telling. Upper-class people are continually informing lower-class ones that they are lacking in something other than what they truly lack: money and power. Sutton-Smith's discussion of class reminded me of Stone's writings on how lower-class people are willing to accept wrestling as a sport in a way that upper- and middle-class people are not. Stone quotes one beer-drinking wrestling fan as he slams his hand on the bar, shouting "I don't give a damn if it is fake! Kill the son-of-a-bitch!" (Stone, 1972:301). Sport means different things to different segments of society, and these groups are likely to cast aspersions on other groups who do not agree with them about the structure and moral nature of sport.

This approach rests on an assumption recently stated explicitly by Joseph Gusfield in his book, *The Culture of Public Problems* (1981), drawing on the work of Kenneth Burke, Hugh D. Duncan, Gregory Stone, and others. Gusfield argues that public life is a drama filled with symbols. Symbols in this playform can be created and manipulated by participants—here for serious ends. We sport researchers should move away from reifying and defining the concepts of sport, play, and games, and recognize that these terms may be used without a conscious realization of all of the implications of the act. Thus, children play without saying or even thinking, "now I will play." They just do it.

These terms frequently are used in order to make a point about the natures of people and civilization, rather than being purely descriptive. For example, Little League baseball is often discussed in light of moral concerns. Those who like this "game" see it in terms of training the child to work within a cooperative environment, training him or her in physical skills, and keeping the child out of trouble. The positive view of Little League baseball occasionally stems from a working-class perspective, which argues that Little League is part of a child's ticket out of the neighborhood—eventually to college (possibly otherwise unattainable) and, in a few cases, to the big money of professional sport. Little League from this point of view is a blessing.

Others see a darker side of their rhetoric. Here the pressure and the exploitation of Little League is cited as well as its lack of freedom. Little League has been transformed from a game to a "sport" with many of the negative implications that Sutton-Smith has touched upon. This perspective is grounded in the upper-middle class view of the world where sport is not a means to anything else but should be only an end in itself. Fun is the only reward—not money or a college education.

Little League baseball, therefore, represents a playground where certain political and economic positions can be staked out in the guise of talking about children's leisure. It is not a question of whether Little League baseball is "right"—but whom it is right for, and who will use it (or its absence) to enforce their view of what proper childhood activity should consist. Similar analyses could be made of other childhood activities—Halloween pranks, quasi-sexual activities, playing video-games, or Boy Scouts. The critical issue is that from the scholarly perspective, we must see these activities as existing in a web of moral meanings, reflecting the structure and divisions of the larger society.

Sport, play, and politics are terms from the same world—the world of symbolic meanings. When we analyze sport and play, we are talking about human nature and our conceptions about what is good and sinful, about political and social systems, and about the proper relationships between individuals and collectivities. From this insight the sociology of sport is made part of the social sciences: From the comprehension of symbols comes understanding of how meaning structures our obdurate reality.

Part 1
Questions for Further Study

Taken as a whole, the chapters in this section are as indicative of the general state of social theory as they are of sport sociology. Contrasting paradigms, differing domain assumption, methodological variation, and conflicting schools of thought are the important stuff of sociology. Not only should we not expect consensus, we should be fearful of sociological unanimity, for no sociologist nor theoretical school has cornered the market on truth.

Although debate may be healthy, it also can be confusing, especially when academicians resort to the use of jargon and wage battles that seem trivial to the uninitiated. We hope the use of jargon has been limited in these chapters. Also, it should be pointed out that what may appear trivial or only a matter of semantics may be crucial in theoretical discussions. The downfall of many students is to assume that serious theoretical discussions can be read lightly. In fact, to appreciate any theoretical work, one must accumulate a certain level of understanding of the theory. Generally, this is possible only through background reading.

One's understanding of social theory will be enhanced gradually the more deeply one delves into the field. One way to accomplish this is through the investigation of specific problems. Listed below are several questions suitable for term papers or class discussions, which might serve to further inform students and increase their understanding of social theory.

The State of Social Theory in Sport Sociology

Why have some general theory perspectives (e.g., systems theory) seemingly been avoided in sport sociology? Conversely, as Kenyon (chapter 1) notes, why has so much attention been paid to structural-functionalist and conflict theory perspectives? What is the dominant paradigm in sport sociology today? Is it a form of positivism as suggested by Ingham (chapter 2), or is it a Marxist paradigm? Should sociologists be expected to treat sport any differently than other subsystems in this society?

The Eliasian Perspective

What is the Eliasian perspective? Dunning (chapter 2) calls it a figurational-developmental perspective. Where would such an approach fit into Kenyon's list of theoretical categories? What does Curtis (chapter 3) mean when he states that Elias' work is an example of unilinear evolution?

How can we explain the seeming lack of communication between European and North American sociologists? What has been the impact of North American social theorists on European sociology?

What are Pearton's domain assumptions? Is Pearton an Eliasian? How might Pearton's work be categorized using Kenyon's typology?

The Play-Sport Relationship

Might sport appropriately be categorized as a subset of play, or are they essentially distinct? What difference does such a definitional resolution make in terms of how sport is understood and studied? What is the paradigm that informs Sutton-Smith's work (chapter 5)? Why does Fine (chapter 6) think that sociologists have spent too much time defining sport? Is such a statement affected by his theoretical paradigm?

As a result of reading the chapters in this section has your understanding of sport been affected? How is your view of sport related to your view of society? What questions would you most like to see researchers in sport sociology address? Do you think your research priorities are affected more by your view of sport or society? Is there any way to separate the two?

PART 2

Substantive Issues

In this section the commitment to theory extends to several substantive areas in the sociology of sport. An interest in socialization has characterized this subfield since its conception, so it is fitting that socialization is the first of these substantive areas. Barry McPherson provides a major contribution (chapter 8) in which he calls for a "new wave" of research in socialization in sport that would combine different theoretical and methodological perspectives. His ideas are applied by Jay Coakley (chapter 9) to youth sport, a popular area of research in sociology of sport. Both contributions are critiqued by Rees (chapter 10).

From a subject that has received a great deal of attention from sociologists of sport, we then turn to one that has received very little. Small group research has been a neglected area in sociology of sport, despite early optimism (see Lüschen, 1969). In the hopes that interest in that field will be rekindled, the editors asked several leading researchers to analyze the area from different theoretical perspectives. Günther Lüschen (chapter 11) adopts primarily a functionalist perspective and calls for a return to analysis at the group and system level. Gary Fine (chapter 12) shows how the symbolic interaction prespective is important in understanding group processes in sport. He suggests that every sport team has its own separate culture or "idioculture," which has to be taken into account when analyzing concepts such as group cohesion and leadership. Because social psychological theories have been more popular than sociological theories in the analysis of sport groups, it was important to include a view from this perspective—specifically, group dynamics (chapter 13). Neil Widmeyer, who has recently done research on group cohesion in sport teams, reviews some of the substantive developments of this field and discusses several relevant theoretical and methodological problems presently being faced by researchers such as himself. The theoretical approaches to research on the sports group represented by Lüschen, Fine, and Widmeyer are reviewed by Merrill Melnick (chapter 14). In summary, the sport group is alive and well and is awaiting research from any or all of these perspectives. Future researchers have the potential to enrich our knowledge of sport groups and at the same time extend social theory.

One of the earliest contributions to the sociology of sport was the critical or "muckracking" approach (see Melnick, 1975). Radical sociologists were critical of the state of college sport (J. Scott, 1971) and professional sport (Hoch, 1972). An interest in intercollegiate athletics has been sustained by sociologists of sport to this day. Analysis of college sport from three theoretical perspectives current in sociology are included here. James Frey (chapter 15) presents a functionalist approach that, knowingly or unknowingly, has guided the thinking of most supporters of college athletics. Eldon Snyder (chapter 16) presents a symbolic interaction analysis of college athletics. He demonstrates that, even in this supposedly regimented world, athletes and coaches define their roles idiosyncratically and show great concern in managing their social identities. A conflict theory perspective is offered by Stanley Eitzen (chapter 17) as central to an understanding of the economic and social problems that presently plague big-time college athletics. These three theoretical perspectives are reviewed by John Massengale (chapter 18) from his unique vantage point as sociologist and practitioner. Massengale conducts research and teaches in the sociology of sport and is also an athletic director.

The final chapters in this section deal with the topic of applied sociology of sport. If sociology of sport is to grow, the knowledge developed must be of use to practitioners involved in sport organizations. The fact is supported by Günther Lüschen (chapter 19), as he develops the idea of action knowledge in sociology of sport. How this knowledge can be translated into sport policy and practice and some of the problems with this process are outlined by Barry McPherson (chapter 20). He provides us with a fascinating "blow by blow" account of his work with youth sport organizations in Ontario. The Lüschen and McPherson contributions are reviewed by Roger Rees in the final chapter of the book. Fittingly, these chapters raise the issue that underlies this book, that is, the need for a strong theoretical base for the sociology of sport. Such a commitment is important if the "critical mass" (Loy, Kenyon & McPherson, 1980) of sociology of sport is to be raised. Only then will applied sociology of sport become commonplace rather than unusual.

CHAPTER 8

Socialization Theory and Research: Toward a "New Wave" of Scholarly Inquiry in a Sport Context[1]

Barry D. McPherson

Ten years ago I completed an extensive review of the basic literature on socialization theory and research prior to initiating my PhD dissertation. Therefore, it was with some excitement and enthusiasm that I accepted the challenge to review the recent literature and identify some postulates and suggestions for future directions concerning youth socialization in a sport context. However, once I began to examine the literature from the past decade, my enthusiam waned and disappointment prevailed.

This intellectual deflation resulted for two related reasons. First, I had expected that by the 1980s some clear, irrefutable postulates or laws should have been firmly entrenched in the literature. This, I did not find to be the case. A second reason for my disenchantment was the unfulfilled hope that substantive knowledge concerning some facets of the process would have approached closure, so that subsequent research efforts could be more focused rather than so eclectic. As I will illustrate throughout this chapter, the last 10 years have been characterized by continued eclecticism in both substantive concerns and theoretical approaches.

Areas of Substantive Concern: An Overview

Pre-1971

Prior to 1971 a structural-functionalist perspective predominated, along with the almost exclusive use of cognitive, developmental, social learning, and role theories. Moreover, most emphasis was on describing and explaining the process whereby infants, children, and adolescents learn to behave as social beings within their particular culture or subculture.

Thus, racial, gender, class, and ethnic variations in the process were identified, although white, middle-class males most frequently were the subjects of research. Throughout these studies, which were initiated within a variety of disciplines, the emphasis tended to be on the product (i.e., a particular skill, attitude, or role) and the degree to which socialization has occurred, rather than on the microdynamics of the process within given social systems. To illustrate, although it is well understood that the family is an important social system and that the parents and older siblings serve as role models, little is known about the dynamics whereby the socializee accepts or rejects varying characteristics and teachings of the role model. Similarly, the degree and process of reverse socialization, wherein the socializee socializes the role models, has received little emphasis.

1971–1981

In the early 1970s relatively few studies of socialization were published. However, since 1975 there has been renewed interest in the process and concept, from both theoretical and empirical perspectives. Concomitant with the growing interest in social gerontology, a large number of articles in the past decade have focused on socialization through the life cycle, with particular emphasis on the early, middle, and later years of adulthood (e.g., Looft, 1973; Rosow, 1974; Mortimer & Simmons, 1978; Rose, 1979). Moreover, the emphasis, especially in studies pertaining to adulthood, has been more on the acquisition of specific skills or roles, than on general facets of social learning. Similarly, with changing roles and power relations between men and women, there has been increased interest in sex-role socialization, sexual behavior, and occupational and political socialization as it pertains to females, increasingly from the feminist perspective (see articles on this topic in the following two journals: *Signs* and *Sex Roles*).

Regardless of the stage in life, the most common areas of substantive concern in the literature during this period, in relative order of frequency, have been: (a) sex-role socialization, with some articles in recent years representing the feminist perspective; (b) occupational, organizational, or professional socialization; (c) theoretical and methodological approaches for studying the process; (d) the role and dynamics of various family structures in the process and product; (e) political socialization; (f) socialization via the mass media, especially television; (g) cross-cultural studies; and (h) linguistic, cognitive, and personality socialization. Increased attention has also been paid to the subprocesses of anticipatory socialization, desocialization (role exits, disengagement), and resocialization at various stages in the life cycle. Furthermore, the process and product of socialization have been studied in relation to such current social concerns as criminal behavior, health behavior, aging and the aged, drug and alcohol use and abuse, intergenerational conflict (i.e., the generation gap), sexual behavior, the physically and mentally disabled, and religious cults and fanaticism. In short, there has been increased interest in individual learning, more so than in cultural transmission, and in the discontinuity and atypical aspects of socialization. Thus, in some respects, the concept has been utilized in recent years in a more applied sense to describe and explain prevailing social concerns in North America.

For the most part, cognitive developmental theories and social learning theories continue to guide studies from a theoretical perspective. However, with the increasing diversity in topics and a growing interest in the process whereby less socially acceptable behaviors are acquired (e.g., premarital sex, drug and alcohol use, joining religious cults), the research studies tend to be more atheoretical. Hence, the study of socialization is eclectic and multidisciplinary in nature and has been based on biological, learning, and cognitive-developmental theories.

To illustrate, cognitive socialization principles are not universal and, quite likely, vary by the social context in which the socialization process occurs. Furthermore, within sociology in particular, the process has increasingly been studied in recent years from a multiparadigmatic perspective. As a result, greater attention was paid to studying facets of the process from such theoretical perspectives as symbolic interactionism, ethnomethodology, exchange theory, and general systems theory. Finally, there has been a continuing debate and tension concerning whether the analysis of the process has viewed man as "oversocialized" or "undersocialized" (cf. Boldt, 1979). This continuing discussion has led to a consideration of the "biosocial" image of man and to the conclusion that both an over- and undersocialized image of man prevails (cf. Strauss, 1978a). As a conceptual compromise, Boldt (1979) suggests that we utilize a "moderately socialized" image of man.

The remainder of this chapter examines some of the issues and future directions derived from a review of the recent socialization literature. Quite clearly each topic comprises a chapter in itself. Therefore, I have selected recently published articles or books that include some heretofore unaddressed issues or represent a unique approach to the study of socialization. They are presented to stimulate thought and scholarly inquiry in future studies on socialization in a sport context. Unfortunately, the literature does not provide the basis for compiling a compendium of postulates at this time.

Recent Theoretical Approaches and Concerns

Because of the interdisciplinary, eclectic approach to the study of the process and the multifaceted character of the process, it is unlikely that any one theoretical perspective will ever adequately account for the process or end product. In recent years social scientists were somewhat more willing to consider alternative theoretical approaches to support explanations, rather than as competing views of the process. To illustrate, Dawe (1970), speaking of the "two sociologies," argues that less emphasis should be placed on the normative approach wherein deviance is viewed as nonconforming and incomplete socialization. He argues that more emphasis should be given to an interpretive approach (e.g., elements of symbolic interactionism, phenomenology, ethnomethodology) wherein the individual seeks to gain control or mastery over his or her situation, relationships, and institutions. In this latter approach the focus of study is on such elements of the process as the definition of the situation, presentation of the self, and negotiation with others.

This more recent approach to the study of socialization has been prevalent within sociology as a result of three interrelated developments. First, an adequate explanation or theory must account for both the transmission of culture and for the development of autonomous human beings. That is, there are two interacting levels of analysis for which different theoretical approaches are most appropriate. Thus, at the macrolevel more universal outcomes occur; conformity to societal norms is the goal; the social order continues despite turnover in the role players; learnings are generalized from one social situation to another; the process is more predictable; and the individual passively responds to socializers and the environment. At this level, social learning theory, role theory, reference group theory, and cognitive and social development theories are more likely to be powerful explanatory frameworks.

On the other hand, where individual learning and situation-specific outcomes are the goal, and where the process is less predictable and depends more on the active involvement of the socializee in determining the outcomes, theories that account for interpersonal interaction and negotiation are more useful. For example, the symbolic interactionist perspective views socialization as an active rather than a passive process. This perspective recognizes that new and novel meanings and definitions of the process can be created; that nonconformity, deviant responses, and maladaptive outcomes are responsible; and, that uncertainty prevails in the process (cf. Mortimer & Simmons, 1978; Yaels & Karp, 1978). Similarly, exchange theory (cf. Nord, 1973) recognizes the importance of social approval in social learning and accounts for the active negotiation by the socializee,[2] whereas expectancy theory suggests that specific aspects of socialization will most likely occur where the expectation of rewards is high. Finally, systems theory (cf. Feiring & Lewis, 1978; Nakayama, 1972) suggests that much can be learned about the socialization process by analyzing the interaction process and meaning within the basic familial subsystem—the triad of mother, father, and child.

A second development promoting greater use of microlevel theories has been the prevailing acceptance in recent years that socialization is a life-long process. Thus, there has been greater interest in socialization during the middle and later years, especially with respect to adaptation to role transitions (e.g., divorce, widowhood, retirement, middle-age unemployment, re-entry of women into the labor force, etc.). As a result, social scientists have recognized that the use of one perspective is not likely to account for the life-long process of socialization, and that particular theoretical perspectives may be most appropriate at different stages in the life cycle. To illustrate, during infancy and early childhood, the functionalist perspective using social and cognitive development theories may be most appropriate to explain the process, wherein as the social being ages, a conflict, exchange, or symbolic interactionist perspective may be more appropriate during adolescence and throughout adulthood (cf. Dowd, 1980; George, 1980).

A third, and perhaps the most influential, factor leading to the increased use of alternative approaches was a revival of the debate concerning whether the analyses have viewed people as "over" or "under" socialized. In recent years at least three publications have sought to resolve this debate. Yaels and Karp (1978) argued that the use of the symbolic interactionist perspective meets the criticisms of Wrong (1964). They also concluded that there is no "over" or "under" socialization, but rather that there are different mechanisms or levels of socialization that must be explained. Similarly, Boldt (1979) suggests that the concern regarding the two conceptions of people can be alleviated by a greater emphasis on symbolic interactionism that shifts the focus from social structure and the outcome of conformity to the process of negotiated interaction, personal meaning, and nonconforming outcomes.

The most recent and comprehensive attempt to resolve this debate seeks to synthesize the two views by presenting a bilevel theory that accounts for the structural and the interactional elements of the process (Wentworth, 1980). Wentworth begins by critiquing the almost dichotomous "sociologistic" and "individualistic" orientations to socialization. The "sociologistic" approach emphasizes social structure, role learning through internalization by a passive individual, and conformity so that an "over-socialized" perspective prevails. The "individualistic" approach, in the early years, concentrated on moral, cognitive, and ethical learning and was mainly studied by psychologists. However, later, sociologists emphasized the active role of the socializee in social learning via negotiated interaction. As a result of this negotiated interaction, social order and conformity may not evolve, thereby leading to the view that people were "undersocialized."

In an effort to present a synthesis, Wentworth (1980) began with the rather logical and simple premise that the social structural elements impinge on the individual who is an active participant in the socializing process. He then suggests that there are five facets to include when viewing the socialization process at the macro- and microlevels of analysis:

1. Investigators must distinguish between socialization as internalization and socialization as interaction. That is, whereas internali-

zation is primarily a cognitive process where the individual passively accepts the elements of the social world, interaction is an active, reciprocal process between the socializer and the socializee and between the self and the environment. In this latter process it must be confirmed that what is taught is learned and accepted.

2. Even though traditional symbolic interactionism involves the view of the participant, Wentworth favors a more objective approach wherein socialization should be studied from the perspective of the observer.

3. The acquisition of cultural rules so that the individual is able to participate in social life is the most important outcome of the process.

4. Greater emphasis needs to be paid to the social "context" or social situation where socialization or "reality construction" occurs. That is, a greater focus is needed on the interactional or ecological setting (cf. Bronfenbrenner, 1979).

5. Power and social control are essential concepts to be included in a theory of socialization because they are essential resources to be acquired and used in social interaction.

In summary, Wentworth's synthesis argues that the process operates on two levels, and that special attention must be paid to the social structure, the specific social contexts where interaction occurs, the acquisition and use of power, the reciprocal process of interaction, and the active role of the socializee.

By implication, future work concerning socialization in a sport context needs to abandon the almost exclusive use of the functionalist perspective and become more theoretically integrated. This does not imply that eclecticism should prevail, but rather that conscious attempts to examine the process from a merged theoretical perspective are needed to advance knowledge. More specifically, a merging of cognitive, developmental, interactionist, and social learning theories and concepts might be fruitful for understanding the acquisition of the affective and cognitive components of the process (cf. Wackman, 1977). Similarly, a merging of role and exchange theory might account for the learning of behavioral components; whereas a reciprocal merging of the personality and social systems might clarify "the consequences that the process of socialization has for the individual in an internal or psychological sense" (Di Renzo, 1977:268) as well as "the mediating processes whereby personality dynamics input into the function of social systems" (Di Renzo, 1977:285). In short, not only is there a need for greater use of microlevel theories but also for the integration and synthesis of theories within sociology and between sociology, psychology, and related disciplines. This should be the basis for the "new wave" of socialization studies.

Recent Methodological Approaches and Concerns

Whereas early studies of socialization were based on observation, interviews, questionnaires, and even some standardized measures of cognitive or maturational development, socialization has become such a "catch-all" concept and process[3] that methodological pluralism and inadequacies prevail. As Greenberger and Sorenson (1974:356) have observed, "research on socialization and human development tends to focus in a piecemeal way on a wide variety of individual traits, attitudes, and values. There are few comprehensive, coherent, and generally accepted themes which organize such variables and guide research."

In an attempt to improve conceptualization, and thereby methodological approaches, Di Renzo (1977) substituted "humanization" for "socialization." He argued that humanization was a more appropriate generic label for several processes of social learning and development, and suggested that there are four distinct, yet integrated, subprocesses, which could serve as the major focus of attention for specific disciplines. These subprocesses, with their major discipline in parentheses are: (a) maturation (biology) of the biological organism across the life cycle; (b) culturation (anthropology), which represents processes and knowledge transmitted to the individual via enculturation or acculturation; (c) socialization (sociology), which pertains to the structure and processes of social learning that are optional and external to the organism; and (d) personality development (psychology), which represents the internal or psychological development of the organism within its own unique qualities or attributes. An illustration of this approach is a model of psychosocial maturity proposed by Greenberger and Sorensen (1974). They combined the sociological component of socialization and the psychological component of personality development to account, from a functionalist perspective, for the requirements of the social system and the development of the individual.

Another attempt to introduce more rigorous conceptualization and methodology has been presented by Triandis (1977). Recognizing that findings on social behavior have not been universal and valid across time, space, and culture, Triandis identified several systems of variables, which he reduced to four: ecological-subsistence, sociocultural, socialization, and individual. These systems are linked together, but variations within each system and the influence they have on variations in other systems are not well understood because multiple measures within the various systems have seldom been utilized. Thus, there is still considerable need for definitive conceptualization, which in turn may lead to more methodological rigor and consistency. In short, greater theoretical and empirical integration continues to be an elusive goal, although the problems of "identification, measurement, and empirical assessment of theoretical linkages between personality systems and social systems" (Di Renzo, 1977:285) have been a principal area of concern in recent years.

In addition to methodological concerns derived from conceptual problems, a number of specific methodological limitations need to be continually addressed and resolved in socialization research. The following appear to be some of the more serious decisions facing those who intend to initiate socialization research in the future:

1. There is a need to study those who have not been socialized, or who have been undersocialized, rather than those who have acquired and internalized specific behaviors, attitudes, values, roles, and so forth.

2. There is an urgent need for longitudinal, panel, and intercohort studies, especially to separate age-related from generational, cultural-historical, and cohort effects (cf. Bengtson and Cutler, 1976).

3. Greater efforts must be made to distinguish between the response to a questionnaire or interview and actual behavior (cf. Baumrind, 1980). This especially applies to studies of children's attitudes (cf. Vaillancourt, 1973).

4. In light of changing outcomes of sex-role socialization, both the stage of development and the sex of the child need to receive more serious attention when studying patterns of childhood socialization. That is, more ethnographic and comparative research on sex differences is clearly needed (cf. Baumrind, 1980; Rosenblatt & Cunningham, 1976).

5. Greater attention should be directed to understanding the impact of the environment or ecology where children are being socialized. This goes beyond the need for more rigid controls of social class and race to include an analysis of the physical and social environment. To illustrate, because of social change, gender-related socialization effects are even more salient today than they were before the onset of increasing and greater gender equality at all ages. In short, the sex differences reported in socialization studies in the 1960s and earlier may be totally inadequate for explanation today—at all stages of the life cycle and within different cultural environments.

6. Greater effort needs to be directed toward controlling real-life phenomena. Within the last decade the utility and validity of the logical, positivist research paradigm has been seriously questioned as representing an overmechanistic, static model of human development. As a result, a need has been expressed for organismic models, which are "naturalistic, longitudinal investigations that treat the person or the family rather than the variable as the

unit and which use multiple stimuli in many representative situations to assess children and their parents" (Baumrind, 1980:648).

7. Related to the above point, Baumrind (1980:650) further notes that "we need hypotheses and research strategies that take into account naturally occurring person-situation interactions and do not reduce human activity to stimulus-response units or to immediate roles and statuses."

8. With increasing recognition of the complexity of the process, greater attempts must be made to utilize multi-directional linear and curvilinear causal models, even though reciprocal causation is difficult to test and verify. This is especially important when temporal factors are considered to be theoretically relevant, and when the influence of reverse or reciprocal socialization effects between individuals (e.g., parent and child) must be analyzed (cf. Bell & Harper, 1977: Bell, 1979; Buss, 1981; Henderson, 1981).

9. Increased attention needs to be given to the interaction of the person with the social context by observing people in typical contexts where natural constraints function to influence behavior. To illustrate, the internalization of "honesty" and the demonstration of this characteristic in daily behavior might vary depending on whether the individual is in a bank or a store with barrels of candy; whether they are engaged in pick-up baseball, a Little League game early in the season, or the championship game; and, on whether the mother, father, younger sibling, or older sibling is present when freshly baked cookies for the school sale are left on the kitchen table.

10. Similarly, generalizations concerning gender differences may be highly situation-specific. For example, the mother may demonstrate aggresive behavior when protecting her family, which is similar to behavior displayed by her spouse in the occupational setting.

11. Considerably greater attention needs to be directed to the development of social competence and child-rearing characteristics and patterns within a number of gender, class, racial, and ethnic subcultures. This is especially true in light of social change within industrialized societies and rapid modernization in developing nations. For example, to what extent does the meaning of "competition," "competitiveness," "aggressiveness," and so on vary over time and across stages in the life cycle? Here is an example where the processes of desocialization and resocialization are not well understood, in general, and with respect to behavior in a sport context.

12. With respect to socialization across the life cycle within the family, greater attention needs to be directed toward identifying cohort versus lineage effects. This is particularly a concern with

socialization during the middle and later years (cf. Bengtson & Cutler, 1976).

13. As suggested earlier in the chapter, greater efforts should be directed to examining the unintended short and long-term positive or negative consequences of various aspects of the socialization process—that is, the "side effects" or "discontinuities," such as those relating to socialization into highly competitive sport before 10 years of age.

14. There should be more analysis of the interaction dynamics within and between social agents and social systems involved in the process at different stages of the life cycle.

15. There is a need for a better understanding of the consequences of the process for the individual in terms of the personal system. That is, how does a change in personality influence values and orientation toward social reality? This illustrates where greater integration of the personality and social systems is needed; conceptually, theoretically, and methodologically.

16. The conceptualization of the process needs to include both passive (i.e., imitation, direct teaching, internalization) and active (i.e., a reciprocal, ongoing process of interaction or negotiation between the socializer and the socializee, or between the self and the environment) aspects of the process. For example, with increasing levels of organization and bureaucratization within youth sport, more learning of values, skills, and orientations may be occurring via direct teachings from a standardized curriculum than via negotiated interaction with socializing agents.

17. Finally, related to most of the above points, there is an increasing need to understand the structure of the social world from the child's perspective. This will enable a more complete explanation of the process with respect to the continuities and discontinuities in the outcome.

In summary, the issues, concerns, and suggestions highlighted above represent those that have been raised in the literature in recent years. Although there are a number of specific methodological concerns, most of the issues relating to research in the area are based on theoretical and conceptual issues that must be resolved first. As in any area of research, fuzzy or incomplete thinking about social phenomena cannot be overcome with sophisticated designs or statistical treatments. Rather, the design and conceptualization of a study must be compatible if the level of understanding is to be enhanced.

Substantive Concerns and the Implications for Future Study in a Sport Context

The remainder of the chapter represents an analysis of substantive issues about socialization that have appeared in the literature since 1971. However, I have not provided a detailed synthesis of the literature, but rather have selected specific ideas from articles that may have particular relevance for the study of socialization concerning sport behavior. As a result, the large body of literature on adult socialization, occupational or professional socialization, and political socialization is neglected, except to provide an overview of current topics of interest and to indicate particular concepts, methods, approaches, and so on that might have relevance for the study of socialization as it pertains to sport during childhood and adolescence. In the other substantive areas, interesting approaches and unique ideas are highlighted to provide suggestions for future scholarly work in this area.

As a caveat, I must indicate that my general impression of this field at the present time is that eclecticism prevails with respect to substantive, theoretical, and methodological concerns. Perhaps, this is partly due to the fact that much of this "socialization" literature is appearing in obscure, "minor-league" journals rather than in the generally accepted mainstream journals, and that emerging fields such as family studies and mental and physical rehabilitation are utilizing the concept with greater frequency. One clear result of this dispersion is that novice investigators seldom have a total awareness or understanding of the literature, issues, and approaches in the more traditional disciplines. This often results in an unnecessary quasi-duplication, but not a replication, of approaches or rationales across areas. The natural outcome of this situation is that there has been relatively little increase in our knowledge about the process or end product—despite the fact that the concept has been utilized to a greater extent with different populations and in different contexts.

The Socialization Process in General

The following represent concerns, approaches, or issues about the process, in general, which merit future consideration in socialization research in a sport context:

1. The progression from passive acceptance of roles to active involvement in the shaping of roles needs to be considered and under-

stood. As a starting point, an article by Thornton and Nardi (1975) should be consulted. They suggest that the process of role acquisition involves temporal progression through four stages: anticipatory, formal, informal, and personal. Each stage is characterized by the type of expectations that predominate and to which role learners must give specific attention. Thornton and Nardi argue that just because the individual occupies the role, it does not mean he or she has been fully socialized. Thus, the role is not fully acquired until the individual has anticipated it; learned anticipatory, formal, and informal expectations included in the role; formulated his or her own expectations about the role; reacted to, reconciled, and internalized these various expectations; and, accepted the final outcome.

2. Whereas much socialization occurs via face-to-face interaction in a dyad, to what extent does television viewing in varying degrees detract from the process? (Chapman, 1972).

3. There is an increasing concern with competence (cf. Baumrind, 1978). Therefore, we need to better understand how and why varying degrees of competence in role performance evolve, and what the outcomes are of varying levels of effective role performance for the self and for society (cf. Hall, 1974).

4. There has been increasing interest in the development of particular facets of moral behavior (e.g., delinquency; premarital sex; tobacco, alcohol, chemical, or drug use and abuse) and the relationship between preceding and subsequent socialization practices and outcomes (cf. Furman & Masters, 1980).

5. Both intrasystem dynamics and intersystem dependencies in the socialization process need to be studied. More specifically, Hartup (1979) suggests that childhood socialization occurs via reciprocal causalities within conjunctive social systems. Similarly, Hawkes (1978) utilizes Litwak and Meyer's theory of shared function to stress the cooperative shared function between families and bureaucracies (e.g., youth sport organizations) with respect to the socialization of children.

6. Although virtually no attention has been directed toward the influence of science and technology on human social behavior, this is a strategic area for future study. For example, on the simplest level, will those who are socialized to accept and utilize technology in their daily lives (e.g., home computers) be more readily able and willing to cope with future social change which is initiated by dramatic advances in science and technology?

Socializing Agencies and Agents

Family

Despite the long-standing tradition of interest in the family as a unit of scholarly inquiry, there has yet to appear an integrative theory to facilitate understanding of the family as a dynamic social system which is present in most societies. Rather, the study of family dynamics still represents a mosaic of diverse topics, techniques, methodologies, concepts, and frameworks—although the structural-functional, interactionist, and family life cycle models have been utilized most frequently. However, within recent years balance theory, game theory, exchange theory, modernization theory, general systems theory, conflict theory, the feminist perspective, Marxist and neomarxist theory, ethnomethodology, phenomenology, and critical theory have been used to try to increase our level of explanation (cf. Glossop, 1980). As a result, the present state of the art is such that at best, a life-span developmental perspective is needed, along with contributions from many disciplines and the use of more than one theoretical perspective. In this way we may more closely approach an integrated synthesis of this phenomenon (cf. Cook & Blau, 1978). This is especially important in light of the impact of social change on the family structure and processes, and in the recognition that the family does not exist in a social vacuum but rather in a changing social and physical environment. The limited list of suggestions that follow are but a few of the more crucial concerns related to the process of socialization within the family context during the 1980s.

1. Although the family is not the sole agent, and may be less influential than in the past, it is still the basic socialization system and the system that interacts with and predetermines the influence of other agencies and agents.
2. The major factors (cf. L. Larson, 1980; Marjoribanks & Walberg, 1976) within the family system that merit consideration concerning childhood and youth socialization are: family social status (size, parental education, and occupation); family structure (size, birth order, spacing); marital relation (source of power, authority structure, degree of sexual and emotional satisfaction); parent-child relationships (degree of support, communication patterns); and personal attributes of the members (age, sex-role identification, personality).
3. The major dimensions of the socialization process must be viewed and studied as interpenetrating and linked processes. These

dimensions include: the structure and process of sociocultural influences on the attitudes, value orientations, and behavior of the individual; the reciprocal influence of individual attributes on the relative impact of these sociocultural influences; and the modes and processes by which the learning of roles takes place (Larson, 1974).

4. Culture is transferred both vertically (from parents to children and vice versa) and horizontally (between siblings) (cf. Tsukada, 1979) and within the same or contiguous generations. The relative and changing influence of the family for culture transfer (e.g., in single parent families for sport consumption and knowledge) needs to be examined more closely (cf. Bengtson, 1975; Feiring & Lewis, 1978; Saal, 1972).

5. The impact of the changing structure of the family (cf. Laslett, 1978) because of single parenting or dual breadwinners, especially in the middle and upper class, has not been studied sufficiently. To illustrate, what is the effect on the various facets of the socialization process of a household headed by a female where the separated father may be a playmate more than a disciplinarian for the children, and where the mother is in the labor force and children are cared for by extrafamilial surrogates?

6. Similarly, what is the impact of family disorganization through divorce or widowhood on the socialization process, and the outcome when reconstituted or blended families emerge after a divorce, either through cohabitation or remarriage? How and in what way do these changes in family structure have an impact on the sport role socialization process?

7. What is the influence on the socialization process of children raised in single versus dual career families? The process may vary because of the extent to which socialization responsibilities are delegated, neglected, or abandoned due to parental career interests.

8. There is a need to account for changing values and lifestyles concerning children and women's roles across society. For example, what is the socialization process for children raised by unmarried teenage mothers, many of whom remain single and on welfare? What is the impact for children born to parents who delay childbearing until they are over 30 years of age? Do these parents have less time and interest for childrearing?

9. With the changing position and status of women in some segments of society, to what extent are fathers more involved in day-to-day child care? If fathers are more involved, what impact does this have on young girls, especially concerning the sex-role identification process and their involvement in physical activity?

That is, is the father becoming a more nurturant and primary parent? If so, what impact does this have on the long-term outcome of the socialization process for males and females, respectively? (cf. Baumrind, 1980; Hoffman, 1977).

10. Within the family greater attention needs to be directed to such dynamics of the process as parent-child by sex interactions at varying ages and the long-term impact of these interactions on the offspring (cf. McBride, 1979); the quality and nature of parent-child relations during childhood and adolescence; the relative influence of the mother versus the father for specific outcomes; and the nature of the process by family size (from one child to many children in a family). To illustrate, McDonald (1977), using a social power theory of parental identification, argues that the more parental power each parent is perceived to have, the greater the degree of adolescent identification with the parent. Similarly, supervision by the parent in salient behavioral domains is positively related to parental value on conformity and negatively related to a parental value on self-reliance (cf. Ellis, Lee, & Peterson, 1978).

11. With respect to the changing role and status of women, what impact does this change have on the socialization process for children exposed to "liberated" versus "traditional" parenting styles? To illustrate, adolescent children of employed mothers were found to differentiate less concerning sex-role concepts than children of nonemployed mothers (Gold & Andres, 1978). A remaining question is: Do children exposed to the more egalitarian, liberated parental style encounter fewer sex-typed toys, receive fewer pressures for rigid, stereotypical sex-role identification, and receive reinforcement and encouragement for different play and sport experiences than children socialized by more traditional parents?

12. Twin studies suggest genetic influences on the development of individual differences in behavioral problems (cf. O'Connor, Foch, Sherry, & Plomin, 1980). Hypotheses based in biosociology might be a fruitful avenue for future inquiry concerning discontinuities and deviations from more normative patterns of socialization.

The School

Compared to the family, relatively few studies on socialization within the school system have been completed in recent years.[4] Perhaps this is not surprising in light of the relative stability in the structure and process of the educational system during the 1970s after the major restructuring which occurred in the 1960s. However, the following points suggest a few avenues that need to be considered in future studies:

1. Rosenbaum (1975) argues that the tracking systems in schools provide different environments for the students, and hence there are differential socialization processes in the upper and lower tracks. More specifically, he found that the upper stratum is exposed to greater opportunities for individual expression and development (i.e., self-direction prevails) whereas the lower stratum homogenizes members and reduces the relevance of prior experience (i.e., conformity prevails). To what extent do these tracking environments influence the sport socialization process within the high school system, and by inference, later in life?
2. Curtis (1974) argues that studies have failed to demonstrate that the school is an independent normative system. That is, there has been a failure to demonstrate that observed student orientations are acquired in school rather in other socialization settings such as the home or community.
3. Berger (1977) has argued that the socialization process within the school fosters sex role stereotypes and therefore hampers the socialization of females into the labor force. Thus, greater attention needs to be directed to gender differences in the process within elementary and high schools, in general, and with respect to sport in particular.

The Mass Media

Most of the interest in the role of the media in socialization has focused on how television serves specific socializing functions. Some of these include: the impact of television programs as socializing agents for mentally retarded children (Baran, 1977); the effects of campaign advertising and newscasts on political socialization (Atkin, 1977); the role of commercials and women in news events in sex-role stereotyping and sex-role identification (Whitlow, 1977; Scheibe, 1979); and the role of gossip columns as instruments of socialization and social control (Levin & Kimmel, 1977).

Brundage (1980) makes a number of points concerning television's role in socialization that merit consideration in future studies.

1. Not only does the child receive and interpret the content of the media, but he or she is also exposed to how parents, siblings, or peers interpret the content of the program(s). Thus, Archie Bunker's orientations may be criticized or reinforced; opinions concerning news events may be devalued or supported; and particular commercials or programs may be utilized to reinforce or discourage particular behavioral or attitudinal predispositions. As a result, television has the potential to reinforce, to contract, to

extinguish, and to extend the influence of other socializing agents. More specifically, it can provide support for, or alternatives to, deeply rooted family values and orientations.

2. Television may or may not assist in the education of a particular child, depending on the content. However, television may interfere with the educational process because viewing televison may interfere with, or turn off, other socialization activities.

3. The influence of television appears to decrease during adolescence as individuals move further from the family.

The future role of television in the socialization process may become more interesting, significant, and educational, both in general, and with respect to specific behavioral, cognitive, and attitudinal domains. For example, with increasing technology, two-way interaction will make television a more dynamic, interactive medium (e.g., via the Telidon system). Similarly, the appearance of speciality 24-hour cable channels enables consumers to "channel" their interests and to elect a range of educational or quasi-educational programs. For example, what is the impact of being socialized in a home where ESPN or the USA Network is available 24 hours a day versus a previous life style wherein even cable television may not have been available? In short, the impact of the availability of cable or satellite television programming on the socialization process in hitherto untouched markets may be a process akin to the diffusion of television sets in homes during the 1950s.

Social Processes and Socialization

Sex-Role Socialization

Not surprisingly, in light of social changes pertaining to the role and status of women, to increased or more open homosexuality, to an increase in the number of families where both parents work, to an increase in delayed marriage and childbearing, and to an increase in single parenting because of divorce, widowhood, and unwed mothers, more attention in the past 10 years has been directed to facets of this process than to any other area in socialization. These social changes have seldom, if ever, been considered in the sport socialization literature where the traditional nuclear family has been assumed to be the normative structure for socialization during childhood and adolescence.

The remainder of this section outlines substantive topics that have been addressed most frequently in this area in recent years.

1. Increased interest has been shown in the nature and extent to which parents hold changing expectations concerning the sex-role identification of the child. Whereas early studies tended to focus on mothers (cf. Langlois & Downs, 1980), in recent years

there has been increasing interest in the father's role in the process for young girls and boys. Fathers interact more with infant sons than with infant daughters, and they perform less nurturant caretaking than mothers (Lamb & Stevenson, 1978). However, with increasing extrafamilial opportunities for mothers, a need exists to examine the changing demands being placed on fathers and adult males for nurturant, caretaking roles (cf. Bearison, 1979; Knox & Kupterer, 1971), and the concomitant influence on the sex-role identification process of male and female children.

2. Interest in changing achievement motivations and work patterns of young mothers (cf. Hoffman, 1972; Klecka & Hiller, 1977) have sought to determine whether employment and a focus on personal career achievement enhances or detracts from the sex-role identification process of young children, especially girls. To date, the evidence is unclear and variations may partially be the result of personal competence, personality and cognitive style, as much as whether the mother works or not.

3. Throughout the literature a debate continues concerning the definition of "sex-role" and "sex-role identification" and how the concept should be measured (cf. McDonald, 1978). For example, McDonald suggests that children may not identify with the same-sex parent, but rather with parental power. Thus, the parent who is perceived to control the resources and decisions in the family is perceived to have more power and becomes, during adolescence, the main source of imitation or modelling. This suggests that the process may vary by age and may differ during adolescence compared to more sex-linked imitation during childhood.

4. To date, most studies have primarily focused on the process from a male perspective—as though it were a more crucial process for males. This view is changing, and future efforts need to focus on the process from both the male and female perspectives.

5. A continuing attempt to explain the process of sex-role learning has resulted in a number of possible alternative and complementary explanations. Some of the more recent explanations suggest that sex-related orientations result from the interaction of cultural values and personality and intellectual abilities that interact with cultural sex-role stereotypes (Birns, 1976), from situational factors rather than relatively immutable sex-based personality patterns (Thune, Manderscheid, & Silbergeld, 1980), from participation in sex-typed activities (Carpenter & Huston-Stein, 1980), and from the existence and perpetuation of gender stratification wherein sex-role values are internalized in a variety of social institutions where women have traditionally played subordinate roles (Vanfossen, 1977). In short, a number of alternative explanations for

the process have some degree of support, but a definitive explanation is lacking.

6. The role of toys, play, and games continues to be a topic of interest and to be perceived as a major mechanism of sex-role socialization (cf. Langlois & Downs, 1980; Lever, 1976, 1978; Wolf, 1975). However, if participation patterns in sex-type activities are changing (cf. Lueptow, 1980),[5] what are the implications for the future role of play, games, and sport as integral elements in the process of sex-role socialization?

7. Finally, although it is frequently assumed that most sex-role socialization occurs in the home, there appears to be renewed interest in the role of teachers and the school, perhaps because they may be required to play a more influential role in this process in the future (cf. Evans, 1979; Hahn, 1978; Schneider & Coutts, 1979).

Occupational and Professional Socialization

In recent years the primarily descriptive approach to examining procedures, processes, problems, and contingencies relating to entry into a specific occupation has continued. Some of the occupations that have been examined, in each case by a single study, include: teachers, dentists, pharmacists, military personnel, seminarians, and ballerinas. In addition, increased attention has been directed to blue collar occupational roles such as police cadets, prostitutes, and electricians. Throughout these studies it was found that much of the occupational socialization process involves some direct teaching, plus a large amount of modeling of superiors by the subordinates. Moreover, most of the emphasis has been on the acquisition of specific behaviors required for successful performance or survival in the job. Thus, the recent study by Laska and Micklin (1979), which stresses the importance of the cognitive dimension in occupational socialization, must be viewed as a new avenue to consider in future studies. In fact, with more complete and realistic anticipatory cognitive socialization, the expectations might better fit the realities of a specific occupation. Similarly, future studies might direct more attention to the role of personality in attraction to, and successful socialization into, specific occupations. As in other areas of socialization, there appears to be an increasing recognition of the inadequacies of the occupational socialization processes for women. Moreover, studies have noted gender differences in job performance, job attitudes, and levels of professional socialization, which may be attributed to the specific socialization process for a given occupation.

Finally, increased attention needs to be directed toward the learning of new occupations, or new roles because of promotion or unemployment during the middle years. To illustrate, Khleit (1975) noted in his

study of the professionalization of school superintendents that the process involves socialization to acquire a new identity. This required a
discontinuity with the previous roles and identity (e.g., as a teacher, principal) and an "unlearning" of previously held and cherished sentiments.
A similar shift in sport occurs when a player moves into a management
role. Similarly, whereas most of the studies have been retrospective in
nature, increased use of longitudinal designs and time lag regression
analyses are needed to control for the temporal effects from the stage of
anticipatory socialization to the stage of fully socialized involvement in
the position.

Political and Cognitive Socialization

The study of political socialization in recent years has shifted from the
learning of affective orientations or political party affiliation by children,
to the impact of specific political events and specific social categories or
events (e.g., adolescent radicalism, Watergate, nationality, race, single
vs. dual parent families) on the present or future political beliefs and
behavior. Perhaps the most important direction that is needed in this field,
as in the sport domain, is to better understand the process of cognitive
socialization in a variety of specific contexts (cf. Washburn, 1977).

With respect to cognitive socialization in general, most studies still focus
on infancy and the childhood years. However, social meanings are transferred from generation to generation and undergo change in the process.
They also require change because of social and technological changes in
society. Thus, in the study of socialization into sport, greater attention
needs to be directed toward the meaning of sport as taught to, and, more
importantly, as perceived by children and adolescents of different ages.
The meaning and social cognition of winning, competition, authority
figures, and consuming versus playing, for example, may be interpreted
and internalized in different ways by different cohorts.

Cultural Variations in Socialization: Class, Race, Ethnicity

Since the early 1970s, there has been considerably more interest in the
study of socialization from cross-cultural (e.g., Kumagai, 1978; Ryback,
Sanders, Lorenz, & Koestenblatt, 1980; Whiting & Whiting, 1975) and
subcultural perspectives (e.g., Aseltine, 1978; Buriel, 1981; De Vos, 1980;
Knight & Kagan, 1977; McCarrey & Weisbord-Hemmingsen, 1980).
Studies of ths nature have clearly identified significant differences in child-
rearing practices across cultures and between minority ethnic groups who
live within the same dominant culture. Of particular interest to scholars
in North America has been the attempt to understand the mechanism
or process whereby individuals are acculturated to some or all of the
elements of the mainstream culture versus being acculturated to the
minority group subculture (cf. Knight & Kagan, 1977). To illustrate, variations in religion, family size, parent's education, adherence to cultural
beliefs and traditions, sex-role demands and expectations, achievement

orientations, place of residence (i.e., ethnic homogeneity vs. ethnic heterogeneity), and family structure can significantly influence the nature and outcome of the process. Moreover, the extent to which the peer group provides alternative or compensatory socializaton to that provided by the family may be strongly influenced by the cultural or ethnic homogeneity or heterogeneity of the peer group (cf. De Vos, 1980). Similarly, the role of the media in perpetuating or changing images or practices of socialization within majority and minority groups must be monitored more closely.

Finally, increased attention in recent years has been directed to social class differences in the process. Whereas earlier studies tended to focus more on descriptive differences by social class in the outcome, more recent studies have centered on the mechanisms whereby these differences arise. For example, Bersani, Gillham, and Napady (1977) found that in low socioeconomic areas teachers and school counselors are the agents who spend the most time talking with youth, whereas in the high socioeconomic areas most discussion occurs with parents. Similarly, Ellis et al. (1978) noted that the middle class places a higher value on self-reliance than on conformity, whereas the reverse holds among blue-collar workers. Values held and espoused are related to the extent to which a particular value has been instrumental in the parent's own success within a variety of institutional contexts. Therefore, value orientations concerning achievement, competitiveness, aggressiveness, and socially acceptable occupational and leisure roles for females need to be examined in order to better understand the socialization process with respect to the sport domain.

Summary and Conclusions

This chapter presents a review of the socialization literature, with a special emphasis on the past decade. Rather than presenting a detailed review of specific studies, which is an impossible task within one chapter because of the diversity of topics found under the rubric "socialization," the chapter highlights significant theoretical, methodological, and substantive issues that need to be addressed in the future, both in general and with respect to sport.

The major conclusion to be drawn from this review is that despite a plethora of work in this area, more questions than answers remain about both the outcome and the process. Although this seems like an obvious, and perhaps trite conclusion, its significance is that the volume of work completed in this substantive area of the social sciences has likely been greater than that in any other area. Yet, we still lack complete and adequate explanations for most facets and stages of the various subprocesses. Therefore, it is clear that considerable conceptual, theoretical, and methodological work of quality remains to be initiated and to be completed with respect to all elements of the various subprocesses that comprise the phenomenon of socialization. In order to facilitate this "new wave" of scholarly inquiry, the following points merit serious consideration:

1. More emphasis should be placed on the process than on the outcome. This is partially related to the need for a greater emphasis on explaining rather than merely describing the outcome.
2. Increased attention should be given to the interaction between the biological, personal, and social systems through the integration of concepts and theories from biosociology, psychology, and sociology.
3. At present, the literature, especially outside mainstream sociology and psychology, is characterized by too many atheoretical and unrelated studies. At this stage in the development of socialization knowledge, the brickyard remains chaotic.
4. Different levels of theoretical analysis need to be integrated and utilized to explain the various levels of socialization (cf. Wentworth, 1980). That is, the micro- and macro-levels need to be integrated to explain different elements of the process and to explain the process at different stages in the life cycle.
5. The need for greater theoretical integration suggests a merging of the interpretive (i.e., an emphasis on negotiated interaction) and the normative (i.e., a structure and function) perspectives (cf. Dawe, 1970). Scholars must be cautioned not to confuse theoretical integration with rampant, unrelated eclecticism. That is, there must be a clear and valid conceptual merging of theoretical perspectives. In some respects, this implies the need for the creative development of synthesized middle-range theories and for scholars trained in different perspectives to work together.
6. A need exists for more emphasis on the dynamics and structure of the various social systems, rather than on merely describing the relative influence of one system compared to another. To illustrate, we know very little about the process of socialization in general, or subprocesses in particular (e.g., sex-role, political, occupational, or sport role socialization) in families that are headed by either a single parent or dual "breadwinners." In short, the impact of social change on the process within specific social systems needs to be studied.
7. Further, with respect to social change, current efforts need to focus on the impact on socialization of changing sex-roles, the influence of science and technology on our daily lives, and specifically, the impact of technological changes that may initiate new forms and uses of the mass media.

8. Future studies need to devote more attention to the process of reciprocal socialization at all stages in the life cycle; and to understanding the processes from the perspective of the socializee—whether the novice be child, adolescent, or adult, or whether they are voluntary, quasi-voluntary (i.e., reluctant conformers), or involuntary (i.e., coerced) participants in the process.

9. Longitudinal studies are needed to separate aging, cohort, and historical-cultural effects in the long-term process across the life course. In addition, longitudinal studies are needed to identify the influence of early life outcomes on the process for events, role transitions, and so forth, which occur at later stages in life.

10. Related to studying socialization as a life-long process is the need to place greater emphasis on the processes of desocialization and resocialization, especially with respect to the process of adjustment to transition points such as divorce, widowhood, the empty nest, or loss of job during the middle years or at mandatory retirement.

11. Another benefit of the longitudinal approach is that it would enable us to comprehend the "side effects" of the process, both in the short and long term. Here, special attention could be given to accounting for "discontinuities" in the process. More specifically, within a sport context, this would facilitate an understanding of the impact of being involved in highly specialized competitive sport programs from an early age (e.g., age-group swimming, gymnastics, figure skating) on social maturity in early adulthood.

12. In the past, those "not socialized" have been considered atypical and have received little scholarly attention. In the future, the "failures," the "drop-outs," and those who opt not to be socialized in some respect merit serious attention. To illustrate, those not socialized into various sport roles may well outnumber those who have been socialized. Maybe it is time we studied those who represent the "normative" pattern of sport involvement.

13. Finally, in all future studies there is a need to more adequately and completely account for variations in the process due to class, race, ethnicity, gender, nationality, and uniqueness in subcultural values and orientations.

In conclusion, much work remains for the creative scholar. I hope the next wave of inquiry will lead to more order in the brickyard and will result in the accumulation of a compendium of "defensible postulates"— an order that I regret to say is difficult to fill at the present stage of development in this substantive area of inquiry.

Notes

1. This paper could not have been written without the library research and conceptual assistance of Dr. Yasuo Yamaguchi.
2. As an aside, I wonder to what extent children are socialized into participant and consumer roles in sport to gain approval from a parent, rather than because they have a high level of intrinsic interest in the activity.
3. To illustrate, socialization is concerned with language acquisition; moral, social, and cognitive development; sex-role development; interpersonal competence; development of the self; personality development; becoming deviant; adaptation to institutional settings; occupational learning; the acquisition of political, religious, and leisure attitudes and behavior; adaptation to physical and mental disabilities; aging phenomenon such as role transitions; minority group acculturation; cross-cultural and subcultural variations; and so forth.
4. In fact, we were able to find only 6 articles with socialization within the schools as the major focus of attention.
5. For example, computerized and electronic games are much less sex-based than toys and games encountered by earlier cohorts. Similarly, in sport, at the elementary school level coeducational games are increasingly prevalent in the curriculum and on the playground.

CHAPTER 9

Socializaton and Youth Sports

Jay J. Coakley

Over the past decade the topic of youth sports has generated an amazing amount of attention. Television news programs and the major national news magazines have featured special programs and stories about the pros and cons of the ever-increasing number of organized sport programs for children. Publications and programs on the local and regional levels have done the same. Among social scientists there have been similar discussions. Much of what social scientists have written consists of critical but impressionistic generalizations about the experiences of the young participants in organized programs. More recently there has been a growing number of systematic investigations of how children are socialized into and through sport participation, but most of these are atheoretical and unrelated to one another. To describe the area of socialization and youth sports as a chaotic brickyard (McPherson, 1981a) remains appropriate.

Before discussing the present state of knowledge in this area, it is necessary to define the terms *socialization* and *youth sports*. First, youth sports refer to formally organized, adult supervised, competitive sport programs for preadolescent children (i.e., children less than 13 years old). Second, socialization refers to a process of social interaction through which people develop, extend, and modify their conceptions of who they are and how they relate to the social world around them. This latter definition emphasizes that socialization

1. occurs through social relationships (real, imagined, or anticipated) with others, especially significant others;
2. involves *more* than a simple one-way process of learning in which a person's self-conception and manner of relating to the rest of the world is passively shaped by other people and social events; and

3. is never complete, that is, it is a constantly emerging process involving the changing interface between a person and the surrounding social world.

These terms are explicitly defined because researchers have been guilty of conceptual ambiguity in many of their investigations of socialization and youth sports. Some have confused formally organized, competitive sport programs with a variety of activities in which physical skills are involved. Others have limited their conception of socialization to simple skill acquisition and the development of measurable character traits and have ignored the dynamic social processes that make up the essence of socialization itself.

Socialization Into Youth Sports

This side of the socialization and youth sports question has received less attention than the issue of how children are influenced through their participation. However, the physical fitness movement among adults has raised new questions about how people are introduced to physical activities and how their participation patterns are formed and altered. This creates new relevance for the topic of how children are socialized *into* youth sports.

There are a few noteworthy theoretical and empirical investigations of this topic. In fact, we are at a good starting point for the development of hypotheses and the initiation of further research. For example, Kenyon and McPherson's (1973) discussion of sport and the process of socialization contains 18 propositions related to the socialization of young people into the role of sport participant. Most of these propositions are yet to be tested and qualified through empirical research. Studies by Susan Greendorfer and her colleagues at the University of Illinois,[1] Snyder and Spreitzer (1976a, 1978), and Mike Smith (1979) have raised a number of questions about the differences between the ways males and females are socialized into sport. Similarly, research by Greendorfer and Ewing (1981) indicates racial variations in socialization patterns leading to sport participation.

Unfortunately, most of the information we have about the process through which children are socialized into sport comes from studies of white, male high school and college athletes or top-level amateurs. In these studies, subjects have usually been asked to recall significant positive influences at various points in their sports careers. Occasionally, their responses have been compared to the responses of subjects who are not elite performers. However, the use of comparison groups has been rare. These studies have increased our understanding of general socialization patterns in the life cycles of *elite athletes*, but they have told us little about the specific processes leading to a child's involvement in organized youth sports. On a general level we know that a child's initial involvement is influenced by: (a) the availability of opportunities; (b) relationships with family members, peers, media role models, and local neighborhood role models; and (c) his or her self-perception as a potential program participant. However, there are numerous questions about each of these factors yet to be investigated. Following are some examples:

- What types of sports and sport program structures are most attractive to children and how do preferences vary by gender, socioeconomic status, race, type of community, geographical location, and country?
- How does the attractiveness of organized, competitive sport programs compare to the attractiveness of other forms of physical activities?
- How does the availability of opportunities vary by gender, socioeconomic status, race, type of community, geographical location, and country?

Questions about relationships

- How is the decision to become involved in an organized sport program tied to specific relationships in a child's life?
- How does the relative significance of different relationships vary for different children?
- What is the difference between encouragement and pressure in a child's relationship with others?
- How are participation decisions influenced by media role models and/or role models in the immediate social environment of the child?

Questions about self-perception

- How is a child's decision to participate tied to identity (i.e., self-conception, body image, self-esteem, and past experience)?
- How is the role of sport participant incorporated into a child's self-conception and everyday life events?
- How is involvement in sport related to issues raised by developmental theorists such as Mead, Piaget, Kohlberg, Bruner, and others?
- How does the media influence the self-perception process in ways that either encourage or discourage sport participation?

In exploring these issues it is necessary to use comparison groups of children who have not chosen to be involved. Furthermore, there is a need for more creative methodological approaches. As McPherson has suggested, there must be attempts to "distinguish between the response to a questionnaire or interview and actual behavior" (see chapter 8). Therefore, qualitative as well as quantitative methods of data collection must be utilized to describe and to analyze the processes of which a child's sport related behavior is a part.

Socialization and Continuing Participation in Youth Sports

The issue of continued involvement in sport falls between the topics of socialization into sport and socialization through sport. The definition given earlier emphasized that socialization is never completed. Therefore, socialization into sport is an ongoing process, and the decision to stay involved is continually problematic. The dynamics of "participation careers" for the preadolescent have generally been overlooked in research on socialization and youth sports. For example, little is known about the circumstances under which participation is maintained, expanded, restricted, shifted, discontinued, and/or resumed by children. Nor is much known about how these various patterns in participation careers vary by gender, socioeconomic status, race, and age, or about how they are related to types of personal experiences such as success or failure. Furthermore, little is known about how success and failure are defined by young participants and how the experiences of young participants are mediated by parents, peers, coaches, and others.

The phenomenon of dropping out of organized sport programs has been investigated by Guppy (1974), McPherson, Guppy, and McKay (1976), Orlick (1973, 1974), and Orlick and Botterill (1975). Each of these exploratory studies provides a basis for raising further questions about who drops out of what programs for what reasons. They also suggest that dropping out is done for many different reasons and that the term "dropping out" describes only a part of what happens when a child fails to return to participate in a particular sport program. Competing nonsport interests, the demands of school, residence changes, shifts to other sports or other sport programs, and new preferences for less structured physical activities are all part of this so-called dropping out phenomenon. Further research is needed to specify the types of changes occurring within a child's participation career as well as the conditions leading to these changes.

Another dimension of a child's participation career is the manner in which sport is integrated into the participant's life. We have little information on the meaning of involvement from the participant's perspective. We know nothing about the extent to which a child's behavior within the context of sport is indicative of internalized values, the process of identification, or merely the result of compliance to overtly expressed expectations coming from coaches, parents, and peers. Qualitative methods such as those used by Faulkner (1974a, 1974b) in his study of professional hockey players are needed to uncover some of these crucial dynamics of sport participation careers during childhood. A good example of the use of this methodology in a youth sport context is provided by G.A. Fine (1979a). With systematic observations he describes how baseball coaches construct moral meanings through their interpretations of events and experiences during a Little League season. Now there is a need to discover how players on youth sport teams construct their own moral meanings. Probably there are some significant differences between adults' and players' interpretations of what occurs in the youth sport experience. As the patterns of these differences are outined, our understanding of socialization and youth sports will greatly expand.[2]

Socialization Through Sport

Participation and "Character" Changes

In 1978 Loy, McPherson, and Kenyon surveyed the literature on this issue and concluded that:

> There is little, if any, valid evidence that participation in [organized] sport is an important or essential element in the socialization process, or that involvement in sport teaches or results in...character building, moral development, a competitive and/or cooperative orientation, good citizenship, or certain valued personality traits. (p. 244)

Similar findings have been reported by others (Loy & Ingham, 1973; Stevenson, 1975). Since 1978 nothing has been learned to dramatically alter this conclusion (King & Chi, 1979; Kleiber & Kelly, 1980; Magill & Ash, 1979). At the moment it is safe to say that most of the observed differences between participants and nonparticipants can be accounted for by: (a) the voluntary and involuntary selection processes connected with organized sport programs, and (b) the fact that many such programs provide adults with unique opportunities to see their children display skills and attributes acquired during normal processes of growth and maturation.

However, this "safe" conclusion is far from being definitive. Research is needed to control for selection and maturation along with other variables such as the conditions of involvement, the nature and duration of the participation experience, and the social feedback associated with participation. Research on the interscholastic athletes strongly suggests that young people are most likely to be affected by participation when it leads to changes in their social status within the family and among close friends, and alters the nature of feedback received in these relationships. This emphasizes the notion that the sport experience takes on meaning through the participants' relationships, especially close, personal relationships. In other words, the most important thing is not what the child does to the ball or what the ball does to the child, but rather how the child's interpretation of the sport experience is mediated through relationships with others (see Watson, 1976, 1977a). As long as research continues to compare participants and nonparticipants through simple cross-sectional analyses of mean scores on a variety of character trait measures, the socialization process itself will never even be described, much less understood.

This emphasis on relationships and social processes suggests that studies on the topic of socialization through sport need a new model to guide research design and analysis. In this model the identity and behavior of the individual would be the dependent variable and social feedback would be the independent variable. Sport participation, always considered to be *the* independent variable in the past, may be best dealt with as an antecedent or intervening variable in this model.

Participation and Achievement Orientation: A Special Case

Critics accuse organized sport programs of teaching impressionable young people to give winning and personal success higher priority than fairness and a concern for others. Support for this criticism is usually grounded in research showing that young people with experience in organized programs rate a victory over others and a demonstration of personal skills higher than playing fair or having fun (Kidd & Woodman, 1975; Mantel & VanderVelden, 1974; Webb, 1969). In other words, participants are likely to develop a "professional orientation" toward their own sport involvement and move away from a "play orientation." However, the research supporting this conclusion is methodologically weak, which raises questions about its validity.

Such studies often use Webb's three-point paper-and-pencil question to "uncover" the priorities of young people when it comes to winning, playing well, and playing fair (or having fun). Usually, all the respondents who give priority to a combination of winning and playing well are classified as having a "professional orientation." Those who give priority to playing fair (or having fun) are classified as having a "play orientation." Research suggests that a play orientation is less common among participants in youth sports than among those who do not participate in formally organized programs.[3] The reason for this may be related to a weakness in the question itself. For example, participants in youth sports are likely to use their experiences in *organized* games as reference points to respond to the question. Those not involved in youth sports are likely to use *informal* games and play activities as reference points. If this is the case, children who participate in youth sports can be expected to rate fairness relatively low compared to their nonparticipating counterparts because in their organized games fairness is taken for granted. Fairness is guaranteed by referees and umpires, and it is not something players have to think about. On the other hand, fairness is a major concern for those whose experiences occur in informal settings. In fact, if it is not a major concern, their games are not likely to last very long, if they ever get started in the first place.

The participants in youth sports are likely to give higher priority to winning and to playing well because organized games are objectively structured so that these concerns are important. They are important regardless of the personal orientations of the players. The higher professionalism scores of the participants may be more a measure of how the setting is formally defined than a measure of personal orientations. Nonparticipants do not play in settings where win-loss records and personal performance statistics are kept, or where adults watch and control game events. In the absence of these situational factors, it is not difficult to see why these young people are less concerned with winning and playing well. If they were in an organized game with adults controlling, watching, and evaluating them, they might not see things in such a playful and "nonprofessional" manner.

Similarly, the participants in youth sports are likely to define playing well, winning, and having fun as one and the same thing (Scanlon & Passer, 1978, 1979). The game itself has been officially structured so that fun is objectively defined in instrumental terms. However, fun in informal games has an emergent quality. It depends on creativity and expression along with playing well; its definition is open, and it becomes more of a concern than for players in an organized game. This concern, however, is less a function of personal orientations than of situational factors surrounding the activity.

In summary, the scores on the commonly used professionalism scale are probably more of an indication of the structural conditions under which games are played than of the enduring personal traits of those questioned. Of course, it must also be remembered that youth sports tend to attract young people who enjoy the instrumental challenges provided by organized games. Therefore, participation is very likely to be the result rather than the cause of professional orientations. This interpretation is strongly supported by a recent study done by Roberts, Kleiber, and Duda (1981).

Participation and "Little Leaguism"

A few years ago Sherif and Rattray (1976) made an interesting observation about the activity patterns of North American children in middle-class families. They noted that television viewing time of these children increases "in direct proportion to the efforts adults make to involve them in organized activities" (1976:102). The inference underlying their observation was that adults may be wasting their time and money on organized programs because the programs themselves do little to teach young people to handle discretionary time.

This possible effect of youth sports was also discussed by Devereaux who has argued that the condition of "'Little Leaguism' is threatening to wipe out the spontaneous culture of free play and games among American children, and that it is therefore robbing our children not just of their childish fun but also of some of their most valuable learning experiences" (1976:37). Goodman (1979) and Opie and Opie (1969) reached similar conclusions in their respective studies. Of course, not everyone agrees with this interpretation of how youth sports have affected young people. Wohl (1970, 1979) argues that organized programs provide people of all ages with incentives and models for their own informal participation. Lever (1976, 1978) suggests that participation in youth sports may be one of the reasons why boys seem better able than girls to create more complex games and group activities in their free time. Similarly, Westkott and Coakley (1981) discussed the possibility that one of the functions of youth sports for girls is to provide females with knowledge of complex game models that can carry over to their informal play groups. Futhermore, organized programs can show girls and young women that playing active and competitive sports on their own is accepted and legitimate.

In summary, we clearly need further research on this question. For example, I have observed that some children are seemingly able to use participation in youth sports as a starting point to get together with friends and to make up numerous games and activities on their own. Organized sport experiences may be valuable catalysts in the development of the physical skills needed to create a wide variety of informal games. However, other children who participate in youth sports do not seem to have the faintest idea of how to create a game on their own. Research is needed to increase our understanding of the conditions under which participation in youth sports either improves or destroys a young person's abilities to initiate and to maintain leisure activities.

Conclusion

This brief and selective review of the literature suggests that we have made little progress in uncovering the dynamics of the socialization processes associated with youth sports, and that we know little about the meanings of involvement from the perspectives of young people themselves. The usefulness of future research in this area depends on: (a) a clear conceptualization of both socialization and youth sports, (b) the use of sound theoretical perspectives to develop hypotheses,[4] and (c) the use of creative methodological approaches to uncover the dynamics and the meaning of behavior among young people in sport and sport-related contexts. McPherson (see chapter 8) has called for a "new wave" of scholarly inquiry into the phenomenon of socialization; this chapter leads to the same conclusion.

Notes

1. See Greendorfer (1977b, 1978, 1979), Greendorfer and Lewko (1978), and Lewko and Ewing (1980).
2. See also Kleinman and Fine (1979) for an informative discussion of how the moral meanings constructed by those in positions of authority relate to social control and the self-conceptions of Little League players. Research by Watson (1976, 1977a) focused on the meanings children attached to the organized sport experience and how these meanings vary by socioeconomic status.
3. An often underestimated finding in this research is the fact that most young people adhere to a play orientation rather than a professional orientation; few young people, even those in organized programs, are so obsessed with winning that they are willing to forsake fairness and fun.
4. A discussion of how sociological theory can be used to guide our understanding of and research on youth sports can be found in Coakley (1981).

Socialization and Sport:
A Response to McPherson and Coakley

C. Roger Rees

This response cannot provide a detailed review of McPherson's survey of 20 years of sociological research on socialization. Some of the theoretical and substantive implications of his review for socialization research in sport will be discussed with particular reference to the youth sport research discussed by Coakley. Both these reviews provide valuable starting points for students interested in doing research in the area of socializaton and sport and for sociologists interested in sport who want to update their knowledge of recent theoretical and substantive developments in the general area of socialization.

According to McPherson, the sociological research in socialization during the 1960s was characterized by an emphasis on outcomes. Sociologists were interested in how the social system functioned to produce a fully socialized individual, and which were the most important agents in this process. Not surprisingly, sociologists were guided in this endeavor by functionalist theory, which at the individual level, is concerned with how the system influences the socializee. As McPherson points out, there were reactions to this approach, for example, the "oversocialized/undersocialized conception of man" debate (Parsons, 1962; Turk, 1965; Wilson, 1964; Wrong, 1961, 1964), but this debate did not change the theoretical perspectives.

Sociologists interested in sport also utilized functionalist theory. Specifically, researchers investigated factors influencing the degree to which children become involved in sports (Kenyon & McPherson, 1973; Snyder & Spreitzer, 1976b), and what, if any, effect this involvement has upon them (Loy & Ingham, 1973). This approach to socialization and sport was criticized (Hoch, 1972; J. Scott, 1971), but these radical critiques failed to suggest alternative theoretical models from which to generate research.

In one sense, by asserting that involvement in sports produced "mindless robots" who obeyed the system without question, these critics provided support for a functionalist perspective.

This perspective has also been applied to youth sports. For example, Webb (1969) and others who have used his approach (see Coakley's review, chapter 9) were interested in how and why childrens' orientations toward play and games changed from a "play orientation" to a "win orientation." While Webb saw this as a logical extension of the socialization process in a society that stresses achievement, others saw it as a result of the differential socialization through sport. Boys had a more "professional orientation" toward participation in sport than girls did because participation in organized sports was more salient to them (Kidd & Woodman, 1975), whereas boys who participated in organized sport programs had a higher "professional orientation" than those who did not (Mantel & VanderVelden, 1974).

Findings such as these were interpreted as part of an "oversocialized conception of youth in sport" and critics claimed that youth sport programs are too competitive, reduce spontaneity and free play in childrens' leisure time pursuits, and do not give children adequate opportunity to interact with their environment (Devereux, 1976). More recently, Sutton-Smith questions this criticism and suggests that sociologists were guilty of painting an idealized picture of childrens' play when contrasting it to organized sport (see chapter 6).

Concentrating upon the effect of the social system upon the individual is only part of the picture. McPherson points out that, in recent years, socialization research is concerned with the process as well as the outcome, with understanding how individuals interact with their environment as well as how they are changed by it. In calling for a "new wave" of research on socialization in a sport content he asks us to pay attention to this social process. Although not as common as research from a functionalist perspective, examples of this approach are in the literature (e.g., Fine, 1979b; Marsh & Harré, 1978). In the area of youth sport it is now understood that the outcomes from involvement depend upon the social context in which involvement takes place (Martens, 1978; Rees, in press; C. Sherif & Rattray, 1976). The way in which children interact with parents, coaches, and peers and interpret this interaction is part of that social context. Too much emphasis on organization in youth sport programs (Devereux, 1976) and high drop-out rates (Orlick, 1974) are perceived as "problems" more by the sociologists studying youth sport than by the participants themselves (see chapter 9, Coakley's critique of the "Webb scale" research). At least such issues as overorganization and dropping out need to be investigated from the childrens' perspective.

However, McPherson (following Wentworth, 1980) also calls for merging theoretical perspectives as part of his new wave of research. He suggests that we deal both with the transmission of culture and with the development of autonomous human beings in a sport context. On a pessimistic note, little evidence from Coakley's review of the sociological research or Gould's (1982) review of the psychological research shows that most researchers in the field of youth sport will be able to do this. Coakley and Gould both note the prevalence of a "shotgun" approach in youth sport research, implying a lack of any theoretical perspective at all. It is a far cry from this to the theoretical and the methodological sophistication required to successfully carry out McPherson's new wave.

On an optimistic note the reviews provided by McPherson and Coakley are a good place for the neophyte researcher (and some veterans) to begin. Many of the points made by McPherson have direct application to youth sport research. For example, sociologists can find in sport a natural laboratory to study such processes as competition and sex-role stereotyping. Young boys and girls now participate together in organized sport at school and in youth leagues to a greater extent than ever before. What effect, if any, does this integration have upon the development sex-role stereotyping, or the reduction of sex-role stereotyping already there? Answers to questions such as these are part of McPherson's new wave. If his directions are followed, sociologists will be able to add to the fund of knowledge about sport and to make a contribution to the development of socialization theory at the same time.

On Small Groups in Sport: Methodological Reflections With Reference to Structural-Functional Approaches

Günther Lüschen

When I was approached to address the topic, "Small Groups in Sport," my immediate response was that I did not feel competent anymore. I had, after all, left this field of study some years ago and had not followed the recent research closely. It was then suggested that I might discuss why I left the field, a response convincing enough to make me take another look at the area as I had done with Hans Lenk (Lenk & Lüschen, 1975) some years ago. Subsequently, my reflections and inquiries into the literature made me not regret my agreement. I shall, however, stray somewhat beyond the assigned topic of structural-functional analysis in small group research—something I am drawn to do because I do not consider myself a close follower of that approach. My comments shall focus on my personal experiences and on some methodological reflections that I hope will jell into something meaningful and will rekindle my own and others' interest in the group dimension of this approach.

Some Notes on Personal Experiences

My scholarly parentage is probably best described as that of a disenchanted student of *geisteswissenschaftliche* pedagogy, who found his position with the help of gestalt philosophy and an empirical version of phenomenology at Graz plus the craftsmanship of Cologne and Michigan social science research. In particular, my philosophical training in the tradition of Franz Brentano and Alexius von Meinong allowed me to integrate my experiences and interests that focused on sociological problems in sport and on valid research methodology alike. Moreover, gestalt philosophy made me sensitive to structural dimensions even in small-scale, face-to-face interactions. In the end, my interests were strictly sociological, and psychological considerations, unless they were the only valid explanation of a given social phenomenon, were either used as a starting point for subsequent sociological reasoning, or, as in the case of individual experiences, as the empirical basis for insights into structural properties of social systems. Besides the issue of small groups as totalities beyond the sum total of individuals, I have always held a perspective that social systems form a reality of their own. However, in terms of data collection, systems cannot be interviewed; individuals can, and they, as part of social systems, from groups to organizations, have experiences that reflect the system.

As far as small group research and sport is concerned, I was always interested in group or social relations aspects, not in matters of individual psychology. Nor did I ever believe in the wisdom of psychological reductionism. I found Homans' (1962:7) statement "small groups are not what we study but where we study it" very misleading. I could possibly finish at this point by saying that I left the field because we lost the group. Following people like Homans directed our attention to individuals, psychological reasoning, and lab experiments where the reality of sport and the sport group were massacred for research expediency and model application of a simple design. After all, we should have been laughed out of the lab by any experienced sportsperson when calling shuffleboard a complex motor task, although from a motor behavioral point of view it may well be. Of course, a social psychologist should not be impressed by notions of complexity in such a task. On the other extreme, symbolic interactionists have not significantly aided us in better understanding the structural dimensions of small group research. Their methodological insistence on the self as a point of departure has made many of them blind to realities of social and institutional structure. As a case in point, Mead's (1934) insight into the *generalized other* was, by many, confused with *significant other*, and small group researchers in sport have never noted Mead's use of the sport team to explain the *generalized other*.

After my postdoctoral experiences at Michigan with Newcomb and Zander, I organized the first international seminar on sociology of sport at the University of Cologne on the topic, "Small Group Research and the Group in Sport" (Lüschen, 1966a). This was in line with my methodological experiences with group dynamics at Ann Arbor and gestalt philosophy at Graz. Given the high variety of group formations in sport and play, I considered the topic most worthy of analysis, both for its own sake and for that of sport in general. Maybe even more important, I wanted to incorporate this borderline area into the sociology of sport. The newly formed International Committee for Sociology of Sport concurred with such reasoning. Moreover, sociology and social psychology at the University of Cologne were, through the Simmel/von Wiese tradition and Rene Konig's interest, reasonably akin to such plans. At this time I engaged in field-experimental studies of the structure of physical education classes conducted under reinforced achievement-pressure, and over time, expected to see structural balances in these formalized large groups. Emerson (1966b) presented his Mt. Everest study on communication feedback under sustained group goal achievement in an extreme situation, subsequently published in *Sociometry*. Elias and Dunning (1966a) made an important extension of the field of study by discussing the phenomenon of "tonus" between opposing sport teams. Lenk (1966) provided further insights into his often quoted study about internal group conflict and high productivity, which could not be explained in terms of individual psychology and linear causality alone. Whereas papers like these provided a reasonable recognition of group or social structure, others focused on psychological or linear social relationships in the group context. Gregory Stone (1966), in a critical review of the field of small group research, addressed the differentiation between *interpersonal* and *structural* relations as particularly crucial. This important article by Stone, unfortunately available only in German, provides a distinction with which we can describe reasonably well what has happened in the field of small groups and sport. If social relations or group commodities were the focus of research, they were and are mostly addressed as problems of interpersonal, not structural relations.

Structural-Functional and Systems Approaches

By the time of the Cologne Seminar, of course, a prominent example of functional analysis already existed. R.F. Bales' (1950) *Interaction Process Analysis* not only resulted in a formidable analytic scheme for the analysis of group process and role structure, but it also had a direct impact on the formulation of the four functional prerequisites that systems must fulfill. At Cologne there was no reference to this methodology. Walter Schafer's (1966) discussion and outline of the social structure of sport groups was analytically rather modest and avoided any systems or functional notions. Subsequently, in the Big Ten Symposium of 1968, I used several concepts of Parsonian systems theory in order to clarify some basic analytic concepts and to direct the field to a stronger recognition of group structure and group environment (Lüschen, 1969:57-66). My concern for structural properties was more or less drowned out in the discussion of Parsons and the cumbersome nature of the Parsonian analytic concepts. These concepts are particularly weak to account for the dynamics of groups and the identification of structural relations of group members. Worth noting is that the analytic rigidity of functional analysis and Balesian systems theory never made any inroads into the study of sport groups. Bales (1970) modified his methodological approach to a more subjective stance.

A more recent attempt reconciles interaction process analysis with attribution theory and finds the two quite compatible (Morgan, 1975). Are we to conclude then that even psychological approaches to the small group will ultimately discover the reality of social structure? With some interest and irony it may be noted that a key concept of group dynamics, namely, cohesiveness, has now entered common language and is used to describe a systems property, that is, social integration. The disciplinary discussion in line with Homans' statement cited earlier and under the power of the psychological establishment turned away even from the term. Now rarely is the issue of small group research discussed as a genuine entity of its own (Borgatta & Baker, 1981a,b); most accounts are found under elaborations and research of social psychology. Lewin's heritage is weak. Moreno's technique of sociometry has a follower in network analysis, which, over the use of powerful mathematical procedures, has shown results on clique formation. This technique may not only lose the group but, over its mathematical models, social reality as well (Alba, 1981). The social group and structural properties in face-to-face interactions are probably best preserved in symbolic interactionism in the tradition of Simmel and Mead. Their mainly phenomenological form of scientific inquiry safeguards against an oversight of group and social structure. Even here, however, one finds the danger of taking the methodological approach to identify structure in individual experience and conscience as a psychological reality. Moreover, some of the symbolic interactionists are unduly sensitive in their attempt to separate themselves from systems and functional traditions. Representatives like Goffman (1961b) and Stryker (1980), however, provide ample evidence for the appearance and the magnitude of groups and social structure in interactional analysis.

Small Group Research In Sport: Its Present State and Prospects

At present not much recognition of group and structural properties exists in the social psychological study of sport. The study of cohesiveness, very prominent over the years in our field, very much stressed the individual dimension and, unlike Lewin's intention, the substance, not the construct notion of the very term. With research into validity of the term (Widmeyer & Martens, 1978) and the more recent observations that situational contexts and tasks have to be accounted for in cohesiveness (Carron & Chelladurai, 1981), there is every hope that the group and elements of social structure will soon regain their position in future analyses (Loy, McPherson, & Kenyon, 1978b).

The study of leadership in groups, a major preoccupation of social psychology until the 1960s, ultimately resulted in a recognition of structural contexts and complexity that goes beyond linear causal models and the simple measurement of personality traits. Behavioral item analyses may still have some attraction in predicting leader effectiveness. Some 20 years after Fiedler's study of leadership (which made prominent reference to sport groups), he developed a more complex scheme to explain leadership in groups on the basis of a contingency model accounting for leader-member relations, task-structure, and position power (Fiedler, 1968, 1981). Clearly related to the necessity of accounting for the structural and group context in leader behavior are the studies of Grusky (1963a, 1963b) on managerial effectiveness. They have now led to a series of replications that all underline the importance of group and social structural contexts (Eitzen & Yetman, 1972; Allen, Panian, & Lotz, 1979).

The study of group performance in sport (Landers, Brawley, & Landers, 1981) demonstrates a recognition of the complexities of small group research and a sensitive use of such basic structural constructs as coaction, competition, group size, task structure, and communication patterns. The ongoing problem of in-group conflict and competition, as they relate to performance and productivity, demonstrates (despite contradictory results) that two-variable, linear measures and notions of simple causality leads to insights in precisely defined situations. Such studies would, of course, need many qualifiers, and often such results are not particularly interesting then. Furthermore, abstract generalizations are possible only with reference to structural contexts and the seeming imprecision for measurement of relational constructs pointed out by Cassirer (1910). Of course, this should be surprising to nobody in light of Malewski's (1964) paradoxical, but quite correct, methodological observation: Theories of low level abstraction need several qualifications, whereas more abstract statements actually have less of a problem with verification. Consequently, any study testing the same hypothesis may lead to different, conflicting results if all qualifiers are not met in a replication.

Some Further Methodological Observations on Groups and Sport

The uniformity of sport groups and sport situations as a methodological problem can, of course, turn into one of its merits. If we are reasonably aware of the context and structural multiplicity of sport groups, then conflicting results in replications of research may be more easily explained. The mitigating factors can probably be understood as caused by only a few variables. Variances between a soccer team and a children's sandlot game are probably more easily explained than those between a group of prisoners and a decision-making community board.

The precision of two-variable unilineal designs, and even their more complex offspring in measurement models, of course, also have to be checked for measurement bias. In line with such problems, and the often trivial and tautological nature of much of social psychological research, McGuire (1973) suggested a shift from critical to creative hypothesis testing, or, in other terms, a shift from our emphasis on the logic of justification to that of discovery. However, this is not an open invitation to sloppy research; quite to the contrary. Creative hypothesis testing in research on sport groups will have to account for structural relations and contexts, and it will probably best be accomplished by more field research instead of laboratory testing. Actually, the natural field of the sport group provides many of the advantages of the lab of which we have not made sufficient use at this time. Lenk's (1977) rowing team studies, Klein and Christiansen's (1966) basketball analyses, and Watson's (1974) observations of competitive children's games provide ample evidence of such potentials.

Instead of summarizing let me propose some propositions that I consider crucial for the future of small group research on sport.

1. In his development of constructs like cohesiveness, locomotion, and force-field, Lewin (1964) was aware of the necessity to overcome the Aristotelian emphasis on substance terminology with more emphasis on relational constructs, as developed by Cassirer (1910). We still emphasize substance terms and avoid relational terms—even in the use of cohesiveness.
2. Lewin (1949), with reference to Cassirer, and despite his engineering background, did not mind notions of imprecision. They could lead to new developments in scientific insight and to the breakdown of what now, after Kuhn (1962), are called scientific paradigms.
3. Although Lewin (1962) and McGuire (1973) considered new avenues of scientific insight to open up by more creativity, it appears reasonable to extend such notions also to stronger use of qualitative observation techniques and phenomenological modes of scientific inquiry. The latter notion of more qualitative methodology, with the true rigor of phenomenological reasoning, allows a better reformulation of group and structural relations from which rigorous quantitative analysis must not be excluded. Also, it allows the advancement of theory—on a more abstract level of "form," or deep-structure if you wish.
4. The pledge for other than observation concepts keyed toward quantitative research, an advancement beyond the individual and

toward group and social structural properties, does not mean the insistence on qualitative method. To the contrary, a multiplicity of method is suggested, where appropriate, even in individual studies. Within phenomenological approaches a multiplicity of perspectives is a necessity for the analysis. Denzin's (1970) notion of "triangulation" in research may also be expanded in this way and, for the complex reality of groups as social systems, thereby regain that level of insight which S-R-models and two-variable analyses hardly touch.

Research Problems

In conclusion, before I suggest some research problems for future systems and structural analysis, one may well ask whether I have dropped the ball or lost the group by default in my preceding discussion because I have not pleaded the case very well. After all, relational constructs à la Cassirer or Stone's category of structural relations imply a dimension of social structure or a notion of Lewin's force-field not, by necessity, a clearly delimited group system. The tonus in intergroup competition of Elias and Dunning does not need a clearly defined overarching system, nor any strong recognition of two group entities. So, is Homans right after all, at least as we may say something about social structure but not much about the group itself? Quite a few of the elaborate and suggestive outlines for small group research (cf. Loy et al., 1978b) seem to back up that conclusion. Not that they follow Homans (1950) all the way in a strictly psychological reductionism, but notions of groups as entities of their own are weak. The small group remains, to a high degree, a strategic point of analysis, not a matter of genuine interest itself. I do not particularly mind such a state of the art as a sociological social psychology. Yet, there is, of course, more to it in small group research when addressing the unit of the group itself.

Beyond some identifiable descriptive variables that rather easily describe such features as group size, group territory and spatial density, group goal, and group task that immediately suggest a research program for sport groups, there are more creative theroretical adventures before us in a structural or systems approach to small groups in sport. One can distinguish structural levels of groups from task, skill, sympathy, communication, and power structures (cf. Cartwright & Zander 1968:485), which are important predictors for outcome variables, whose measurement is now possible with multivariate approaches. The structural or systems approach to small groups in sport would help us better predict group effectiveness with practical payoffs for sport.

Lewin's interest in relational terms invites the recognition of the dynamics of groups, which is a true epistemological advancement, not one for practical purposes only as is often suggested. This interest should also extend into the dimension of time in order to better understand group information and change. So far, we have used research over time mainly for experimental t_1-t_2 designs or have, at best, followed the life of groups through qualitative observations (Whyte, 1943). Time-series are a powerful way to observe and analyze structure and process over a bundle of key variables.

Two additional areas appear of importance in small group analysis:

1. Structural impacts of the group environment are obvious and need more recognition, from the immediate social environment to cultural factors, than we have given them so far. Such external and impersonal factors as racial discrimination have been analyzed for sport teams (Loy & McElvogue, 1971), but there is a range of other structural impacts and interchanges. What is the impact of a bureaucracy or formal organization at large on such groups as football teams, Little League teams, or a physical education class? We should not expect a direct and lineal causality but a negotiated order. Social class background of members on a sport team certainly has consequences for the structure of such a team. Landecker's (1970) integration of social status characteristics within groups versus social class cleavages in society at large suggests an inverse relationship. Structural interchanges of this kind have strong impacts on group structure and process in sport as well.

2. Groups are not isolated within the system of sport. Typically they engage other groups in competition and form relationships that have their own dynamics and structure. Elias and Dunning's (1966b) concept of "tonus" is an attempt to understand such interdependencies. The concept of "association" that binds opposing teams together at the same time that they fiercely fight each other is another. Can such relationships still be represented in multivariate statistical measures, or has the qualitative observation of such social structure (Lüschen, 1970) to suffice? What comes into focus is obviously a dimension of a general form of interdependence that reveals a dialectical structure. Here our statistical analyses may register in conflicting results, incompatibilities that have to be comprehended on an abstract level by phenomenological reasoning. Again, it will need a number of observations and rigid analyses by deductively advanced tests before such insight can be advanced.

In these final suggestions for research under a structural and systems approach, I have left out the construct of function altogether. The implicit notion of final cause and teleological procedure is certainly transferable into an efficient cause argument and thus may become easy for observational purposes. Also, Lewin's relational terms are sufficiently concrete to engage us in systems notions that avoid the often insurmountable measurement and observation problems of an analytic scheme of functional prerequisites. For the time being I do not want to engage in a lengthy argument over functional analysis in the study of small groups in sport. The construct of groups as organized wholes, or systems that are linked to other systems and are part of a social environment of other organizations at large and society, is suggestive enough for a program that I would rather refer to as structural analysis. Outcome variables like winning, effectiveness, or survival of a team are sufficiently concrete for research. They are also very practical—and they keep system notions of an essentially functional nature alive.

Small Groups and Sport:
A Symbolic Interactionist Perspective

Gary Alan Fine

The sport team is one of the most common social organizations in American life. For this reason, if for no other, sport teams provide a sociologically significant setting for understanding interaction. My goal in this chapter is to present some insights into the structure and meaning of sport teams from a symbolic interactionist perspective. However, before I attempt this task, I shall briefly describe the major premises of symbolic interactionist thought.

The symbolic interactionist approach to social life was developed by Charles Horton Cooley, George Herbert Mead, Herbert Blumer, Erving Goffman, and Gregory Stone, among others. Blumer (1969), who coined the term, argued that three premises are crucial to the perspective. First, human beings act toward things on the basis of the meanings that these objects have for them. Therefore, objects (or actions) have no a priori stimulus value. Second, the meanings of these stimuli emerge through social interaction. Third, and most important, these meanings are not static but are modified through an interpretive process. Meanings, therefore, are not reified but are potentially subject to interpersonal negotiation. Through this assumption the symbolic interactionist perspective orients itself to change. A further assumption is that social meanings are shared through communication, and, consequently, causes of action are not primarily biological and subconscious, but are social and conscious. The primary method of differentiating the symbolic interactionist approach from the functionist approach or the group dynamics approach is that symbolic interactionists focus on the *meanings* created in team sport and on how these meanings influence the play. This emphasizes that in different situations social meanings may be significantly different, even with the same players. Although this brief synopsis of symbolic interactionist thought is both too simplified for those who know the theory well and too brief for those who don't know it at all, I hope it will suffice.

Sports and games are a particularly appropriate social world for symbolic interactionists to examine because these forms of activities are symbolic worlds par excellence. They are spheres of activities in which the acts within them have no inherent meaning (Goffman, 1961b); what meanings exist are created by social actors—through rules, conventions, contexts, and negotiations. Consider the following example suggested by McCall and Simmons:

> A rather young man, in a park in the Bronx, is standing quietly but very alertly in the afternoon sun. Suddenly he tenses and scurries a few tentative steps to his right, still rather frozen, his gaze locked on a man only a few feet away. This other man makes a sudden movement with his right arm, and the first fellow breaks into sudden flight. Twenty or thirty yards away, still another fellow starts to run to cut him off, and the first man falls on his face, skidding, and bouncing roughly along the ground for several feet as a result of his great momentum. (1970:94)

The "social object" being created is, of course, a stolen base. What is a stolen base? As a physical object it is nothing; rather, it is a coordination of movements, which we have defined as a meaningful type of behavior. A stolen base is the relationship among a set of behaviors. As the description points out, if we remove the contextual clues, it is difficult to determine what is happening. Sport is like that: Its meaning is socially generated. Its biological function, if such exists, is well hidden by layers of social meaning.

Some sports, those I shall be discussing, are sports only because of the presence of others. To conceive of solitaire baseball, football, or even tennis is impossible. These activities require an opposition, and in the case of team sports colleagues who play different roles in the sport structure. Although it would be valuable to consider how interactionists have discussed play and games, I will confine my attention to the symbolic interactionist approach to team sport. Regrettably, there has been little symbolic interactionist research to deal with team sport, in contrast with individual play or social games which has been well discussed (e.g., Mead, 1934; Stone, 1965; Goffman, 1961b). This chapter will examine several concepts which can be and have been used by interactionists to examine team sport but by no means covering all possible topics. I have chosen to emphasize: (a) the generalized other, (b) sport ritual, (c) rhetoric as a sense-making device, (d) momentum and history, (e) small group culture, and (f) coping with failure.

The Generalized Other

When George Herbert Mead was describing the concept of the generalized other, he used the example of a baseball team to explain what he meant:

> The organized community or a social group which gives to the individual his unity of self may be called "the generalized other." The attitude of the generalized other is the attitude of the whole community. Thus, for example, in the case of such a social group as a ball team, the team is the generalized other in so far as it enters—an organized process or social activity—into the experience of any one of the individual members of it. (Mead, 1934:154)

The team player has a relationship with all of the others on the team. For the centerfielder to know how to play centerfield, he or she must be conscious of his or her fellow players, what they should be doing, and what they are doing. This sense of place is developed from the interrelationships among selves. However, these relationships by themselves do not comprise the generalized other. The generalized other refers specifically to the relationship between the individual player and the team on which he or she plays. For the individual to develop a self, he or she must be able to take the attitudes of others into account and must be aware of how they view their world—in this case, baseball. By generalizing the attitudes of specific others toward the various components of their shared social activity, the individual develops an alignment to his or her activity.

This concept of the generalized other allows us to understand how a group of sporting individuals can be seen as a team, rather than simply a collection of coacting individuals. By understanding the construct of the generalized other—i.e., the ability to recognize the salience and motivating power of the social unit—we can comprehend the development of social cohesion and shared goals. Further, this serves as a point of entry for the study of deviance in sport. Why, we might ask, do players act aggressively, even violently, in sport? One part of any answer should rely upon the player's perspective of the generalized other. Put differently, how does the player believe that his or her teammates expect him or her to act in any given situation? The generalized other represents the locus for normative expectations for the player, as exemplified by players who feel a special responsibility to the team when they put on their "Dodger blues" or "Yankee pinstripes." To understand sports as a collective or team enterprise, it is necessary to recognize that not only do relationships exist among selves, but there is also a relationship between the player's self-conception and his or her conception of the team.

Sport Ritual

Sport teams are, of course, task-oriented groups with winning as their primary goal. Winning games is not as easy a phenomenon as some coaches make it out to be. Wanting to win is one thing, but actually winning is something else. Teams must defeat other teams who are also trying as hard as they can to achieve the same goal. Because success may depend on forces outside the control of the player, it is not surprising that team members will recognize the uncertainty inherent in their activities. As Malinowski wrote about magic

> We find magic wherever the elements of chance and accident, and the emotional play between hope and fear have a wide and extensive range. We do not find magic wherever the pursuit is certain, reliable, and well under the control of rational methods. (cited by Gmelch, 1971:39; see Malinowski, 1954)

Anthropologists have focused their studies of magic on such uncertain activities as hunting, fishing, weather prediction, and the like. Expanding these topics, it is easy to see how this also applies to sports. In a classic examination of superstitions in professional baseball, George Gmelch examined what he termed "baseball magic"—those rituals and taboos used by professional baseball players in the course of their professional activity. These rituals are supposed to have sufficient symbolic power to insure a favorable outcome for the player, as in the following examples:

> After each pitch, ex-major leaguer Lou Skeins used to reach into his back pocket to touch a crucifix, straighten his cap, and clutch his genitals. Detroit infielder Tim Maring wore the same clothes and put them on exactly in the same order each day during a batting streak. (Gmelch, 1971:40)

Gmelch's discussion focuses exclusively on individual rituals and does not discuss the forms that team rituals can take. Although team rituals typically are not as extensive or bizarre as the rituals of individuals, they do exist—particularly in the period immediately prior to the game. Van Gennep (1960/1909) called this period the "liminal period" in his theory of rites of passage—the period of change between two major states of existence. One Little League baseball team I studied would gather immediately prior to a game, standing in a tight circle with their hands clasped in the middle, and then would raise their arms in unison with a loud cheer. Another team had a meeting immediately prior to the first pitch of the game on the pitching mound, including the team's pitcher, catcher, and infielders. A third team insisted on always taking the first base dugout, believing that the other dugout would bring them bad luck.

Still other teams had particular ways in which they arranged their bats to insure a successful outcome in the game. Such rituals appear to provide players with some additional confidence in their team, and, perhaps, these rituals also provide the security of knowing that there is some stability in their sporting career—eliminating one possible source of anxiety.

Perhaps the most frequent and easily observed ritual among sport teams is cheering. Cheering is a highly visible (or actually audible) activity. Karen Larson (1980) emphasizes that baseball chatter (of which cheering is a large part) serves a ritual function in sport. She claims that baseball chatter is communication that is not designed to be informational, but rather is relational. That is, this sport ritual provides a means by which players can symbolically affirm their team relationships. Cooperative in-group relationships and competitive out-group relationships are defined and emphasized through cheering and chatter. She further argues that:

> The ritualized communication that surrounds and is part of a softball game constitutes a meta-game, where the real and the ritual meet and intertwine, forming a pattern of behavior which is itself a model of the interface between that which is game and that which is not game. (Larson, 1980:14)

By this she indicates the central symbolic importance of communication, and that baseball talk has a similar relationship to serious talk as sport has to work. The ritual component of chatter gives it its meaning as play, just as the rules of the sporting event give it its role as play. We find that both cheering and sport are set apart from the serious world by the socially constructed boundaries that separate playing meanings from the meanings of mundane reality. Further, the fact that these activities are shared by other members of a team means that this playful reality constitutes a social world, rather than an idiosyncratic world-view.

Sport Rhetoric

Talk is an important component of most sporting events, but what do people talk about while they are playing? This analysis extends the examination of cheers and chatter, which are by no means the only talk that occurs within the context of sport. Indeed, when talking about the rhetoric of sport, it is particularly valuable to describe those moral communications embedded in coaches' lectures to their teams and players' moral invocations (Synder & Spreitzer, 1979). Cheers, chatter, and slogans (Snyder, 1972) represent the telegraphed, abbreviated form of these moral messages.

What meanings are communicated within the sport setting, and how are situational aspects of sport used to make these points? At least within the context of Little League baseball, four themes regularly emerge as morally relevant: effort, sportsmanship, teamwork, and the importance of victory and defeat (Fine, 1979a; Kleinman & Fine, 1979). Because I am concerned here with the importance of the small group in sport, I shall briefly discuss how teamwork is used as a symbolic construct in Little League baseball—although this analysis applies to many other areas as well.

Teamwork is important at all ages, but for preadolescents particular emphasis is required. Developmental psychologists see preadolescence as a time of transition, when preadolescents are changing their egocentric emphasis to a greater concern with others and with their position in groups. As Piaget (1962/1932) has noted, this change corresponds to a shift in orientation to game rules.

Coaches regularly stress the value of teamwork, not just for its pragmatic utility, but for its moral consequences as well. One coach commented that he felt that Little League baseball is as important for preadolescents as the army is for young men because it teaches them to work as a unit. Coaches particularly emphasize the importance of teamwork at the beginning of the season and whenever they believe they see a lack of cooperation.

> One coach reminds his players in a preseason practice: "Pull for your team. We don't have room for a bunch of individuals. Every one of us must do our best. Last year we had a lot of prima donnas, and we only came in third." (Field notes)
> The coach says to his team before the first game of the season: "On the Cardinal team everyone plays. We're not the Cardinals. We took the I out. We're the Cards, or you have to say Cardinals without the I which sounds funny." (Field notes)

Coaches also use teamwork rhetoric after games—victory or defeat—to comment on the game that just ended.

> A coach comments after a come-from-behind victory: "Isn't that nice to come back and win it. It was a team effort. Everybody played well." (Field notes)
> A coach remarks after a pre-season loss: "No thinking out there. No aggression is being shown on balls. Nobody wants to take charge out there. You're a team; you got to play as a team." (Field notes)

The coach is not responding to a clear indicator of a concrete phenomenon. Rather, these comments are situationally constructed, indicating that several players are making mistakes in sequence, or that there is a confluence of superior plays, which occur within an athletic sequence ("as part of the same play"). One boy or girl making an exceptional throw and his or her teammate making an exceptional catch is defined as an example of teamwork. As with all forms of athletic rhetoric, the mention of teamwork is a part of the adults' interpretive process—a process that creates morally significant issues from the physical movements of children.

Although this example is directly connected to Little League baseball, moral rhetorics are a central part of team sport. This talk serves as a symbolic motivator for the team. Even though, as in the case of teamwork, the physical referent may be ambiguous and ill-defined, the flexibility of rhetoric allows it to be used in a variety of social situations by coaches and players and even referees (Askins, Carter, & Wood, 1981) to construct their reality and to provide the moral grounding for future behaviors.

Momentum and History

Interactionists believe that groups are always "in process." By that I mean that groups are characterized by a dynamic tension—the group is always changing and is aware of this change. Peter and Patricia Adler (1978) deal with this issue while examining how momentum operates in sport. They argue that sport activities have emotional tides associated with them. A team (or player) that feels that its play is characterized by "momentum" will likely do better than a team without the same feeling. The social construct of momentum is, in effect, a definition of the situation, and like all situational definitions, it has effects in the "real world" of behavior. This, of course, is what athletes mean when they talk about the power of positive thinking, although momentum goes beyond this. Momentum has a historical component to it, in that momentum is connected to those events that have transpired immediately prior to the present game, and to which teams are responding. In addition, specific events have the potential to alter momentum. However, for any set of actions or events to be related to momentum, they must be defined as such by members of the team. Here a connection exists between sport rhetoric (as discussed above) and momentum.

Symbolic interactionists recognize the historical components of sport— particularly the history of a season. One important way in which most team sports differ from many individual sports is that in team sports, the individual game is embedded within a season. Each game is not only an end in itself, rather the game is one part of a skein of events that, taken together, constitute success. The goal in most team sports is to compile the best record for the season and to win the championship, which is usually based, in part, on the team's seasonal record. This structure of sport means that the attention of the team will not only be on what is happening on any given day, but will have both a retrospective (historical) and a prospective focus. Thus, a sport team is concerned with its evolving history and believes that strategic change can alter its past record.

How is this historical character of sport expressed? The most obvious and direct sense in which sport and history merge is through record-keeping and the compilation of statistics. In baseball these include such numerical indicators as victories, defeats, batting average, homeruns, earned run average, strike-outs (for batters and for pitchers), bases on balls (again for batters and pitchers), errors, and stolen bases. As John Schulian notes: "When it comes to baseball, the statistician is a poet" (1981:3). Whereas not all team sports have such extensive record keeping systems, all do maintain records.

In addition, team sports are composed of events (plays) strung together. Some of these plays are notable in that they have a lasting impact on participants and spectators. These plays have, in the words of Erving Goffman, a long "referential afterlife" (Goffman, 1976). As with interaction sequences in general, not all plays in sport have equal immediate or future significance. Those particularly salient events provide memory markers around which evaluations of future performance and typifications of the "essence" of the season can be based. Most teams have a few plays or games that they refer to long after the event itself has transpired. Along with the more objective feature of records and statistics, these "great moments" ground baseball in the history of the season. They allow players and spectators to construct meaningful typifications of the season.

Players are continually judging their attitudes and activities in light of what has happened that season. The perception that a team has or lacks momentum is a direct result of how they see their relative position during the season, and whether they perceive it to be rising, falling, or remaining constant. Teams generate meanings for themselves, a key fact for the symbolic interactionist perspective on group dynamics.

Team Culture

Team members typically come to know each other quite well during a season. As a consequence they develop a set of norms, artifacts, and expressions, which I refer to as their *culture*. Because meaning derives from interaction and culture, a set of shared understandings is clearly implicated in the symbolic interactionist approach.

I have argued previously (1979b) that every group creates a culture of its own, which I have termed its *idioculture*. An idioculture consists of a system of knowledge, beliefs, behaviors, and customs shared by members of an interacting group to which members can refer and can employ as the basis of further interaction. Members recognize that they have shared experiences and that these experiences can be referred to with the expectation that they will be understood by other members. Further, they can be employed to construct a social reality. The concept seems admirably suited to a study of sport teams, and I applied it to my examination of Little League baseball teams. Teams with their spirit of community try to differentiate themselves from other teams. They do this through culture creation. Through the creation of culture, teams attempt to address problems that are facing them (H. Becker & Geer, 1960).

I shall consider one example of how cultural creation operates. During the middle of the season, the Beanville Rangers (a pseudonym) created and enforced a rule that no player could eat ice cream while sitting on the bench during a game. This rule was triggered by a combination of circumstances: It occurred in the context of a Little League game in which the Rangers, by this time accustomed to victory, were being beaten. On the bench one of the nonplaying low-status players was eating an ice cream cone. This situation triggered the decision by the high-status, older players (not the coach) that ice cream could not be eaten on the bench (although gum could be chewed). The rule was compatible with the policy and perspectives of professional sport teams. It did not deal with any taboo or threatening areas of children's culture, and it is comparable to the rules that children frequently make (Piaget, 1962/1932; Cooley, 1964/1902). The rule was functional in relieving the frustration that the older players felt during the game and in tending to get the attention of the younger members on the game. Further, the presence of any set of rules or rituals creates a sense of group cohesion (Cartwright & Zander, 1953) and satisfaction (Borgatta & Bales, 1953). Finally, this rule was proposed by the high-status members to control the low-status members. Later in the season an older, high-status player did eat ice cream on the bench and was not criticized by other team members, although the rule remained in force for other team members.

Culture serves to enhance group cohesion. This culture is not given to the team, but rather it emerges from their play. In other words, the team, in addition to creating a win-loss record, also creates a set of meanings. Unfortunately, the area of team sport culture has not been extensively explored, but the question of how team culture operates differently among winning and losing teams is worthy of additional research.

Failure

Not all players or teams can succeed at sport. Sport is objectively "zero-sum" for teams (one winner and one loser in each contest). As a result, sport generates an equal number of winners and losers. Considering the season as a whole, all teams (except one) are losers. Admitting that "moral victories" and subjective satisfaction exist, most teams are at least somewhat disappointed in their performances. How do losers deal with the symbolic consequences of their defeat, and how do sport organizations inform their players that they have not met adequate standards—that is, failed? To understand the moral significance of failure we must recognize that for most active sportspeople, sports ability is closely connected to their identity, presentation of self, and self-esteem. Success matters, not just for the rewards that it brings, but also because it says something about one's identity.

Ball (1976) argued that there are basically two "scripts" for convincing a player of his or her failure. The first, following Garfinkel (1956), is "degradation;" the second is Goffman's (1952) concept of "cooling-out." Degradation involves dramatization: focusing on the public separation of the failure from his or her position and its related identity by the destruction of that identity. Cooling-out involves routinization and the private estrangement of the failure from his or her position and his or her no longer completely legitimate identity. Ball claimed that the degraded are forcibly removed, and the cooled-out are "conned" out and left to disappear on their own, although with organizational support.

As Harris and Eitzen (1978) describe, these tactics may have quite dramatic effects on the athletic failure because so much of his or her self is invested in these roles. Failure in sport, for the individual, is symbolically tied to death—the death of a key part of the individual's self.

Both of these articles (Ball, 1976; Harris & Eitzen, 1978) on the symbolic consequences of failure deal with how individual athletes deal with and are made to deal with failure. However, failure is also a consequence of team sports. As Ball notes: "Sports teams are, in fact, one of the few places where the less able may be protected from failure—this is the case where their relative lack of ability may be 'covered' by the presence of others who are extremely able" (Ball, 1976:726, citing Goode, 1967:15). Just as this statement is accurate, the reverse is also true. A good player may be tainted with failure because of the team for which he or she plays—a curse which players for the 1981 Chicago Cubs, or New Orleans Saints, can certainly appreciate. Failure rubs off on the individual, just as does success. Failure is not only an individual problem, but also a team problem. Teams that lose a lot must somehow deal with their losses.

How they deal with defeat depends on several factors: economic, definitional, and psychological. Obviously, professional teams, where the players and coaches play as work, must take defeat seriously, because they are failing in their vocation. These losses have implications for their professional employment. A losing team not only loses games, but it loses fans. This loss of fans is a loss of revenue for the team owner—a very serious problem, and one that may result in scapegoating a coach or player. Teams in this situation cannot afford to become depressed or withdrawn after losses, as they are not supposed to become overly emotional. They just are expected to work harder or more skillfully, or be replaced with someone who can work that hard or that skillfully. In Little League and other sport areas not economically grounded, defeat does not matter in this monetary sense. Players will not be excluded from the team just because they lose, although team defeat may affect the reputation of individual players (such as a pitcher who loses all his or her games because his or her teammates cannot field).

Some teams, particularly teams that do not represent a community (i.e., a school or town), may claim not to care about losing. They, in effect, define the goal of sport as having fun instead of winning. Little League teams, which lack ability and recognize that they do, often will resort to this definition. By expressing one of the core values of Little League—that playing, not winning, is most important—they insulate themselves from the self-destructive aspects of their defeats. Other teams cannot get away with taking such a casual attitude to winning and losing. They expect to win, and when this is not forthcoming, they become very upset and seek scapegoats, becoming on occasion abusive towards umpires, the other team, or teammates. Because their expectations were high, defeat for these teams is not seen as acceptable.

Both success and failure carry with them symbolic meaning about self and group. However, these meanings are not inevitable and are subject to social construction by the members of the team. An unsuccessful team can define itself in several ways, and this process of group definition is central to the symbolic interactionist approach to sport.

Conclusion

Sport is a particularly appropriate area for symbolic interactionist analysis because numerous symbolic meanings are created within this bounded social world. The process by which these meanings are constructed is easily accessible to the sociological observer. Further, because we are observing something that is so obviously a function of the existence of the team, rather than of a collection of individuals, we can examine the collective process of meaning construction. Symbolic values are crucial to sport: winning and losing, morality and sportsmanship, teamwork and individual effort. Further, major symbolic interactionist constructs such as self, generalized other, role, position, and identity are relevant to any analysis of sport.

I have not attempted in this chapter to do anything more than to present several concepts that have been used by symbolic interactionists to deal with the concept of the sport team. I hope, some of these concepts are potentially useful to those whose research is outside of this scholarly tradition. Possibly, these ideas will spur those who consider themselves to be symbolic interactionists to explore further the world of team sport as a locale in which some of the constructs of the perspective can generate additional constructs that, in turn, can be used by other researchers exploring other content areas.

Theoretical and Methodological Perspectives of Group Dynamics in the Study of Small Groups in Sport

W. Neil Widmeyer

What is group dynamics? The term *group dynamics* originated with Kurt Lewin. However, group dynamics did not bring Lewin into the limelight of the scientific community. Rather, he attracted attention because he did not rely on traditional mechanistic associationism to study human behavior; instead, he went to the more precise sciences of physics and mathematics where, respectively, he borrowed the concept of "field" and aspects of topological geometry to formulate his now famous field theory.

At times group dynamics has not been treated as synonymous with the sum total of field theory but rather with some aspect of it. For example, some writers define group dynamics as *group research* and dwell on Lewin's emphasis of the experimental study of group life. By treating group dynamics and empiricism as synonymous, these authors ignore Lewin's great concern for theory construction. Another view says because group dynamics is field theory and because the primary concern of field theory is group cohesiveness, *ergo* group dynamics is "the study of group cohesion." Such a view is reflected in Pirtle's (1972) description of group dynamics as "the study of factors that hold groups together."

Cartwright (1968), in discussing the origins of group dynamics, points out that people frequently use the term to refer to *a political ideology* of group organization that emphasizes democratic leadership and participation of members in group decisions. Cartwright goes on to say that to some people, group dynamics refers to *a number of techniques* such as role playing, buzz sessions, group observation, and so forth—all of which are employed extensively in training programs designed to improve the human relations skills of management personnel.

Finally, defining group dynamics as *group psychology*, Durkin (1964) implies that group dynamics is an approach that focuses more on the individual in the group than do other methods of small group analysis.

At this point, it must be recognized that group dynamics has been viewed as

1. field theory,
2. experimental laboratory investigation,
3. the study of group cohesion,
4. an ideology embracing democratic action,
5. a set of management training techniques, and
6. the psychological approach to groups.

Despite the relevance of each of these views of group dynamics, each by itself underrepresents the term. More complete than any of these partial views is the more general perspective of Cartwright who views group dynamics as a field of study devoted to understanding the nature of group life. Specifically, this involves understanding (a) the nature of groups, (b) the laws of group development, (c) interrelationships among groups, (d) interrelationships among groups and individuals, and (e) interrelationships among groups and larger institutions.

As previously noted, group dynamics emphasizes both theory and research in the analysis of group life. Research provides the data upon which a theory can be built, and the theory, in turn, organizes the known data into a framework to guide future investigations from which data can support, reject, or modify existing theory. Therefore, there is not a choice between theory and research, but rather choice exists among kinds of theory and among kinds of empirical methods. Thus, the remainder of the chapter is devoted to discussing various theoretical and methodological perspectives employed in group dynamics.

Theoretical Approaches to the Study of Group Dynamics

Deutsch (1968) points out that, despite his emphasis on theoretical analysis, Lewin wrote very little on the theory of group dynamics. Therefore, one must turn to more modern scholars for guidance. Recently, M. Shaw (1981) proposed a scheme to classify theoretical approaches to the study of group dynamics, which closely parallels that outlined by Kenyon in Chapter 1. Shaw distinguishes first between *theoretical orientations*, which are general approaches that apply to a broad range of social contexts (i.e., not just to groups), and the very *limited theories,* which apply to one aspect (i.e., a specific phenomenon) of the group. The theoretical orientations that Shaw cites are field theory and stimulus-response reinforcement theory, whereas the examples he gives of limited theories are theories of leadership and conformity. Shaw suggests that between general theoretical orientations and specific limited theories lie theories that deal with *middle range phenomena,* which are not as broad as social behavior in general or as narrow as any one specific aspect of behavior. One such middle range phenomenon is small group behavior. According to Shaw, the theories that have dealt with small group behavior are (a) Cattell's group syntality theory, (b) Thibaut and Kelly's exchange theory, (c) Schutz's theory of interpersonal relations, and (d) Benoit-Smullyan's group congruency theory.

After presenting their list of "theories," "theoretical approaches," "models," or "theoretical orientations," most authors conclude with the "motherhood statement" that although no one theory can explain all of group behavior, each adds something to the understanding of group life. In contrast to such expressions of satisfaction with the status quo are the proclamations of Shaw (1981) and Zander (1979). Shaw says,

> Any discipline must provide for the integration of theoretical formulations. Group dynamics has largely failed in this respect. . .a few attempts have been made, with varying degrees of success. But for the most part these theories are capable of encompassing only limited amounts of information gleaned from small group research. One can appeal to the complexity of the phenomena as a reason for the failure of group dynamics to devise an adequate theory, but the fact remains that no existing theory can adequately organize the empirical data of group dynamics (cf. Kaul & Bednar, 1978; Ruzicka, Palisi, & Berven, 1979). Such a theory is sorely needed. (1981:449)

Similarly, Zander states,

> There are few well-developed theories about behavior in groups. The theories that do exist, moreover, seldom aid in understanding groups as such, or even the behavior of members in behalf of their groups, because the theories often are based on ideas taken from individual psychology, and these are primarily concerned with the actions of individuals for the good of those individuals. (1979:423)

Have theoretical approaches been effectively employed in the study of the small group in sport when they have been unsuccessfully applied in the study of small groups in general?

Theoretical Approaches to the Study of Sport Groups

First, to the best of my knowledge neither of the major theoretical orientations identified by Shaw, *field theory* and *stimulus-response reinforcement theory*, have been tested or used as a guide while studying the group life of athletic teams. In addition, very rarely have the theories that Shaw identified as dealing with the middle range phenomenon of small groups been applied to sport groups. Conspicuously absent is *group congruency theory*, and although factor analysis techniques have been used extensively in small group research, both inside and outside of sport, they have rarely, if ever, been used in conjunction with *Cattell's theory of syntality*. Social reinforcement has been studied a great deal in sport settings, but it is normally tied to individual rather than group behavior, and, therefore, it is safe to say that *social exchange theory* has also been neglected in the analysis of sport teams.

FIRO, the *theory of interpersonal relations* developed and refined by Schutz (1955, 1958), has been used to analyze behavior in sport groups. This theory argues that all individuals experience needs to give and to express inclusion, control, and affection. For compatibility to exist in any interpersonal relationship, an equilibrium between the needs of oneself and those of the others involved, is necessary. Carron and Bennett (1977) used FIRO to examine the factors related to effective interaction between coaches and athletes. They found that "the interpersonal relationship within incompatible coach-athlete dyads was characterized by relatively detached, withdrawn, isolated behavior on the part of both the coach and athlete" (Carron & Bennett, 1977:677). To explain why affection and control were not discriminating factors, Carron and Bennett point out that in situations where such incompatibility exists, athletes often quit or are "cut" from the team. In another study, Pease, Locke, an Burlingame (1971) used the FIRO-B scale and found that, indeed, player-coach incompatibility was a large factor in the athlete's decision to quit the team. Using the Schutz model, Carron (1978) found that the lack of affection and inclusion behavior by coaches combined with the athlete's need in these areas led to incompatibility in the coach-athlete dyad. Finally, Carron and Garvie (1978) examined the relationship between coach-athlete compatibility and the performance of Olympic and FISU Games wrestlers; they found that certain aspects of compatibility were related to effective performance. Many small group analysts discount these studies, arguing that the coach-athlete dyad does not constitute a group.

The majority, if not all, of the theoretical perspectives that have been and are presently being utilized in the analysis of sport teams are theories that deal with a specific aspect rather than the sum total of group life. The most prevalent are theories of

1. group leadership,
2. group motivation, and
3. group performance.

Theories of Group Leadership

The study of leadership was concerned initially with How does one become a leader? and later with How does one become an effective leader?

Early trait theories, which postulated that individuals became leaders because they possessed certain personal characteristics, received little empirical support, either inside or outside of sport settings. In response, situational theories proposed that individuals became leaders because of the situations they experienced. These theories led to the establishment of many leadership training courses despite the fact that few situational variables were universally shown to contribute to the emergence of leaders.

One of the earliest responses to the question, How does one become an effective leader, came from Lewin, Lippitt, and White (1939). Their work involving "autocratic," "democratic," and "laissez-faire" styles of leadership reflected a trait theory approach insomuch as it implied that the relative effectiveness of the various leadership styles held up regardless of the situation. Situationalists believed that just as the situation could determine the leader, so also could it determine the effective leader. Gradually, scholars came to realize that situational and personal factors need to be considered simultaneously when determining how individuals become effective leaders. Undoubtedly, the most recognized of such interactionist perspectives was that advanced by Fiedler (1964). This theory, known as Fiedler's Contingency Model, predicted which type of leader behavior (i.e., "task oriented" or "relationship oriented") was most favorable in situations ranked according to leader-member relations, leader position power, and task structure.

The analysis of leadership in sport groups has gone through the same evolutionary process. The trait approach has been used to compare coaches with noncoaches (e.g., Sage, 1972b), coaches at one level of play with those at another level (e.g., Walsh & Carron, 1977), and successful coaches with uunsuccessful coaches (e.g., Sage, 1972a). As was the case in the nonsport literature, the results have been conflicting. Although some studies (Ogilvie & Tutko, 1966) have shown that coaches are typically conservative, dogmatic, and manipulative, others (Sage, 1972a; Walsh & Carron, 1977) have not been able to demonstrate these findings. In spite of the obvious fruitlessness of the trait approach, some researchers still use it to study leadership in small groups.

A situational theory that has been used extensively to predict leadership in sport is Grusky's theory of formal structure. This theory, often referred to as Grusky's model of managerial succession, identifies group members as high or low interactors based upon how central they are to the "action" of the group. Grusky argues that the centrality of one's position, and thus one's "interactiveness," influences the kind of role skills that one learns, which, in turn, influences one's chances of moving into a leadership position in an organization. Grusky's initial demonstration that baseball managers tend to have been players from central positions has stimulated a great deal of research of this phenomenon, both at various playing levels and in a wide variety of sports. For an extensive review of this research, the reader is directed to the Loy et al. (1978) text. Insofar as the theory itself is concerned, Loy, McPherson, and Kenyon point out certain problems that exist with Grusky's original conceptualization. In many sports (e.g., hockey and basketball) players do not remain in fixed positions; thus, the static notion of spatial centrality needs to be replaced by the more dynamic concept of functional centrality. Chelladruai and Carron (1977) draw attention to the fact that it may not be the sport itself that dictates centrality, but rather it may be the coaching strategy employed. For example, within the game of football one defensive secondary may play a zone, whereas other teams may elect to play a man-to-man defense. The authors imply that those who participated in the dependent task (i.e., the zone defense) would be more likely to be recruited to leadership positions than would those who played the man-to-man defense, which did not require coordination of efforts with fellow players. Even with these shortcomings, the theory has generated many scholarly investigations. However, some would suggest that it is doomed to failure in that it considers only situational factors while ignoring differences among individuals.

An interactionist approach to the study of leadership in sport is very rare. In spite of its origin in sport and its extensive use outside athletic settings, Fiedler's model has rarely been tested in sport, and when it has, hardly ever has it been supported. The greatest criticism of Fiedler's work has centered on his Least Preferred Co-worker (LPC) scale, which has been used to assess the behavioral orientations of leaders. Reviewers have suggested that Fiedler ignored certain important situational variables (qualities and expectations of the group members). In addition, Carron (1980) pointed out that Fiedler's construct of leader-member relations requires complex measurement, and, in the studies to date (Danielson, 1978; Inciong, 1974), there have been virtually no variations in this parameter in the coaching situations examined. It can be said, therefore, that Fiedler's model has helped very little in understanding leadership behavior in sport groups.

Recently, Chelladurai (1978) developed an interactionist model (Figure 1), which not only takes into account the characteristics of the leaders, the members, and the situation, but also identifies prescribed leader behavior and preferred leader behavior. This model indicates how all five of these classes of variables influence actual leader behavior and how the latter two mediate the actual leader behavior-group performance relationship and the actual leader behavior-group satisfaction relationship. Although this model has not yet been used extensively in sport, my opinion is that it has greater potential than any of its predecessors to provide a framework to explain *how* leader behavior in sport relates to team performance and to the satisfaction of team members.

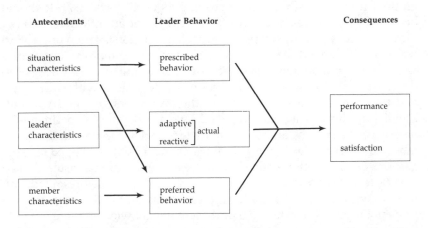

Figure 1: A multidimensional model of leadership. (Chelladurai, 1978; reproduced with permission of the author)

Theories of Group Motivation in Sport

At one time it was generally accepted that the goals of a group represented the sum of, or perhaps a compromise among, the goals of individual group members. In contrast to this view are the observations of Zander, who notes that individuals involved in group decision-making

> Often suppress any inclination to put their own needs first, pay little attention to each other's personal desires, and believe it to be an ethical matter to behave in this way. They concentrate instead on what the total group should do. Choices are made on the basis of what is "good for the group," . . . .It is understandable then that members' motives to achieve success may not only be dispositions to obtain personal rewards, but may also be inclinations to attain satisfactory outcomes for the group. (1971:2)

Zander and his colleagues, at the University of Michigan Research Center for Group Dynamics, have studied group motives very extensively. Their investigations have focused on the antecedents and consequences of group goals in achievement situations. The theoretical position underly-

ing this research is really no different than the widely accepted model
of individual achievement motivation formulated by Atkinson and Feather
(1966). Indeed, Zander's scheme recognizes that in any achievement situation a group's tendency to achieve success is a function of the group's
desire to achieve success, the perceived probability of group success, and
the incentive value of group success. Carron points out, "The desire for
group success (DGS) is a group oriented motive, the basis of which is
the group members' disposition to derive pride and satisfaction with the
group if it is successful in accomplishing its task" (1980:197). It should
be noted that the desire for group success is not an inflexible trait but
rather a motive that develops in particular situations. The work of Forward (1969) showed that the individual and group motives for success
were both independent and additive. In addition, Zander (1974)
demonstrated that these two motives could be at odds with each other,
and that contrary to popular belief, the group motive could win out.
Zander and his colleagues conducted several laboratory experiments to
determine the circumstances that promoted the development of the group
motive for success. From these findings Zander (1978) developed ten suggestions as to how the motive to achieve success could be fostered in an
athletic team. Space does not allow the entire recipe to be presented; suffice to say, however, that all ten are variations on the theme of making
pride in the team important. To the best of my knowledge, there has only
been one attempt to apply these suggestions to a field setting involving
physical activity. Brawley, at the University of Waterloo (Canada), is
presently using Zander's recipe in an attempt to develop the motive to
achieve success within a group of firefighters involved in an exercise
program.

   The same problems that have plagued individual achievement motivation theory are present in Zander's group achievement motivation theory.
These problems include: operationalizing desire for group success and
perceived probability of group success as well as understanding how the
intrinsic incentive for group success is influenced by available extrinsic
rewards. Individual achievement motivation theory has proven more
helpful in understanding why one achievement task is selected over
another, or why a particular level of achievement is expected, than it has
been in explaining why one individual performs better than another in
an achievement situation. Likewise, even though it appears that group
achievement motives are linked to group performance, the nature of these
links are not as clear at this time as the links between group achievement
motives and group aspiration level are.

Theories of Group Performance in Sport

The aspect of the sport group that has been most frequently examined
is its performance. In view of the fact that sport is extremely performance

oriented this is not surprising. Unfortunately, most investigations of the performance of sport groups have not involved theory but have simply examined how teams possessing a greater amount of variable "X" (e.g., task motivation) perform in relation to teams possessing lesser amounts of variable "X." This process has been repeated with variables "Y," "Z," and many others. No theoretical rationale exists to select the variables that have been examined; consequently, this area of study earned the reputation of being an excellent example of the shotgun approach to research. Eventually researchers realized that they needed some framework to identify variables that were most likely to influence group performance.

Hackman and Morris (1975) point out that even though thousands of studies of group performance have been reported (Hare, 1972; McGrath & Altman, 1966), very little is known about *why* some groups are more effective than others. They believe that the key to understanding group effectiveness lies in the ongoing interaction process that takes place among group members. They argue that group process can improve as well as impair group task effectiveness. Unlike Steiner (1972), who spoke only of process losses, Hackman and Morris suggest that the interaction among group members may be beneficial in that it can help to catch errors. Likewise, Collins and Guetzkow (1964) believe that group interaction can lead to the "assembly effect bonuses" that come from the stimulation of one individual by another. In reviewing the group performance literature, Hackman and Morris conclude that something important happens in group interaction, which can affect performance outcome, but "just what that 'something' is—whether it is more likely to enhance or depress group effectiveness" is unknown (1975:49). The authors then present a paradigm (Figure 2) to identify relationships among group input variables, group process variables, and group output variables. The basic assumption underlying their framework is that input factors influence output variables through the interaction process. Specifically, they suggest and demonstrate through past research that the group interaction process influences (a) the level of effort brought to the task, (b) the task performance strategies of the members, and (c) the level of knowledge and skill available to the group. Understanding how each of these three types of variables is influenced by the interaction process can help one to understand how each relates to performance outcome.

In sport, there have been numerous examinations of how individual-level factors such as abilities, personalities, attitudes, and motives of group members relate to team performance. Also, there have been several investigations of how "group-level factors" such as cohesion relate to team performance. However the Hackman and Morris model identifies an entire class of input variables (environment-level factors) and certain output variables (other outcomes), which have been rarely examined in sport. By ignoring interaction process variables, social scientists of sport have

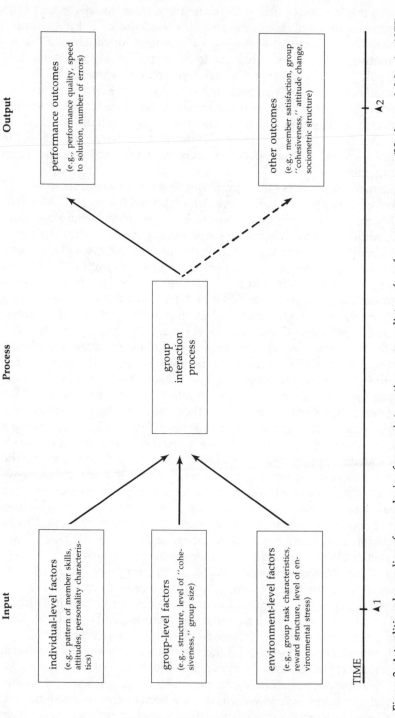

Figure 2. A traditional paradigm for analysis of group interaction as a mediator of performance outcomes (Hackman & Morris, 1975).

Note: From *Social psychology: A brief introduction* by J.E. McGrath, 1964, Orlando, FL: Academic Press. Copyright 1964 by Academic Press. Reprinted by permission.

not been able to understand *how* and *why* input variables are related to output variables.

Uninvestigated Aspects of the Group Life of Sport Teams

Certain aspects of group life, which have been investigated extensively outside of sport, have rarely, if ever, been analyzed in athletic teams. These neglected areas of study concerning sport groups include: (a) group development, (b) coalition formation, and (c) social pressures on members. The absence of such topics in sport group research is difficult to understand for two major reasons. First, each of the topics has relevance for sport; and second, theories have been developed in each of these areas that have successfully guided the research of that area in groups outside of sport.

That sport groups go through stages of development, that subgroups form within sport groups, and that members of sport groups experience social pressures all seem to go without saying. Thus, knowing how and why each of these occur seems vital if one is to understand the group life of athletic teams. For example, knowing about the stages that groups pass through could explain why relationships between variables such as cohesion and success are strong in some situations and weak in others. Cohesion can be strongly related to success in a newly formed group but rather weakly associated with success in a well-established group. This occurs if the cohesion is based upon interpersonal attraction and if interpersonal attraction influenced group success at the early stages of group development but not once groups became established. Other equally plausible cases can be advanced to demonstrate the importance of examining each of the other two major topics neglected in sport.

To exemplify the claim that theories do exist in these three areas and that they have guided research, I direct your attention to the area of coalition formation. Simmel's (1950) notion that power differences are the basis of subgroup formations is borne out in Caplow's (1956) theory that "weakness is strength" and Gamson's (1961) concept of the "cheapest winning coalition." Even though both these coalition theories have stood the test of time, not to mention many empirical investigations, they have been supplemented by newer, highly regarded perspectives such as bargaining theory (Komorita & Chertkoff, 1973), balance theory (Webster & Smith, 1978), as well as the path model of Lawler and Youngs (1975).

In his recent and very extensive review of social coalitions, Baker states that coalition theory "is alive and well and likely to remain so" (1981:645). To appreciate that viable theoretical perspectives exist in the other two areas, the reader is directed to Zander's (1979) overview of small group processes.

Recent Methodological Perspectives in Group Dynamics

Because it is easier to subjectively criticize than it is to objectively summarize, it is extremely tempting to turn a section entitled "Methodological Perspectives" into one entitled "Methodological Problems." In an effort to avoid this trap, I focus on recent methodological advances in small group research. Undoubtedly, many methodological advances have occurred in the analysis of small group behavior. The present chapter restricts itself to a presentation of five recent advances in group dynamics research. These are

1. recognition of differences among group tasks;
2. controlling for and/or accounting for ability variables;
3. consideration of several variables simultaneously;
4. recognition that previous statistical techniques could not identify causality; and
5. recognition that the group is more than its mean score.

The discussion of each of these advances is framed within research dealing primarily with group performance. This does not mean they do not apply to other aspects of group life; rather, it simply reflects my familiarity with their applicability to group performance research.

Recognition of Group Task Differences

Scientists, regardless of their field of study, have come to realize that they cannot generalize the findings of their investigations to task situations that are different from those found in their original research. Because the number of possible tasks in any field of endeavor is usually very large, scholars have sought to categorize tasks in some way that is meaningful for that discipline. Since the two most often cited criteria for a small group are interaction and interdependence, it follows that the tasks of small groups should in some way be differentiated in terms of these characteristics. Thus, researchers have distinguished between interacting and coacting tasks and between independent and interdependent tasks.

Recognizing these task differences allows one to understand why two variables are more strongly related in one situation than in another. For example, cohesion has been shown to be positively related to performance outcome in interacting or interdependent sport tasks such as basketball (e.g., Widmeyer & Martens, 1978), whereas this has not been the case with coacting or independent tasks such as bowling (e.g., Landers & Lüschen, 1974). This is understandable if one recognizes that independent or coacting tasks do not require coordination, and, therefore, a process variable such as cohesion has little opportunity to prevent a coordination loss or bring about a coordination gain within such tasks.

A more elaborate scheme for classifying the tasks of small groups was devised by Steiner (1972) who first distinguished between divisible tasks (i.e., ones that could be subdivided) and unitary tasks (i.e., ones that had to be completed by one person). Unitary tasks were further subdivided into disjunctive tasks, conjunctive tasks, additive tasks, and discretionary tasks. In a disjunctive task, every member of the team must complete the task, for example, to swim across a lake, and the group's performance is equated to the performance of the best member. This team swimming endeavor could be a conjunctive task if the team's performance is equated to the performance of the weakest team member. In additive tasks, the group's performance is equal to the sum of the performance of each member. Additive tasks may be sequential (e.g., a relay event), or they may be simultaneous (e.g., a rowing event). Discretionary tasks are like additive tasks in that all members' scores are considered in computing a group score; however, members' contributions are differentially weighted. Although most group sport tasks are either additive or divisible, it is recognized that certain ones do take on conjunctive or disjunctive features. For example, a popular coaching strategy in basketball and football involves isolating the team's best offensive player on the opponent's weakest defensive player, thus trying to create a disjunctive task for the offense and a conjunctive task for the defense. Identifying the nature of the task can aid in understanding how certain input variables or process variables are related to performance outcome. In a disjunctive task it is better to have a large number of group members with heterogeneous ability levels, whereas in a conjunctive task a small number of individuals with homogeneous ability levels provides the best potential productivity. Also, it follows that process variables such as cohesion and leadership are more influential within additive, discretionary, or divisible tasks in which coordination is required than they are within disjunctive or conjunctive tasks. These examples indicate that the formulation and the subsequent recognition of a logically based scheme for classifying the tasks facing athletic teams can and already does contribute to explaining and predicting behavior within such small groups.

Controlling for and/or Accounting for Ability Variables

In a study examining the relationship between cohesion and performance outcome, Melnick and Chemers state, "a team's playing ability represents a confounding variable when a researcher seeks to determine the relationship between nonperformance variables and task effectiveness" (1974:5). What Melnick and Chemers are saying is that ability is such a strong overriding variable in the performance of athletic teams that it often masks the effects of other influences. Davis (1969) is somewhat more blunt in stating that five geniuses will outperform five morons in a problem-solving task even if the cohesion of the morons far exceeds that of the geniuses. It is not difficult to suggest the parallel that five Kareem Abdul-Jabaars would outperform five Neil Widmeyers in basketball, regardless of the cohesion level of the latter group. Recognition of the powerful contribution that ability makes to performance outcome has led researchers either to control for ability through some sort of equalizing technique (e.g., Widmeyer, 1977), or to account for its effect through some statistical technique (e.g., Widmeyer & Gosset, 1978).

Consideration of Several Variables Simultaneously

To say that group life is extremely complex is an understatement. In spite of the widespread recognition of this fact, those who have investigated small groups have, until very recently, usually considered only two variables at a time. Stogdill (1972) concluded his extensive review of the cohesion literature by stating that high cohesiveness by itself does not lead to high productivity. Instead, he suggested that cohesiveness and productivity tend to be positively related under conditions of high group motivation and negatively related under conditions of low group motivation. Only recently have such interactive effects of group variables been examined. That this has occurred is largely the result of theoretical advances such as the Hackman and Morris model, which stressed group process, and of methodological refinements such as the adoption of multiple regression analysis with continuous data instead of employing t-tests to compare artificially dichotomized groups.

Recognition That Previous Statistical Techniques Could Not Identify Causality

Several studies of sport groups have measured two variables at one time and have said, or implied very strongly, that the one caused a variation in the other when, in fact, such causality was not demonstrated. For example, the cohesion of athletic teams has been measured at the end of a season, and at the very same point in time, these teams, based upon their seasonal won-lost records, have been classified as successful or unsuccessful. Then, after comparing the mean cohesion scores of the successful group with those of the unsuccessful group, authors have suggested that cohesion caused success. Anyone can argue that in such an example, success could just as easily have caused cohesion. Researchers attempted to correct this problem by assessing cohesion at the beginning of the season, before any performance had occurred, and then relating this preseason cohesion to year-end performance record. Although this is a better technique than correlating two simultaneously taken measures, it still does not prove causality in that the performance record could result from any number of intervening influences.

Sport sociologists have for some time employed path analysis as a method for "studying the direct and indirect effects of variables taken as causes of variables taken as effects" (Kerlinger & Pedhazur, 1973:305). Only within the last few years, however, have social psychologists of sport "latched on" to this statistical technique. Kerlinger and Pedhazur (1973) are quick to point out that path analysis is not a method to find causes, but instead is a method to analyze the causal relations proposed by the researcher. Recognition by those who study the dynamics of sport groups that correlational techniques cannot demonstrate causality and that path analysis is certainly no panacea will most definitely lead to more conservative conclusions regarding small group research in sport.

Recognition That the Group Is More Than Its Mean Score

Until very recently, the standard—and almost the sole—method for describing a particular group characteristic was to present the mean value of all the scores achieved by individual group members on that characteristic. This technique is inappropriate for several reasons.

First, describing a group solely by its mean score suggests that the variation in scores among group members in unimportant. To say that a group whose members' cohesion scores are 5, 5, 6, 7, and 7 is the same as a group whose members' scores are 3, 4, 6, 8, and 9 because they have identical means ignores the effects of group homogeneity. Recently, Gosset (1980) operationalized cohesion variability as the standard deviation scores in the cohesion values he obtained for the members of the intercollegiate basketball and hockey teams that he examined. Although cohesion variability by itself was not a significant predictor of performance outcome, the combination of cohesion variability and average (i.e., mean) team cohesion predicted 37% of the variance in team performance outcome as compared to the 22%, which was predicted by average (i.e., mean) cohesion alone. His data revealed that among teams with the same mean cohesion, those teams with low cohesion variability performed better than those with high cohesion variability.

Second, the mean score may be an inappropriate representative of a group characteristic because it treats the scores of all members equally. Because some players are more involved in creating the group product, their input and process scores should weigh more heavily than those of other group members in the formulation of a group score. Indeed, Gray and Gruber's (1981) finding that the cohesion scores of the core players were significantly greater than those of the fringe players implies that more relevant data concerning the prediction of team performance outcome may be available if starting status is taken into consideration when formulating a group score for any characteristic.

Recently, John Loy and I studied group composition-group performance relationships in doubles tennis teams. In addition to examining the amount of ability and the variability in ability, which in this case was the difference in ability between the one player and the other, we investigated how well the abilities of one team member fit with those of the other member. We found that the serve-volley compatibility combined with the forehand-backhand compatibility of team members predicted performance outcome better than individual or total tennis abilities did. Thus, the importance of the "assembly effect" occurring among group members is another reason why the group mean should not be the sole representative of the group.

Recognizing that the group is more than its mean score is not only recognizing that variations in member characteristics are significant and that compatibility of member characteristics are important. It is also recognizing that the group exhibits properties of its own rather than simply being the sum of those of its members. Group cohesion is accepted as a group phenomenon, yet investigators continue to measure the attractions that groups hold for *individuals*, rather than attempting to obtain a measure of *group* integration!

Methodological Problems in Group Dynamics Today

Notwithstanding these methodological advances, several problems associated with studying group dynamics of athletic teams still exist. I will focus on one problem that Loy and I encountered in our investigations of doubles tennis teams. It is not uncommon to compute group scores from individual scores. In some investigations, such as the well-known Klein and Christiansen (1966) study, individuals are members of more than one group. In such cases it can be argued that conceptually each team is unique. Nevertheless the fact remains that the values of any one team are not independent from the values of any other team to which that member belongs. Correlation coefficients and/or multiple regression coefficients computed with such values are most likely overinflated. This problem is not new, and it is certainly not unique to the small group in sport or even to the social sciences in general. At the moment statisticians do not have a method to compute statistics accurately from data containing cases that are not totally independent from each other. Those who study group dynamics should be aware of this problem and should make cautious conclusions from data where it exists.

Concluding Remarks

In summary, group dynamics is a field of study devoted to understanding (a) the nature of groups, (b) the laws of group development, (c) interrelationships among groups, (d) interrelationships among groups and individuals, and (e) interrelationships among groups and large institutions. Although general theoretical orientations that explain a broad range of social behavior and theories of middle range designed specifically for the small group have been used to explain group life in general, only certain very limited theories have been used to explain aspects of life within athletic teams. This situation is not as bad as it first appears. As Kenyon (see chapter 1) points out, theory is important, but it is not a panacea; scholarship should be "ranked" above theory.

I contend that the study of the dynamics of sport groups can indeed be considered a scholarly pursuit if, that is, social scientists take advantage of such methodological advances as

1. recognition of differences among group tasks;
2. techniques for controlling and/or accounting for ability variables;
3. techniques for considering several variables simultaneously;
4. recognition that previous statistical techniques could not identify causality; and
5. recognition that the group is more than its mean score.

Small Group Research in Sport—Theory and Method: A Response to Lüschen, Fine, and Widmeyer

Merrill J. Melnick

Reply to Lüschen

Lüschen's candid, introspective analysis of the sport group research field and his reasons for leaving it, several years ago, provides a thought-provoking and stimulating point of departure for this chapter. Although revealing some "rustiness" in places, for example, some unfamiliarity with the contemporary literature, Lüschen has, in the main, offered an insightful and telling critique of the field. His decision to leave the sport group to pursue other areas of interest has been the field's loss, and one hopes that professional meetings such as this one will rekindle his interest in looking once more at this most challenging of social systems.

Multiplicity of Research Perspectives

Although I am essentially in agreement with Lüschen's criticism of what has, unfortunately, become an "overpsychologized" treatment of the small group in sport, I am not as willing to abandon the psychological perspective for understanding sport group life as he seems to be. To be sure, the unique and special character of the sport group has often been compromised and even lost sight of when subjected to excessive psychological reductionism, artificial laboratory experimentation, and the simplistic, two-variable, unilinear research design that Lüschen so dislikes. All of this is sufficient to "turn off" anyone interested in the sport group, and so Lüschen's "parting of the ways" with the field was and is quite understandable. Further, the sport group researcher's failure to differentiate between intermember relations and group *structural* relations has accounted in no small way for the snail-like development of the field as well as its failure to command the attention of researchers interested in sport systems in general. That the sport group research field has failed to recognize the important roles that group structure and group environment play in accounting for and explaining team behavior is a point Lüschen makes very well.

However, in the same way that Lüschen has called for a multiplicity of research methodologies for studying the sport group, I would like to similarly suggest that a multiplicity of academic perspectives and theoretical orientations are also required to understand the rich and complex nature of team sport life. That is, a *sociological* social psychology might help better focus attention on the structural properties of sport groups, but it should not be allowed to stifle the use of other valid perspectives, such as psychological, social psychological, psychoanalytic, and so forth. No one perspective, in my judgment, has a monopoly on explanatory power.

The fact is, certain group member *psychological* characteristics contribute in an important way to group structure, group process, and group performance—they cannot and should not be ignored. For example, such individual psychological traits as "desire for group success" (Zander, 1974), inclusion, affection, and control needs (Carron & Bennett, 1977), affiliation motivation (Sorrentino & Sheppard, 1978), individual prominence (M. Shaw, 1959), achievement motivation (Klein & Christiansen, 1969), and "will to win" (Dorsey, Lawson, & Pezer, 1980) all have important implications for social interaction and group behavior. In addition, the homogeneity or heterogeneity of certain group member psychological characteristics, for example, achievement motivation, has also been identified as contributing in a significant way to group effectiveness. Lastly, intermember relations, such as friendship patterns, are known to have a direct influence on group structural arrangements and, ultimately, group performance. For example, studies by Slepicka (1975), Yaffe (1974), and Klein and Christiansen (1969) all show how friendship relations directly influence the distribution of passes in volleyball, soccer, and basketball, respectively. In short, Lüschen's call for a more sociologically oriented perspective in sport group research is an important one and surely cannot be ignored. However, if the main and interactional effects of all the input, process, and output variables that help to explain the complexities and perplexities of team sport behavior are to be fully understood, not one but several academic perspectives will have to be consulted.

Structural Analysis in Sport Group Research

Lüschen should be happy to hear that his plea for structural analysis in sport group research postdates some notable efforts already made in this direction. McGrath's (1964) frame-of-reference for analyzing small groups has provided guidance for this researcher as well as, I am sure, for several others. In McGrath's schema, group structure, a major group input variable, is divided into work, power, communication, and affect substructures. Each is seen as having influence on group process, development, and performance. His other two input variables include group member composition factors and task/environment. The latter recognizes the fact that group behavior is very much affected by the properties of the task and the environmental conditions under which the task is performed.

On another front, Greendorfer's (1977a) *organizational analysis* of a college football team represents a promising attempt at understanding sport group behavior within a large social context, one which takes into account the impact of formal, social organizations on team life. With respect to sport group leadership, Chelladurai's (1980) multidimensional model of leader effectiveness recognizes the importance of group structure and context by proposing that leader behavior is a function of group member, leader, and *situation* characteristics. Generally speaking, cohesiveness is no longer looked upon today as a static group characteristic linked to the personal inclinations of individual group members, but rather as a *process* variable existing at a higher level of abstraction than "a-t-g" (attraction-to-group) and referring more to the *relational* characteristics of the group field.

As a final example of the appearance of structural considerations in sport group research, most researchers interested in group performance now recognize that group member composition variables, for example, skill, no longer adequately predict performance effectiveness. Reference to situational (e.g., group size, task structure) and relational factors (e.g., status consensus, clique formation) is now the rule more than the exception. So, while the systematic recognition of structural relations in sport group research has not reached the level of general acceptance that Lüschen would prefer to see, there is considerable evidence that the momentum has indeed swung in this direction.

Future Research Directions

The methodological suggestions and research challenges that Lüschen offers to present and future sport group researchers are especially keen and well worth reemphasizing. I strongly second his call for more natural field studies, creative hypothesis testing, and qualitative data. Sport group researchers will need to further address themselves, as Lüschen points out, to the structural complexity of sport groups, the ways in which the social environment impacts on group structure and function, the cyclical history of sport groups as revealed by time series data, and the dynamic, dialetic relationship that exists when opposing sport groups engage one another. With the exception of Elias and Dunning's (1966a) seminal work in this area, sport group researchers have, by and large, totally ignored the effect that particular sport groups have on the behavior and performance of other sport groups. The interactional effects that result when athletic teams possessing distinctively different compositional, structural, leadership, and cohesiveness characteristics engage one another in competition is something we know hardly anything about.

To summarize, Lüschen has rendered a considerable service to the field of sport group research by calling attention to what has been, up until recently, its haphazard treatment and, oftentimes, embarrassing neglect of *structural analysis*. Groups are, indeed, unique and complex social systems closely linked by common predicament to other sport groups, and all are part of a social environment composed of other social systems and more general societal influences. The sooner these relational constructs and structural contexts are more fully recognized and appreciated, the sooner the sport group research field will be able to unravel the mysteries that explain sport group behavior.

Reply to Fine

Judged purely on the basis of how well he accomplished the task he defined for himself, Fine's paper must be considered "successful." He selected several concepts favored by symbolic interactionists and demonstrated how they can be used in the study of sport teams. Whether these concepts are useful in an empirical, causal sense to sport group researchers is another question, which I will take up shortly. In any event, Fine's analysis of the symbolic richness of the team sport milieu is persuasive. Indeed, one wonders why this perspective has been employed so sparingly by researchers interested in understanding team sport life.

Advantages of Symbolic Interactionist Analysis

Examples of the many symbolic elements present within team sports abound and Fine has done an excellent job in calling our attention to them. Team values, norms, rituals, cheers, chatter, signals, plays, statistics, and reactions to success and failure all offer convincing proof that team sports are a particularly appropriate arena for symbolic interactionist analysis. The rich and colorful narrative of the symbolic interactionist is a welcome addition to the sometimes cold and dispassionate sport group research literature one so frequently encounters. Moreover, Fine has demonstrated in his own research with Little League baseball teams the unquestioned utility of the symbolic interactionist perspective for understanding the more "difficult to reach" team sport nuances, such as the moral consequences of coaching rhetoric, the ways in which team culture is created, and so on.

What I am suggesting is that symbolic interactionism offers the sport group researcher, so inclined, a theoretical perspective for capturing those subtle and evasive aspects of team life that "mainstream" sport group researchers are likely to miss. As a way of helping us to better understand the idiosyncratic nature of the social world of a sport group and how that social world is constructed, symbolic interactionism has much to offer. Moreover, Fine is to be commended for making a successful case on its behalf.

Shortcomings of Symbolic Interactionism

Like all major theoretical orientations, symbolic interactionism has its share of detractors who are quick to point out what they perceive to be its shortcomings. Fine frequently refers to the idiosyncratic nature of team sport life and, by so doing, reveals his understandable commitment to a basic premise crucial to the interactionist perspective, namely, that objects have no a priori value—that the creation of a team's social reality is a subjective process, which derives from the special meanings that group members assign to the structural and cultural stimuli around them. Critics have spoken most loudly on this point. Are individual sport teams really all that unique? Are team positions, roles, prestige hierarchies, values, norms, sanctioning systems, rituals, superstitions, and the like as different from team to team as the symbolic interactionist would have us believe? Are there not some *universalistic* features of team sport life that are characteristic of *all* sport teams, regardless of team member composition or circumstance?

What some critics have suggested is that in their desire to move as far away as possible from structural-functionalism, interactionists have developed a theoretical position that is just as deficient and lopsided as functionalism, except in the opposite direction (Broadbent, 1974). Therefore, what we have is an "*undersocialized* conception of team sport life," one that fails to recognize those institutionalized values, norms, habits, routines, and customs extant within the larger social world of sport. These factors exercise their influence upon each and every group member, separate and apart from those social and cultural elements that operate within the carefully circumscribed boundaries of a particular team. The former are not subject to continuous discussion, negotiation, interpretation, and reinterpretation. For example, must team values such as loyalty, altruism, sportsmanship, and respect for authority be learned anew with each and every sport team membership? Are the role responsibilities assigned to particular playing positions so different from team to team that lengthy apprenticeships have to be served before a role aspirant can perform effectively? Is there really that much variance among team playing abilities, practice sessions, game strategies, and playbooks? Perhaps, it was a negative answer to this last question that led Goldstein (1979) to advance the provocative thesis that at the highest levels of competition, chance factors mainly decide game outcome, not skill, ability, or cultural trappings.

To be sure, each team will develop its own special and unique personality and way of doing things. My point is that the roots of social order characteristics of most sport teams are not as idiosyncratic as the interactionist would have us believe. An attempt to understand the structural and cultural uniqueness of sport teams is certainly a worthy endeavor but should not dissuade us from searching for those lawlike generalizations that can help explain sport team behavior in the generic sense.

Although detailed, multihued descriptions of sport team life make for interesting and colorful reading, my personal biases make me anxious to find answers to specific, practical questions. For example, what can the symbolic interactionist tell us about how shared symbolic meanings impact upon, or influence specific team behaviors? On this question Fine has little to say and, perhaps, that's the way it should be because it was not his intention to engage in such speculation. However, these questions still need to be asked and to be answered. How do sport rituals, sport rhetoric, and team cultures, for example, affect winning, losing, cohesiveness, leadership, intramember conflict, clique formation, and scapegoating? Are there certain group-generated meanings that have a direct bearing on a team's performance? For example, is a collective sense of team momentum a prerequisite or corequisite for a winning streak? In terms of its future prospects for success, does it really matter what symbolic meaning a team attaches to failure? In short, even in the absence of related empirical work, speculations about the relationships between specific symbolic interactionist concepts and specific team behaviors seem in order. Unless some attempt is made to anchor such concepts as the generalized other and the idioculture, for example, to specific dimensions of sport group behavior, they will continue to make interesting reading but will continue to be of limited, practical value.

Finally, if the group process of symbolic meaning construction is as crucial an element in team life as Fine suggests, then it would be interesting to speculate on the role coaches can, or should play in the process. For example, should the coach pay particular heed to the type of chatter his or her team prefers? Should team rituals be allowed to naturally evolve, or should the coach deliberately plan for them? Just how much freedom, if any, should team members be given in selecting such important idiocultural symbols as values, norms, and sanctions? In short, what role should the coach play in the construction of his or her team's social world?

I hope these and other questions will stimulate further discussion and analysis of the symbolic interactionist perspective and the role it can play in explicating the psychosocial dimensions of sport team life.

Reply to Widmeyer

On first appearances, group dynamics can hardly be described as a major theoretical approach to the study of small groups. Be that as it may, as a field of study concerned with using scientific methods to determine why groups behave the way they do, group dynamics does indeed draw its inspiration from several major theoretical perspectives, for example, field theory, interaction theory, and psychoanalytic theory. The group dynamicist's abiding interest in the nature of groups, the laws that govern their development, and the social interaction and social influence processes that occur between and among members is sufficient qualification, in my judgment, to participate in a general session on theory and method in sport group research.

Essentially, what Widmeyer has attempted to do (in my judgment, quite successfully) is to offer an overview of the current status of the sport group research field. I see no value in reacting to or debating the merits of the concept *group dynamics*. For me, it is a ubiquitous, multipurpose concept that can be used to refer to (a) the complex forces that act upon every group throughout its existence and cause it to behave the way it does; (b) a body of basic knowledge about group behavior that has accumulated from past research; (c) a growing body of applied small group principles and techniques; and (d) a formal, social scientific field of study (Knowles & Knowles, 1972). I am more concerned with whether or not Widmeyer has rendered a fair and accurate appraisal of the sport group research field. In my judgment, he has indeed. He identified for us those "limited theories" in the areas of group structure, leadership, motivation, and performance that currently enjoy favor among sport group researchers. He suggested several aspects of sport team life, which remain, unfortunately, uninvestigated areas. He astutely summarized several recent methodological advancements that have occurred in the analysis of sport group behavior. All things considered, one has reason to feel more than a twinge of guarded optimism about the future of the sport group research field after reading Widmeyer's remarks. I would now like to address the implied, optimistic tone of his chapter.

Optimistic Outlook

Two recently published state-of-the-art discourses on the subfield of sociology of sport predict a rather gloomy future for sport group research. One author noted that the study of the athletic team has *declined* over the past several years (Lüschen, 1980), while the other observed that sport sociologists ". . .have practically abandoned research from a small group perspective" (Greendorfer, 1981:383). I received a considerably different impression after reading Widmeyer's chapter. For example, to learn that interest in the sport group extends beyond the mind-numbing debate over whether cohesiveness is an antecedent or a consequence of team performance was refreshing. Widmeyer observes that in the areas of group structure, leadership, motivation, and performance, theory and research are going forward. Specifically, my own recent perusal of the contemporary research literature revealed no less than 24 sport group research studies published within the last 6 years. These studies investigated a wide and diverse assortment of variables including physical and personality characteristics of group members, interpersonal attraction, social interaction, coach-athlete compatibility, team momentum, intermember conflict, clique formation, leadership, team performance, reactions to success and failure, and audience effects (Melnick, 1983).

Of further interest has been the development of models and data-gathering instruments specific to the study of sport groups, for example, Chelladurai's (1980) interactionist model to explain sport leader behavior. On the methodological front there is also reason for optimism. The level of sophistication of sport group research has improved considerably over the past 10 years. The discovery of team task differences and the need to control for team ability variance, the use of multiple regression analysis, and the recognized importance of team member homogeneity/heterogeneity have all helped improve upon the highly descriptive and simplistic sport group research of the past. However, I wonder whether Widmeyer shares my concern about whether this "new, improved research" will ever reach the practitioner in the field. That is to say, unless deliberate efforts are made to share this research with the coaching profession, for example, the translation of these research findings into everyday practice will go wanting. That is not to say that the formal study of a sport group is not a worthy scholarly endeavor in and of itself. What I am suggesting is that it is an unfortunate state of affairs when research findings and recommendations that can have direct, practical pay-offs never see the light of day because of their limited dissemination. I believe that coaches are willing and able to profit from our research, provided they are given the opportunity to do so.

Widmeyer has offered us a far-ranging chapter that touches on many aspects of group dynamics as it applies to the study of sport teams. He is critical of the field, particularly its judicious use of small group theory and its methodological failings. He is also generous in his praise of those sport group researchers whose work has extended the theoretical and empirical boundaries of this challenging field of specialization. To take exception with, or to find fault with a chapter that is essentially an overview of the work that has been done to date is difficult. I find myself basically in agreement with his reading and critique of the current "state of the art." With respect to his discussion of group performance theories, this is especially true. His criticism of Steiner's (1972) model of group effectiveness is a telling one because everyday sport experience informs us that *group process* has the potential to facilitate and to enhance group performance, that it need not always impair group task effectiveness as Steiner suggests. The modestly skilled basketball team that is able to play outstanding ball is testimony to the fact that something special can indeed occur when group members interact in mutually supportive ways— that they are capable of performing well above what their individual skills and abilities suggest. For this reason I believe a systems paradigm holds great potential for explaining sport group behavior, especially, group performance. Not only does it recognize the obvious but important relationship between group input and output variables, but it also emphasizes the important role that *group process* variables play in mediating that input. My suspicion is that social interaction is the key element in explaining the performance effectiveness of interacting sport groups.

To summarize, Widmeyer is to be commended for his successful handling of a most ambitious task. He has provided us with an accurate and stimulating overview of the group dynamics field as well as the ways in which it has been and is being applied to the study of sport teams. Rather than be dismayed by the record to-date, Widmeyer has given us considerable reason to believe that the formal and systematic study of sport groups is alive and well and has a promising future.

College Athletics: Problems of a Functional Analysis

James H. Frey

Applying the structural-functional paradigm to sport seems to be a "natural" exercise. Sport, at any level, is usually discussed, defended, or criticized by academics, journalists, boosters, and participants in terms of the contributions sport makes to individual growth, group cohesion, societal stability, and the like. If it is true that any regular behavior pattern, normative structure, or value configuration can be analyzed in functional terms, that is, in terms of its social consequences (Johnson, 1981), then certainly sport, and in this case the intercollegiate variety, can be assessed in this manner. Few question the fact that college sports hold a prominent place in the behavior, social life, and belief systems, either symbolically or participatory, of a large portion of our population.

The functional paradigm is well represented within sport sociology. This is the case whether the underlying perspective on social organization views society as held together by normative consensus or by differential power relations. Allardt (1967), Coakley, (1982), Dunning (1967), Edwards (1973), Eitzen and Sage (1978), Lüschen (1967), and Stevenson and Nixon (1972) are examples of sport sociologists who have evaluated the social consequences of sport for the maintenance of a system or for the undermining or disruption of that system. The more traditional functional view is expressed quite well by Dunning in the case of personality system.

It is likely that any sport or game which shows some degree of persistence over time will be found to perform certain functions in the sense of yielding satisfactions of some kind or another for those who participate, whether directly as actors, or less directly as spectators. (1967:147)

Dunning goes on to assert that sport provides that participant with "tension excitement," a pleasurable experience that serves as a functional substitute for similar experiences lacking in work and home.

Even the critics of the ordinarily positive assessments of sport very often will counter with functional statements of their own. Only the direction of the consequence is different. For example, Edwards states,

A review of evident and informal opinions does not allow any conclusive evaluation of the claim that sports participation prepares an athlete for life. It does suggest that there are many cases in which participation is *detrimental* (emphasis added) to his adjustment in greater society. (1973:325)

Edwards applies a similar analysis to the various components, for example, competition, mental fitness, physical fitness. In both cases the logic of the functional argument is the same: A configuration or pattern (sport participation) exists; therefore, it must have consequences. In one case, they are functional (contributory in the Parsonian sense), and, in the other, they are dysfunctional or noncontributory (in the Mertonian sense). Neither analysis specifies under what conditions either is true. This analytic deficiency, plus other problems with functional analysis, goes a long way in telling us why the functional paradigm is somewhat passé in mainstream sociology today and why it should be in sport sociology.

The criticisms of functional sociology, such as conservatism, esoteric language, ahistorical, tautological reasoning, exaggerations of harmony, and banality (Johnson, 1981; Zeitlin, 1973) apply to functional sport sociology as well. Attacks on functionalism, however, actually represent criticism of what was formerly mainstream sociology, and as Goode (1973:65) states, "criticizing functionalism is like beating a dead horse." It is difficult today to find a sociologist who would admit to adhering to an approach that includes teleological reasoning, is resistent to the analysis of conflict or social change, and contains a belief that all standard features of a system tend to have positive consequences. The earlier prominence of functionalism may at least be partially explained by the efforts of sociologists to distinguish the subject matter of their discipline and to establish the scientific status of sociological work. The result was the grasp of a more immediate and visible ex post facto analytic approach as opposed to building theoretical models with an empirical base. Several factors served to replace or to push aside functional analysis in sociology. They are

1. the rise to prominence of alternative paradigms, namely, conflict theory (Horowitz, 1967; Mills, 1956), and "Sociologies of Every-

day Life" as expressed in symbolic interaction (Goffman, 1959), and phenomenologically based existential sociology (Douglas et al., 1980);

2. the general movement from concern with "big theory" to concern with micro and "little theories" (Warshay, 1975); and

3. the lack of consensus on how to "do" sociology (Gove, 1979).

The same phenomenon, I predict, will also occur in the sociology of sport.

The sociology of sport, in general, and intercollegiate sport in particular, still depend a great deal upon functional analysis. We have reached the stage where there is considerable literature on the positive or the negative consequences of intercollegiate sport for participants, community, and society. Even though one could be assured, as were our mainstream predecessors, that he or she was "doing sociology," when applying the functional paradigm to sport, conceptual confusion and methodological ambiguity remain. These problems are especially acute for the study of intercollegiate sport because it remains the least developed, both theoretically and methodologically, of any area of sport studies. After a discussion of the components of functional analysis, I will attempt to show that this approach to the study of sport has not resulted in our knowing a great deal, in the scientific sense, about intercollegiate athletics.

Functional Analysis: Brief Overview

The analysis of social reality occurs at several levels (Johnson, 1981). The level of the individual focuses on action and behavior. The interpersonal level, as exemplified by the symbolic interaction and exchange perspectives, focuses on the interaction of individuals and is couched in symbolic meaning, negotiation, cooperation, and other mechanisms of mutual adjustment. The structural level is based on observations of persistent regularities as they are artifacts of status and role arrangements. The functional perspective and the Marxist conflict approach fall in the latter context.

Basic Tenets

In contrast to the paradigms that emphasize the subjective nature of social reality and those that focus on the overt, observable behavior of individuals, the structural-functional view asserts that social phenomena are real apart from individuals (Ritzer, 1975). Social facts, or characteristics of a social system (as they are called in functional analysis), have a reality of their own and, by virtue of their externality, exercise constraint over individual behavior and interactions. Society exists independent of its members and operates according to its own principles. Thus, a system has "needs" that are separate from those of individual members. In addition, the parts of any system are interdependent with reciprocal relationships established by agreement and a desire to keep the system "at equilibrium" (Gouldner, 1959).

For Durkheim, often marked as the source of this view of reality, the system needed mechanisms to maintain social order or stability. This theme was elaborated by Parsons when he asserted that all social systems must meet certain requirements if they are to survive. These systemic needs fall into the categories of Adaptation, Goal attainment, Integration, and Latent pattern maintenance (AGIL) (Parsons, Bales, & Shils, 1953). In addition, a system needs mechanisms of reward, conflict resolution, value training, social control, problem solving, territorial defense, as well as devices to obtain the cooperation of members. Institutions, comprised of role and status systems that, in turn, were reinforced by value configurations internalized and agreed upon by most members,[1] articulated these mechanisms. Any activity or event was then interpreted in terms of its consequences for the operation of these institutions (i.e., maintenance of the equilibrium of the system).

Robert Merton brings some conceptual clarity to functionalism with his elaboration of the concept of "function." Any item is still evaluated in terms of its consequences for the system in question, but these consequences can be dysfunctional (negative), intended (manifest), latent (unintended), or nonfunctional (irrelevant) as well as functional (contributory) (Merton, 1968). Merton also suggests that some items may be functional for some structures within a system and dysfunctional for others. Merton was not ready to accept Parson's premise of functional prerequisities, but he did assert that social order was the result of the net balance of functions over dysfunctions.

Few sociologists today would assert that functionalism represents a theory of social behavior. Rather, it is a strategy for analysis, or a "context of inquiry," or a certain kind of sociological orientation. It was never a specific structure of empirical propositions (Goode, 1973). As a mode of inquiry functional analysis begins by asking two basic questions:

1. What basic functional requirements must be fulfilled for a society, or any social system, to survive as a viable system, and how are these functions fulfilled?
2. For any given pattern of behavior, what are the overall social consequences or effects on the larger system in which the pattern is involved?

Functional analysis proceeds to answer these questions by appealing to a modified teleological approach that arrives at an explanation not by reference to causes that bring about effects, but by reference to *ends* that provide the purpose or goal of its action (Hempel, 1959:277). First, functional analysis identifies a social pattern (e.g., college athletics). Second, it explains the persistence or the regularity of the pattern by establishing its consequences (e.g., social cohesion, character development) for the larger system of which it is a part. Third, it identifies the functions the pattern performs that cannot be adequately filled by equivalent activities (indispensibility factor). Fourth, functional reciprocity or compensatory arrangements of this pattern with others is documented. Functionalism actually begins its analysis with the "effect" and works back to the "cause" in a sort of ex post facto fashion. Ultimately, the goal of functional analysis is to explain the role of each part in keeping a system in proper working order. This has led to a raft of critical or antifunctionalist sentiment.

Criticisms

The problems of functionalism are well known and readily accessible (Hempel, 1959; Merton, 1968; Mills, 1956). Antifunctionalists assert that (a) society is not a harmonious unity; (b) social patterns are not indispensible; (c) standardized sociocultural forms do not result in only positive contributions; (d) the social system is not totally self-regulatory and resistent to change; and (e) teleological reasoning (i.e., the end is the cause of the steps toward it) is not acceptable (Dahrendorf, 1959; Goode, 1973).

Functionalism was viewed as essentially conservative with its focus on the status quo. Functionalists were depicted as investigators without intellectual nerve, preferring order and resisting change. Even the die-hard antifunctionalists could not locate a sociologist who ascribed to the functional tenets criticized by the antifunctionalists. According to many, attacks on functionalism were actually attacks on the content of mainstream sociology (Berger, 1971; Davis, 1959; Goode, 1973) as it existed from approximately 1940 to 1970.[2]

Much of the criticism of the content of mainstream sociology has merit. Sociologists (translation: functionalists) neglected motivation by self-interest in favor of normative consensus; they neglected the importance of force and power in system maintenance; they have not adequately accounted for larger societal factors that might have produced more variability in behavior; they neglected social change; and their theoretical sophistication is less than desirable (Goode, 1973). However, some of the criticism is defensible. True, sociological content may seem conservative, but it is also true that norms play a great role in ordinary behavior; people prefer certainty, and social forces do not move with haste (Berger, 1971). Yet, at the same time, sociology cannot be conservative because we know that sociology has made contributions to social change, problem resolution, and critical analysis of society.

Although we are not ready to accede to Davis' assertion that "any good sociologist is a functionalist," possibly functionalists, as good sociologists, were seeking to establish relationships between parts, forces, or patterns. Their problem was to approach the analysis by noting the effect and "looking backward" for the cause. Thus, a social structure or institutional pattern exists because it contributes to the maintenance of the system—the proof of its existence. This psuedoexplanation is difficult to test and does not account very well for functional alternatives, dysfunctions, latent and unintended consequences, or the establishment of variation in the degree to which a pattern is functional or not. Either a social pattern contributes, or it does not.

Some assert that this type of explanatory procedure is not what functionalists actually intended (Turner, 1982). Rather, the writing style of a statement like "athletics exist because it is functional for social cohesion in the larger collectivity" suggests a teleological approach. This statement can be reinterpreted to mean: "The structure of the larger collectivity as a self-maintaining system is such that structures will be created by the system that produce needed activities. The collectivity requires cohesion and therefore creates athletics to maintain cohesion." Thus, the system, via feedback control, creates its functioning parts. This statement is more like a typical causal statement and not one that is bound in teleological reasoning.[3]

Functionalism became attractive to sociologists because it gave them an explanatory tool at a time when the discipline was in its infancy and not able, or ready, to make causal assertions about social life. Goode (1973) asserts that function substituted for cause because sociologists were too embarrassed to use the latter term. Typically, the analyses of intercollegiate athletics follow the teleological model of functionalism. The result has been that we really cannot explain much about this social pattern, due largely to three factors. First, because of the political stake opponents and proponents have in justifying the existence of athletics, neither side was ready or willing to apply a critical analysis, that is, apply a model that would account for differences or variation. Perhaps we were afraid of what the model would tell us.[4] Second, it was easy to speak in terms of functional analysis because there was little agreement on what needed to be studied, how to go about studying athletics, what was good evidence, and whether sport should be studied in and of itself or should be a vehicle to study general sociological phenomena. The result was a "brickyard"—no cumulative knowledge of any depth (McPherson, 1978). Third, sociology of sport was reaching for its *cause celebre*.

In mainstream sociology and in sport sociology it is desirable to reformulate or to modify the language of functionalism—dysfunction, nonfunction, eufunction, functional prerequisites—and to speak, instead, in terms of "cause and effect." This will result in more rigorous problem definition and consequent assertions about the nature of relationships. Functional alternatives will then become multiple causes. References to the "continued existence of society" or other distant and untraceable phenomena will no longer be acceptable. Specificity and theoretical rigor should be the order of the day. Rather than a continued discussion of the positive and negative consequences of intercollegiate athletics, it would be of greater scientific value to begin looking at this social pattern as it provides the context for theoretical study or as a variable in a larger model under test.

Intercollegiate Athletics: The Functional Tradition

Functions and Dysfunctions

If we say that intercollegiate athletics is functional, then what are we really saying? In the terms of the paradigm we are saying that "college athletics as a social pattern exhibits some consequences," and "these consequences are viewed as essentially positive." Therefore, college athletics, as a persistent social pattern, continues to exist because it makes positive contributions to the maintenance of the systems of which it is a part. The high congruence of societal values with those associated with sport in general, plus the fact that those who evaluate the consequences of athletics as highly positive tend to be those who have substantial emotional and economic investment in sport (Cross, 1977; Novak, 1975; Wooden, 1972), has contributed to the institutionalization of intercollegiate athletics in its present form. The normative and institutional underpinnings of college sport have served to enhance its priority and sustenance in the community and higher education systems to which it belongs.

On the other hand, negative or dysfunctional consequences of athletics on campus have also been brought to our attention. The detractors assert that this social pattern produces effects that are harmful to participant, community, campus, and society (Edwards, 1973; Scott, 1971). Recent scandals of grade fixing, payoffs, educational compromise, and even out-and-out violation of the law accentuate these adverse effects. Yet, the motivation to participate in key athletic status and role positions provides a surplus of willing applicants; college sport continues to maintain significant cultural and structural support. In the Mertonian sense, apparently, functions outweigh dysfunctions. As Gouldner would note, the reciprocal interdependence of athletics with education, family, political, and economic entities is institutionalized with a favorable return for all parties. Table 1 suggests that intercollegiate athletics are on solid ground if one weighs the functions over the dysfunctions. A careful review of the literature on college sports reveals that a version of functional analysis has been applied whether the tone of that literature is supportive or critical.

Table 1. Summary of Functions and Dysfunctions of College Athletics, by System Level

System	Functions	Dysfunctions
Individual/ Personality	1. Character development (e.g., courage, humbleness) 2. Acquisition of social skills 3. Tension release 4. Educational attainment 5. Occupational attainment 6. Occupational success 7. Educational opportunity 8. Physical fitness 9. Prestige 10. Tension/excitement 11. Identity formation 12. Affective association	1. Character detraction 2. Negative aggression 3. Educational detraction 4. Exploitation of larger subsystems (i.e., powerlessness) 5. Role conflict and stress 6. Dehumanizing and delusionary 7. Value distortion

Education (Subsystem)	1. Integration of student body
	2. Reduction of conflict
	3. Unity of members across class lines
	4. Social control
	  a. Displaced aggression
	  b. Norm affirmation
	5. Prestige
	6. Community visibility
	7. Academic communities visibility
	8. Generalized political and economic influence/support
	9. Informal membership retention and support beyond formal break (i.e., graduation)
	10. Attraction of membership
	11. Promotion of "town and gown" affiliation
		1. Detraction from educational mission
		2. Promotion of hostility/ conflict

Community (Subsystem)	1. Unity of members across social categories
	2. Democratization of interpersonal relations—"talking sports"
	3. Social control
	  a. Displaced aggression
	  b. Norm affirmation
	  c. Safety valve/tension management
	4. Entertainment—tension excitement
	5. Economic—flow of new capital
		1. Creation of false consciousness
		2. Diversion of attention from social problems
		3. Reinforcement of class distinctions
		4. Promotion of hostility and conflict

Cont.

Table 1. Cont.

Society		
	6. Opportunity for association for political and economic elite 7. Identity and visibility via boosterism 8. Community legitimacy—"big league"	
Society	1. Socialization to accepted values, norms (e.g., conformity) 2. Safety valve/tension release at class level 3. Ritualistic expression of American life—norm and value affirmation 4. Reinforcement of sex, age, and racial role allocations	1. Socialization to norms and behavior which are demeaning or potentially disruptive (e.g., dishonesty, circumventing rules) 2. Intergroup/class hostility 3. Diversion of attention from exploitive social structure 4. Reinforcement of sexism, racism, and unequal distribution of resources

Note. Further discussion of each of the functions or dysfunctions listed can be found in one or all of the following: Blackburn and Nyikos (1974), Cady (1978), Coakley (1979), Edwards (1973), Eitzen and Sage (1978), Frey (1979, 1982), and Scott (1971).

Functional Autonomy

Thus, undoubtedly functional analysis can and will continue to be applied to the analysis of intercollegiate athletics. For example, beyond the notion of positive or negative function we can reconceptualize the loss of academic/institutional control of athletics in terms of Gouldner's (1959) treatment of functional autonomy. He asserts that each part of a system is dependent on other parts, with some parts being more dependent than others. Dependence is, thus, a matter of degree. Athletic departments, as a result of their responsibility to raise their own resources and to be closely connected with an extra-education, community-based booster coalition, exhibit a high degree of functional autonomy. These departments can survive separation from the larger institution, on which they are not significantly dependent for economic and political reasons, if they can establish a way to legitimize the break of the traditional association of athletics and education.

Furthermore, it is possible to analyze the trends in college athletics in functional terms by reference to Parsons' (1951) need-prerequisites for systems. The professionalization, commercialization, and rationalization of sport of the college variety represent a process whereby college sport has moved from its prominent place as a reinforcer of normative patterns (latent pattern maintenance) and a mechanism of social control (integrative), to a position promoting the economic (adaptive) and political (goal attainment) needs of significant collectivities within the system. This will make change even more difficult because the factors of power and economy are more formidable and meaningful to a system than those of value training and solidarity. Thus, conformity and cooperation can be obtained by coercion if necessary.

Shortcomings of the Functional Paradigm

If face validity can provide the criteria for evaluating what we know about college athletics by using the functional paradigm, then it appears that we can believe ourselves to be quite knowledgable. However, a closer look tells us we cannot explain very much about college athletics as either an independent sociologial phenomenon or as a research site for the study of more general sociological problems (e.g., occupational socialization). Marxian or conflict perspective, also essentially a macro-approach, does not offer much improvement in the knowledge base because it also is caught up in the tautological analysis and polemical subterfuge. Both avoid building theoretical models or engaging in systematic research, particularly when analyzing factors at the community, institutional, and societal levels.

By focusing on the positive or negative consequences of athletics, both the functionalist and Marxist approaches were forced to an either/or situation to the neglect of the notion of variability. For example, it is asserted that participation in college athletics either builds character or detracts from the same. Left unexplained are: At what point does participation move from reinforcement to detraction? Is there a difference in the development of "character" by players' social background, nature of the game, program size, coach's background, degree of athletic socialization, and so on? If college athletics support educational goals, when does it detract from these goals? The same line of reasoning applies to the analysis of the relation of athletic participation to academic achievement, occupational success, individual prestige, and personality change or development. If we talk about "cause" and forget our ideological attachments, then analytic rigor, as well as the knowlege base, improve considerably.

What Is Needed

If analytic rigor improves, then so also will our research. Beyond the level of the individual/personality system, we really understand very little in an empirical sense about the relationship of college athletics to the other systems. In many ways this logical outcome of applying a conceptual paradigm, either Marxist or functional, utilizes concepts and assertions about reality. For example, "X supports the maintenance of the system" or "an individual is alienated by virtue of his or her exploited labor" which are virtually untestable. Sport sociology needs the application of sophisticated research, qualitative or quantitative, without the *excess* conceptual baggage of prominent paradigms, and oriented to the norms of science, in order to add to its knowledge of the meaning of sport, particularly college sport to social and personality systems. Thus, sport sociology is confronted with the same problems as mainstream sociology—the improvement of content through attention to factors previously unaccounted for, increasing theoretical sophistication, and the employment of more rigor in research. This means, in effect, that we must move beyond the strict application of a functionalist approach and must take advantage of the diversity in methodological and theroretical orientations that currently exist in sociology. Each should be utilized where appropriate and with the goal of building cumulative knowledge.

Notes

1. Parson's scheme is better known, but others have suggested a similar configuration of system needs. Aberle et al. (1950) assert that four conditions must be avoided if a system is to survive. These are (a) biological extinction of members, (b) membership apathy, (c) war, and (d) absorption into another society. They also suggest nine functional prerequisites.
2. A recent review symposium on the content and the editorial policy of sociological journals published in *Contemporary Sociology* contained few references to functionalism and certainly did not find functionalism, or, for that matter, any theoretical view, dominant in sociology. If anything, diversity and disagreement prevail (Gove, 1979).
3. My thanks to a colleague, Dr. Loren Reichert, for drawing my attention to this distinction.
4. Gove, in his review of the substantive content of journals, asserts that this is a basic problem to all of sociology. He states: "Many sociologists have strong ideological commitments to a particular image of what society should be like, and these ideological commitments strongly shape their work and their judgments of others" (1979:801).

Athletics and Higher Education: A Symbolic Interaction Perspective

Eldon E. Snyder

Sociological theories, according to Sorokin (1956), may be nothing more than attempts to explain some contemporary event in terms of what "seems right" to the theorist and the audience. In this vein, Gouldner (1970) suggests that the mark of a good theory is the gut-level feeling that it fits the historical moment, or that it makes sense of events otherwise too disjointed and random to understand. One theory, however, may be inadequate to provide a complete explanation of reality. Ritzer (1975) notes that sociology is a multiple paradigm science, and different paradigms and theoretical perspectives focus on particular aspects of what is going on. Each approaches the subject from a different angle. A comprehensive study of social behavior may profit from the incorporation of several theoretical perspectives; each seems right in providing its own unique view and makes sense of some portion of social reality.

A primary characteristic of sport in higher education is that athletic departments tend to institutionalize the role expectations of administrators, coaches, players, and trainers. Structural-functional and conflict theories are suitable for viewing the way athletic departments facilitate the maintenance of the system and constrain behavior. These two theoretical perspectives are often mirror images of each other and are useful for studying complex organizations, authority structures, social control, institutionalized roles, and socialization of individuals into these roles. Yet, ironically, sport has the built-in characteristic of instability. That is, the inherent lack of predictability in the outcome of athletic contests leaves the primary goals of formal sport—winning and fiscal solvency— always uncertain. Furthermore, these theories do not go far enough in considering the possibility that persons may not simply "respond" to external stimuli. Individuals may choose not to abide by the constraints imposed upon them. For example, members of athletic departments do not always blindly seek goals set for them by others. Indeed, under certain conditions athletes, coaches, trainers, and administrators rationally select conflicting goals, and social structures are negotiated and transformed. Thus, whereas the institutionalization of formal sport organizations reduces the fluidity and problematic nature of behavior (as contrasted to everyday activities), a brief reflection suggests that even in the bureaucratic structure of collegiate athletic departments behavior is not rigidly determined, fixed, and immutable. In fact, Blumer uses a sport metaphor to illustrate this point: "although most football plays can be predefined and precharted, when the ball is intercepted the situation becomes undefined, and self-indication and interpretation are necessary" (Wallace & Wolf, 1980:245). Therefore, collegiate athletic programs are invariably "in process," problematic, emergent, and "under construction." The symbolic interactionist perspective is particularly useful in focusing on those occasions that are unexpected, dynamic, processual, as well as the "close up" view of how individuals define, reflect, and make decisions.

Basic Assumptions of the Symbolic Interactionist Perspective

The primary objective of this chapter is to use the basic assumptions of symbolic interactionism as a perspective to view athletics in higher education. No attempt to deal with the nuances and schools of thought within symbolic interactionism is made. Consequently, no attention is given to the detailed differences between Stryker's (1980) "social structural" version of symbolic interactionism, the alleged methodological differences between Mead and Blumer (Blumer, 1980; McPhail & Rexroat, 1979, 1980), or the closely related theories of ethnomethodology and phenomenology (Douglas et al., 1980). Rather, the basic premises of symbolic interactionism will be outlined; then a discussion of how this perspective can be used in the analysis of some aspects of collegiate sport will be presented.

A generalized version of the symbolic interactionist framework is explicated as follows:

1. A basic premise of symbolic interactionism has evolved from George H. Mead (1934). Human communication and behavior are dependent on *significant symbols* that label and classify the world and allow for cooperative behavior among people. A symbol is significant because it transmits meanings that are shared by others in a group. As children learn to talk, the significant sym-

bols are acquired that represent salient elements and meanings in a situation necessary for mutual social interaction. The meanings of things are not inherent within the object; rather, meaning is a social product and is socially created.

2. Because the meanings transmitted by significant symbols are the basis for social interaction, cooperative behavior is possible only if people acquire approximately the same meanings, and they understand the actions of others by *putting themselves in the place of others* (take the role of the other) and act accordingly.

3. *Meanings may be modified* and things redefined. In complex societies meanings may vary by subgroup, they may be "in transition" and emergent because rapid social change requires a reexamination and realignment of previous meanings and courses of action. The redefinition of meanings occurs through social interaction.

4. On a personal level the meanings of things are understood and modified through an *interpretive (reflective) process*. The interpretive process includes the overall configuration of objects and acts perceived by the individual and is termed the definition of the situation. Although the symbolic interactionist position does not reject the importance of social structures (status, role, ranking, authority relation, and the like), "they are important only as they enter into the process of interpretation and definition out of which joint actions are formed" (Blumer, 1969:75). Therefore, individuals are capable of reflective behavior about objects, others, and themselves (i.e., they organize their social world). In the course of interpreting and aligning one's actions to others, interactions are often seen as negotiated, emergent, and unpredictable. The problematic and flexible nature of interaction increases in situations of conflicting meanings and interpretation.

5. The acquisition of meanings and the ability for reflective thought includes not only the social environment, but also meanings and *reflections (self-definitions) about one's self*. As a consequence of self-reflection the individuals are better able to control their behavior and anticipate the response of others to alternative acts. The meanings attached to one's self vary according to the situation. In this respect the "identities" are parts of one's self-perception that one announces in varying situations. These identities, like other meanings, are developed and verified through social interaction with others. Also, self-perceptions may be modified and redefined. Furthermore, one's identities may be inconsistent and in conflict with each other, and one's self-perception (or perceptions) may be threatened and changed by contrasting meanings attached to the individual by significant others.

In short, the symbolic interactionist perspective stresses the process of constructing, defining, and negotiating the actions of individuals. Most symbolic interaction analysis has been social-psychological with a focus on individuals' self-perceptions, the social definitions that impinge on the individual as well as the individual's perceptions, and the interpersonal processes that influence opinions and actions. However, the interactionist perspective may also be used for organizational analysis, for example, to examine the informal as opposed to the formal attributes of an organization (Denzin, 1977, 1978; Goffman, 1961a; Selznick, 1948). More specifically, Denzin argues that the interactionist perspective may focus on organizations "as negotiated productions that differentially constrain their members; they are seen as moving patterns of accommodative adjustment among organized parties" (1977:905). Thus, in the following discussion of the symbolic interactionist perspective and athletics in higher education, much of the focus will be social psychological; however, this perspective will also apply to the analysis of athletic departments as complex organizations.

The Symbolic Interactionist Perspective and Athletics in Higher Education

The major thrust of this chapter is to illustrate the use of symbolic interactionism in the context of athletics in higher education. Central to symbolic interactionism is the concept of shared meanings (symbols) that have emerged within the collectivity. In the following section the meanings and values that serve to define the sport situation are outlined. These shared meanings represent the script whereby participants can better understand what others are doing and can direct their own behavior in light of this knowledge.

The Collegiate Sport World: Meanings and Definitions

In the consideration of collegiate sports, the concept of a social world is useful. Shibutani (1955) identified four aspects of social worlds. Each is a universe of *regularized mutual response*, an *arena* of social organization, a *cultural area* with boundaries established by an effective *communication system*. Social worlds studied by interactionists included ethnic, racial, deviant, occupational, religious, recreational, and sexual groups. In each social world related clusters of activity, and a system of beliefs and meanings exist. The social world of collegiate athletics, like other activity systems, rests upon a system of beliefs (a code or creed) that is shared by its members (cf. Nash, 1980). Edwards (1973) describes the American sport creed in terms of such values as hard work, perseverance, competition, and physical and mental fitness. The slogans that are often placed in athletic locker rooms provide qualitative examples of the sport creed (Snyder, 1972):

> The harder I work the luckier I get.
> The will to win is the will to work.
> If you can't put out, get out.
> We issue everything but guts.
> If it doesn't matter if you win or lose, why keep score?
> It takes a cool head to win a hot game.
> Live by the code or get out.
> There is no I in team.

These slogans suggest that athletes are aggressive, competitive, skilled, disciplined, and team-oriented hard workers. These meanings of the sport world provide loosely articulated ways of thinking and ways of evaluating others and one's self-performance. These meanings and beliefs related to the sport world are also embodied in media guides published by most collegiate athletic departments. The success of intercollegiate athletic departments at major universities is determined primarily by their winning records and gate receipts in the revenue sports. The head coach of these sports is responsible for the team's performance. Coaches, like people in other occupational roles, project an image in terms of approved social attributes. Goffman (1967:5) developed this notion in his definition of *face* as the "positive social value a person effectively claims for himself by the line others assume he has taken during a particular contact."

According to Goffman, we spend considerable energy in "face work," that is, in managing others' impressions of us so we can maintain a favorable image. The descriptions provided in the media guides represent the attempt, usually by the Sports Information Director of the athletic department, to manage the readers' impressions of the coach and his or her legitimacy for the position (as well as information about the team). The descriptions of the head coaches and statements by them in the media guides are revealing in providing further data regarding the desired attributes of the coaches and players. In short, they represent shared meanings associated with intercollegiate athletics. The following are sample statements selected from recent media guides for major university football teams:

> The most important traits necessary for a top-notch football player include a willingness to hit, a burning desire to improve each day and the will to prepare and expect to win.

I don't believe in playing without a scoreboard. I don't feel there
is any accomplishment with a tie.

All our efforts are aimed at making each individual realize his full
potential. It takes a great deal of sacrifice and discipline on the part
of each player, but it pays dividends not only now, but later in life.

I believe in discipline and enthusiasm in everything you do in life.
We'll be strictly team-oriented, we'll win or lose as a team.

The desired subjective characteristics demonstrated in risky and fateful
situations display these shared meanings of the collegiate sport world,
as in other competitive arenas. Goffman (1967:214-239) distinguishes such
traits as courage, gameness, integrity, gallantry, and composure. Collegiate sports are often fateful and chancy situations where these character
traits are valued; to display them is to be heroic. Presumably these
characteristics contribute to the primary function of revenue sports in major universities—to be "a winner." In general, college athletes have had
a history of success (i.e., winning) throughout their athletic careers, and
their self-perceptions reflect this focal meaning of the sport world. One
university varsity basketball player described his early athletic success
as follows:[1]

Interviewer: What were your athletic interests in junior high?

Player: I dropped baseball because of all the sports I played that was
  probably my worst. It seemed like when I was younger I played
  every sport—whatever season it was—if it was football I went out
  for football, if it was track, well I went out for track.

Interviewer: Would you say you were better than most kids your age?

Player: I was good. I started in every sport that I played. So I kept
  it up because I enjoyed playing and standing out.

Furthermore, the focal value of winning in the collegiate sport world tends
to override other values. Interviews with collegiate athletes indicate that,
on occasion, pain-killing drugs are used to keep a player in the line-up
regardless of the physical consequences; and the emphasis on practices
and games in the sport season may have undesirable academic consequences for players.

One tradition of interactionism is that it is antideterministic; at first
glance the social world perspective appears contrary to the notions of
fluidity, process, fragmentation, and creativity. Yet, within the collegiate
sport world meanings are not as well defined and deterministic as it may
seem (Strauss, 1978a). For example, players and coaches often hold different views about the objectives of the game. Thus, although winning
is primary for the coach, interviews with varsity athletes indicate that for

the maintenance of their own identity, the opportunity to get in the game and achieve some personal success is probably more important. Furthermore, team members frequently construct meanings, in the form of jokes and nicknames, and enter into collusion against the coach and formal meanings associated with sport. This is evident in the following account:

> *Player:* This year the team has been closer than any team I've ever been on.
>
> *Interviewer:* It this true for all team members, whether they are starting or not?
>
> *Player:* Yea, we seem to get along because we had a common enemy, the coach. Like even before the games, we got to the point when he was out of the locker room the whole team was joking about him, and then when he would come in it was just like a quiet chuckle.

The social world of collegiate sport shows segmentation based on differences such as revenue or nonrevenue sports, size of college or university, men and women's sports. Also, conflicts appear at the intersections of the athletic department and the larger university structure. Additionally, the different meanings are likely to change over a period of time. In short, the salience of process, conflict, and multiple realities that are central to the interactionist position are manifest in the meanings associated with collegiate sport.

Collegiate Sport and Self-Identity: Construction and Maintenance

A cornerstone of symbolic interactionism is that individuals attribute meanings and reflect on themselves; accordingly these self-perceptions vary with the many spheres of their lives. These identities represent "names" or labels that tell people what to expect during a given interaction, for example, player, team captain, assistant coach, head coach, and so on (Feldman, 1979:400). The nature of identites is that they are situational and changeable; thus, Klapp (1969:5) emphasizes that identity is "a fragile mechanism whose equilibrium needs constant maintenance and support from the proper environment, and it is quite easy for something to go wrong with it." An examination of one's identities along a timeline reveals a mixture of identities of varying degrees of salience and prominence; some are rigid and long lasting (e.g., gender identity), whereas others quickly fade away. Furthermore, identities from multiple spheres may compliment or conflict with each other. For example, within sociology of sport one research tradition has considered the possible conflict or complementarity of the "student-athlete" identities. The identity associated with the athlete role is the primary focus of this discussion.

Interviews by the author with college athletes provide summary data to describe the construction of players' identities as athletes. This analysis is consistent with the symbolic interactionist tradition that has emphasized the concept of a "career" for the emergence of one's self-perception (Hughes, 1937). Athletes at major universities are likely to develop a conception of themselves as "good athletes" as early as grade school or junior high school. Interviews with athletes indicate that when they are asked, "How important, on a scale of 1 to 10, were sports to you when you were in junior high school and high school?," most athletes said a 9 or 10 in junior high and a 10 in high school.

Most athletes, since their elementary school years, were supported in the construction of their identities by social networks of parents, friends, coaches, and the media. One athlete pointed out that, "By 7th grade I was so much more athletically developed, I had to play with the 8th grade in basketball, and in baseball I was moved up because I was too good for the kids I was playing with." The same athlete received a key to the gymnasium during his high school years to practice anytime he wished. This preferential treatment was a strong social validation of his self-perception as an outstanding athlete. When asked about the positive aspects of sport in high school, another player answered,

Probably the recognition, because when I began playing in front of people in the town they began to know me because I played basketball. That was kind of neat because I didn't know a lot of people and they would come up to me and say, "hi, how are you doing?" and "great game" and stuff like that.

Most athletes interviewed by the author indicated that at their school they were the player who was most associated with their sport. Furthermore, the volume of letters they received from college recruiters enhanced and supported their perceived athletic abilities. In summary, the accolades and recognition they received from many sources—family, friends, coaches, media, general community, and recruiters—provided support for a processual construction of their athletic identity prior to their university participation.

The preceding discussion suggests that individuals learn to anchor their self perceptions to sport. Because society values and rewards sport performances, these expectations are internalized to maximize the pleasant outcomes and enhance self-esteem. In fact, participation in sport for some people is so salient that their self-worth is primarily sustained by their sport role. For example, Ernest Becker (1971:68) proposes the metaphor of an "inner newsreel" that reviews for us the symbols that give us a feeling of self-esteem. Consequently, we are continually testing and rehearsing the ways we are significant and important. In short, we learn how to best maintain our self-esteem and to avoid anxiety based on the expectations of others.

This principle of self-esteem maintenance must, however, be constantly reinforced, repaired, and reconstructed. This conceptualization is consistent with the ideas of Goffman (1959, 1967) that people actively manage the impressions of others in order to *maintain face*, that is, the positive social value a person claims for himself or herself. Thus, for example, the self-esteem of an athlete is defined in terms of one's performance. Failure in a sport performance represents an inability to satisfy the standards of the athletic goals that, in turn, threatens one's identity as an athlete (Ball, 1976; Harris & Eitzen, 1978). In effect, one who fails is a deviant from the normative expectations of the athletic role, and one's identity is not verified as adequate, particularly by the coach. As such, the resultant embarrassment, humiliation, degradation, and loss of self-esteem may lead to an eventual disengagement from the role. Throughout junior and senior high school this process serves to screen persons who are defined as nonathletic. Although this has a significant impact on youngsters' self-esteem, their athletic identity is less ingrained than among college athletes. The following portions of interviews taped by the author illustrate two university athletes' reactions to failure:

> *Interviewer:* So you really have no explanation for why you would be starting for a while then become a substitute?

> *Varsity basketball player:* No, not really. Well, when he thinks you're not playing well, it's whatever he thinks. Like when I was a junior, believe it or not, I was the leading scorer on the team and when he took me out of the line-up I just kind of disappeared. He just figured I wasn't playing up to my capabilities. It was like here I am starting one game and the next practice, he doesn't even play me in practice. He just sits me there for two hours and I'm getting stiff and saying, "Wow, put me in for something."

> *Interviewer:* What were your feelings about yourself when you were not playing?

> *Player:* I was thinking, "maybe I'm not any good anymore; how could I lose it overnight." When I was playing I was everybody's friend, all the coaching staff would make it a point to talk to me. When I wasn't playing it's like, "go over there and shoot by yourself," and I'd walk by them (the staff) and they would just look the other way.

> *Varsity football player:* Well, my parents took my side. They always thought I should be playing and they were down on the coaches.

Another varsity athlete who failed to live up to performance expectations reflected on the difficulty of dealing with parents and friends who provided social support for his athletic identity.

Interviewer: What did your friends in your home town think?

Player: It's quite a shock to go back and see all your old high school buddies, and they ask you, "How'd you do this year?" All I could say was, "Well I got to play one game or two games or something like that. It's not very much fun."

Additional accounts of personal responses to failure are documented by a variety of sport biographies as well as the reactions to failure outlined by Ball (1976), that is, the "degradation" versus "cooled-out" models. The interaction between coaches and players is a potential adversive relationship. The player maintains his or her self-esteem by having the opportunity to play and to validate the athlete identity. On the other hand, the coach's identity is maintained by winning games. Thus, for many players there is likely to be a dissonance in their personal perceptions of athletic ability and their coach's perceptions.

Erving Goffman's (1961b) observations suggest ingenious strategies that are often used as adjustments for a person whose identity is threatened. For example, one of the adjustments frequently used by athletes is to increase the distance between their self-perception and the role. That is, in response to the coach's threat to one's self-esteem the player may establish some type of self-preserving distance from the athlete role and its definitions. A senior reserve quarterback expressed this distance as, "just a matter of putting in my time—you just want to keep your scholarship—that's the way it was for me." A reserve varsity basketball player said, "at the end of the year I was dying for it to be over. I just hated going to practice everyday and seeing those people again." Adjustments may also be self-preserving by projecting the blame away from oneself and onto the coach. In effect, the player is denying the coach's definition of his ability and is "rejecting one's rejector" (Goffman, 1961a:315). A varsity athlete gave this illustration:

I think that people who aren't starting and who really think they should be, have a legitimate beef. They have an antagonistic view of the coach; like, he's not starting me because maybe my hair is too long or he doesn't like my attitude, or he doesn't like what I'm doing in my personal life or something totally different than his actual play on the field—he starts searching for reasons.

In summary, the collegiate athlete comes into an athletic program that is filled with outstanding athletes. There, many of them discover discrepancies between their self-definition of ability and their coach's perceptions. Consequently, the players often assert themselves in attempts to save face and reconstruct or adjust their athletic identities. In the next part of this chapter this analysis is extended to the way coaches often use aligning actions as a means to maintain a cherished identity—as a successful coach.

The Coach and Aligning Actions: Maintenance of Identity

The concept of impression management also applies to the better understanding of some forms of behavior among coaches. The occupational identity of a coach—at least in a major university—ordinarily rests on his or her ability to win athletic contests. The validity of this assumption, however, varies by type of sport and the level of competition within a college or university context. Athletic contests, by definition, have a problematic outcome; thus, while coaches are charged with complete liability for the outcome, they have only limited control over the result (Edwards, 1973:139). In short, numerous possibilities for failure face the coaching role. Under these conditions failure represents "misalignment," and the ongoing social interaction and coaching identity are threatened. Aligning actions by coaches are adjustments made with others (e.g., the athletic director, university president, fans, alumni, faculty, friends, etc.) to interpret, to reconstruct, and to smooth out the discrepancy between social expectation (to win) and action (losses).

Several forms of aligning actions exist; specifically, the discussion focuses on disclaimers and accounts. A disclaimer is a verbal device used "in advance of an action that the person thinks may discredit him or her in the eyes of others" (Stokes & Hewitt, 1976:845). Accounts, on the other hand, are linguistic devices employed after the untoward action, that is, failure to win (Scott & Lyman, 1968). Two types of accounts are excuses and justifications. Excuses are accounts wherein one admits the act in question is bad, wrong, or undesirable but denies full responsibility. Justifications, on the other hand, are verbal accounts whereby the individual admits responsibility for the act but attempts to justify the behavior by redefining it in positive, rather than negative terms. Aligning actions are attempts to manage impressions by providing new social meanings and to repair social relationships and identities that are threatened by the questionable behavior. However, it should be emphasized that aligning actions are not always honored by others, and their usefulness will "wear thin" with continued failures, and the coach's position and identity will be jeopardized.

The following clichés are expressions that are examples of aligning actions frequently used by coaches:

Disclaimers (before the fact)
  "We have too many injuries."
  "We are definitely the underdogs."

"You can't run a zoo without the animals."
"This is a rebuilding year."

Excuses (after the fact, but a denial of full responsibility)
"They are lucky."
"That's the way the ball bounces."
"We had an unlucky draw."
"We were robbed."
"The game was poorly officiated."

Justifications (after the fact, accepts full responsibility, but there is a positive outcome)
"We showed a lot of heart."
"This team has a lot of class."
"We played so well, it's a shame we lost."
"Even though we lost we demonstrated a lot of character."
"It was a moral victory."

Although aligning actions may be considered distorted definitions of reality, they may be accurate and valid explanations. For example, a team may face a difficult game and lose because of a number of injuries or less talented players. Furthermore, coaches may openly admit to failures without employing an alignment mechanism. Perhaps, it is the highly successful coaches who can assume full responsibility for failure and feel little threat to their identity when they occasionally lose.

Elsewhere, it has been suggested that the explication of aligning actions may profit from the research studies of attribution theory (Snyder & Spreitzer, 1979). Thus, one speculates that the most successful coaches will be more likely to assume full responsibility for their losses (i.e., internal locus of control), whereas less sucessful coaches will frequently employ aligning actions, with the least successful coaches using excuses (external locus of control).

Athletic Organizations: Negotiated Order

Symbolic interactionism is often assumed to be primarily applicable to the study of the individual and interpersonal relationships. Yet, there is increased recognition of how this perspective is also relevant for the analysis of organizations. Specifically, interactionism stresses the way in which behavior, including people's behavior within and between organizations, is antideterministic in the sense that it is continually being negotiated, created, constructed, and emergent (Denzin, 1978; Gerson, 1976; Strauss, 1978b). An athletic department at a major university constitutes an organization where resources and constraints in the forms of power, coercion, control, money, skill, and personal identity are basic resources to be negotiated (Denzin, 1978:90; Gerson, 1976). Within and between athletic departments (including the National Collegiate Athletic

Association), people vary in "degrees of control over one another and
. . .the ability to expand their spheres of influence beyond the specific
confines of their particular subworlds of specialization" (Denzin, 1978:90).
The present discussion derives, in part, from an analysis of complex
organizations by Gross (1978) and Denzin (1978) who have argued that
organizations typically focus on performance and the attainment of specific
goals. Furthermore, such organizations are "inherently criminogenic"
because personal motives built into their structure induce members to
engage in criminal activities to achieve the performance objectives. Similarly, sport organizations in higher education are performance oriented, and
the continual uncertainty inherent in the outcomes of sport provides a
strain toward deviance that may be partially explained by the Mertonian
theory of the divergence between means and goals. One would not argue
that all or most athletic departments are "criminogenic" in terms of violations of the federal, state, or NCAA statutes, regulations, and policies.
Yet, when one observes the relational structure of athletics in higher
education, there are multiple spheres of influence, shifting realities,
manipulative strategies, situational ambiguities, and negotiated orders
that are primarily designed toward performance—usually winning and
financial solvency. Survival strategies are evident in the informal structure of athletic organizations where deviance is most likely to be manifest,
and there are many cases that could be cited to support this assumption.
Space does not permit a comprehensive discussion of the intertwining
relationships and negotiated order of athletics in higher education. Rather,
the following thumbnail sketch highlights some aspects of organizational
behavior that are appropriate for the symbolic interactionist approach.
    One characteristic of symbolic interactionism is that social structure,
that is, an athletic organization, is not a static structure "out there."
Rather, organizations are viewed as structures in process, and negotiations between organizational units are determined by the resources
available as well as the limits and constraints on the respective segments
of the organization. An examination of athletic organizations readily
reveals variations in components of resources and constraints that fluc-
tuate in the course of negotiations over a period of time. Thus, a major
university football coach with the ability to win can enhance the prestige
of the athletic department, balance the athletic budget by game receipts,
bowl games, and television money, and can, therefore, negotiate from
a position of power within the athletic department, the university, the
alumni, and, perhaps, the state legislature.
    However, even a "football power" has some university and NCAA con-
straints. Such resources and constraints are not, however, static. For example, the negotiations of the major Division I-A football schools (collectively known as the College Football Association) with NBC-TV forced
the NCAA to reopen negotiation within its own ranks. The major football schools are likely to improve their relative position within the NCAA

within the near future. Athletic organizations as arenas for negotiated order are also illustrated by the reverberations throughout scholastic and collegiate sport in the last decade by the enforcement of Title IX legislation. Within an athletic department the relative resources and constraints are likely to be influenced by such issues as the following:

• The philosophy of the university toward athletics
• The relative importance of nonrevenue sports *vis-á-vis* revenue sports
• The impact of Title IX
• The strength of the alumni or booster group on the athletic program
• The athletic affiliation and league rules and policies, that is, NCAA, NAIA, Big Eight, Big Ten, and so forth
• The relative success of a specific sport, its win-loss record
• The influence of the coach, that is, his or her record and degree of charismatic leadership

Another area of potential negotiation involves the proposal by the Center for Athletes' Rights and Education for a bill of rights for scholastic and collegiate athletes, including the right to unionize and to share revenues generated by athletic endeavors. An analysis of negotiations within athletic organizations reveals that they are located in larger social structures (that are also in process), and the negotiations may be examined both ways—toward the larger contexts or down to the personal segments of the organization such as the coach attempting to recruit a player, coach-player relationships, and relationships with the media, alumni, and other "interest groups."

In summary, this brief sketch suggests that the symbolic interactionist perspective may be used to illuminate the negotiated relationships within sport organizations. Parenthetically, it should be pointed out that this analysis is consistent with many of the tenets of conflict theory, for example, the use of power, coercion, and other resources to bring about change. Inter- and intraorganization negotiations to maintain organizational well-being and to achieve personal motives within sport are likely to take place between such parties as the NCAA, NAIA, athletic conference affiliation, athletic director, university administration, coaches of the respective sports, players, athletic boosters, and fans ("basking in reflected glory"). With rising athletic expenses and the potential for increased television revenues, it is probable that future negotiations will shift in favor of the spectator sports most suitable for television coverage. Furthermore, the increased emphasis on performance in the revenue sports is likely to promote a spiraling of legal and illegal efforts to gain an advantage, or at least maintain a parity ("everyone else is doing it"), with competing teams. These organizational processes may be further illuminated by an application of the interactionist perspective when used in conjunction with the conflict and functionalist perspectives.

Conclusion and Future Prospects

This chapter has suggested the utility of the symbolic interactionist perspective to illuminate aspects of athletics in higher education. The problematic, processual, and emergent nature of this sport context is particularly suitable for the interactionist analysis. Specific areas of consideration included the meanings and definitions associated with the sport world, aspects of the construction and maintenance of identity by players and coaches, and the manner in which interactionism illuminates the negotiated order of athletic organizations.

One might reasonably expect that the future of athletics in higher education will be primarily influenced by the availability of financial resources. The willingness of the television networks to pay large sums of money for the primary spectator sports will likely increase the chasm between revenue and nonrevenue sports. This split will be reflected in the meanings associated with the respective sports, including the degree of personal identity invested in the sport role by players and coaches. This does not mean that a sport such as tennis is unimportant to the participant and coach, but a tennis player is less likely to be on a full grant-in-aid and to have the same pressures associated with the sport as a football or basketball player does. Furthermore, a coach of a nonrevenue sport is more likely to have his or her identity invested in teaching as well as coaching. These distinctions between the roles of players and coaches of revenue and nonrevenue sports are likely to become more evident in the future.

Additionally, the financial exigencies and ability of the major universities to generate income through sport will likely result in a greater range of diversity between the major football power universities and the smaller universities and colleges. Presumably, the major football powers will wield more power in the negotiations within the NCAA. With the primary focus on the revenue sports, we expect the overall number of sports at most universities to decline. These predictions are, of course, speculative; nevertheless, the processual and emergent nature of athletics at all levels may be better understood by using the symbolic interactionist interpretation.

Finally, although collective violence, social unrest, and collective protests in sport contexts are generally associated with international competition (e.g., European and Latin American soccer competition), university athletic events are potential arenas for such dramatic events. Symbolic interactionism and collective behavior have a long academic affinity within the Chicago School of Sociology. If collective violence, unrest, and protests emerge as part of athletics in higher education, symbolic interactionism is offered as a relevant perspective for the analysis of these social phenomena.

Note

1. As part of the preparation of this chapter, I conducted 10 semistructured (taped) interviews with varsity athletes of several sports. In general, these interview data provided illustrative examples and support for the predetermined conceptual and theoretical premises. However, some of the data generated preliminary descriptions and explanations that approximate an inductive approach (Glaser & Strauss, 1967).

Athletics and Higher Education:
A Conflict Perspective

D. Stanley Eitzen

The conflict perspective has a long tradition in sociology with such early giants as Marx and Weber and later theorists such as Mills, Dahrendorf, Habermas, Collins, Chambliss, Domhoff, Zeitlin, and Useem. These theorists and others provided a unique and important paradigm to understand social structure, social source of social problems, and social change.

A problem in applying this perspective to social phenomena is that the vision and emphasis of conflict theorists varies considerably. Conflict theorists may be Marxists, neo-Marxists, or non-Marxists. Among the neo-Marxists there is a debate between the instrumentalists and the structuralists. Critical theorists from the Frankfurt school are also included, as are some phenomenologists. The analytical focus of conflict theorists may be on power structures, the role of institutions in legitimizing the status quo, how individuals are dominated through the shaping of their consciousnesses and worldviews, the connection between personal troubles of individuals and structure of society, or the efforts by the advantaged to retain power and by the disadvantaged to increase theirs.

The variation in emphasis and concern among conflict theorists does not imply that this perspective is too inconsistent or fragmented for use by contemporary social scientists. On the contrary, conflict theory has rich potential to understand society, social organization, and human behavior. This chapter applies the insights of the conflict perspective to athletics in higher education. To accomplish this, the chapter is divided into three parts. The first enumerates the fundamental assumptions upon which most conflict theorists agree. The second part applies these assumptions to the analysis of athletics in higher education. And finally the conclusion discusses the utility of using the conflict perspective to understand the structure and problems of sport in general.

The Assumptions of Conflict Theory

The conflict perspective, although not a unified theory, does have a unique way of interpreting social life that unites its somewhat diverse adherents. This section will present the general principles common to conflict theorists (taken in part from Bowles & Gintis, 1976; R. Collins, 1975; Hansen, 1976; Johnson, 1981; Lenski, 1966; Parenti, 1978; Reasons & Perdue, 1981; Turner, 1974).

Social Structure

Foremost, the conflict perspective is sociological. The primary unit of analysis is social structure. The focus is not on individual behavior or social interaction but on patterns of action and networks of interaction in social organizations. The social organizations may be friendship groups, voluntary associations, or athletic teams. Typically conflict theorists concentrate on large-scale social organizations such as bureaucracies and communities and most often total societies and their institutions. To the extent that conflict theorists are concerned with individual behavior, it is always as these behaviors are affected by the conditions of social structure. Explanation, then, is never reduced to psychological variables but remains at the structural level, thereby retaining sociological purity.

A major premise of the conflict perspective is that conflict is endemic in social organizations resulting from social structure itself. The things that people desire such as property, prestige, and power are not distributed equally in social organizations, resulting in a fundamental cleavage between the advantaged and the disadvantaged (Dahrendorf, 1959; Marx & Engels, 1951). Related to the above is the assumption of conflict theorists that group interests are the basic elements of social life. Those persons in a similar social condition will organize to maximize their effectiveness in the struggles to preserve or to promote vital group interests.

Power

Next, the powerful use their power to keep themselves in power. They are effective in controlling the powerless in three fundamental ways. Foremost, they, by definition, hold the legitimate power (including the use of force). Any threat to this power is considered illegitimate, and the dissenters are coerced to conform or to face punishment. Next, again by definition, the powerful control the decisionmaking apparatus. At the societal level, for example, the state and the law are instruments of the powerful (Wolfe, 1978). Finally, the powerful control the dissemination of information thus achieving ideological conformity among members. At the societal level, this is accomplished by controlling media, schools, churches, and other institutions. Through the socialization process individuals are taught the cultural norms, values, and ideologies and, thus, to accept the status quo as normal and right, thereby preserving the interests of the dominant (Bowles & Gintis, 1976; Parenti, 1978). This last process is a most effective social control mechanism, even resulting in individuals defining conditions against their interest as appropriate—a condition that Marx called false consciousness (Marx, in Johnson, 1981:130-131).

Another assumption common to conflict theorists is that the inequities in wealth, power, and prestige, plus the coercion and exploitation by the powerful aimed at the disadvantaged, inevitably lead to conflicts between them. There is a dynamic tension between the haves and the have-nots with discrimination and power plays. This tension and the resulting struggles shape the relations within the social organization and the direction and magnitude of social change within it (Chambliss & Ryther, 1975:55-56).

Political Economy

A prominent assumption of the conflict perspective is that understanding society or any of its institutions requires the analysis of the political economy. Power and wealth are inextricably intertwined, and they dominate the rest of society. Therefore, the analyst must consider the type of economy, the ways that members are socialized for production and consumption, and the distribution of power (Hoch, 1972:1-15). In short, although conflict theorists may be interested in a number of social institutions, they show a distinct preference in their description, analysis, and explanation for the two "master" institutions of the economy and the polity (Forcese & Richer, 1975:92-101).

Consequences for Individuals

Another assumption of the conflict perspective has to do with the consequences of social structure for individuals. Conflict theorists believe that the conditions of social organization, domination, and exploitation are not impersonal forces but have alienating, repressive, and frustrating effects on individuals. The important concept here is alienation, which refers to feelings of estrangement resulting from the lack of control over the conditions of one's own life (see Horton, 1966; Marx & Engels, 1963). The individual may feel alienated from work, from the products of labor, from others, and from himself or herself. Feelings of powerlessness and estrangement prevail in social organizations characterized by impersonal bureaucracy, undemocratic decision making, inequality, and where system needs supersede individual needs.

The final assumption of the conflict perspective is that human beings are the architects of social organization and history. Individuals as members of groups define their form and content. The extent to which the powerless accomplish radical change depends on their understanding of the bias of the system and their ability to mobilize others in the same condition (Anderson & Gibson, 1978:7). In short, social conditions are subject to the collective actions of human actors (Flacks & Turkel, 1978:193–194).

Implications of the Conflict Perspective

Taken seriously, the assumptions of the conflict perspective focus the attention of social analysts in particular directions. To begin, central to a conflict analysis is that the institutions of society are reflections of the larger society, in general, and the "master" institutions of the economy and polity, in particular. For example, changes in a contemporary American institution, whether it be in education, religion, or sport, must be viewed in the societal context, especially in terms of the material conditions of social life, technological changes, economic structure, primacy of the accumulation of wealth by individuals and corporations, and increasing rationalization (bureaucratization) of social and economic life (Sewart, 1981).

The second implication of the conflict perspective is a basic mood of skepticism about cultural and social patterns. A fundamental distrust of existing power arrangements exists because they are, by definition, oppressive to the powerless segments. Ideologies are questioned because they support the status quo. Myths are measured against reality. This critical examination of social structure and culture demystifies and demythologizes.

The conflict perspective directs attention toward social problems emanating from structural arrangements. The conflict analyst asks: Under these social arrangements who gets what and why? Who benefits, and who does not? The distribution of resources and power are the keys to understanding social problems because the powerless are dominated by the powerful; therefore, they are thwarted in achieving their basic needs. This emphasis, however, runs counter to the typical explanations social scientists employ for social ills. The choice is seen in an example supplied by Thomas Szasz.

> Suppose that a person wishes to study slavery. How would he go about doing so? First, he might study slaves. He would then find that such persons are generally brutish, poor, and uneducated, and he might conclude that slavery is their "natural" or appropriate social status....Another student "biased" by contempt for the institution of slavery, might proceed differently. He would maintain that there can be no slave without a master holding him in bondage; and he would accordingly consider slavery a type of human *relationship* and

more generally, a *social institution*, supported by custom, law, religion, and force. From this point of view, the study of masters is at least as relevant to the study of slavery as is the study of slaves. (1970:123–124).

Those theorists who focus on the traits and behaviors of the powerless as explanations for the perpetuation of their disadvantaged position are accused by conflict theorists of "blaming the victim" (Ryan, 1976). Conflict theorists are biased in the other direction—siding with the members of the underclass (Becker, 1967) and blaming the system for social problems.

Finally, a major implication of the conflict perspective is that human beings create, sustain, and change the social forms within which they conduct their lives. This means that social conditions are subject to human intervention, transformation, and improvement (Flacks & Turkel, 1978:193–194).

Athletics and Higher Education[1]

The first intercollegiate football game was played between Rutgers and Princeton in 1869. The most significant feature about this game and the early years of intercollegiate competition was that the activities were organized by students with little interest or interference from school administrators. Soon, however, administrators began to believe that the visibility of college sports had important public relations value, aided student recruitment, increased loyalty among students and alumni, and attracted financial support from alumni and legislatures. Thus, the programs increasingly became dominated by administrators and alumni.

During this century, college sports have become big business, with huge television revenues, mammoth stadiums and arenas, and annual athletic budgets approaching $10 million for individual schools. In short, in the past 100 years college sports have shifted from player/student control to outside control; from an informal, ad hoc organization, to layers of bureaucracy (in each university and in the overall organization of collegiate athletics); and from an activity centered on the intrinsic rewards of participation to one centered on extrinsic rewards for nonparticipants. The conflict perspective helps us to understand these dramatic changes and their attendant consequences.

---

[1]The discussion in this chapter is limited to American universities with big-time sports programs for males in the major revenue sports of football and basketball.

The Organization of Power in College Athletics

Beginning as a loose confederation of universities in 1906, the National Collegiate Athletic Association (NCAA) has become the dominant control agent over collegiate athletics (Stern, 1979). The NCAA provides uniform rules for playing, rules for the safety of athletes, their eligibility, the number of scholarships, and the proper recruitment procedures. The NCAA also organizes championships, certifies bowl games, and negotiates television contracts.

The NCAA operates as a monopoly. It controls television rights. It requires athletes who transfer schools before graduation to lose a year of eligibility, thus inhibiting the freedom of athletes and increasing the power of the schools over them. It has enormous and exclusive power as a moral arbiter, acting as accuser and judge in cases involving NCAA rule violations. Its edicts affect playing and coaching careers as well as collegiate finances (Good, 1979b:14). The NCAA has been accused of protecting its interests by not penalizing the most successful schools because to do so would hurt television and bowl game revenues (Good, 1979a). Furthermore, the NCAA has a tendency to direct its penalties at athletes by removing their playing eligibility, rather than punishing coaches, alums, or schools that offered the illegal inducements. The NCAA has also lobbied extensively in Washington, D.C. to weaken the regulations of Title IX, which, if enforced, would bring equality in programs for men and women (DeCrow, 1980) and, it is alleged, weaken the revenue potential of men's sports programs. Ironically, while the NCAA has fought to maintain male superiority in athletic programs, it has at the same time employed various power maneuvers to destroy the Association for Intercollegiate Athletics for Women (AIAW) and take over collegiate sport for men and women (Krotee, 1981).

A major consequence of the NCAA's monopoly powers is that the rules keep the wages of the workers (players) at a minimum. The remuneration of players is limited to an education (room, board, tuition, fees, and books). Although exceptional basketball players can become professionals prior to graduation, exceptional football players cannot (unless they play in Canada) because the NCAA has an agreement with the National Football League that dictates that a player is not eligible for the draft until his class graduates.

At the school level, power over the athletic program is often held by a corporation separate from the university control structure. Alums and others outside the university community may actually hold the ultimate power over the programs. Athletic directors and coaches serve at the discretion of a board composed primarily of financial contributors to the program. Depending on the school, professors and students may have some representation (but always as minorities) on such a board. Athletes are rarely, if ever, allowed to sit on the governing board.

At the team level, athletic squads are almost universally dictatorships. Rules are made and enforced from the top. Game strategy and line-ups are the exclusive province of the coaches. There is no option for players if they want to participate—they must accept the dictates of the coach.

Power in college athletic programs, then, is held at every level by nonathletes and even nonuniversity personnel. The athletes serve their schools at the risk of personal injury, for low wages, and with no power. Most accept their powerlessness because they have been socialized to accept authority; they feel it is in their best interest (false consciousness), and/or they have accepted the myth that if they accept the hierarchical system and work hard, they will succeed in the long run as well-paid professionals.

Conflict theorists are not surprised by the institutionalized powerlessness of athletes (Edwards, 1973). Nor are they shocked by the efforts of the powerful to keep the powerless powerless.

Big-Time Collegiate Sport as Big Business

Sport in a capitalist society is organized so that it is almost impossible to separate the business aspects from the play on the field. Nowhere is this more clearly the case than in big-time collegiate sport. As some examples of the money generated by winning programs in big-time college sports, consider the following:

- ABC-TV and CBS-TV together will pay $263.5 million to broadcast football games between NCAA member schools from 1982–1985. The schools appearing in a nationally televised game will each receive $550,000 in 1982 and $650,000 in 1985. In addition, if teams agree to switch the date or the site of a game from its original schedule to accommodate television, ABC-TV will pay them an "incentive fee" of $250,000.
- The 1982–1983 athletic budget for Ohio State University exceeded $10 million and that of the University of Oklahoma was $9.5 billion.
- January 1, 1983, Michigan and UCLA each received $2.9 million to play in the Rose Bowl. Penn State and Georgia received $1.8 million per school to participate in the Sugar Bowl. The Cotton Bowl teams—Pittsburgh and SMU—each received $1.7 million.

Operating a big-time collegiate athletic program is clearly a business proposition. Because the big monies from television, bowl games, and tournaments flow toward the winners, there are excessive demands to win. This necessity of winning has put incredible pressures on athletic directors and coaches to produce (Ostler, 1981). Desperate to win, coaches (and school administrators) often engaged in a number of illegal and unethical practices detrimental to athletes and the goals of higher education.

- Prospective athletes have been given illegal inducements for their services. (Denlinger & Shapiro, 1975; Black, 1978)
- Gifted athletes have been allowed to play when they should be academically ineligible. "Eligibility" is maintained by falsifying transcripts, enrolling in phantom courses, and having surrogates take tests. (Hammel, 1980; Hanford, 1974; Underwood, 1980)
- Academically marginal athletes have been guided away from potentially difficult courses to maintain their eligibility but thereby impeding progress towards a degree. In essence, the object is to get them through the educational process without an education. (Underwood, 1980)
- The myth of making it as a professional has been perpetuated. Scholastically handicapped players are lured to colleges to pursue an impossible dream of a professional sports career (only 150 rookies make it as professional football players each year as do only about 50 basketball players). (Underwood, 1980:41, 60)
- Players have been given cortisone or other drugs so that they can play with injuries. (Underwood, 1981a:68)
- Some coaches, in their zeal to be successful, have been guilty of behaviors that brutalize and demean their athletes. (Shaw, 1972)

This insight was also recognized by the judge in the trial of former University of New Mexico basketball coach, Norman Ellenberger. After the jury found Ellenberger guilty on 21 counts of fraud for which he should have gone to the state penitentiary for not less than 21 years, District Judge Philip Baiamonte placed him on unsupervised probation saying,

> I am being asked to sentence a man who is simply one cog in the entire machine, the entire system that exists, not only here but over the entire country called college ball. In effect, you see, I am being asked to sentence a man because he got caught, not because his conduct was unacceptable. The clear testimony in this case is that everybody looked the other way until he got caught....What's going through my mind at this point is the question, really, of how fair is it to incarcerate in prison a coach who is basically doing what almost everybody in this community wanted him to do—win basketball games at any cost and by whatever means might be necessary to do that. It seems that the prevailing attitude was, "It's not how the game was played, but whether or not you win or lose that counts." (1981:A6)

The point is that the pursuit of money has prostituted the university and the purpose of sport. Education is not the goal. The physical and the emotional welfare of athletes are secondary to their athletic performance. Sport as a pleasurable activity is an irrelevant consideration in the climate of big-time collegiate sport. Winning and the money generated are paramount. The evils resulting in this milieu are not the result of the malevolent personalities of coaches, but of a perverse system. The perversion is captured in the following statement by Taubman:

> At places like Ohio State, Alabama, Texas, Notre Dame, USC, Michigan, and Oklahoma, they've forgotten football is just a game. It has become a big business, completely disconnected from the fundamental purposes of academic institutions. The goal of college ball is no longer for young men to test and strengthen their bodies, to learn about teamwork, and to have a good time. All that matters is winning, moving up in the national rankings, and grabbing a bigger share of the TV dollar that comes with appearances on NCAA's game of the week on ABC. To achieve these aims, schools and coaches not only bend and break the National Collegiate Athletics Association (NCAA) rules governing college football but, far more destructively, violate the intellectual integrity and principles of the American university system. (1978:91)

And what of the athletes? Athletes in big-time/high-pressure programs are likely to be cynical about their educations, realizing that they are athletes first and students second, if at all. They are poorly paid mercenaries. With few exceptions, their educations are a sham. Very often they are even physically separated from the rest of the student body in athletic dorms. They are also likely to become alienated because of their powerlessness, restricted freedoms, meager wages, the feeling that they are interchangeable parts in the sports machine, and the eventual realization that they will never have even a chance to try out for a professional team.

Most significantly, the athletes have been robbed of the joys of sports participation. The goals of the activity are not play, spontaneous expression, fun, and other nonutilitarian qualities. Sport in a capitalist society has become

> like any other commodity—something to be marketed, packaged, and sold to a mass audience....When sport becomes an activity of *dis*-play, it destroys what is valuable in sport altogether. Sport becomes transformed into a spectacle, played for and shaped into a form which will be "consumed" by spectators searching for titillating entertain-

ment. That which is valuable in sport is subordinated to the demands
of the market. (Sewart, 1981:47, 49)

The athletes thus are workers. Their activities become regimented,
stripped of individuality, and monotonous, just as they are under
the conditions of modern labor. (Sewart, 1981:47)

For Marx the alienation of workers within the capitalist mode of production takes several forms:

> The worker is alienated from the product of his labor: He has no con-
> trol over the commodities he produces, rather they control him. The
> worker is alienated from the means of production: He no longer con-
> trols the sphere of his life called work which becomes estranged to
> him. The outcome of this divorce of life from life activity is self-
> estrangement: The worker increasingly comes to see himself as an
> alienated tool of someone else's production process, his own body
> as a secondary instrument in a means-ends existence. (Sugden,
> 1981:59)

A new organization, the Center for Athletes Rights and Education
(CARE), has been formed recently to work for the benefit of college
athletes (Middleton, 1981). The intent is to organize chapters of athletes
at colleges and universities, to aid athletes in disputes with their coaches
and athletic departments, to form unions to bargain for increased educational and financial benefits such as safe playing conditions and financial
assistance to athletes until their degrees are obtained. Conflict theorists
anticipate that this movement will have considerable difficulty in suc-
ceeding because of the resistance from two sources: (a) officials from the
universities and their agent, the NCAA, because if the plans of CARE
are implemented, their power and advantage will be reduced significantly;
and (b) the majority of athletes who have been socialized to accept sport
as work, their powerlessness, and their being used for the economic
benefit of others (false consciousness).

Conclusions

Each sociological perspective provides the analyst of social life with a lens
to focus attention on certain elements. Each perspective influences what
is looked for, what is seen, and how the phenomena are explained. The
conflict perspective specifically directs attention to the political economy
of social structure. The analyst asks, Who gets what and why? Whose
interests are best served by the existing social arrangements, and whose
are not? Who makes the decisions? How is the distribution of power

related to the holding of economic resources? How is the system of inequities perpetuated? These questions illustrate how the conflict perspective specializes in understanding the relationship between social structure and social problems.

This chapter has shown the utility of the conflict perspective in understanding the problems found in big-time university programs. The conflict perspective has much wider potential for the understanding of sport in other arenas as well as sport in society (see Brohm, 1978; Gruneau, 1975; Hoch, 1972; Sewart, 1981; Sugden, 1981). Sport as an institution is a microcosm of society. Sport serves to perpetuate the status quo through the socialization of dominant values, the fostering of elitism, the promotion of prevailing societal myths, and the perpetuation in obvious and subtle ways of the stratification system by class, race, and sex. The understanding of sport and society is not complete without the analyses and insights of the conflict perspective. The unique contributions of the conflict perspective are crucial to the understanding of social structure, and that understanding is the central task of sociology.

Athletics, Higher Education, and Social Theory: A Response to Frey, Snyder, and Eitzen

John D. Massengale

My goal here is to summarize, discuss, and react to the chapters presented by authors Frey, Snyder, and Eitzen, which considered the theoretical perspectives of functionalism, conflict, and symbolic interactionism, respectively. This task will be attempted primarily from the posture of pure practicality because my own background, one of a sport sociologist who has also spent 11 years as a college football coach, and currently chairs a combined Department of Health, Physical Education, and Athletics at a regional state university, affords me a perspective that may provide some meaningful insights into this discussion.

Functionalism

Functional analysis of athletics in higher education, particularly in terms of social consequences, is not merely the most popular sociological method of inquire; it is overwhelmingly the most popular. Although other methods of inquiry have slowly but surely found their way into the serious study of sport, the functional model persists as the predominant method in athletics.

If attacks on functionalism are really attacks on mainstream sociology, then attacks on functionalism in the study of sport, particularly athletics, might be construed by some as attacks on the study of American society, and the American educational system that perpetuates the mainstream. Frey correctly identified the major limitations of functional analysis, explained it clearly, and appropriately contends that functionalism simply identifies social patterns, while establishing regularity in those social patterns, and does little else than keep the system in working order.

Frey's description of the state of serious analysis in intercollegiate athletics appears to be accurate. Explanation without adequate empirical data is, indeed, voluminous, and conceptual confusion and methodological indecision are evident in the literature. However, I cannot agree with Frey's contention that we appear to know a lot but explain very little. On the contrary, I suspect *we do not know a lot, and tend to explain too much.*

Frey suggests that functionalism became attractive to sociologists because it gave them a bona fide research tool when the discipline was in its infancy. The same reasoning probably holds true for sport sociology. However, the overuse of functional analysis might be caused by factors other than the three that have been offered, or at least in addition to those three.

For instance, functional analysis emerged as the preferred method because it is easy, or because early sport sociologists, often casually referred to as "first generation sport sociologists," who served as role models in this emerging subdiscipline, have a limited competence with other methods. Most were from physical education rather than from sociology, most had their research training in education or physical education rather than sociology, and many still cannot competently use a variety of modern sociological research methods. Indeed, sophisticated methods of sociobehavioral research are often neglected in the fields of education and physical education. Furthermore, what often appears to be a genuine lack of interest in the sociology of sport by graduate students in sociology, can also be a contributing factor. After all, many of us have been told on more than one occasion that the serious study of sport by talented young sociologists, seeking an area of expertise, would be perceived by many colleagues as professional suicide.

Perhaps, too, functionalism emerged as the favorite because it was the only method of inquiry allowed by the athletic establishment. Coaches with deadlines to meet and contests to win simply do not have time to be cooperative with researchers. Coaches characteristically endorse two kinds of research: the kind that helps them to win and the kind that cannot possibly result in any interference with what they perceive to be necessary to win. The inflexibility of coaches regarding cooperative research efforts is further complicated by the opinion of many members of the athletic establishment, who tend to view sport sociologists as troublemakers attempting to disrupt the status quo found in the American athletic system.

Under the circumstances, it is easy to agree with Frey's position that there is no real future in the strict application of the functionalist approach, and that we must build theoretical sophistication and employ more rigor in research and analysis. However, dropping the language of functionalism, which amounts to dropping functionalism itself, while talking in terms of "cause," is an incomplete strategy. I suggest that we greatly improve functionalism, use it as a more thorough foundation, improve our credibility among those in intercollegiate athletics, and then move the sociological study of competitive athletics into an era of sophistication.

Symbolic Interaction

Snyder's presentation is an outstanding illustration of the fact that the study of social behavior profits greatly from the use of many different theoretical perspectives, each making its own unique contribution. Symbolic interaction is an especially unique theoretical perspective, and its uniqueness intensifies when incorporated into an analysis of intercollegiate athletics.

Although symbolic interactionism is often assumed to be primarily applicable to the study of individual and interpersonal relationships, I am pleased that Snyder clearly indicated that it is also an appropriate perspective for the analysis of organizations. Intercollegiate athletics is a self-perpetuating and very fluid set of complex formal organizations, which features a depth of complexity that is seldom appreciated by sociologists. Symbolic interactionism seems to be a perfect fit because intercollegiate athletics features constant stressful situations among individuals and groups, within and between organizations. Role bargains are negotiated, social systems are created, processes for power and exchange are constructed. Continual coercion, control, economic influence, and personal identities emerge to various extents. The ability to expand spheres of influence and utilize manipulative skill become professional specializations as well as criteria to evaluate personal performance.

I wholeheartedly support Snyder's position that intercollegiate athletic programs are invariably in process, problematic, emergent, and under construction and that the symbolic interactionist perspective is particularly useful in focusing on those occasions that are unexpected, dynamic, and processual. Also, symbolic interaction always contains the potential to supply a "close-up" view of how individuals define, reflect, and make decisions. However, I cannot support Snyder's contention that sport has a built-in characteristic of instability, especially in the form of intercollegiate athletics, and would argue that intercollegiate athletics is one of the most stable programs found in higher education. Processes analyzed through symbolic interaction supply college athletics with its stability. The instability associated with winning and losing, which eventually effects fiscal solvency, normally results in a high "turnover" of coaches and players. Playing and coaching are those spheres of intercollegiate athletics, which, in an otherwise stable organization, are uncertain and unstable. Even during hard times, a variety of other educational programs are often discontinued before intercollegiate athletics suffer seriously. The exception to this situation is found at smaller institutions, particularly small private institutions that lack program and fiscal flexibility.

A system that supports, maintains, and perpetuates intercollegiate athletics at the expense of sound academic investment certainly deserves analysis from several different perspectives. Symbolic interactionism as one of those perspectives deserves considerable attention. Symbolic interaction has the possibility of going directly to central causes and components of any social process and permits analysis and interpretation by a researcher with fresh uncontaminated insight. Also, symbolic interaction features the possibility of gaining cooperative support from administrative decision makers in intercollegiate athletics because projects can be designed to relate directly to specific job interests and career aspirations.

Snyder should be congratulated for the clarity with which he describes how a symbolic interactionist can conduct much needed research without rejecting the importance of functionalism, social structures, rankings, or any other cornerstones of mainstream sociology. Indeed, it takes little imagination to picture how symbolic interactionism can supplement almost anything that might be done by a sport sociologist involved in the study of college athletics.

The untapped potential of symbolic interactionism in intercollegiate athletics is clearly evident in several interesting examples presented by Snyder. Two are particularly interesting and relevant to a person in my position.

First, the idea of *maintaining face* among administrators, coaches, players, fans, boosters, and parents suggests settings characterized by instability, loss of esteem, identity problems, embarassment, humiliation, degradation, and exclusion. Such characteristics indicate a set of far-reaching dysfunctional social situations that we do not even begin to fully understand. This, then, appears to be a perfect arena for the symbolic interactionist.

Another example is the complex negotiations between the NCAA, AIAW, and CFA. If the CFA ever gets out of federal appeals court and becomes a working reality, then the NCAA must adjust and compromise or face self-destruction. On the other hand the NCAA made the necessary changes regarding women's athletics and negotiated both successfully and legally with the AIAW, and avoided self-destruction while the AIAW did not. Bureaucratic situations such as these are suitable arenas for the symbolic interactionist.

Before closing on symbolic interaction, I offer a final note. I concur completely with Snyder's view that athletic departments are not "criminogenic" in regard to violation of federal, state, or NCAA statutes, regulations, and policies. Athletic departments are genuine complex organizations trying to conduct business like other complex organizations, doing things in the American way as they are done at IBM, General Motors, or on Capitol Hill.

The Conflict Perspective

Few would find fault with Eitzen's contention that the unique contributions of the conflict perspective are crucial to the understanding of social structure. However, identifying real conflict within intercollegiate athletics remains a barrier to its serious analysis. With the exception of a few short years during the late 1960s, athletics in higher education has not witnessed persons with similar social conditions organizing in an attempt to maximize their effectiveness in the struggle to persevere or to promote vital group interests. On the other hand, intercollegiate athletics witnessed the process of the powerful using their power to keep themselves in power, with regularity, and little or no opposition. That kind of power in intercollegiate athletics has become so legitimate and so institutionalized that the use of force that normally accompanies legitimate power has seldom been needed. Decision makers in intercollegiate athletics have been so successful in disseminating information and molding ideology that the use of government and law has been held to a minimum. The athletic establishment in higher education, directly or indirectly, influences significantly our society's media and schools, thereby preserving the status quo.

Conflict theorists persist in presenting inequities in wealth, power, and prestige, which ultimately lead to coercion and exploitation. However, these inequities are seldom accurately perceived within college athletics, particularly by the players who, unless they are playing very little or have somehow had their consciousness level raised, seem unaware of such inequities.

Athletes, coaches, and educators tend to support the central theme of conflict analysis, namely, that the institutions of a society are reflections of the larger society and that the American athletic system is such an institution. However, fundamental distrust of an existing power, a necessary ingredient for the conflict perspective, is often missing from college athletics.

Eitzen's description of the NCAA is highly analytical, very accurate, and most appropriate. The legitimate power of the NCAA might be the most salient factor referred to by Eitzen, particularly when that power is used to control and to subdue conflict. Rules are made and enforced from the top, obeyed at all levels, and remain the very backbone of modern college athletics.

An interesting and most appropriate factor discussed by Eitzen is the concept of "false consciousness." Most people in intercollegiate athletics, particularly players and younger coaches, tend to accept their powerlessness because they have been socialized to accept authority and have been made to feel that it is in their best interest. The real issue in this situation is whether or not subservience is in their best interest. This situation will never be an important problem in intercollegiate athletics until it is perceived as an important problem by those who actually work in intercollegiate athletics. The institutionalized powerlessness of athletics is accepted. An educational process without an education is accepted. Athletics as the greatest hypocrisy in higher education is accepted.

Conflict theory can do nothing to alter this situation until the situation is defined as being in need of alteration. The contemporary administration of college athletics is clearly acceptable and is most often what our society wants. Intercollegiate athletic personnel are simply not alienated and resist being told that they should become alienated.

Eitzen's chapter is invaluable to those who agree that an analysis of intercollegiate athletics is incomplete without the conflict perspective, while at the same time it fails to realize that conflict theory itself is totally inadequate for the study of athletics in higher education. Status quo, elitism, societal myths, and the obvious accompanying stratification will always exist; but this does not mean that the social structure of intercollegiate athletics is dysfunctional, nor does it imply that intercollegiate athletics is a social problem.

CHAPTER 19

The Practical Uses of Sociology of Sport: Some Methodological Issues

Günther Lüschen

The topic of the practical uses of sport sociology is not often discussed. Some early pledges from East Europe to make sociology of sport more "practical" (Erbach, 1966; Wohl, 1966) were probably mistaken for being only old Marxist and/or political concepts masquerading as "practical uses." Only a few discussions explicitly address this issue (Gruneau, 1978a).[1] The situation is well illustrated by Loy, Kenyon, and McPherson; addressing the problems of ideology and those of the sociology of physical education, they detect a "catch-22" situation.

> On the one hand unless sport sociologists in physical education address themselves to applied research problems in order to provide useful professional knowledge, they will not be well received by fellow faculty in departments and schools of physical education. On the other hand, if sport sociologists in physical education strictly confine themselves to applied research, they are unlikely to establish a simulative body of knowledge with a sociological base and thus fail to legitimate the sociology of sport as a subdiscipline of scholarly inquiry. (1980:104)

Most of us probably agree with that statement. Yet, on closer inspection, the statement becomes increasingly problematic and cuts short the potential of my discussion. Moreover, the statement is not even correct. If academic respectability is our goal as sociologists of sport, then sociologists as a whole would probably be most impressed by an "applied" field that demonstrates an understanding of social science insights and methodology. After all, sociology itself has yet to resolve this critical link between theory and practice. What Loy, Kenyon, and McPherson lament in this statement can be interpreted as one of the merits of this field. As an aside, I disagree with this evaluation insofar as there is to date no respectable and genuine treatment of physical education by sociologists of sport. Besides mobility studies of athletes in U.S. schools, studies in sociology of sport are, at best, implicitly educationally oriented. Certainly, this is one of the ironies of the field. Consequently, this discussion focuses on this problem—that, so far, the practical dimension of the sociology of sport has not been adequately understood.

Loy, McPherson, and Kenyon (1978b), in light of the above statement, gave us no leads or solutions in their comprehensive treatment on sport and social systems. For them, the problem of practical uses is, at best, implicit if extant at all. They certainly do not deal with the problem in a systematic way. Another position, akin to the above, is the genuine fear in sociology circles that to raise problems of practical uses, impoverishes and restricts the richness and the originality of theory.

Finally, the Marxist position, raised for substance and methodological sake, says there is a unity of theory and praxis. Marxists claim that praxis should always be addressed in theorizing in order to incorporate the dynamics of social change. As long as this is not raised in terms of crude Marxism, no objection to such a dimensional extension of theory exists.

The positions described above are, in my opinion, untenable with regard to the problem of practical uses of social science knowledge. I do not advocate a normative system for planning; rather, I advocate a system of knowledge geared to practical action. In the tradition of Kant, Brentano, James, and Popper, to name some of the more prominent people, I advocate a system of knowledge that is an attempt to advance the level of rationality in decision making and practical action. The understanding is that an absolute stage of knowledge is impossible, and that such a system of knowledge has to proceed with a notion of openness and dynamic change.

Sociology has not yet come to terms with this problem. A glimpse of the complexity of the practical uses of sociology comes from the continuous debate over the value-freeness of sociology. Many sociologists have not read Weber carefully or have not tried in any way to resolve this profound methodological issue. Sociology repeatedly tries to resolve everything around theory and practice via the "value problem." Resolution is not easy, and, unless sociology addresses the problem head on and in a methodological context, we may well meet our Waterloo with regard to the theory-practice dilemma. Understanding the theory-practice problem in sociology proper is, at best, limited and, indeed *wrong* in many respects. The solution to this problem for sociology of sport is of exemplary importance for sociology itself, as well as for the genuine and important practical and policy problems for sport and physical education.[2]

For my present purposes, then, the practical uses of a sociology of sport are discussed along the following three lines:

1. The development of "action knowledge"
2. The analysis and understanding of implementation and policy-making in sport
3. The training of sport professionals and executives in sociology

The Development of "Action Knowledge"

No doubt the body of sociological knowledge, in general, and sociology of sport, in particular, provide insights that lead to a better explanation and deeper understanding of this system and of behavior in sport. This knowledge also provides insights that can lead to direct action by athletes, practitioners, and sport executives alike. With regard to the latter, Max Weber reminded us that the sociologist can tell the policymaker what he or she *can* do, perhaps what he or she *wants* to do—but never what he or she *should* do. Behind this is the clear conception of sociology as a non-normative science. Many sociologists adhere to Weber's position and thus refrain from any practical considerations in this field of study. Yet, our insistence that sociology has and should have practical uses seemingly puts it into the position of a normative discipline.

On a propositional basis, sociology of sport explains how levels of success relate to a specific sociocultural context, or how team efficiency is determined by group structure and leadership style. As suggested elsewhere (Lüschen & Sage, 1981), sociology of sport understands this system at large as ambivalent and dialectic. Such explanations and notions of meaning have no immediate implications for action. Such insights are useful, and practitioners make them the basis of their decisions. However, this type of knowledge is *explanatory*, whereby the term implies a wide range of meaning beyond a strict notion of causality. Beyond explanatory knowledge there is, however, a form called *action knowledge*. This type of knowledge incorporates the research results of sociology of sport, the broader meaning of sport action or its system, and the situative complexities of knowledge implementation. With regard to the latter, sociologists like James Coleman (1972) or Scott and Shore (1979) make a similar point; they argue that such an approach will be directed toward policy, not disciplinary concerns. Yet, there is no reason to view application and disciplinary problems as incompatible (cf. Scott & Shore, 1979). Moreover, incorporation of situative concerns of implementation and planning still stays clear of normative prescription.

The concept of action knowledge obviously faces severe obstacles, not only from positions like those of Scott and Shore, or from those mentioned in the introduction. This concept also faces complexities difficult to master in and of themselves. Justifications for proceeding with such an approach exist. Notions of truth in theory (as advanced by pragmatism with its strong account of situative contexts) and epistemological positions in the discussion of inductive reasoning indicate these justifications. To date, the logical problems at induction have not been resolved (Stegmüller, 1971). However, the best solution thus far supports exactly our concern for practical uses. Hans Reichenbach (1938) argued that although no sufficient condition resolves induction, a necessary condition determines the practical need to take action in ordinary life and, therefore, the need to account for this need in scientific reasoning. A justification for action knowledge in epistemological positions gives priority to the problem rather than to method and theory (Feyerabend, 1979; Popper, 1959). Furthermore, there are practical problems; scientific knowledge expands at such a rapid pace that the storage limits of our libraries are strained. Ironically, a paradox arises—collectively, we know more and more, yet, individually, less and less of what we know can be used. Explanatory knowledge leads to a tremendous overflow of information, only part of which can be implemented for practical uses. At the same time, society and its institutions become more complex and require more planning and knowledge. Consequently, not only a logical base emerges, but also a strong practical need for action knowledge. So, how can we describe the structure of action knowledge?

The Structure of Action Knowledge

Action knowledge, in general, does not mean simple recommendations of a concrete and normative nature. Insights in sociology of an explanatory or descriptive nature are useful for practical action. Here I do not refer to quasi-theories in sociology, although recommendations for action may often be based on spurious relationships, or on wrong theoretical concerns, or on none at all. Obtained appropriately, these insights are still useful for action programs, as are the common-sense experiences of coaches. Nobody should take the experiences of coaches and sport politicians lightly, as their insights often result from very controlled and refined situations. In their own way, they are rational solutions to action problems and differ from the irrational practices of magic that are used elsewhere in sport. The program of action knowledge aims for a deeper and more rational understanding based on explanatory knowledge and situative considerations. Although this might be conceived of as the emergence of prescription in propositional form, propositions can be developed, but they may be far from normative prescriptions. Essentially there are two types of propositional bodies of knowledge that differ in the degree of prescribed action.

First, in sport, rigidly defined situations in many ways are standardized across many instances of contests or group behavior. Consequently, insights provided by one ad hoc field observation or experiment provide generalizable information for sport practice. Here are some research results that depict rather narrowly defined situations and are typical of many that coaches or teachers experience:

1. Reinforcement of competition leads to increased aggression in interpersonal relations (Lüschen, 1966b, Sherif, 1973; Sherif & Sherif, 1961).
2. Interpersonal rivalry and conflict in sports teams need not impede team effectiveness, at least not in co-acting groups, where a coach may channel conflict into an incentive for performance (Földesi, 1978; Lenk, 1977).
3. Competition and spectatorship have an effect of increased performance (Martens, 1975; Tripplett, 1898). Home crowds are an added incentive (Schwartz & Barskey, 1977).
4. Psychological distance of the leader facilitates success of basketball teams (Fiedler, 1960).
5. Communication content in an extremely testing situation is inversely related to prospects for a successful outcome (Emerson, 1966b).

Note that results are very specific and spell out the situative context and individual variables in even greater detail than indicated above. Thus, for comparable situations in sport they may provide immediate practical uses, combined with the common sense experiences of coaches they will lead to a substantial decline of risk in decision making.

The second type of research provides no direct suggestion for action, gives rather broad explanation and understanding and, yet, may be useful for action in educational or general policies of sport alike. Results like the following belong to this sector:

1. Nations with central government politically pushing for international change, with a cultural context that favors success and asceticism are those displaying high international performance in sport (Ball, 1972; Seppänen, 1981).
2. Participation in sport increases with higher social status/class (Gruneau, 1975; Lüschen, 1963).
3. Recruitment into top teams in elite educational institutions is related to higher educational and class background (Berryman & Loy, 1976).
4. Discrimination and differential recruitment of ethnic groups occurs in sport parallel to a minority's position in society overall (Edwards, 1980; Yuchtman-Yaar & Semyonov, 1979), and may lead to specific position assignments (Ball, 1973a; Loy & McElvogue, 1971), but may produce inconsistent enumerations with minority superstars commanding the highest salaries (Scully, 1974).

Such results may lead to consequences for building Olympic teams, for recruitment of minorities or lower class members, and for a positive evaluation of sport's position within education. As becomes immediately obvious, the above results are not even remote prescriptions for action; rather, they lead to policy alternatives judged on preconceived values and goals by the policy-maker or the system. Thus, nations less central, less oriented toward international politics, and rather outer-wordly directed in their culture may well decide to do nothing about improving their Olympic teams. More likely, it will not even become a policy issue. For the visible prospects of success among black athletes, responsible leaders may well redirect the commitments of black youngsters (Edwards, 1980).

The Formal Level of Theory

Action knowledge has to relate to a secondary more formal level of theory. It provides insights into the complexities and the generalized meanings of the system, probably suggesting recommendations of caution, particularly in light of often narrow information. At the same time, such theorizing on a secondary level, resulting in notions of form, function, or cybernetic control, may provide a reduction of system complexity. The debate over an understanding of systems and functional analysis continues, and our attention is called to the potentialities of an approach to sociology that has been widely discredited in the recent past. Critics hold that such principles of system operation are based on subjective values and point to the extraordinary difficulties of defining and investigating the explanans, (Hempel, 1965). However, the reduction of complexity occurs constantly in organizational and political action. In a carefully developed theory, it may well provide the critical link between instructive necessities and propositional sociological explanatory knowledge, which will fall short with the amount of information provided. In a system like sport, relational terms (Cassirer, 1910) such as effectiveness, efficiency, fidelity, and responsiveness (Lüschen, 1979) provide guidelines for policy action and for its analysis.

Implementation and Change

The complexity of society and of the sport system will also result in caution for rational policy and knowledge implementation. Whereas planning becomes a necessity in modern society and in organizations like sport. Tenbruck (1972) contends that the connection between explanatory knowledge and policy are not altogether rational. Tenbruck further contends that planning and implementation have their limits because of preference complexities and openness of modern society. Thus, action knowledge contains a notion of risk and indeterminateness for all purposeful action. Add to this the fact that there are always unforeseen consequences of purposeful action, and the principle of action knowledge should state firmly that implementation and change will be recommended only within limits. Action knowledge is more a state of "muddling through" than of "utopian engineering." One way to limit the risk and to increase the fidelity of a specific policy and implementation is the use of action research. Despite its high cost, it may be particularly practical for implementation of change in sport.

This understanding of action knowledge, in light of the complexities of the system and process, leaves the policy actor considerable discretion, be it an individual practitioner, policy-maker, or an organization as a whole. He or she leaves the actor with an increased amount of information, which leads to more rational decision making, and it sensitizes the actor to crucial points of orientation in abstract systems terms. Such constructs have a level of concreteness for the actor that is not well understood in the social sciences. The situation of the actor, who implements social science knowledge and develops practical actions and policy, is in and of itself an empirical problem for study. The practical uses of a sociology of sport can thus be viewed in strictly explanatory dimensions for the analysis of the process of the practitioner's and policymaker's conduct and organizational process in sport. In the end, our understanding of the policy process feeds back into action knowledge as well.

The Process of Implementation and Policy-Making

This major dimension of the practical uses of sociology of sport needs a separate treatment in our elaboration because it contributes to explanatory knowledge as much as to action knowledge. This process analysis raises issues for future theory and research, issues that, so far, are only touched upon in some approaches to organizational and small groups research.

Broadly speaking, in our reviews of existing research, we can refer to two levels of purposeful action: (1) an interpersonal level with implementation problems in groups, teams, and school classes to name the most obvious units, and (2) the policy level for sport at large within organizations, federations, school systems, and even such conglomerates as the mass media.

Leadership and Purposeful Action Within Groups

Studies of leadership in sport refer heavily to efficient leadership and team success. Democratic leadership style was supposedly good for satisfaction of members and resulted also in higher performance, particularly with psychological distance of the leader (Fiedler, 1960). A recent more careful scrutiny resulted in an understanding of effective leadership according to which leader-member relations, power of the leader, and task complexity account for good leadership (Myers & Fiedler, 1966). Grusky (1963a), after a careful analysis, held that coaches in baseball were not particularly influential in determining team success; rather, their function as scapegoats was much more important overall than previously thought. There are very instructive follow-ups which indicate the earlier observations of a high number of qualifications as a necessity in detailed research (Allen, Panian, and Lotz, 1979; Eitzen & Yetman, 1972).

The Study of Organizational Action, Knowledge Implementation, or Policy-Making

This study is one of the more important and most challenging areas to have surfaced in the social sciences in the last decade. Limited rationality, a high number of variables influencing the process, unforeseen and undesirable consequences of purposeful action, and problems of transitivity in a supposedly causal chain appear simultaneously. Simon (1962) referred to the necessity of understanding the rationality or organizational complexity at the same time that actors in the system are not necessarily rational. Lindblom (1980), addressing the difficulties of policy analysis, recently argued that universal principles rather than variables need to be used. He gives up on the notion of linear causality and step-by-step implementation. Instead, systematic causality, uniqueness of each situation, openness of the system, and organization of knowledge and insight around constructs are related to our four analytic terms and to structural foci of each organization of the policy situation. Will this result in more irrationality and subjectivism? Actually, it will not, because it tries to understand the policy-making process with an attempt to increase the level of rationality. However, it needs a broader understanding of research method and scientific reasoning. Multiplicity of method is of the essence, and phenomenological reasoning will have to be revitalized as a supplement to inductive and deductive reasoning. In a way, it is a call "Back to Weber," an acknowledgement of interpretive sociology—although with more epistemological reflection than Weber and most of his modern representatives provide.

Crozier and Friedberg (1980) gave an instructive example in organizational analysis in what they call "strategic analysis" and a "restricted phenomenological approach" to understanding problems of rationality and the allocation of power in organizations. Crozier's (1964) earlier notion of "zones of uncertainty" related to power allocation appears to be very helpful in analyzing executive behavior in sport organizations (Yerles, 1980). Voluntary organizations in sport are, by definition, fairly indeterminate and leave the executives the opportunity to enlarge "zones of uncertainty," which, in turn, result in relatively high power and long endurance in sport executive positions.

Principles of effectiveness, so central in the activity of sport itself, seem only of limited concern beyond the level of team management in sport federations. Thus, discrepancies between policy goals and results appear to be high in a number of National Olympic Committees (Lüschen, 1979).

In general, empirical analysis of policy-making and planning in sport has just begun and needs more efforts in the future than the sociology of sport has been able to provide. The situation in sociology is not much different and, at this time, represents incompatabilities rather than genuine results and theoretical insights. Policy analysis in sport appears to be particularly well suited to aid a better understanding of the "uncertain connection" between knowledge and policy (Lynn, 1978). For sport practice itself, it is a necessity.

The Training of Sport Professionals in Sociology

Although a body of action knowledge can be provided and insights for policy-making and planning will result from future research, one notion puts to use immediate knowledge in the sociology of sport as part of the education of such sport professionals as teachers, coaches, administrators, journalists, and executives. Beyond intellectual curiosity for social science knowledge, with ever more differentiation of the system and an ever-expanding role of sport professionals, the necessity to make social science part of their education exists. They certainly need it to better understand their own position and action in modern sport. Yet, they should also have a command of immediately applicable knowledge and policy-relevant social science, which would provide a more in-depth understanding of a system to which they belong. On such a basis, more rational and better decisions of sport practice are possible. This has implications for the uses of explanatory and action knowledge, it makes any knowledge implementation more efficient, and, with competent personnel, it introduces a rationality into the system that sport as a loosely organized and administered system often does not have.

Conclusion

The future scholars in sociology of sport must squarely address the practical uses of their scholarly activities. This challenging task will not be resolved easily and is a profoundly methodological and theoretical question itself. The program of action knowledge generally does not provide dramatic or simple results—some low-level propositions with a built-in situative precision notwithstanding. Action knowledge is fairly open in direction; yet, it is more precise and provides more rationality than ordinary planning or policy-making afford. One aspect of action knowledge is the incorporation of explanatory knowledge about the implementation and policy-making process. This area warrants a major research concern by itself. A better understanding of executive conduct and of the structure of organizations or systems of implementation in sport go hand in hand with it.

For the sociology of sport as a discipline, action knowledge and policy analyses are major parts of scholarly training. There is, of course, no reason to make this compulsory, nor is there a need to see this discipline only in terms of its practical uses. After all, supposedly purely theoretical concerns often become immensely practical. My remarks above concerning the logic of scientific reasoning suggest that in the structure of theorizing and human insight, this is nothing surprising. With Reichenbach (1938), we may argue that we use practical necessities as a basis for decision making (or in theorizing for that matter) all the time. If nothing else, our insistence on action knowledge makes such connections clearer and makes them a research topic in and of themselves. If we have a clearer understanding of our practical interests, it helps immeasurably. Instead of assailing the notion as potentially ideological, we might also take it on its merits and start a genuine methodological understanding of the practical uses of our field.

Notes

1. Gruneau (1978a), in a critical review of the praxis dimension in the analyses of the sociologists of sport, addresses a number of the same questions to follow in my concern for epistemological clarification. Although my argument tries to separate the relevancy and personal commitment dimension in order to better understand and rationalize such connections, Gruneau's reference to the value problem via Max Weber, or the union of thought and action in Marx, or critical theory, addresses the theory-practice issue as equally important. Whether there is, indeed, as he asserts in light of some publications, a latent recognition of the problem in the subdiscipline of sociology of sport may be debated; there is certainly only a limited understanding of the connection between theory and practice or the problem of transfer of social science knowledge. Evaluation, a topic mentioned by Gruneau, is, in recent research efforts, an incomplete answer to a much broader problem.
2. One may note here, there is no reference to physical education as kinesiology. After all, a rigid understanding of that field of study will, by definition, "miss the boat" on sociologically understanding the theory-practice dimension.

CHAPTER 20

Policy-Oriented Research in Youth Sport: An Analysis of the Process and Product

Barry D. McPherson

Prior to 1970 much of the sport research and policy development of action-oriented social scientists and social activists focused on minority groups, particularly the black athlete. However, in 1971 Ed Devereux (1976) presented an insightful and critical paper that drew attention to yet another social problem, namely, the changing function, structure, and outcomes of competitive sport for children. Devereux argues that children are being deprived of valuable learning experiences and childish fun because of the trend toward "Little Leagueism." In this contemporary form of "play," children's sport has moved from a child-centered, spontaneous model of free play (e.g., backyard, corner lot baseball) to a highly organized adult-centered model (Figure 1) of quasi-professional sport (e.g., Little League Baseball).

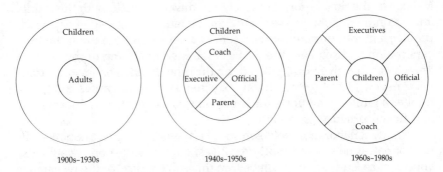

Figure 1. A schematic diagram indicating proportionate change in youth sport from a child dominated world to an adult dominated world.

Emergence of Research in Youth Sport

Stimulated by this essay, scholars began to give more attention to this domain, as reflected by two major conferences in 1971 and 1974 (cf. Albinson & Andrews, 1976; Magill, Ash, & Smoll, 1982) and by the appearance of numerous articles and books pertaining to children's sport (cf. Coakley, 1979; Fine, 1979a, 1979b; Jensen & Heim, 1981; Martens, 1978; McPherson, Guppy & McKay, 1976; Orlick & Botterill, 1975; Smoll & Smith, 1978). Yet, at the same time more voluntary, part-time, or full-time positions for adults were being created within the private and government sector to organize sport programs for children and adolescents. Some of the employees of these youth sport organizations sought to escalate the degree, complexity, and intensity of competition, often with the aim of producing "gold" medalists and elite professional athletes. Others sought to study and ameliorate some of the practices and problems that had become prevalent. Thus, youth sport organizations were often directed by overzealous (but well-meaning) laymen with little or no training.[1] In addition, youth sport attracted the attention of university professors who sought to study the world of children's sport. They too brought a variety of motives, values, and expectations to the social system of children's sport.

Accompanying this increasing interest in youth sport was a growing skepticism by the public concerning the value of university-based research. This was enhanced by the view that university scholars were aloof, elitist, and impractical. Moreover, they were perceived to be out of touch with reality,[2] and their research was considered too theoretical and of little relevance in the "real" social world. At the same time, sport scientists who did foray into the field and become involved in applied, policy-oriented research were often criticized by their colleagues for engaging in "soft," unsophisticated, or "nonscientific" research. In some cases this was justified because of the low quality research[3] that resulted. Moreover, the final report often collected dust on a shelf, with the results and recommendations never being implemented. Thus, to study social problems in the community represented a deviation from the normative expectation that scholars should be committed to adding to the body of knowledge in a given discipline. If, on the other hand, a behavioral scientist pursued "pure" research only, lay members of the profession (practitioners) faulted his efforts for being selfish, explorative, self-centered, and unconcerned with society.

In short, collaboration between social scientists and practitioners (full-time or part-time salaried sport executives, government sport consultants, volunteer executives, etc.) can be fraught with conflict for the researcher as he or she attempts to develop and maintain an identity within two unique social worlds. Similarly, a practitioner who works with a researcher must be careful to maintain his or her identity as a practical, problem-solver and not be seen as "selling-out" to the interests of the researcher. That is, the interests of the layman must be protected and the practitioner must not become too closely identified with the "ivory tower." Otherwise, credibility among one's peers may be lost.[4]

Mutually beneficial collaboration between researcher and practitioner is possible and desirable and must be initiated for the benefit of society, despite the inherent problems that can arise to inhibit or destroy such a process. As Suchman (1967:165) noted, "The public must be given what it needs or it will learn to like what it gets." This statement is particularly appropriate when one considers the contemporary world of competitive sport for children. Throughout the 1960s the professional model of organized sport (with the accompanying rules, philosophy, values, beliefs, practices, norms, and expectations) came to be accepted as "the" model for youth sport, regardless of the age of the participants. For example, the structure, purpose, and rules of "All-Star" hockey in Canada (and even recreational House League hockey) has been isomorphic to that found in the National Hockey League. Parents, coaches, executives, and, naturally, children have accepted the professional model as the only model. As a result, there has been an aversion to policy changes at the minor level that would lead to changes in the game, even if the changes made the game more suitable to the physical and psychological maturity of the child.

In effect, except for a few critics, the rules, philosophy, and structure of youth sport are seldom questioned, however inappropriate or ineffective they may be. That is, there has been widespread public support to maintain the status quo, even though to some observers the status quo has become something other than what it was many years before. However, in recent years, at least in Canada, the social system of children's sport has benefited from the presence of objective, critical thinkers who consider the needs of the child first, and those of the adult volunteer second. These individuals are questioning current practices but at the same time are seeking and are demanding evidence before they change current policies or rules. These sport executives or government sport consultants have sought the assistance of "academic" personnel in order to study the present system and to determine whether change is needed. Some of the changes, sought directly or indirectly, have been related to

1. the behavior of parents;
2. the attitudes and philosophies about the meaning, rules, and objectives of the sport;
3. the cognitive style of the volunteer (e.g., "there is only one "right" way and that's the way it has been and will be," even if the right way is no longer appropriate or was incorrect in the first place!);

4. the leadership capabilities of adult volunteers (especially with respect to their ability to make correct and logical decisions);
5. the interaction patterns between players and officials, coaches and officials, coaches and parents, executives and coaches; and
6. the structure and normative order of the sport (e.g., rule changes, teaching specific skills at specific ages, adapting playing field dimensions to the age of the participant).

Presented in this chapter are a description and an analysis of the process and problems the author experienced during two distinctly different policy-oriented field studies concerning children's sport. In both studies, a university-based researcher, identified with the sociology of sport, worked with, for, and sometimes against policy-oriented practitioners, including full-time professional employees of sport organizations, volunteer sport executives, paid professional coaches, and civil servants and elected representatives at the municipal and provincial government level. The ultimate goal of both of these projects was (a) to identify whether change was needed in the particular sport and, if so, to what degree; (b) to determine whether there was support for or opposition to new directions; and (c) to indicate via concrete, applicable recommendations how change might be initiated. Hence, the concern was more with contributing to social policy in children's sport than with contributing, at least directly, to existing knowledge in the sociology of sport.[5]

This chapter presents and discusses some models for an applied policy-oriented social systems analysis of youth in the hope that sport sociologists will continue to utilize their concepts and research skills to bridge the gap between practitioner and researcher. In this way, by working with sport organizations, sport sociologists can help to diagnose problems and to seek solutions.

As a guiding principle, the main client, the child, must always receive priority in any decisions made. At the same time, the sport sociologist must strive to adhere to the basic principles of high quality, ethically neutral research (cf. McPherson, 1978:75–76). Consequently, the contribution to both applied and theoretical knowledge about sport phenomena can be enhanced in the following ways as suggested by Williams (1976:89–99):

1. Sensitizing individuals qua individuals, or as policymakers and practitioners, in various occupations and organizations to factors and relationships that otherwise would be unnoticed, unknown, or misjudged.
2. Providing factual descriptions and conceptual mapping of important features of social life, past and present, in our own society and elsewhere.

3. Pointing out erroneous assumptions and beliefs; exposing stereotypes and myths; "debunking."
4. Calling attention to hitherto unnoticed elements and relationships (e.g., latent functions, unanticipated consequences, counterintuitive regularities, surprising outcomes, paradoxical relationships).
5. Reconceptualizing the social world; providing new perspectives (e.g., white-collar crime, secondary deviance, "positive" features of conflict, cultural fictions, institutionalized evasion of institutional norms).
6. Specifying the location and prevalence of various beliefs, values, preferences, and behavior patterns within and among organizations, communities, societies, or other collectivities.
7. Providing research methods, techniques, and study designs for generating and analyzing information relevant to practical activities in medicine, education, industry, government, religion, and so on.
8. Providing accessible and suitably codified sociological information to decision makers in all types of organizations and associations.
9. Measuring the outcomes of programs of action through sociologically informed research and assessment procedures.
10. Analyzing ideologies and social programs to reveal logical structure, factual bases, relations to interests of various social formations, and probable consequences.

Critique of Research on Youth Sport

Despite the apparent growing interest and concern about "problems" in youth sport, scholarly work on the topic is still relatively sporadic and sparse. Moreover, many of the articles have been reviews or conceptual analyses that present little empirical evidence upon which to initiate social change or to make specific policy decisions. For example, commenting on the lack of research in the area of age-group programs in all sports, Sage (1974) stated that

Any discussion of this topic invariably depresses me because there is such a lack of empirical work on which to base an argument for or against these programs....The physicians and physiologists have the best documentation and it deals with the physiological aspects of participation, but it is pitifully limited. Psychologists have almost nothing except their professional hunches.

The same conclusion can be derived about the sociology and social psychology of sport.

Although there have been a number of empirical studies in recent years, these have tended

1. to focus on only one social group (usually children or coaches) within the social system;[6]
2. to be based on limited samples within one sport in a single region or community, the results of which are then extrapolated to other sports;
3. to focus on many sports in the same study and therefore depend on global questions rather than sport-specific questions;[7]
4. to focus on only one age group or to attempt to include all ages under the rubric of youth sport;
5. to present descriptive information with no attempt at analysis or prescription;
6. to be unidisciplinary in orientation; and
7. to be based on small, nonrepresentative samples so that many of the attitudes, opinions, and beliefs expressed represent the isolated experiences of specific individuals or specific segments of a given community.

The end result of these concerns is that an inaccurate portrayal may be depicted, unwarranted criticism may be leveled, and incorrect or unnecessary decisions may be made. These outcomes can have serious ramifications for the individuals involved and for the social system within that specific sport. Furthermore, the personal biases of a few opinion-leaders or of influential executives may be readily accepted as normative by the various client groups (e.g., children, parents, officials, the media). In effect, there is often little consultation between decision makers (paid or volunteer executives), and the direct (children) and indirect (parents) clients concerning the structure, rules, and philosophy of their leisure-time activities.

In the following studies, it was not possible to cope with all of the concerns previously mentioned. However, most of them were addressed in these two studies, which sought to initiate change and to assist in policy decisions concerning children's competitive sport. In each case a university-based researcher worked in collaboration with volunteer laymen, civil servants, and full-time sport executives. For each study the background, methods, results, and outcome are described and analyzed from the perspective of the major investigator. Hopefully ethical neutrality has been maintained and both sides of the coin, with respect to the process and aftermath, have been completely described. Although the next two sections are largely descriptive, the third section presents a posthoc analysis and discussion of the collaborative policy-oriented research process in children's sport.

A Study of Age-Group Swimming: A Survey of Swimmers, Parents, and Coaches

Background and Purpose

In 1977 the Executive Director and the Board of Directors of the Ontario Section of the Canadian Amateur Swimming Association decided to evaluate the age group swimming (AGS) program in the province. This decision was precipitated by a number of concerns that had been brought to their attention directly (by coaches, parents, swimmers, and executives of local swim clubs) or indirectly (through articles or letters to the editors of swim magazines, through attendance at conferences and workshops, or by reading conceptual or research articles in professional journals). These concerns included:

- At what age should competitive swimming begin?
- Is the competitive structure by age as it presently exists the best structure?
- What are the present training practices employed by coaches?
- At what age should competitive swimming begin?
- Are there any problems with the reward (awards) system as it presently exists?
- What relative emphasis should be placed on teaching versus training?
- At what distances should swimmers train and compete, and at what distances do swimmers seem to be most interested in competing?
- What are the positive and negative aspects of the objectives of the AGS program as they presently exist?
- What effects do age and sex differences have on the success of the AGS program?
- What impact does AGS have upon family life?
- What training practices are presently utilized by coaches?
- What techniques of teaching skills are presently used by coaches?
- What learning principles are presently used by coaches?
- What are the motivating devices or mechanisms used by coaches and parents?
- What impact does a highly competitive program have upon the physical and psychological growth and development of a child?

- How does a child learn to adapt to stress?
- Which injuries seem to be most likely to occur in a competitive swimming program?

Being comprised of well-educated laymen,[8] the board decided to analyze the present program but to initiate changes only if they would be in the best interest of the child or adolescent.[9] I was contacted to carry out a social "audit" of the system of age group swimming in Ontario in order to determine if the goals of the program were being met. Based on the results of the study, recommendations were to be made to the board of directors who would then decide whether program changes were to be initiated.

Method

Having agreed to undertake the study, the principal investigator met with the executive director and his staff to gain a thorough understanding of the social structure and social actors within the AGS system in Ontario. This included such factors as the political aspects involved in decision making, key power figures, and other influential elites. This step was essential in order to seek the cooperation and input of all significant others early in the process. Moreover, potential users of the results needed to be identified early in the research process. Otherwise, regardless of the findings and recommendations, needed changes could be blocked or avoided if a significant power group or individual was overlooked or not consulted.

It became very apparent that the coaches comprised a potentially powerful group because they had recently become formally organized as the Ontario Swimming Coaches Association. Many of the coaches, unlike other sports, were full- or part-time *paid* professionals who were employed by local swim clubs throughout the province. As a result, many of them perceived themselves, and perhaps rightly so, as *the* experts on age group swimming. Hence, this group was invited to send three consultants to serve as an advisory group to the research team. In addition to this important reference group, there were two university-based researchers who had published numerous research articles on swimming, one of whom was also a highly successful university and AGS coach. These were resources and significant others in the AGS world that needed to be consulted and included in the project in some way.[10] Finally, because the study was to be funded by a negotiated grant from the Sport and Fitness Division of the provincial government, a research officer in that division was invited to serve as a consultant at the planning and analysis stages of the process.[11] The structure of the AGS system and a trichotomized model of the research structure are presented in Figure 2.

Sponsor	Government ministry		CASA (Ontario Section) Board of Directors	
Research Team	Government research officer	University researchers	Executive Director of the CASA (Ontario Section)	Representatives of the the Ontario Swimming Coaches Association
Subjects	Parents	Swimmers	Coaches	

Figure 2. The structure of the Age Group Swimming system in Ontario.

Having gained an understanding of the external social structure that might impinge on the study, the next step was to assemble a research team to identify the key elements in the internal structure of the AGS world. Because of the nature of the concerns expressed by the initiators of the project, it was decided to assemble an interdisciplinary team that would provide expertise pertaining to (a) the macrosocial system; (b) the individual with respect to personality, coaching methods, and motivation as they related to training and performance; (c) the motor learning and performance aspects; (d) the medical aspects of competitive swimming; (e) the physiological aspects of training and competing; and (f) the growth and development outcomes of competitive sport programs. Once the research team was assembled, each member first completed a review of literature to determine the current state of knowledge in his or her area of expertise (cf. McPherson, Marteniuk, Tihanyi, Rushall, & Clarke, 1980a).

Based on the review of literature, the research team generated a series of questions designed to elicit current knowledge, attitudes, behaviors, and opinions about various facets of the AGS for which current evidence was not available in the province of Ontario. Each question pertained to either the sociological, psychological (learning, motivation), or physiological (training, medical aspects) domain of AGS. A questionnaire was designed for parents, swimmers, and coaches because it was decided that these social factors were the most central participants in the system.[12] In order to compare the responses of the three groups, a number of the questions were repeated in each inventory. In this way it was possible to identify areas of consensus or conflict among parents, coaches, and swimmers.

After the research team completed questionnaires in draft form, a panel of coaches critiqued the questionnaires. This review sought to determine if all substantive concerns had been met, to identify the areas not considered germane within the province at that point in time, and to identify any problems in the meaning and wording of questions. Once the suggested revisions had been made, the instruments were pretested with coaches, parents, and swimmers. In addition, 20 swimmers under 12 years of age were interviewed to determine their ability to respond to the questions. Based on these pilot tests, final revisions in wording and format were completed, and the final versions were constructed.

In order to obtain a representative sample of those involved in AGS, the sample was randomly selected from the list of 2,832 swimmers registered with the Ontario Section of the Canadian Amateur Swimming Association. The population was then subdivided into the six competitive regions. Based on the proportion of swimmers in each region, compared to the total population of swimmers, it was determined that all swimmers would be surveyed in three regions with the smallest number of members. In the three regions with the largest membership, swimmers would be randomly selected. Hence, a systematic random sampling procedure was utilized to sample 80% of the swimmers in the 12 years of age and under age groups, and 50% of those from 13 to 16 years of age. This systematic random sampling procedure accounted for the proportion of competitive swimmers by age in those regions.

The total sample was comprised of 1,860 swimmers. Within this sample, 1,230 swimmers were only sent a questionnaire, while for the other 630, a questionnaire was sent to both the swimmer and to his or her parent. The "family package" was also stratified by region, sex, and age. Finally, the total population of 204 coaches was used as the third subsample. Thus, there were three subsamples: the swimmers, the parents, and the coaches.

Each questionnaire was designed to include questions pertaining to the particular group being studied. Hence, although similar questions appeared on each instrument for the purpose of comparing the responses of different social groups, each question was worded so that it was appropriate for the swimmer, the parent, or the coach. The questionnaires were mailed to all three groups along with a letter of introduction from the CASA (Ontario section). This letter indicated that the study was supported and requested by the executive director, by the board of directors, and by the Swimming Coaches Association. Each package contained a self-addressed, stamped return envelope. If the swimmer was under 12 years of age, a note was included to the parent who was *least involved* in the child's swimming program. This note asked that the less-involved parent in the child's swim program interview the child, thereby assuring that all questions were understood and completed. The family package requested that the *most involved* parent complete the parent questionnaire.

Results

The response rate for the three groups was as follows: swimmers, 60%; parents, 52.8%; and coaches, 50.9%. The lower response rate by the coaches was interesting to note. This may have resulted from the fact that some of them, as we heard via the "grapevine," felt threatened by this study. That is, they could be criticized if there was consensus that some specific practices and goals, or a philosophy, were viewed as detrimental to performance or led to children dropping out of swimming. Moreover, the initiation of the survey had the potential to raise issues previously not considered by swimmers or parents and thus generate a conflict situation. However, as the results[13] (McPherson, Marteniuk, Tihanyi, & Clarke, 1980b) suggest, there was general agreement that the system as it existed was functioning well but was not perfect or ideal.

It is beyond the scope of this chapter to present in detail the specific results of the AGS study. However, it is important to note that in addition to reporting the frequency responses for each of the questions by each of the three groups, the responses by the three groups to similar questions were compared in the following areas of concern: (a) the objectives and structure of the program; (b) the problem of attrition; (c) the system of motivation and rewards being used; (d) the attitudes and practices concerning competition and pressure to win; and (e) the methods of instruction being employed, the training techniques, and the practice procedures. This analysis resulted in 29 specific conclusions pertaining to the coaches, 18 specific conclusions pertaining to the parents, and 22 conclusions pertaining specifically to the swimmers. Based on the analyses and conclusions, 13 specific recommendations were directed for action toward the executive director, the board of directors, the Swim Coaches Association, and the executives of local swim clubs.

The Outcome: Consensus, Reorientation, and Minor Adjustments to the Status Quo

Upon completion of a draft of the final report, a copy was submitted to the executive director and the representatives of the coaches association. The executive director responded positively, suggesting that this document would promote discussion and stimulate the introduction of some adjustments to the system. Some of these included less parental involvement at the pool; more communication between coaches and swimmers pertaining to motivation; more understanding by coaches of scientifically based learning and training principles; the amount of time devoted to training and competing at the younger age groups; and the need for a better system of disseminating swimming information to coaches, swimmers, and parents. The representatives of the coaches association thought the report was interesting but refused to recommend that it be read and discussed by their members.[14] To my knowledge, it was never discussed at one of their meetings.

The major investigator presented the final report to the board of directors and responded to questions about the results and implications at a lengthy meeting. The result of this meeting was a general feeling that the AGS system was functioning well and the decision was made, correctly I believe, that major changes in rules and structure were not needed. The board had a summary of the report printed, and a copy was sent to the president of each local swim club. Again, from the "grapevine" (via the executive director), it was noted that the report was formally discussed at only a few local executive meetings. However, the idea and recommendations in the report did reorient the philosophies of some clubs, which had been moving toward an elite model designed to produce age group champions at any cost. Of course, this is only anecdotal evidence. The ideal situation would have been to initiate a follow-up survey of local swim club executives to determine to what extent ideas in the report were discussed, and to what extent reorientation of goals and minor adjustments to the status quo were initiated.

The Minor Hockey Study:
A Parent Survey and Public Forums

Background and Purpose

Although this study was also conducted within the province of Ontario, the background, purpose, methods, and outcomes are considerably different than the study of AGS. These variations clearly illustrate differences between youth sports that can be traced to historical, cultural,[15] structural, organizational, personality, and political factors. Space constraints do not permit a complete delineation of all of these factors. However, those concerned with understanding and improving youth sport must consider these factors in any analysis of a youth sport system.

The *indirect* impetus for this study stemmed from two specific incidents that were symptomatic of a changing social environment in minor hockey. The first involved the conviction of a 16-year-old in 1973 for manslaughter as a result of a fight *outside* an arena after a House League[16] game. The second incident was a violent play-off series between two Junior B teams in April 1974 in which one of the teams finally withdrew from the series to protect its players. This team, which was suspended by the governing hockey body, was either praised or abused by various sectors of the public.

As a result of this latter incident, a public inquiry into violence in amateur hockey was commissioned by the attorney general of the province (cf. McMurtry, 1974). One recommendation of the McMurtry report was the establishment of an Ontario Hockey Council (OHC) to establish and to monitor the purpose and objectives of amateur hockey. Clearly, this recommendation reflected the lack of adequate leadership and the need for an advisory group of qualified people to provide leadership. The council was established in 1975 by the government agency responsible for sport and fitness. However, for political reasons, the membership was not that intended by McMurtry. Rather than a council comprised of persons with specific facets of hockey expertise (e.g., philosophers, sociologists, psychologists, physiologists, lawyers, social workers, recreation directors, etc.), the council was comprised of two volunteer executives (the president and vice-president) from each of the seven CAHA affiliated hockey associations (i.e., all-star hockey) in the province, plus five "academic" or "professional" experts who served as *nonvoting* chairmen of subcommittees. Hence, the council was dominated by individuals who were more concerned with financial matters and legislation pertaining to territory, boundaries, competition, and championships than with promoting the philosophical and developmental aspects of the game for children.

With the inception of the OHC, a number of educational packages (newsletters, booklets, films, TV shorts) were prepared by the various subcommittees. These were delivered to players, parents, coaches, and officials in an effort to improve the social and cognitive environment within minor hockey. As chairman of the Parent Education Committee, I had attempted to convince the council to hold their four meetings per year in different communities. In this way members of the hockey public (parents, players, coaches, local association executives) could be invited to express their opinions and concerns about the philosphy and structure of minor hockey. Not surprisingly, this concept received absolutely no support, primarily because the hockey executives expected that they would receive criticism about their leadership.[17] As a result, the council existed until 1979 as one of the best-kept secrets in hockey. The educational programs attained moderate success, but this varied greatly from region to region, depending on whether the materials were distributed or not by the hockey organizations.[18]

The *direct* impetus for this study derived from four somewhat related events that occurred in late 1978 and early 1979. First, a team of Canadian professional hockey players was defeated by a Soviet team in a series of games. This, moreso than ever in the past, raised comments in the press and debate by the public concerning the deterioration of the basic skill level of Canadian players "because of the emphasis on fighting and other violent acts." In effect, the Canadian ego had been deflated and a national consciousness had been raised. This created a climate among the public whereby it was the appropriate time to initiate new approaches to the game.[19]

A second factor was the appointment of a new Minister for Culture and Recreation (MCR), the agency responsible for funding the Ontario Hockey Council. For the first time the MCR was headed by a minister genuinely interested in and concerned about hockey, particularly minor hockey. He was also concerned about the increasing number of letters received by his ministry from parents concerning problems they could not get resolved by discussion with the executives of organized hockey.

The third factor was the designation of 1979 as "The Year of the Child." As chairman of the Parent Education Committee, I proposed that the council undertake a special project during this year to increase its visibility and to demonstrate that it was truly committed to improving hockey for children. This idea of a special project, initially, did not receive any support from the members of the council.

The fourth element in the sequence was the request in February 1979 by the minister to meet face-to-face with the Hockey Council. At that meeting he indicated that as much as he was against government interference in the activities of voluntary organizations, his ministry was committing excessive resources to resolving complaints about minor hockey. Therefore, he wanted to give the council, which represented organized hockey, a chance to exhibit leadership and to improve the minor hockey environment. If the council was not interested or able, he would have to intervene.[20] Moreover, because of some prior prompting behind the scenes,[21] he requested that the chairman of the Parent Education Committee initiate a study of minor hockey in Ontario that he would fund. The purpose of the study was threefold:

1. To solicit opinions from parents about a number of current issues, for example: possible rule changes, an emphasis on teaching skills versus playing games, the increasing cost in time and money to play hockey, the quality of leadership by coaches, officials, and executives, the behavior of parents, and so on.
2. To provide the public with an opportunity to support or oppose some recent proposals to introduce changes in minor hockey (e.g., eliminate bodychecking for those under 12 years of age). In this way the adults (e.g., parents) would feel they had been consulted, the executives who favored change would know whether they had support or not, and those executives who favored maintaining the status quo would know whether to dogmatically proceed as usual, or whether to become more democratic and progressive in their deliberations and decisions.
3. To bring to the attention of the public (and thereby indirectly educate) concerns and issues of which they may have been unaware. It was hoped that the questions in the survey and the discussions at the forums would serve as a catalyst to stimulate people to ask questions and to discuss issues pertaining to minor hockey, thereby stimulating self-initiated change within the system.

In short, the study was designed to obtain information that could be used to guide decision makers, to serve as a stimulus to get adults communicating in a rational manner with each other about minor hockey, and to indicate that there were some alternative rules, structure, and philosophy that could be attempted in minor hockey. Thus, the direct purpose of the survey and forums was to create a mechanism that would initiate a minor social movement wherein the public would demand that the executives consider and implement change to create a more positive educational environment within youth hockey.

Methods

Given a mandate to proceed, although reluctantly by most members of council,[22] I began by generating a strategy for giving and receiving information to and from the public. Again, an analysis of the principal groups, key actors, and the social structure was completed (Figure 3).

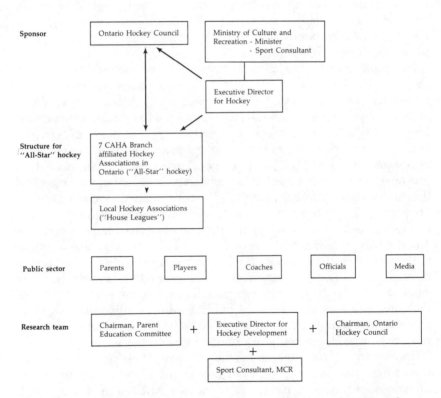

Figure 3. The structure of the amateur hockey system in Ontario, Canada.

The study was conducted in two complementary phases. Phase 1 involved a mail survey of parents of players who were playing "All-Star" hockey. This group was selected because their addresses were on file in the branch offices. Because addresses were not available for the "House

League" players and, therefore, their parents, Phase II consisted of 31 public forums throughout the province where interested citizens (adults and children) could receive[23] and give[24] information pertaining to minor hockey. The forums were chaired by the chairman of the OHC and the chairman of the Parent Education Committee.

Once the general design was completed, the minister held a press conference to inform the public about the purpose and format of the study. More importantly, the press conference served to alert the media and the public that minor hockey was now viewed as a social concern that merited serious attention.[25]

The seven page, 23-item survey was pretested for comprehension and then mailed in March 1979 to 78,754 addresses throughout the province. A total of 31,302 questionnaires (39.8%)[26] were returned without any follow-up procedures. This extremely high response rate for a public survey indicated an enormous interest in and concern about minor hockey by parents. Particularly impressive were the number of parents (80% of the 39.8% who responded) who wrote detailed comments in response to the four open-ended questions.[27]

The results for all of the "closed" questions were analyzed for all 31,302 respondents. However, because of the massive response to the open-ended questions, a subsample of 6,000 was selected for analysis on each of the four questions. The results were analyzed first for all respondents, and then the following factors were introduced as control variables: region of the province, percentage of the child's games attended by parents, level of competition by age (i.e., novice, atom, pee-wee, bantam, midget, or juvenile), the distance travelled to play games, and the parental view that there is too much violence in amateur hockey and in their child's league. Frequency distributions and cross tabulations were computed.

As soon as the frequency distributions were available, a preliminary report[28] was prepared, and a second press conference was held just prior to the start of the next hockey season (i.e., September 1979). At this conference, the significant findings, with annotated comments, were presented by the principal investigator. The conference also announced the dates and locations of the 31 public forums, outlined their format, and encouraged the public to attend and be heard, especially if they had not yet had an opportunity to provide input to the study.

Upon completion of the forums, the principal investigator wrote a final report that included the results of the parent survey; a summary, by categories, of the ideas, issues, and concerns raised at the forums; and, a number of recommendations, which were presented to the minister and then released to the public at a final press conference.[29]

Results

Again, it is beyond the scope of this paper to present detailed results of the study.[30] However, in general, results from the parent survey indicated there was little difference in opinion by geographical region, by amount of involvement in the child's activity (e.g., percentage of games attended by parents), or by time commitment (e.g., the distance travelled to play games). However, parents of children at the novice (8 to 9 years), atom (9 to 10 years), and juvenile (17 years) levels generally seemed to comment less and to have fewer concerns than those whose child was playing pee-wee (11 to 12 years), bantam (13 to 14 years), or midget (15 to 16 years) hockey. This suggests that the parents of the youngest age levels may still be "learning" about minor hockey, and that parents of the oldest age group (i.e., juvenile) may have become less involved. Further, it may also reflect the frequently held opinion that minor hockey is more competitive and serious (e.g., career socialization) at the pee-wee, bantam, and midget levels. Finally, those who felt that there was too much violence in amateur hockey and in their child's league were more concerned that the behavior of parents in minor hockey must be modified, and were more in favor of a greater emphasis on the teaching and practicing of fundamental hockey skills.

In general, the major findings of the parent survey indicated that: (a) parents want more emphasis on the teaching of skills and less emphasis on playing a large number of games; (b) parents are in favor of eliminating bodychecking for pee-wee age players and below; (c) parents believe there is a great need for improvement in parental behavior and attitudes; (d) the cost for hockey is becoming an increasing burden; (e) all competitive coaches should be certified; (f) verbal abuse of officials is increasing by players, coaches, and parents; and (g) referees do not call enough stick abuse penalties (i.e., slashing, high sticking, etc.). The report includes a number of the specific comments written by parents on the questionnaire as examples of the ideas and concerns expressed (McPherson & Davidson, 1980:24-28).

Similarly, the report includes a number of the ideas and statements presented by those who attended the forums or submitted written statements (McPherson & Davidson, 1980:74-99). The majority of the concerns or ideas expressed were related to the objectives and philosophy of minor hockey, the organization (structure and executives) of minor hockey, parental involvement, financial matters, and coaching and officiating.

Based on the quantitative and qualitative findings of the survey and the discussions at the forums, a number of recommendations were proposed in order to generate discussion in every community throughout the province. More specifically, the following are the areas in which recommendations were made with the number of recommendations pertaining to each in parentheses:

- the aims, objectives, and philosophy of minor hockey (15)
- the organization (structure and executives) of minor hockey (18)

- coaching (19)
- officiating (12)
- parents (9)
- players (7)
- the teaching and development of fundamental skills (11)
- the playing rules for minor hockey (11)
- the financing of minor hockey (7)
- the media and minor hockey (3)
- local and provincial governments (4)
- professional and junior hockey (1)
- minor hockey in comparison to other organized children's sport (4)
- general recommendations (8)

The Outcome: Conflict, Threats, Conciliation, Change

Created through political maneuvers, the outcome of this study led to further politically based actions and reactions because of the vested interests of the various subgroups involved in minor hockey. Again, the details must be described in order to appreciate the difficulties of policy-oriented collaborative research. First, as a caveat, had the principal investigator been content to undertake this study, submit a final report to the sponsor, and return to his "ivory tower," this study would have been an expensive "white elephant" that would have gathered dust on shelves. Similarly, had the minister been content to reap the publicity from the report when it was first released, and then let it be filed and sink to obscurity, the impact of the report would have been minimal. However, as the following scenario illustrates, the principal investigator and the minister and his staff were committed to aggressive advocacy on the basis of the statements and evidence in the report. As a result, they joined forces to ensure that the recommendations in the report were considered seriously by the volunteer hockey executives, particularly at the branch or regional level.

Upon completion of the first draft of the final report, the principal investigator shared a copy with the Executive Director for Hockey Development and with members of the Parent Education Committee.[31] Because one major recommendation was that the minister should formally respond to the report, this draft was then presented to the minister and his staff. The minister met with the executive director and the principal investigator to discuss steps he might take when the report was released. At the press conference announcing the release of the report, the minister would respond in the following three ways to indicate that he supported the report and that he was committed to stimulating a new environment within minor hockey in Ontario:

1. The OHC would become an incorporated nonprofit organization, totally free of government involvement except for funding, so that hockey "volunteers" could provide leadership and see that recommendations in the report were considered and implemented. This newly reconstituted body was to be comprised of seven branch executives plus two representatives from the public sector to be appointed by the minister.

2. In order to enable this new body to implement some of the recommendations, particularly with respect to hiring full time regional coordinators, the ministry would provide up to $2 million over a 3-year period to this newly incorporated body.

3. But, if hockey volunteers could not work together with representatives of the public sector and refused to consider and act on the recommendations, it was within his right and responsibility as minister to create a Hockey Advisory Council, comprised solely of representatives of the public sector, to insure that children were exposed to an educationally sound hockey environment.

Thus, the minister preferred to use the "carrot" approach (#1 and #2 above) but would resort to the "pitchfork" approach (#3 above) if necessary to insure that action pertaining to the recommendations was initiated. The die was now cast for a subsequent 5 months of conflict and turmoil within minor hockey—none of which took place on the ice, and none of which involved the children!

On February 28, 1980, a press conference was held in Toronto to announce the release of the report and the minister's reaction. At the same time, over 75,000 summaries of the report were distributed as feedback to hockey parents throughout the province. The initial reaction of the media was essentially supportive and favorable, although a few reporters sought to create controversy by asking other sport governing bodies for their reaction to the fact that hockey was receiving $2 million for developmental programs. Thus, the public was generally satisfied and, as numerous letters to the editor indicated, felt that the report and the recommendations were acceptable and workable: That is, previous dissatisfaction led to an endorsement of change and a willingness to move in new directions.

However, there were those within the hockey system who were satisfied with the status quo and who were prepared to resist change, thereby opposing the report and the suggested recommendations. Chief among these were the presidents of two of the largest hockey branches in the province, both of whom dominated two other presidents by verbal intimidation and threats. The reaction[32] of this group and their supporters was as follows:

- They had not been consulted about the content of the final report.

- They did not want regional coordinators (full-time personnel to assist the volunteer to do a better job) because they were a threat to the "volunteer."
- They did not want the $2 million because it represented more government interference.
- The report was a biased, inaccurate, nonrepresentative "textbook" view of minor hockey.[33]
- They did not want public sector representation on the newly incorporated body because they would be "government appointees" (spies?).
- They did not want the OHC to be reconstituted, but rather would have preferred to see it cease to exist so they could continue to rule minor hockey as they had in the past.[34]

Once the press became aware of this dissension within the ranks of organized hockey, they fanned the fire to "sell newspapers" by seeking quotes almost weekly from representatives of either faction. Hence, what should have been discussed and rationalized "behind closed doors" became a public issue. The lines were drawn very clearly and, interestingly, reflected education and age lines. Allied with the "young turks" (the principal investigator and the executive director, both of whom were under 40) who favored change were the presidents of three of the branch associations (all of whom were under 45 years of age and well-educated) and the minister and his staff. Allied with the "old guard" were the less-educated (high school or less) and "older" (55+) presidents of four branch associations, although primarily only two of these were committed to confrontation; the other two became their "puppets."

It is beyond the scope of this article to chronicle all the events that transpired between February 28, 1980, and July 31, 1980, when the issues were finally resolved. However, a few include

- a great effort by the "old guard" to claim government interference in a voluntary organization;
- efforts to discredit the report as being unrepresentative of the views of those involved in minor hockey (despite a response by 31,302 parents and the 31 public forums);
- attempts to disparage the principal investigator as not "a volunteer," as not a "hockey person," as being "too academic," and as being only interested in the publicity he received;
- an inability of the "old guard" to understand or consider the recommendations in the report, most of which pertained to the developmental aspects of the game rather than to the legislative aspects (the sacred domain of the executives);
- a portrayal of the concept of regional full-time hockey development coordinators as a threat to the volunteer;

- a fear of regional coordinators delivering more to the local community than would the branch executives, thus threatening the presidents who opposed this concept;
- one branch (for reasons that are still not clear but which again revolve around personalities rather than ideas or issues[35]) pulling out of the OHC, two others threatening to do likewise;
- a series of supposedly secret meetings with the minister by both factions;
- a number of heated council meetings at which consensus would apparently be attained, only to be overturned 1 or 2 days later when a president, allied with the "old guard," would reverse his decision and say his association could not support that view; and
- the wearing down of the "old guard" as the "young turks" gave them a few concessions, most of which were relatively meaningless in the long run.

Through all of this, the local hockey associations and the general public[36] were supportive of the recommendations in the report and totally confused by the off-ice conflict.

In effect, what had occurred among a few of the branch executives was that they had forgotten about the report itself, and what it was attempting to do, as they fought zealously to protect their hitherto uncontested domain of legislating and organizing minor hockey. In reality, the report made relatively few recommendations concerning legislation, but rather focused more on how to improve the environment in the game and how to increase the skill level of the participants. Thus, we see that an evaluation process had become increasingly political because it yielded conclusions about the "worth" of programs administered by volunteers. The initial high rate of nonacceptance of the report resulted from a perceived threat to both the organizations and to the avocational group (i.e., the volunteer executives).

The result of the "battle" was a reconstituted hockey council, which reflected

- an emphasis on the developmental rather than the legislative aspects of the game;
- the appointment of regional coordinators in three of the five branches;
- the appointment of two public sector voting delegates to the council;
- withdrawal of the ministry from active involvement in minor hockey;
- a budget which increased the opportunity to develop educational packages for coaches, officials, players, executives, and parents;

- the resignation from the committee (to save face) of two self-serving "bad apples" in the minor hockey executive board;
- a consideration by all branches of how and why each recommendation in the report should or could be acted upon;
- a willingness to experiment with new rules and new ideas if they have the potential to improve the hockey experience for children;
- more pressure on executives to communicate with and to be responsive and accountable to the parents and players; and
- a greater awareness that the child, not the adult executive, must come first in any decision.

In short, the report was openly discussed and the recommendations were seriously and objectively considered before being accepted or rejected. As a caveat, it was never expected by the principal investigator that all of the recommendations would be implemented in full throughout the province. Rather, it was hoped that some recommendations might be viewed as appropriate for some communities or regions, and if this was the case, they would be implemented on at least a trial basis.

Analysis and Discussion

Having described the purpose, methods, results, and outcomes of two large policy-oriented field research studies, this section presents a post hoc analysis of the process, plus a prescription for future studies.

The Social Context of Social Research

Field research does not take place in a vacuum. Rather, the research effort is another form of organized social activity in which interaction and feedback occur continuously. On one level, this interaction appears to occur only, or mainly, between the investigator and the respondent. However, other levels may intrude in varying degrees at different stages in the research process. These include interaction between the investigator and the sponsor, the investigator and special interest groups, the media and the investigator, the media and the special interest groups, the sponsor and the media, special interest groups and the target population, and the investigator and academic colleagues. In the case of the hockey study, these interactions were fraught with conflict, disagreements, or lobbying as one group sought to suppress the report, while the other sought to have the recommendations discussed widely.

Because field research is often a social and political process, it may require the investigator to carefully manage both social identity and the social situation. For example, the public forums, if they were to produce useful information, had to be staged very carefully so as not to threaten representatives of the target population. In order to create an open, communicative environment, a significant hockey executive in each community was invited to sit at the head of the table to introduce the principal investigators as colleagues. To add to this atmosphere at the forums, casual dress was the norm, first names were used, and "hockey" jokes were intentionally included in the presentation made by the cochairmen in their opening remarks. Special care was taken to indicate the varied and considerable hockey experience of both cochairmen. That is, we were not naive observers or "academics"; on the contrary, we were concerned, experienced "hockey people" who were present to listen to parents' ideas in order to make hockey a better experience for their children.

At various times some of the remarks directed toward the coinvestigators were hostile. Rather than becoming defensive and debating the point, we diffused the hostility by thanking parents for their opinions and by indicating the comments would be considered with the other ideas presented. In other words, although confrontation and debate would have been possible and enjoyable in many cases, we intentionally absorbed the "shots" rather than expressing an opinion or invoking an argument.

At a few of the forums, no matter how we tried to establish an open dialogue, the wariness of prospective respondents prevailed either because of their reluctance to speak in public, or because of the suspicion that we were on a witch hunt to destroy minor hockey. In each case we tried a variety of techniques, all of which eventually led to a public discussion and exchange of ideas. These techniques included the following:

- asking leading questions such as, "We haven't had much opportunity to hear from mothers at the previous forums—I would be really interested in what some of the mothers think because they probably spend more time watching the kids play hockey than do the fathers";
- providing feedback concerning some of the issues raised at earlier forums, especially those in nearby communities;
- adjourning for doughnuts and coffee and approaching individuals on a one-to-one basis;
- asking a well-known local hockey figure in the audience to speak first; and
- relating some humorous anecdotes reported on the questionnaire or at earlier forums.

In short, it was essential that we "staged" our social identity and that the interaction format was managed carefully to maximize both the quantity and quality of input from the public.[37]

Another aspect of collaborative field research that creates special problems for a university researcher within the social domain is that of interacting with lay people. This occurs during the planning, implementation, analysis, and reporting stages of the project. One example of a problem area in this domain is the tendency of the university researcher to become impatient and irritated with lengthy, unproductive meetings held by lay people in voluntary organizations. This can occur initially when they are deciding whether to implement a project and later when deciding whether to adopt and implement policy recommendations.

A behavioral scientist must be aware of and learn to have patience with the fact that the diffusion and adoption of new knowledge into any volunteer organization, particularly in those run by volunteers where members of the lower middle class predominate (as in hockey), is likely to be difficult, to be met with resistance, and to be characterized by seemingly endless delays. As Cottrell and Sheldon (1964:127–128) note with respect to the medical profession,

> the structure of medical institutions is frequently more rigid and authoritarian than the somewhat more informal and much less authoritarian pattern of academic life in which the social scientist is trained.

Sport, and particularly youth sport, which is basically organized by untrained volunteers, could very easily be substituted for "medical institutions" in the above quote. Moreover, whereas the researcher may be mainly "task"oriented, the volunteers may be more "process" or "social" oriented.

Another problem-creating difference between behavioral scientists and practitioners is that of status incongruity. Whereas scientists have years of education, many of the volunteers have little education beyond the minimum legal requirement. Moreover, there is often an age difference in that the older volunteer executive is interacting with a younger behavioral scientist (i.e., a "young turk"). Hence, the situation arises wherein the "old guard" makes decisions based on work by young professionals who may be perceived to lack "experience." In this situation, the behavioral scientist can be made to feel like a child giving advice to adults. In effect, this situation results from age-based role conflict, a division of labor that reflects status and age differences, and perhaps even divergent and conflicting values which represent two unique age cohorts or cultures. Such subcultural differences within the social situation, if unrecognized or misunderstood, can often lead to unrealistic expectations on both sides. The differences can also very easily lead to feelings of frustration, indignation, and overt conflict that may jeopardize the project.

Another potential source of conflict revolves around perceived role responsibilities where, traditionally, a dichotomy existed. That is, those within the voluntary organization are generally perceived to have greater expertise and more interest in identifying needs, specifying policy goals, and in planning, formulating, and implementing policies. In contrast, the social scientist is more concerned with formulating research objectives; designing, sampling, and measuring; analyzing data; and arriving at conclusions in the form of policy recommendations. Today, much policy-oriented research is not bound or guided by any specific theoretical tradition, but rather utilizes and adapts concepts and methodological tools from a variety of disciplines and research experiences. In fact, van de Vall and Bolas (1980), in a recent discussion of the emergence of a professional paradigm in sociology, reported that client-oriented projects that utilize ideographic rather than nomothetic concepts have greater policy impacts.[38] That is, the theoretical perspective and method is grounded in the specific problem. Hence, a symbiotic relationship between scientist and layman is necessary in order that the scientist can be given assistance in identifying the problem and in understanding the social structure of that social system. Then, the scientist, using his or her expertise, plans a study to seek a solution to the problem.[39]

A need exists, however, for practitioners to actively participate in the research process.[40] If they participate, they have a better understanding of the process and outcome, they will be more committed to considering recommendations, and they will become more objective and less protective or defensive concerning their roles and their organizations. Similarly, the researcher, by interacting with laymen, is more likely to become immersed to some extent in the value system of the target group. Although this should not influence the design or the implementation of the study, it may influence which recommendations get highlighted in a final report or at press conferences.[41] At the same time, policymakers want the researcher to continue to be involved in the organizational side of the dichotomy in order to increase the likelihood of change occurring and to legitimate the impact of the policy changes. It might also be the case that if lobbying for implementation or recommendations is needed, the investigator may be seen to have few or no vested interests, at least compared to those within the formal structure of the voluntary organization.[42] Taking an active role in the organization's activities does not imply distortion of the data, providing a system of collaboration is present to insure checks on the collection and interpretation of information gathered during the research process.

In summary, policy-oriented field research is a social process that requires the collaboration of both layman and scientist. However, with this collaborative system professional responsibilities, on either side, must not be sacrificed because the outcome can have an impact on many whose lives may be altered or changed by the implementation of specific recommendations. Furthermore, the investigator must be careful not to bias the research process or the policy recommendations in the direction of a sponsoring agency that may have vested interests. In both studies described in this chapter, the reverse was true in that bias, if present, was directed toward the major target group, namely, the child. Clearly, any bias present in both studies was not in favor of the secondary consumer group, namely, the adults who organize children's sport.[43]

Finally, the researcher must be careful not to advocate a policy without data, or to advocate a policy not warranted by or consistent with the data. This is where objective laymen and academic colleagues can play a critical role by critiquing drafts of a final report. Yet, at the same time, there needs to be room for investigators to express opinions based on qualitative experiences and previous knowledge, rather than on strictly empirical evidence—this fine line also needs input from practitioners to insure that opinions are grounded in experiences.

Some Models for Collaborative Field Research

To date, field research seems to have been characterized by two dichotomous approaches: conflict or consensus. In the conflict model, social scientists study the oppressors to unmask the underlying causes of the problem. Much of the basis for the social problem is attributed to the dominant institutions that control information and decision making. The investigator who adheres to these assumptions places himself or herself on the side of the controlled, powerless, or exploited members of society, and the research process involves overcoming the barriers that the dominant power elite place upon entry and access to the data. Thus, methods may involve confrontation politics, spy tactics, or coercion. In short, conflict is built into the research process because not all of those within the system wish the study to be initiated because of potential personal losses. Moreover, conflict is inherent in that the researcher seeks data that those in control may not wish to have released beyond their domain. Some have implied that this approach is unethical in that it does not require the informed consent of those who become subjects in the study and because it is partisan in orientation (cf. Blau, 1964).

In contrast, the consensus methodology involves obtaining informed consent and voluntary cooperation of those studied. Moreover, consensus-oriented methodologists are generally willing to cease their research when elites block access to the data. Thus, this methodology may be viewed by some (notably conflict methodologists) as a method of preserving the status quo because the investigator is a "hired hand" of the power elite and lacks control over the application process.

Thus, at first glance, one might consider the swimming study to be an example of the consensus model, whereas the hockey study involved a conflict approach—at least in the early stages and after the release of the final report. However, research in the real world is more complex than a simple dichotomy of conflict versus consensus, or "bad guys" versus "good guys." As Hessler, New, and May (1980:321) noted, "Whether the research strategy is conservative or critical depends more upon the researcher's understanding of the social system under investigation than upon the conceptual model." They further state that we must not only consider the researcher and the subjects, but also the sponsor and the larger community which receives or lives with the results as they are applied. In fact, not all, or not even a majority of the target population may share the commitment and fervor of the researcher to initiate change. Rather, many might prefer to maintain the status quo, especially if they are unaware of the issues and do not know about alternatives (e.g., the hockey and swimming parents).

It appears that a researcher cannot adhere rigidly to either a conflict or a consensus model or, if so, potential solutions for problems may not surface.[44] That is, the complex relationships existing among the researcher, the sponsor, the media, vested interest groups, and the group targeted to receive the application of the research results must not be ignored. Hessler et al. (1980:332) believe that solutions will not occur as long as social scientists adhere to either the conflict or the consensus model, thereby failing to differentiate between the power and exchange dimensions of research vis-à-vis sponsors, target population, and researchers. As an alternative, they propose an exchange model.

In the exchange model (Hessler et al., 1980), individuals who supply rewarding services (e.g., information, humor, praise) in turn obligate recipients who must reciprocate (e.g., give information). That is, there should be a reciprocal process of give and take among actors. When power dominates the research process, asymmetry prevails. Inevitably, most exchange relationships involve some degree of power, which leads to some degree of social control.[45]

However, by including some degree of mutual sharing of control (e.g., the OHC was given a mandate by the minister to work out a solution to considering the recommendations in the report), the possibility of the researcher or the subjects being in a totally dependent position is precluded, even though power strategies can dominate the research process at some stage. Moreover, in an exchange model the chances are greater that the researcher will gain access to types of data and levels of meaning not available to those who adhere to a conflict or consensus approach.

In summary, both studies reported in this chapter were primarily based on an exchange methodology wherein the investigator collaborated with practitioners and subjects in carrying out the study. This approach, via forums and questionnaires that seek to provide as well as receive information, raises client consciousness and hence facilitates the diffusion and adoption of new ideas, rules, and policies. Although objectivity prevailed, it was the objectives of the major client (i.e., the children) that prevailed over those of a vested interest group (i.e., executives of branch associations). In short, as Hessler et al. (1979:341) note, "Researchers place themselves into different exchange and power structures, depending on their goals, their commitment to different group interests, and the very practical matter of gaining research entry." This model also goes a long way toward generating a sense of client-consciousness among the research team and other vested interest groups.[46] In short, an exchange model of policy-oriented youth sport research involves sharing control over the application of findings between the researcher and the target population who lack power to effect social change by themselves. Thus, future studies of the social system of children's sport should adhere to an exchange perspective, particularly between the researcher and the major client groups.[47] Rather than viewing children's play as an adult-centered model or a child-centered model, perhaps an integrated or exchange model should be considered. This would involve two-way interaction to determine congruency (e.g., on structure, rewards, competition, etc.) among actors (children and adults), and might be more appropriate and successful in both understanding the social system and in prescribing and initiating change.

Conclusion

This chapter has indicated some of the problems and prospects of working with lay collaborators within the domain of policy-oriented research concerning youth sport. In 1980, W.F. Whyte announced the following theme for the 1981 Annual Meeting of the American Sociological Association: "Exploring the Frontiers of the Possible: Social Inventions for Solving Human Problems." In his elaboration of this theme, Whyte noted that in the past our prescriptions have rarely appeared helpful to practitioners because the solutions are too general and vague, and it is difficult to translate general statements into specific actions. He described a social invention as "a new and apparently promising strategy designed to solve some persistent and serious human problem" (Whyte, 1980:1). He then appealed for a fruitful reorientation of the direction of sociological research to strengthen the capacity of sociologists to discover solutions to human problems.

Far be it for me to claim that the models presented in this paper represent "social inventions," or exemplars, or that they approach the "frontier of the possible." However, what was attempted and what has resulted has had significant impact on the organizations involved, in particular, on interorganizational relations (e.g., between branch executives in minor hockey and between government and organized sport governing bodies); on human interactions (e.g., between researcher and layman, between adult and child, between parent and executive); on policies pertaining to the philosophy, rules, and structure of minor sport in Ontario; and, above all, on the general social environment in which children compete in sport, especially in hockey. As a result of the hockey study, a new coordinating body has been formed to develop minor hockey; a new set of interorganizational relations (e.g., government and the private nonprofit sector) have been established; a new set of procedures for shaping human interactions and activities (e.g., new playing rules for the youngest age groups have been created; greater consultation between executives and players or parents) has transpired; and new policies pertaining to rules[48] or structure have been implemented. Thus, the models of collaborative research presented here are offered to stimulate further policy-oriented research in youth sport.

Notes

1. For example, even among those with a business or physical education background, few had completed courses in psychology, sociology of sport, psychology of sport, growth and development, physiology, or biomechanics where the emphasis or focus was on children or adolescents.
2. For example, while working on the hockey study described in this chapter, I received an anonymous letter that included an application for a psychoanalytically based workshop on reality-therapy. An accompanying note suggested that I should attend this workshop instead of "interfering" with minor hockey.
3. Probably a high correlaton between the quality of "pure" and "applied" research exists. Low-quality "applied" research might be the expected outcome of one who produces low-quality "pure" or theoretical research.
4. This, in fact, happened to both the "layman" coinvestigator and the government consultant involved in the study of minor hockey. They were stigmatized for "selling out" and "being uppity" because they cooperated with a university professor and because they supported the final report. In the case of the coinvestigator, he lost a number of friends, although he has few regrets. As he says, "I made new friends and finally learned what some of my supposedly close allies and friends were really like."
5. However, this chapter and other papers cited in the references are direct byproducts of the data collected and the experiences encountered in these two field studies. That is, the university-based researcher does not have to neglect his or her contributions to the discipline, as the data can usually be used for "academic, discipline-oriented" work as well.
6. For example, parents are seldom included; yet, we know they are "significant others" who often register the children for sport before the child knows what it is all about; they encourage the child to participate with varying degrees of pressure; and they establish performance expectations for their child.
7. For example, the most comprehensive and thorough study to date, the three-part interdisciplinary Michigan Youth Sport Study, used global questions designed to obtain information from participants in a variety of sports. Whereas results can be analyzed by sport, questions may have been interpreted differently by those involved in different sports. Moreover, some pertinent questions related to a specific sport may not have been asked, thereby limiting the completeness of information upon which to explain the findings and upon which to base decisions (cf. Seefeldt, Blievernicht, Bruce, & Gilliam, 1976, 1978a, 1978b).
8. For example, most had a university degree, and the chairman had just recently been appointed as a provincial judge. This educational background

differs markedly from the norm (some high school) for minor hockey executives.

9. It is important in all research in this area to recognize the wide age range (approximately 6 to 16 years) of participants and to be aware that different rules, structure, and philosophy might be needed for the various age groups within "youth" sport.

10. One became a member of the research team to represent the physiology and growth and development component in the interdisciplinary team that was selected. The other wrote an extensive review of literature in his area of expertise, and this was included in the final report.

11. This individual became intrinsically involved far beyond the responsibilities related to his job and made a significant contribution, which exceeded that expected from a civil servant!

12. A questionnaire was also designed for executives of local swim clubs and former age group swimmers, but budget constraints prevented a survey of these particular components of the system.

13. A copy of the complete report is available at cost from the CASA (Ontario Section), 1220 Sheppard Ave. East, Willowdale, Ontario, Canada M2K 2X1. In addition, the data are available on tape from the Leisure Studies Data Bank Department of Recreation, University of Waterloo, Waterloo, Ontario, Canada N2L 3G1.

14. They did agree however, after some persuasion, to have their names listed in the final report as consultants to the study.

15. The importance of hockey within the value system and lifestyle of Canadians is important for the reader to understand. As one individual has suggested, "Hockey is Canada's culture." Thus, for many parents, minor hockey for their children is a "serious" matter, moreso perhaps than Little League baseball is for parents in the United States.

16. "House League" hockey, as opposed to "All-Star" hockey, is organized by the hockey association in each community. At this level of hockey, a player is assigned to a team rather than competing for a position on an elite team. This level of hockey involves less time and travel and is generally considered to be "less serious" and "less competitive" than All Star hockey, which involves representing one's community (town or city).

17. Many of these volunteer executives adhere to the basic premises that because one is a volunteer, what he or she does is "correct" and is not to be criticized under any circumstances, regardless of whether his or her actions are in the best interest of the child.

18. Whether the materials were distributed or not was often directly related to the philosophical view of the executives. Stories of materials being delivered to executives for distribution to players or parents, only to end up in a basement or the garbage, were not uncommon.

19. Many of these changes were not really new as they had been advocated for at least 5 years (by university coaches, provincial and national technical directors of hockey, university professors with expertise in hockey, etc.,) but had been ignored by the volunteer hockey executives who are responsible for legislation and leadership.

20. This event was really the catalyst because these lay volunteers fear and abhor government interference in their domain, other than to provide funds. This belief in "government-at-arms-length" and the belief in the "divine right of the volunteer to run minor hockey"—regardless of whether it is done well or not—are important to appreciate.

21. The Executive Director of Hockey in Ontario and I presented a draft of a parent questionnaire and the concept of public forums to the minister as a suggestion of how the environment in minor hockey might be studied and changed during "The Year of the Child."

22. Many members thought the public would be apathetic, that interest would wane, and that any results would be discredited because of a lack of response and interest.

23. The first half hour of each forum involved a brief summary of the results of the parent survey, plus an orientation to sources of information about hockey that are available for parents, players, coaches, and officials.

24. Citizens were invited to appear at the forum to express their ideas orally, or they were encouraged to submit written statements, briefs, or letters if anonymity was desired.

25. As will be noted, the use of press conferences at specific times was a deliberate strategy to increase public knowledge, awareness, and consciousness about the study and about the environment in minor hockey. Whereas the minister, no doubt, used the press conferences for political purposes, the principal investigator used them to highlight salient points and concerns that reporters could not ignore. As a result, minor hockey for the first time received "front page" coverage, was the focus of written editorials (on the editorial page, not the sport page), editorial page cartoons, Letters to the Editor, lead stories on radio and television news shows, and a major topic of "phone-in" radio shows. In short, the press conference and subsequent coverage encouraged the media and the public to "come out of the closet" and to express their concerns and ideas about minor hockey with conviction.

26. In reality, the response rate was considerably higher because a number of homes received more than one copy of the questionnaire as a result of the duplication of names on some of the mailing lists.

27. Many of the respondents attached handwritten or typed comments which ran from one to five pages in length. Others wrote extensively in the space provided on the questionnaire.

28. Prompt completion of a report and immediate release of the results are important if credibility is to be maintained and if action is to be initiated while the issue is "hot."

29. At this point, the aftermath began in earnest; this will be detailed below in the section entitled "Outcome."

30. A copy of the final report (McPherson & Davidson, 1980) can be obtained for $2.00 from the Ontario Government Bookstore, 880 Bay Street, Toronto, Canada. In addition, the data set for the parent survey is stored in the Leisure Studies Data Bank, Department of Recreation, University of Waterloo, Waterloo, Ontario, Canada N2L 3G1.

31. The members of the OHC were not consulted at this point for a variety of reasons, the main one being that they, with their conservative orientation, would have tried to delay public release of the report indefinitely by wanting to have a say in dotting every "i" and crossing every "t." This omission later proved to be a tactical error because it gave some of them ammunition whereby they could claim they had not been consulted and therefore the report was not "an OHC Report."

32. Many of these reactions were based on personalities: the two individuals most in opposition were poorly educated, egocentered individuals who had risen to the top of their organization by verbal intimidation of others, rather than solely on leadership skills. For both, the presidency and the right to wear

that jacket, were peak moments in their lives—they had achieved a position visible to the public. There is little doubt but that these two self-seeking personalities initiated and prolonged the conflict that resulted from the release of the report.

33. The first line of attack concerning policy-oriented research is often the methodology (sampling, questions, analytic techniques, etc.), although the real basis may be ideology or change. That is, when conclusions enter the public domain, methods are questioned.

34. In fact, this was another factor in the confrontation. The principal investigators and the OHC were receiving more press "ink" than the presidents and their respective associations.

35. In fact, the principal investigator was cited as being partly to blame for this withdrawal. He had mentioned in a supposedly private conversation that part of the problem with minor hockey is the quality of leadership, namely, that some executives are incompetent because they cannot function objectively without putting their own interests or ego ahead of the child. This comment appeared in a newspaper report with the headline, "Hockey Executives are Incompetent."

36. In fact, most editorials, Letters to the Editor and to the minister were extremely supportive and urged hockey associations to consider the ideas in the report. Moreover, as time went on many media personnel reversed their initial view and admitted, as one headline stated, "I am willing to eat crow over the bodychecking rule."

37. For example, after the first two forums I had to put a muzzle on my lay collaborator. Being a gregarious, outgoing individual, he got caught up in his role as cochairman and felt compelled to respond with an answer, story, or solution to each comment from the floor. After we convinced him that it was not "the Lloyd Davidson show," he became more of a facilitator and less of a participant. In fact, he became quite adept at providing cues that kept a respondent on "track," and in encouraging reluctant attendees to speak out.

38. Ideographic concepts are of low abstraction and are generated from, or grounded in, the data in order to better understand the specific problem. Nomothetic concepts are more formal, general, and abstract and have been validated in the literature.

39. In effect, true collaboration demands mutual understanding and trust, something that was always present in the swimming study, but that varied greatly among various actors in the hockey study.

40. Practitioners can assist by identifying problem areas or people; by providing feedback about opposition to the study; by clarifying the wording and meaning of questions; by facilitating contact with respondents; by forming part of the data gathering teams (e.g., the forums); by interpreting findings and suggesting needed policy changes; by improving the vocabulary in the final report; and so forth.

41. For example, given the opportunity to speak after the report was released, I often emphasized my personal preferences for certain recommendations. These preferences, however, were based on my intuition that there was a great deal of concern and support for change in these areas (e.g., change the high sticking rule for children, pay more attention to the needs of House League players, reduce travel, have a ratio of two practices for every game).

42. On more than one occasion, I was totally frustrated and annoyed to the point where I was ready to resign from the OHC. However, objective, open-minded branch presidents and the minister and his staff stressed that if I gave up the ship, the battle would be lost because mine was a credible opinion

to which the public would listen. Plus, I was one of the few people who could fight the establishment in hockey without personally having anything to lose. That is, they had no "hammer" over me as they did over some of the other volunteer executives.

43. Some adults who favored the status quo suspected that the investigators, with government encouragement, were on a witch hunt to get adults out of youth hockey and to destroy the good intentions of adult volunteers who devoted their leisure time to working with children.

44. At certain times in the research process, expediency may force a researcher to adopt a conflict model in order for action to occur. For example, it was clearly necessary to adopt a conflict stance when the final hockey report was tabled and consensus concerning implementation of the recommendations appeared to be impossible, at least initially.

45. For example, in the hockey study the major investigator had power, by virtue of intimate knowledge of the survey and forum concerns and of his mandate, to make recommendations. Similarly, the Minister of Culture and Recreation had both financial and legislative power. The investigator also had another version of the report, which could have been an exposé of inadequate leadership in minor hockey.

46. For example, some members of the OHC later admitted that as a result of the report and the aftermath, they had undergone a self-examination. They recognized that they were out of touch with the child and the local executives, and that future decisions and directions would be taken only after greater consultation with local executives, parents, and players.

47. A need to be more client-centered in the field exists. This process should begin by determining the social significance of field research to the various client groups, each of which must be identified early in the research process.

48. For example, in most communities, teams receive two points for a victory, one for a tie and zero for a loss. However, in one innovative community each hockey team is given 10 points at the start of the game, and if there are no infractions the winning team gets 12 points, the losers 10 points. Points are subtracted for infractions such as not giving players equal ice time (5 points), a major penalty (3 points), a misconduct penalty (2 points), exceeding the maximum number of penalty minutes per game (3 points). Thus, a team could lose a game but retain its 10 points for normative play and thereby gain more points than the team that won the game by scoring more goals, but that deviated from the rules and was penalized for its behavior while winning.

Action Knowledge and Policy Research: A Response to Lüschen and McPherson

C. Roger Rees

A recurring criticism of the field of sport sociology has been that it has not produced applied knowledge that can be used to answer "real" problems in the world of sport. Specifically, our field has been criticized for a functionalist research perspective, which tends to support the status quo (Scott, 1972), for its separation from physical education, itself an applied field, (Greendorfer, 1977c), and for its failure to tackle applied problems (Melnick, 1975, 1981). Thus, it is encouraging to review these chapters that call for the development of action knowledge in the sociology of sport (Lüschen, chapter 19) and show sociologists in the process of applying their knowledge (McPherson, chapter 20). Concern with the application of knowledge is certainly a thriving issue in the present field of sociology. Rossi and Whyte (1983), two leading practitioners in applied sociology, have pointed out that interest in applied-side sociology provides a valid measure of the financial health of the profession. As times get harder, interest in application rises (Rossi & Whyte, 1983). If this is the case, sociologists of sport should be very interested in application because the job market in academe is quite bleak. Sport sociologists can look with envy at other areas of the sport science (particularly exercise physiology) that have well-developed areas of application. If the subfield of sport sociology is to develop, it too must seek applied markets. Thus, there is both theoretical and practical interest in these papers.

Traditionally, sociologists have shown ambivalence toward applied research. According to Rossi (1980) and Rossi and Whyte (1983), sociologists have felt that basic research was somehow better than applied research. This issue has been relevant to the development of sport sociology because concern with academic legitimation may have led early scholars to subscribe to the value-free approach in their research (Melnick, 1981). Furthermore, because of the historical links between sport sociology and physical education, the basic versus applied issue has particular significance. Loy has pointed out a "catch-22" for sport sociologists housed in physical education departments. On the one hand, they are expected to do applied research by their physical education colleagues, which will not be accepted as high status by their sociology colleagues; on the other hand, basic research will not be accepted by physical educationalists (Loy, Kenyon & McPherson, 1980:104).

Recently Rossi and Whyte (1983) have suggested that the line between applied research and basic research is fuzzy. They cite several cases of basic research applied over time. Similar examples can be found in sport sociology. By applying Grusky's theory of organizational structure to professional sport, sociologists have demonstrated the "stacking" phenomenon in professional football and baseball (see Curtis & Loy, 1979, for a review). This has raised the level of consciousness about racial bias in sport and stimulated applied research in that area (Braddock, 1980).

In one sense all sociology of sport is applied, because of its subject matter, and the problem is how to convince potential users that the knowledge developed is valuable to them. Certainly Lüschen's call for the development of "action knowledge" is a step in the right direction, and it is logical to accept his assertion that this knowledge be used to train sport professionals such as teachers, coaches, and administrators. However, the gap between what is and what ought to be is very great. Although administrators of physical education programs in our universities agree that the present knowledge developed by sociology of sport is of value to physical education students, such knowledge is rarely part of their required curriculum (Southard, 1982; 1983). To convince sport professionals of the importance of sociological knowledge if they do not receive instruction in it is difficult. This state of affairs puts sociology of sport in a unique position relative to other sociological subfields that have a strong applied component (e.g., military sociology, criminal justice). To think of a criminal justice program without a sociological component is difficult; yet, Southard's research shows that physical education teachers and coaches (who typically get their training in physical education departments) may have no exposure to sociology of sport whatsoever.

Another problem confronting those who would extend applied sociology to contexts outside physical education and athletics is what Loy, Kenyon and McPherson (1980) have called the "critical mass" of knowledge. Is there enough quality research in sport sociology to warrant its consideration by clientele in the applied sector? Although sociologists have traditionally considered applied research to be less scientifically rigorous than basic research, Rossi and Whyte (1983) reject this claim and suggest that, if anything, the reverse is true. Because errors made as a result of sloppy applied research can be costly in both human and economic terms, the highest standards of methodology and statistical analysis are necessary. Although applied research may not mean less rigorous research, it may mean different research if the experience in other areas of the sport sciences is any indication. In sport psychology, where an applied perspective is very strong, recent literature reviews have been critical of the lack of theory testing (Dishman, 1983; Landers, 1983). They may share Loy's concern that the development of knowledge in the subfield, either sport psychology or sport sociology, may be threatened by an applied perspective.

Nevertheless, the chapter by McPherson is an example of quality research with practical application. In fact, it is a good example of the use of action knowledge that Lüschen is suggesting. McPherson gives a blow-by-blow account of how to persuade youth sport practitioners to make decisions based upon rationality (or at least based upon rationality as it is perceived by the sport sociologist). This task is not easy, given the power structure and vested interests in such bureaucratic organizations as youth league hockey. To be successful, sport sociologists need to manage their social identities during interaction with the organizational leaders and the public (itself a form of applied sociology). That the sport sociologist must go to much trouble to bring about change attests to the problem confronting applied sociology of sport in the future.

However, this review should not end on a pessimistic note. Applied sociology is gaining academic acceptance (Freeman, 1983), and much of the prejudice toward it within sociology is being reduced (Rossi & Whyte, 1983). Whyte (1980) gave examples of productive dialogue between sociologists and nonsociologists, which helped to solve human problems. These "social inventions" occur when the sociologist interacts on an equal footing with other scholars and practitioners interested in social problems. The hockey study in Ontario described by McPherson is an example of such a social invention. Similar social inventions could take place in fields such as gerontology (Streib, 1983), leisure (McPherson & Kozlik, 1980), and in fact, all areas in which involvement in sport and physical activity takes place.

Part 2
Questions for Further Study

In part 2 several substantive areas in the sociology of sport were analyzed from different theoretical perspectives. The theories are examples of what Kenyon (chapter 1) calls grand theories. Because they differ significantly in their domain assumptions, they may lead to different views of social reality in sport. How is the researcher able to reconcile these differences when using such theories to explain sport sociologically? Listed below are several unanswered questions for each substantive area. These questions may be suitable for term papers or class projects.

Socialization

Is the "new wave" of research in socialization and sport a realistic idea, given the chaotic situation in the parent discipline noted by McPherson in his review? How is the theoretical integration suggested by McPherson going to take place? Will not such theoretical and methodological sophistication (e.g., longitudinal studies) require a commitment of time and money that is unrealistic, given the present situation in higher education in which researchers in social science are being asked to teach more courses and are finding research funding increasingly difficult to obtain?

Small Group Research in Sport

Are the theoretical perspectives outlined in this section irreconcilable in small group research in sport? For example, if there is an increase in analysis at the group and system level, as suggested by Lüschen, how is Fine's idiosyncratic culture of sports groups preserved? How would Widmeyer and others who have measured group cohesion in sport with Likert-type scales treat Fine's proposal? Is the key to understanding the sport group to be found in the social interaction of group members, as Melnick suggests? In order to investigate this issue, how is social interaction conceptualized and measured? Will graph theory and network analysis replace sociometry?

Athletics and Higher Education

Sociologists of sport have always been concerned about intercollegiate athletics, but this concern has led to little practical change in this institution. Because sociologists are rarely involved in policy decisions, their revelations about the problems in athletics, which were summarized by Eitzen, rarely get considered by policymakers. Even if athletic administrators did discuss "social problems" in intercollegiate athletics, Frey suggests that they would be likely to reject such views as radical and left-wing. To what degree should sociologists of sport extend the conflict perspective into personal action against perceived inequities in college athletics (e.g., the Center for Athletes' Rights)? On the other hand, to what degree are the excesses of college athletics common to the system as a whole, to certain big-time programs, or particular revenue-producing sports (e.g., football and basketball) within such programs?

Applied Sociology of Sport

Given the practical issues raised in the previous sections of this summary, how realistic a proposition is applied sociology of sport? What exactly is "action knowledge," and how can sports practitioners be persuaded to pay money to sociologists of sport for applying it in specific contexts? Although McPherson was able to find funding for his hockey research, his study also demonstrated that it is very difficult to translate research findings into social change. Will sociologists of sport have to become more like psychologists of sport and try to convince coaches that their knowledge can produce "winners"? Is there an ethical problem in this approach if the sociologist realizes that the variables he or she is assessing are more complicated than the coach may think (e.g., the relationship between group cohesion and team success)? Does theory become irrelevant in this type of research? Sociologists who conduct applied research say that it does not, but psychologists of sport have recently noticed the lack of theory testing in their field at the present time (see Rees, chapter 21).

References

Aberle, D.F., A.K. Cohen, A.K. Davis, M.J. Levy and F.X. Sutton
1950 "The functional prerequisites of a society." Ethics 60:100-111.

Adler, P. and P. Adler
1978 "The role of momentum in sport." Urban Life 7:153-176.

Alba, R.D.
1981 "From small groups to social networks: mathematical approaches to group structure." American Behavioral Scientist 24:681-694.

Albinson, J. and G. Andrews (eds.)
1976 Child in Sport and Physical Activity. Baltimore: University Park Press.

Allardt, E.
1967 "Basic approaches in comparative sociological research and study of sport." International Review of Sport Sociology 2:89-108.

Allen, M.P., S.K. Panian and R.E. Lotz
1979 "Managerial succession and organizational performance: a recalcitrant problem revisited." Administrative Science Quarterly 24:167-180.

Anderson, C.H. and J.R. Gibson
1978 Toward a New Sociology, 3rd ed. Homewood, IL: Dorsey.

Ardrey, R.
1966 The Territorial Imperative. New York: Atheneum.

Arms, R., G. Russell and M. Sandilands
1980 Effects of Viewing Aggressive Sports or the Hostility of Spectators. Pp. 133-142 in R. Suinn (ed.), Psychology in Sports: Methods and Applications. Minneapolis, MN: Burgess.

Aseltine, G.
1978 "Family socialization preceptions among black and white high school students." Journal of Negro Education 43:256-265.

Askins, R.L., T.J. Carter and M. Wood
1981 "Rule enforcement in a public setting: the case of basketball officiating." Qualitative Sociology 4:87-101.

Atkin, C.
  1977 "Effects of campaign advertising and newscasts on children."
        Journalism Quarterly 54:503-508.
Atkinson, J. and N. Feather
  1966 A Theory of Achievement Motivation. New York: John Wiley
        and Sons.
Atyeo, D.
  1979 Blood and Guts: Violence in Sport. New York: Paddington Press.
Babcock, B. (ed.)
  1978 The Reversible World. Ithaca, NY: Cornell University Press.
Baiamonte, P.
  1981 "Baiamonte's pre-sentencing remarks." Albuquerque Journal,
        July 9, p. A6.
Baker, P.
  1981 "Social coalitions." American Behavioral Scientist, 24:633-647.
Bales, R.F.
  1950 Interaction Process Analysis. Cambridge, MA: Addison-Wesley.
  1970 Personality and Interpersonal Behavior. New York: Holt,
        Rinehart, and Winston.
Ball, D.W.
  1972 "Olympic games competition." International Journal of Com-
        parative Sociology 13:186-200.
  1973a "Ascription and position: a comparative analysis of stacking in
        professional football." Canadian Review of Sociology and An-
        thropology 10:97-111.
  1973b "Marx and the game of Monopoly." Fourth International ICSS
        Symposium, Bucharest, Romania. SIRLS Document B 0345.
  1975 "A note on method in the sociological study of sport." Pp. 39-47
        in D.W. Ball and J.W. Loy (eds.), Sport and the Social Order:
        Contributions to the Sociology of Sport. Reading, MA: Addison-
        Wesley.
  1976 "Failure in sport." American Sociological Review 41:726-739.
Ball, D.W. and J.W. Loy (eds.)
  1975 Sport and Social Order: Contributions to the Sociology of Sport.
        Reading, MA: Addison-Wesley.
Bandura, A. and R. Walters
  1963 Social Learning and Personality Development. New York: Holt,
        Rinehart & Winston.
Baran, S.
  1977 "Television programs as socializing agents for mentally retarded
        children." AV Communication Review 25:281-289.
Bass, B.M.
  1980 "Team productivity and individual member competence." Small
        Group Behavior 11(4):431-504.

Bateson, G.
  1972   Steps to an Ecology of Mind. New York: Chandler.
Baumrind, D.
  1978   "Parental disciplinary patterns and social competence in children." Youth and Society 9:239-276.
  1980   "New directions in socialization research." American Psychologist 35:639-652.
Beamish, R.
  1982   "Sport, value and the fetishism of commodities: central issues of alienated sport." Pp. 81-102 in A.G. Ingham and E.F. Broom (eds.), Career Patterns and Career Contingencies in Sport. Proceedings, 1st Regional Symposium, International Committee for the Sociology of Sport, May-June, 1981, University of British Columbia, Vancouver.
Bearison, D.
  1979   "Sex-linked patterns of socialization." Sex Roles 5:11-18.
Becker, E.
  1971   The Birth and Death of Meaning. New York: Free Press.
Becker, H.S.
  1967   "Whose side are we on?" Social Problems 14 (Winter):239-247.
Becker, H.S. and B. Geer
  1960   "Latent culture: a note on the theory of latent social roles." Administrative Science Quarterly 5:304-313.
Bell, R.
  1979   "Parent, child and reciprocal influences." American Psychologist 34:821-826.
Bell, R. and L. Harper
  1977   Child Effects on Adults. New York: John Wiley and Sons.
Bend, E. and B. Petrie
  1977   "Sport participation, scholastic. . ., and social mobility." Pp. 1-44 in R.S. Hutton (ed.), Exercise and Sport Sciences Reviews, Vol. 5. Santa Barbara, CA: Journal Publishing.
Bengtson, V.
  1975   "Generation and family effects in value socialization." American Sociological Review 40:358-371.
Bengtson, V. and N. Cutler
  1976   "Generations and intergenerational relations: perspectives on age groups and social change." Pp. 130-159 in R. Binstock and E. Shanas (eds.), Handbook of Aging and the Social Sciences. New York: Van Nostrand Reinhold Co.
Benton, T.
  1977   Philosophical Foundations of the Three Sociologies. London: Routledge & Kegan Paul.

Berger, G.
  1977   "The socialization of American females as a dysfunctional pro-
         cess: selected research." Journal of Research and Development
         in Education 10:3-11.
Berger, P.
  1971   "Sociology and freedom." American Sociologist 6:1-5.
Berger, P.L., B. Berger and H. Kellner
  1973   The Homeless Mind: Modernization and Consciousness. Garden
         City, NY: Vintage.
Berkowitz, L.
  1962   Aggression: A Social Psychological Analysis. New York: McGraw-
         Hill.
Bernstein, R.J.
  1976   The Restructuring of Social and Political Theory. Philadelphia:
         University of Pennsylvania Press/Harcourt, Brace, & Jovanovich.
Berryman, J. and J. Loy
  1976   "Secondary schools and ivy-league letters." British Journal of
         Sociology 27:61-77.
Bersani, C., J. Gillham and D. Napady
  1977   "Perceived expectations and role behavior of socialization agents:
         the case of the school counselor and SES areas." The Sociological
         Quarterly 18:384-398.
Birns, B.
  1976   "The emergence and socialization of sex differences in the earliest
         years." Merrill-Palmer Quarterly 22:229-254.
Birrell, S.
  1981   "Sport as ritual: interpretations from Durkheim to Goffman."
         Social Forces 60(2):354-376.
Black, S.
  1978   "The most ruthless game in sports." New West 24 (November
         20):81-102.
Blackburn, R.T. and M.S. Nyikos
  1974   "College football and Mr. Chips: all in the family." Phi Delta
         Kappan 56:110-113.
Blalock, H.M.
  1969   Theory Construction. Englewood Cliffs, NJ: Prentice-Hall.
  1979   "Measurement and conceptual problems: the major obstacle to
         integrating theory and research." American Sociological Review
         44:881-894.
Blau, P.
  1964   Exchange and Power in Social Life. New York: John Wiley and
         Sons.

Blau, P.M. and O.D. Duncan
  1967 The American Occupational Structure. New York: Jossey-Bass, Inc.
Blumer, H.
  1969 Symbolic Interactionism. Englewood Cliffs, NJ: Prentice-Hall.
  1980 "Comment: Mead and Blumer: the convergent methodological perspectives of social behaviorism and symbolic interactionism." American Sociological Review 45:409-419.
Boas, F.
  1963 The Mind of Primitive Man. New York: Collier. (Originally published, 1911)
Boldt, E.
  1979 "Homo sociologicus: under and/over-socialized." Society 3:1-5.
Borgatta, E.F. and P.M. Baker (eds.)
  1981a Small groups: an agenda for research and theory. American Behavioral Scientist (Special Issue) 24(5):601-717.
Borgatta, E.F. and P.M.Baker
  1981b "The small group movement." American Behavioral Scientist 24:607-618.
Borgatta, E.G. and R.F. Bales
  1953 "Task and accumulation of experience as factors in the interaction of small groups." Sociometry 16:239-252.
Bowles, S. and H. Gintis
  1976 Schooling in Capitalist America. New York: Basic Books.
Braddock, J.
  1980 Institutional Discrimination: A Study of Managerial Recruitment in Professional Football. Washington, DC: National Football League Players Association.
Broadbent, R.S.
  1974 "Notes on the sociology of the absurd." Pacific Sociological Review 17:35-45.
Brohm, J.M.
  1976 Critique Du Sport. Paris: Christian Bourgois.
  1978 Sport: A Prison of Measured Time. London: Ink Links.
Bronfenbrenner, U.
  1979 The Ecology of Human Development. Cambridge, MA: Harvard University Press.
Brundage, D.
  1980 "Mutual supports of home, school and community in the socialization of children." Pp. 150-177 in D. Radcliffe (ed.), The Family and the Socialization of Children. Ottawa: Social Science and Humanities Research Council of Canada.

Buriel, R.
   1981   "The relation of Anglo- and Mexican-American children's locus
           of control beliefs to parents' and teachers' socialization prac-
           tices." Child Development 51:104-113.
Buss, D.
   1981   "Predicting parent-child interactions from children's activity
           level." Developmental Psychology 17:59-65.
Cady, E.H.
   1978   The Big Game: College Sports and American Life. Knoxville:
           University of Tennessee Press.
Caplow, T.
   1956   "A theory of coalitions in the triad." American Sociological
           Review 21:489-493.
Carpenter, C. and A. Huston-Stein
   1980   "Activity structure and sex-typed behavior in preschool chil-
           dren." Child Development 51(3):862-872.

Carron, A.
   1978   "Role behavior and coach-athlete interaction." International
           Review of Sport Sociology 13:51-65.
   1980   Social Psychology of Sport. Ithaca, NY: Movement Press.
   1981   "Sport Psychology in the 1980s: status, direction and challenges
           in the domain of group dynamics." Paper presented at the
           Annual Meeting of the North American Society for the
           Psychology of Sport and Physical Activity, Monterey, CA, June
           2.
Carron, A. and B. Bennett
   1977   "Compatibility in the coach-athlete dyad." Research Quarter-
           ly 48:671-679.
Carron, A. and P. Chelladurai
   1981   "The dynamics of group cohesion in sport." International Jour-
           nal of Sport Psychology 3(2):123-139.

Carron, A. and G. Garvie
   1978   "Compatibility and successful performance." Perceptual and
           Motor Skills 46:1121-1122.
Cartwright, D.
   1968   "The nature of group cohesiveness." Pp. 91-109 in D. Cart-
           wright and A. Zander (eds.), Group Dynamics. New York:
           Harper and Row.
Cartwright, D. and A. Zander (eds.)
   1953   Group Dynamics (1st Ed.). Evanston, IL: Row, Peterson.
   1968   Group Dynamics (3rd Ed.). New York: Harper and Row.
Cassirer, E.
   1910   Substanzbegriff und Funktionsbegriff. Berlin: B. Cassirer.

Cavallo, D.
1981 Muscles and Morals: Organized Playgrounds and Urban Reform, 1880-1920. Philadelphia: University of Pennsylvania Press.
Chambliss, W.J. and T.E. Ryther
1975 Sociology. New York: McGraw-Hill.
Chapman, I.
1972 "The dyad: social and para-social." International Journal of Contemporary Sociology 9:182-187.
Chataway, C. and P. Goodhart
1968 War Without Weapons. London: Allen.
Chelladurai, P.
1978 Multidimensional Model of Leadership. Unpublished doctoral dissertation, University of Waterloo, Ontario.
1980 "Leadership in sport organizations." Journal of Applied Sport Sciences 5:226-231.
Chelladurai, P. and A. Carron
1977 "A reanalysis of formal structure in sport." Canadian Journal of Applied Sport Science 2:9-14.
Chesney, K.
1970 The Victorian Underworld. Newton Abbot, Devon, Canada: Readers Union Group.
Chicago Tribune
1980 (Quote by P. Rozelle) October 8, Section 4:14.
Coakley, J.J.
1978 Sport in Society: Issues and Controversies. St. Louis: Mosby.
1979 "Play group versus organized competitive team: a comparison." Pp. 118-127 in D.S. Eitzen (ed.), Sport in Contemporary Society: An Anthology. New York: St. Martin's Press.
1981 "Sociological theory and organized youth sports." Paper presented at the meetings of the American Alliance for Health, Physical Education, Recreation, and Dance. Boston.
1982 Sport in Society: Issues and Controversies (2nd Ed.). St. Louis: Mosby.
Coleman, J.
1972 Policy Research in the Social Sciences. Morristown, NJ: General Learning Press.
Coles, R.W.
1975 "Football as a 'surrogate' religion?" Pp. 61-77 in M. Hill (ed.), Sociological Yearbook of Religion, No. 8. London: SCM Press Ltd.
Collins, R.
1975 Conflict Sociology: Toward an Explanatory Science. New York: Academic Press.

Collins, E. and H. Guetzkow
  1964 A Social Psychology of Group Processes for Decision Making.
        New York: John Wiley and Sons.
Cook, N. and Z. Blau
  1978 "Parent behavior: an interdisciplinary perspective on its socializa-
        tion effects." Youth and Society 9:231-238.
Cooley, C.H.
  1964 Human Nature and the Social Order. New York: Schocken.
        (Originally published, 1902.)
Corrigan, P.
  1977 The Dialectics of Doing Nothing. New York: Macmillan.
Cottrell, L. and E. Sheldon
  1964 "Problems of collaboration between social scientists and the prac-
        ticing professions." The Annals of the American Academy of
        Social Science 346:127-128.
Coulson, M.A. and C. Riddell
  1980 Approaching Sociology. London: Routledge & Kegan.
Covenay, P.
  1967 The Image of Childhood. Baltimore: Penguin.
Cross, G.L.
  1977 Presidents Can't Punt. Norman: Oklahoma University Press.
Crozier, M.
  1964 The Bureaucratic Phenomenon. Chicago: University of Chicago
        Press.
Crozier, M. and E. Friedberg
  1980 Actors and Systems. The Politics of Collective Action. Chicago:
        University of Chicago Press.
Csikszentmihalyi, M.
  1975 Beyond Boredom and Anxiety. San Francisco: Jossey-Bass.
Cullen, J.B. and F.T. Cullen
  1975 "The structural and contextual conditions of group norm viola-
        tion." International Review of Sports Sociology 10(2):69-78.
Curtis, J.E., D.M. Connor and J. Harp
  1970 "An emergent professional community: French and English
        sociologists and anthropologists in Canada." Social Science In-
        formation 9(4):113-136.
Curtis, J.E. and J.W. Loy
  1979 "Race/ethnicity and relative centrality of playing position in team
        sports." Pp. 285-313 in R.S. Hutton (ed.), Exercise and Sport
        Sciences Reviews: Vol. 6. Philadelphia: The Franklin Institute
        Press.
Curtis, J.E. and J.W. Petras
  1970 "Introduction." Pp. 1-85 in J.E. Curtis and J.W. Petras (eds.),
        The Sociology of Knowledge: A Reader. New York: Praeger.

Curtis, R.
1974 "The issue of schools as social systems: Socialization effects from lengths of membership." The Sociological Quarterly 15(2):277-293.
Dahrendorf, R.
1959 Class and Class Conflict in Industrial Society. Stanford: Stanford University Press.
Danielson, R.
1978 "Contingency model of leadership effectiveness: for empirical investigation of its application in sport." Pp. 345-354 in F. Landry and W.A.R. Urban (eds.), Motor Learning, Sport Psychology, Pedagogy and Didactics of Physical Activity. Miami: Symposia Specialists. (A collection of the formal papers presented at the International Congress of Physical Activity Sciences, Quebec City, July 11-16, 1976.)
Davis, J.H.
1969 Group Performance. Reading, MA: Addison-Wesley.
Davis, K.
1959 "The myth of functional analysis as a special method of sociology and anthropology." American Sociological Review 24:757-772.
Dawe, A.
1970 "The two sociologies." British Journal of Sociology 21:207-218.
DeCrow, K.
1980 "Hardlining Title IX." Civil Rights Quarterly Perspectives 12 (Summer):16-23.
DeKoven, B.
1978 The Well Played Game. New York: Anchor Books.
Denlinger, K. and L. Shapiro
1975 Athletes for Sale. New York: Thomas Y. Crowell.
Denzin, N.
1970 The Research Act: Chicago: Aldine.
1977 "Notes on the criminogenic hypothesis: a case study of the American liquor industry." American Sociological Review 42:905-920.
1978 "Crime and the American liquor industry." Pp. 87-118 in N. Denzin (ed.), Studies in Symbolic Interaction, Vol. 1. Greenwich, CT: Jai Press, Inc.
Deutsch, M.
1968 "Field theory in social psychology." Vol 1. Pp. 412-487 in G. Lindzey and E. Aronson (eds.), The Handbook of Social Psychology (2nd Ed.). Reading, MA: Addison-Wesley.
Devereux, E.
1976 "Backyard versus Little League baseball: the impoverishment of children's games." Pp. 37-56 in D. Landers (ed.), Social Problems in Athletics. Urbana, IL: University of Illinois Press.

De Vos, G.
  1980 "Ethnic adaptation and minority status." Journal of Cross-
         Cultural Psychology 11:101-124.
DeWar, C.K.
  1980 "Spectator fights at professional baseball games." Review of
         Sport and Leisure 1(June):12-25.
Di Renzo, G.
  1977 "Socialization, personality, and social systems." Annual Review
         of Sociology 3:261-295.
Dishman, R.K.
  1983 "Identity crisis in North American sport psychology: academics
         in professional issues." Journal of Sport Psychology 5(2):123-134.
Dollard, J., L. Doob, N. Miller, O. Mowrer and R. Sears
  1939 Frustration and Aggression. New Haven, CT: Yale University
         Press.
Donnelly, P.
  1978 Group Cohesion and Sport. CAHPER Monograph. Calgary:
         University Press.
Dorsey, B., P. Lawson and V. Pezer
  1980 "The relationship between women's basketball performance and
         the will to win." Canadian Journal of Applied Sport Sciences
         5:91-93.
Douglas, J.D., P.A. Adler, A. Fontana, C.R. Freeman and J. Kotarba
  1980 Introduction to the Sociologies of Everyday Life. Boston: Allyn
         and Bacon.
Dowd, J.
  1980 Stratification Among the Aged. Monterey, CA: Brooks Cole.
Dunning, E.
  1967 "Notes on some conceptual and theoretical problems in the
         sociology of sport." International Review of Sport Sociology
         2:143-150.
  1973 "The structural-functional properties of folk-games and modern
         sports: a sociological analysis." Sportwissenschaft 3(3):215-232.
  1979 "The figurational dynamics of modern sport." Sportwissenschaft
         9:341-359.
  1980 "Social bonding and the socio-genesis of violence." Conference
         Proceedings, Bio-Social Aspects of Sport, London.
  1983 "Social bonding and violence in sport." Pp. 129-146 in J. Gold-
         stein (ed.), Sports Violence. New York: Springer-Verlag.
Dunning, E. and K. Sheard
  1976 "The bifurcation of Rubgy Union and Rugby League: a case study
         of organizational conflict and change." International Review of
         Sport Sociology 11(2):31-72.
  1979 Barbarians, Gentlemen and Players. New York: New York
         University Press.

Durkheim, E.
1964   The Division of Labour in Society. New York: Macmillan.
1976   The Elementary Forms of the Religious Life. London: George Allen & Unwin.
Durkin, H.
1964   The Group in Depth. New York: International Universities Press.
Edwards, H.
1973   Sociology of Sport. New York: Irwin-Dorsey.
1980   The Structure That Must Be. New York: Free Press.
Edwards, H. and V. Rackages
1977   "The dynamics of violence in American sport." Journal of Sport and Social Issues 1(2):3-31.
Eibl-Eibesfieldt, I.
1971   Love and Hate: The Natural History of Behavior Patterns. London: Methuen.
Eitzen, D. and G.H. Sage
1978   Sociology of American Sport. Dubuque, IA: Wm. C. Brown.
Eitzen, D.S. and N. Yetman
1972   "Managerial change, longevity and organizational effectiveness." Administrative Science Quarterly 17(1):110-116.
Elias, N.
1974   "The sciences: Towards a theory." Pp. 21-42 in R. Whitley (ed.), Social Processes of Scientific Development. London: Routledge & Kegan Paul.
1978a The Civilizing Process: The History of Manners. New York: Urizen Books; Oxford: Blackwell.
1978b What is Sociology? London: Hutchinson.
Elias, N. and E. Dunning
1966a "Dynamics of group sports with special reference to football." British Journal of Sociology 17:388-401.
1966b "Zur Dynamic von Sportgruppen." Pp. 118-134 in G. Lüschen (ed.) Kleingruppenforschung und Gruppe im Sport. Köln and Opladen: Westdeutscher Verlag. (English version in British Journal of Sociology.)
1969   "The quest for excitement in leisure." Society and Leisure, (2).
1970   "The quest for excitement in unexciting societies." Pp. 31-51 in G. Lüschen (ed.), A Cross-Cultural Analysis of Sports and Games. Champaign, IL: Stipes.
Ellis, G., G. Lee and L. Peterson
1978   "Supervision and conformity: a cross-cultural analysis of parental socialization values." American Journal of Sociology 84:386-403.
Emerson, R.M.
1966a "Mount Everest." Pp. 135-176 in G. Lüschen (ed.), Kleingruppenforschung und Gruppe im Sport. Köln and

Opladen: Westdeutscher Verlag. (English version in Sociometry 29(3):213-227.

1966b "Mount Everest: a case study of communication feedback and sustained group goal-striving." Sociometry 29:213-227.

Erbach, G.
1966 "The science of sport and sports sociology: questions related to the development and problems of structure." International Review of Sport Sociology 1:97-126.

Evans, T.
1979 "Creativity, sex-role socialization and pupil-teacher interactions in early schooling." The Sociological Review 27:139-155.

Eysenck, H.J. and D.K. Nias
1978 Sex, Violence, and the Media. London: Maurice, Temple, Smith.

Fagen, R.
1980 Animal Play Behavior. Oxford: Oxford University Press.

Faulkner, R.
1974a "Coming of age in organizations: a comparative study of career contingencies and adult socialization." Sociology of Work and Occupations 1(2):131-173.
1974b "Making violence by doing work: selves, situations, and the world of professional hockey." Sociology of Work and Occupations 1(3):288-312.

Feiring, C. and M. Lewis
1978 "The child as a member of the family system." Behavioral Science 23:225-233.

Feldman, S.
1979 "Nested identities." Pp. 399-418 in N. Denzin (ed.), Studies in Symbolic Interaction, Vol. 2. Greenwich, CT: Jai Press.

Feyerabend, P.
1979 Erkenntnis fur freie Menschen. Frankfurt: Suhrkamp.

Fiedler, F.E.
1960 "The leader's psychological distance and group effectiveness." Pp. 586-606 in D. Cartwright and A. Zander (eds.), Group Dynamics. Evanston, IL: Row, Peterson.
1964 "A contingency model of leadership effectiveness." Pp. 150-190 in L. Berkowitz (ed.), Advances in Experimental Social Psychology, Vol. 1. New York: Academic Press.
1968 "Personality and situational determinants of leadership effectiveness." Pp. 362-380 in D. Cartwright and A. Zander (eds.), Group Dynamics. New York: Harper and Row.
1981 "Leadership effectiveness." American Behavioral Scientist 24(5):619-632.

Fine, G.A.
  1979a "Preadolescent socialization through organized athletics: the construction of moral meanings in Little League baseball." Pp. 79-105 in M. Krotee (ed.), The Dimensions of Sport Sociology. West Point, NY: Leisure Press.
  1979b "Small group culture creation: the idioculture of Little League Baseball teams." American Sociological Review 44:733-745.

Flacks, R. and G. Turkel
  1978 "Radical sociology: the emergence of neo-Marxian perspectives in U.S. sociology." Annual Review of Sociology 4:193-238.

Fluegelman, A.
  1976 The New Games Book. New York: Dolphin.

Földesi, T.
  1978 "Investigation for the objective measurement of cooperative ability among the members of rowing teams." International Review of Sport Sociology 13:48-70.

Forcese, D. and S. Richer
  1975 Issues in Canadian Society. Scarborough, Ontario: Prentice-Hall.

Forward, J.
  1969 "Group achievement motivation and individual motives to achieve success and avoid failure." Journal of Personality 37:297-309.

Freeman, H.E.
  1983 "Introduction." In H.E. Freeman, R.R. Dynes, P.H. Rossi and W.F. Whyte (eds.), Applied Sociology: Roles and Activities of Sociologists in Diverse Settings. San Francisco: Jossey-Bass.

Freese, L.
  1980 "Formal theorizing." Annual Review of Sociology 6:187-212.
  1981 "The formalization of theory and method." American Behavioral Scientist (January) 24:345-363.

Frey, J.H.
  1979 "The coming demise of intercollegiate athletics." Arena Review 3:34-43.
  1982 The Governance of Intercollegiate Athletics. West Point, NY: Leisure Press.

Fromm, E.
  1977 The Anatomy of Human Destructiveness. New York: Penguin.

Furlong, W.B.
  1980 "Violence in sport." New York Times Magazine (Nov. 30),
        Pp. 41, 122-134.
Furman, W. and J. Masters
  1980 "Peer interactions, sociometric status, and resistance to
        deviation in young children." Developmental Psychology
        16:229-236.
Gamson, W.
  1961 "A theory of coalition formation." American Sociological Review
        26:373-382.
Garfinkel, H.
  1956 "Conditions of successful degradation ceremonies." American
        Journal of Sociology 61:420-424.
Garvey, K.
  1977 Play. Cambridge, MA: Harvard University Press.
Gaskell, G. and R. Pearton
  1979 "Aggression and sport." Pp. 263-295 in J. Goldstein (ed.), Sports,
        Games and Play. Hillsdale, NJ: Lawrence Erlbaum Associates.
George, L.
  1980 Role Transitions in Later Life. Monterey, CA: Brooks/Cole.
Gerson, E.
  1976 "On quality of life." American Sociological Review 41:793-806.
Giddens, A.
  1976 New Rules of Sociological Method. London: Hutchinson.
  1979 Central Problems in Social Theory. London: Hutchinson.
Glaser, B. and A. Strauss
  1967 The Discovery of Grounded Theory. Chicago: Aldine.
Gleichmann, P., J. Goudsblom and H. Korte (eds.)
  1977 Human Figuration. Amsterdam: Amsterdams Sociologisch
        Tijdschrift.
Glossop, R.
  1980 "Trends in family studies: towards an appropriate discourse."
        Pp. 186-244 in D. Radcliffe (ed.), The Family and the Socializa-
        tion of Children. Ottawa: Social Sciences and Humanities
        Research Council of Canada.
Gmelch, G.J.
  1971 "Baseball magic." Trans-Action 8:39-41, 54.
Goffman, E.
  1952 "Cooling the mark out: some adaptations to failure." Psychiatry
        15:451-463.
  1959 The Presentation of Self in Everyday Life. New York: Doubleday.
  1961a Asylums. Garden City, NY: Doubleday.
  1961b Encounters: Two Studies in the Sociology of Interaction. Indian-
        apolis: Bobbs-Merrill.
  1967 Interaction Ritual. Garden City, NY: Doubleday.

1976 "Replies and responses." Language in Society 5:257-313.

1981 Forms of Talk. Philadelphia: University of Pennsylvania Press.

Gold, D. and D. Andres

1978 "Comparisons of adolescent children with employed and nonemployed mothers." Merrill-Palmer Quarterly 24:243-254.

Goldstein, J.H.

1975 Aggression and Crimes of Violence. Oxford: Oxford University Press.

1979 "Outcomes in professional team sports: chance, skill and situational factors." Pp. 401-408 in J.H. Goldstein (ed.), Sports, Games and Play. Hillsdale: Lawrence Erlbaum Associates.

Goldstein, J. and R. Arms

1971 "Effects of observing athletic contests on hostility." Sociometry 34(1):83-90.

Good, P.

1979a "The shocking inequalities of the NCAA." Sport 68 (January):35-38.

1979b "Reform—or be reformed." Sport 68 (April):14, 104.

Goode, W.J.

1967 "Protection of the inept." American Sociological Review 32:5-19.

1973 Explorations in Social Theory. New York: Oxford University Press.

Goodman, G.

1979 Choosing Sides: Playground and Street Life on the Lower East Side. New York: Schocken.

Gosset, D.

1980 Cohesion Variability as a Predictor Variable in the Cohesion Performance Outcome Relationship. Unpublished master's thesis, University of Waterloo, Waterloo, Ontario.

Goudsblom, J.

1977 Sociology in the Balance. Oxford: Oxford University Press.

Gould, D.

1982 "Sport psychology in the 1980's: status, direction and challenge in youth sport research." Journal of Sport Psychology 4:203-218.

Gouldner, A.W.

1959 "Reciprocity and autonomy in functional theory." Pp. 241-270 in L. Gross (ed.), Symposium in Sociological Theory. New York: Harper and Row.

1970 The Coming Crisis of Western Sociology. New York: Basic Books.

Gove, W.R.

1979 "The review process and its consequences in the major sociology journals." Contemporary Sociology 8:799-804.

Graham, H.D. and T.R. Gurr

1969 The History of Violence in America: Historical and Comparative Perspectives. New York: Bantam Books.

Gray, G. and J. Gruber
  1981 "The relationships between elements of team cohesiveness and team success at various levels of basketball competition." Paper presented at American Association for Health, Physical Education and Recreation. Milwaukee.
Greenberger, E. and H. Sorensen
  1974 "Toward a concept of psychosocial maturity." Journal of Youth and Adolescence 3:329-358.
Greendorfer, S.
  1977a "Intercollegiate football: an approach toward rationalization." International Review of Sport Sociology 12:27-34.
  1977b "Role of socializing agents in female sport involvement." Research Quarterly 48:304-310.
  1977c "Sociology of sport: knowledge for what?" Quest 28:58-65.
  1978 "Socialization into sport." Pp. 115-140 in C. Oglesby (ed.), Women and Sport. Philadelphia: Lea and Febiger.
  1979 "Differences in childhood socialization influences of women involved in sport and women not involved in sport." Pp. 59-72 in M. Krotee (ed.), The Dimensions of Sport Sociology. West Point, NY: Leisure Press.
  1981 "Emergence of and future prospects for sociology of sport." Pp. 379-398 in G.A. Brooks (ed.), Perspectives on the Academic Discipline of Physical Education. Champaign, IL: Human Kinetics.
Greendorfer, S. and M. Ewing
  1981 "Race and gender differences in children's socialization into sport." Research Quarterly for Exercise and Sport 52:301-310.
Greendorfer, S. and J. Lewko
  1978 "Role of family members in sport socialization of children." Research Quarterly 49:146-152.
Gross, E.
  1978 "Organizational crime: a theoretical perspective." Pp. 55-85 in N. Denzin (ed.), Studies in Symbolic Interaction, Vol. 1. Greenwich, CT: Jai Press.
Gross, J.
  1981 "A women reporter in Yankee country." The New York Times Magazine (October 25):32-45.
Gruneau, R.S.
  1975 "Sport, social differentiation and social inequality." Pp. 121-184 in D.W. Ball and J.W. Loy (eds.), Sport and Social Order. Reading, MA: Addison-Wesley.
  1978a "Conflicting standards and problems of personal action in the sociology of sport." Quest 30:80-90.

1978b "Elites, class and corporate power in Canadian sport: some preliminary findings." Pp. 201-242 in F. Landry and W.A.R. Orban (eds.), Sociology and Legal Aspects of Sports and Leisure. Miami: Symposia Specialists.

1981 Class, Sports and Social Development: A Study in Social Theory and Historical Sociology. Unpublished doctoral dissertation, University of Massachusetts, Amherst.

Grusky, O.
1963a "Managerial succession and organizational effectiveness." American Journal of Sociology 69:21-31.

1963b "The effects of formal structure on management recruitment: a study of baseball organization." Sociometry 26:345-353.

Guppy, L.
1974 The Effect of Selected Socialization Practices on the Sport Achievement Orientations of Male and Female Adolescents. Unpublished master's thesis, University of Waterloo, Ontario.

Gusfield, J.
1981 The Culture of Public Problems. Chicago: University of Chicago Press.

Guttman, A.
1978 From Ritual to Record: The Nature of Modern Sport. New York: University of Columbia Press.

Haag, H.
1979 "Development and structure of a theoretical framework for sport science (Sportwissenschaft)." Quest 31(1):25-35.

Hackman, J. and C. Morris
1975 "Group tasks, group interaction process, and group performance effectiveness: a review and proposed integration." Pp. 45-99 in I. Berkowitz (ed.), Advances in Experimental Social Psychology, Vol. 8. New York: Academic Press.

Hahn, C.
1978 "Review of research on sex roles: implications for social studies research." Theory and Research in Social Education 6:73-99.

Hall, B.
1974 "'Competence' and its assessment in a professional training situation." The Australian and New Zealand Journal of Sociology 10:221-222.

Hammel, B.
1980 "The passing game: student athletes as illegal receivers." Phi Delta Kappan (September):7-13.

Hanford, G.H.
1974 An Inquiry into the Need for and Feasibility of a National Study of Intercollegiate Athletics. Washington, DC: American Council on Education.

Hans, J.S.
  1981   The Play of the World. Amherst, MA: University of Massa-
         chusetts Press.
Hansen, D.A.
  1976   An Invitation to Critical Sociology. New York: The Free Press.
Hare, A.
  1972   Handbook of Small Group Research. New York: The Free Press.
Harrington, J.A.
  1968   Soccer Hooliganism. Bristol: John Wright and Sons.
Harris, D. and D.S. Eitzen
  1978   "The consequences of failure." Urban Life 7:177-188.
Harrison, P.
  1974   "Soccer's tribal wars." New Society 29 (September 5).
Hartup, W.
  1979   "The social worlds of childhood." American Psychologist
         34:944-950.
Hasdorf, A. and H. Cantril
  1954   "They saw a game." Journal of Abnormal and Social Psychology
         49:129-134.
Hauser, P.M.
  1981   "Sociology's progress toward science." The American
         Sociologist 16(1):62-64.
Hawkes, G.
  1978   "Who will rear our children?" The Family Coordinator
         27:159-166.
Heinila, K.
  1966   "Notes on inter group conflict in sport." International Review
         of Sports Sociology 1:31-38.
  1967   "Kuntien Liikuntatoiminnan Suunnittein." (Community plan-
         ning in sport and physical activities.) Pp. 163-180 in Kunnan Kult-
         tuuripolitiikka, Suomen Kultuurirahasto.
Helmes, R.C.
  1978   "Ideology and social control in Canadian sport: A theoretical
         review." Working Papers in the Sociological Study of Sports and
         Leisure 1(4):1-54. Kingston, Ontario: Queen's University.
  1982   "The philosophy of science and the problem of alienated sport
         labor." Pp. 103-185 in A.G. Ingham and E.F. Broom (eds.),
         Career Patterns and Career Contingencies in Sport. First Regional
         Symposium, International Committee for the Sociology of Sport,
         May-June, 1981, University of British Columbia, Vancouver.
Hempel, C.G.
  1959   "The logic of functional analysis." Pp. 271-310 in L. Gross (ed.),
         Symposium on Sociological Theory. New York: Harper and Row.
  1965   Aspects of Scientific Explanation. New York: Free Press.
Henderson, R.

1981   Parent-Child Interaction: Theory, Research and Prospects. New York: Academic Press.

Hessler, R., P. New and J.T. May

1979   "Power, exchange and research-development link." Human Organization 38:334-342.

1980   "Conflict, consensus and exchange." Social Problems 27:320-332.

Hoch, P.

1972   Rip Off the Big Game: The Exploitation of Sports by the Power Elite. New York: Anchor Books.

Hoffman, L.

1972   "Early childhood experiences and women's achievement motives." Journal of Social Issues 28:129-155.

1977   "Changes in family roles, socialization, and sex differences." American Psychologist 32:644-657.

Homans, G.C.

1950   The Human Group. New York: Harcourt, Brace.

1962   Social Behavior: Its Elementary Forms. New York: Harcourt, Brace, World.

1980   "Discovery and the discovered in social theory." Pp. 17-22 in H.M. Blalock (ed.), Sociological Theory and Research. New York: Free Press.

Horowitz, I.L.

1967   Power, Politics and People. New York: Oxford University Press.

Horton, J.

1966   "Order and conflict theories of social problems as competing ideologies." American Journal of Sociology 71:701-713.

Hughes, E.

1937   "Institutional office and the person." American Journal of Sociology 43:404-413.

Hughes, R. and J. Coakley

1978   "Player violence and the social organization of contact sport." Journal of Sport Behavior 1(4):155-168.

Huizinga, J.

1955   Homo Ludens. Boston, MA: Beacon Press.

Inciong, P.

1974   Leadership Styles and Team Success. Unpublished doctoral dissertation, University of Utah, Salt Lake City.

James, C.W.

1963   Beyond a Boundry. London: Stanley Paul.

Jensen, R. and J. Heim (eds.)

1981   The Child in Sport. Toronto: Ontario Research Council on Leisure.

Johnson, D.P.

1981   Sociological Theory: Classical Founders and Contemporary Perspectives. New York: John Wiley and Sons.

Kane, J.
  1976 "Personality and physical ability." In G. Kenyon (ed.), Contemporary Psychology in Sport. Chicago: Chicago Athletic Institute.
Kaul, T.J. and R.L. Bednar
  1978 "Conceptualizing group research: a publishing analysis." Small Group Behavior 9:173-191.
Kenyon, G. and B. McPherson
  1973 "Becoming involved in physical activity and sport: a process of socialization." Pp. 303-332 in G.L. Rarick (ed.), Physical Activity: Human Growth and Development. New York: Academic Press.
  1981 "The significance of social theory in the development of sport sociology." Paper presented at the Second Annual Conference of the North American Society for the Sociology of Sport, Fort Worth, TX.
Kerlinger, F. and E. Pedhazur
  1973 Multiple Regression in Behavioral Research. New York: Holt, Rinehart and Winston.
Kessen, W.
  1979 "The American child and other cultural inventions." American Psychologist 34:815-820.
Khleit, B.
  1975 "Professionalization of school superintendents: a sociocultural study of an elite program." Human Organization 34:301-308.
Kidd, B.
  1978 The Political Economy of Sport. Sociology of Sport Monograph Series. Ottawa: CAHPER.
Kidd, T. and W. Woodman
  1975 "Sex and orientations toward winning in sport." Research Quarterly 46(4):476-483.
King, J. and P. Chi
  1979 "Social structure, sex roles, and personality: comparisons of male/female athletes/nonathletes." Pp. 115-148 in J. Goldstein (ed.), Sports, Games and Play. Hillsdale, NY: Lawrence Erlbaum.
Kiviaho, P. and U. Mustikkamaa
  1978 "Intra-group conflict in sport audiences during inter-group competition: a test of the conflict-integration hypothesis." Pp. 267-282 in F. Landry and W.A.B. Orban (eds.), Sociology of Sport: Sociological Studies and Administrative, Economic and Legal Aspects of Sports and Leisure. Miami, FL: Symposia Specialists.
Klapp, O.
  1969 Collective Search for Identity. New York: Holt, Rinehart, Winston.

Klecka, C. and D. Hiller
1977 "Adolescent gender-role socialization. Sex-Roles 3:241-255.
Kleiber, D. and J. Kelly
1980 "Leisure, socialization, and the life cycle." Pp. 91-137 in S. Iso-Ahola (ed.), Social Psychological Perspectives on Leisure and Recreation. Springfield, IL: Charles C. Thomas.
Klein, M. and G. Christiansen
1966 "Gruppenkomposition, Gruppenstruktur und Effektivitat von Basketballmannschaften." Pp. 180-191 in G. Lüschen (ed.), Kleingruppenforschung und Gruppe im Sport, Köln and Opladen: Westdeutscher Verlag.
1969 "Group composition, group structure, and group effectiveness of basketball teams." Pp. 397-407 in J. Loy and G. Kenyon (eds.), Sport, Culture, and Society: A Reader on the Sociology of Sport. London: Macmillan.
Kleinman, S. and G. Fine
1979 "Rhetoric and action in moral organizations—social control of Little Leaguers and ministry students." Urban Life 8(3):275-294.
Knapp, M. and H. Knapp
1976 One Potato, Two Potato: New York: Norton.
Knight, G. and S. Kagan
1977 "Acculturation of prosocial and competitive behaviors among second- and third-generation Mexican-American children." Journal of Cross-Cultural Psychology 8:273-284.
Knowles, M. and H. Knowles
1972 Introduction to Group Dynamics. New York: Association Press.
Knox, W. and H. Kupterer
1971 "Discontinuity in the socialization of males in the United States." Merrill-Palmer Quarterly 17:251-261.
Komorita, S. and J. Chertkoff
1973 "A bargaining theory of coalition formation." Psychological Review 80:149-162.
Korr, C.P.
1982 "Class and community—The formation and control of an English professional football club." Pp. 4-19 on A.G. Ingham and E.F. Broom (eds.), Career Patterns and Career Contingencies in Sport. Proceedings of the ICSS First Regional Symposium, Vancouver.
Krotee, M.L.
1981 "The battle of the sexes: a brawl in the locker room." Journal of Sport and Social Issues 5:15-23.
Kuhlman, W.
1975 "Violence in professional sports." Wisconsin Law Review 3:771-790.

Kuhn, T.S.
  1962 The Structure of Scientific Revolutions. Chicago, IL: University
        of Chicago Press.
  1970 The Structure of Scientific Revolutions. Chicago, IL University
        of Chicago Press. (Originally published in 1962).
Kumagai, F.
  1978 "Socialization of youth in Japan and the United States." Jour-
        nal of Comparative Family Studies 9:335-346.
Lakoff, G. and M. Johnson
  1980 Metaphors We Live By. Chicago: University of Chicago Press.
Lamb, M. and M. Stevenson
  1978 "Father-infant relationships: their nature and importance."
        Youth and Society 9:277-298.
Landecker, W.S.
  1970 "Status congruence, class crystallization and social cleavage."
        Sociology and Social Research 54(3):343-355.
Landers, D.M.
  1983 "Whatever happened to theory testing in sport psychology?"
        Journal of Sport Psychology 5(2):135-151.
Landers, D., L.R. Brawley and D. Landers
  1981 "Group performance, interaction and leadership." Pp. 297-315
        in G. Lüschen and G. Sage (eds.), Handbook of Social Science
        of Sport. Champaign, IL: Stipes.
Landers, D. and G. Lüschen
  1974 "Team performance outcome and cohesiveness of competitive
        co-acting groups." International Review of Sport Sociology
        9:57-69.
Langlois, J. and A. Downs
  1980 "Mothers, fathers, and peers as socializing agents of sex-typed
        play behavior in young children." Child Development 51:1237-
        1247.
LaPiere, R.
  1934 "Attitudes versus actions." Social Forces 13:230-237.
Larson, K.
  1980 "'Keep up the chatter': ritual communications in American sum-
        mer softball." Paper presented at the annual meeting of the
        American Anthropological Association, Washington, DC.
Larson, L.
  1974 "An examination of the salience hierarchy during adolescence:
        the influence of the family. Adolescence 9:317-332.
  1980 "The multicultural dimension and family variability." Pp. 47-81
        in D. Radcliffe (ed.), The Family and the Socialization of
        Children. Ottawa: Social Sciences and the Humanities Research
        Council of Canada.

Laska, S. and M. Micklin
  1979 "The knowledge dimension of occupational socialization: role models and their social influence." Youth and Society 10:360-378.
Laslett, B.
  1978 "Family membership, past and present." Social Problems 25:476-490.
Lawler, E. and G. Youngs
  1975 "Coalition formulation: an integrative model." Sociometry 38:1-17.
Lefebvre, L.M. and M.W. Passer
  1974 "The effects of game location and importance on aggression in team sport." IRSS 5(2).
Leitgeb, A.
  1955 Das Verhaltinis Awischen Sport Und Gesellschaft. (The Relation Between Sport and Society.) Unpublished doctoral dissertation, University of Graz, Graz, Austria.
Lenk, H.
  1965 Konflikt and Leistung in Spitzensportmannschaften. (Conflict and Achievement in Championship Crews.) Soziale Welt 16(4):307-347.
  1966 Maximale Leistung trotz inneren Konflikten. Pp. 168-172 in G. Lüschen (ed.), Kleingruppenforschung und Gruppe im Sport, Köln and Opladen: Westdeutscher Verlag. (English version, pp. 343-396 in J.W. Loy and G.S. Kenyon (eds.), Sport, Culture and Society. London: Macmillan.)
  1973 'Manipulation' oder 'Emanzipation' im Leistungssport? Die Entfremdungsthese und das Selbst des Athleten. ('Manipulation' or 'Emancipation' in high performance sports? The thesis of alienation and the self of the athlete.) Pp. 67-108 in H. Lenk, S. Moser and E. Beyer (eds.), Philosophie Des Sports. Schorndorf, German Federal Republic: Verlag Karl Hofmann.
  1977 Team Dynamics. Champaign, IL: Stipes.
Lenk, H. and G. Lüschen
  1975 "Epistemological problems and the personality and social system in social psychology." Theory and Decision 6:333-355.
Lenski, G.E.
  1966 Power and Privilege: A Theory of Social Stratification. New York: McGraw-Hill.
Lever, J.
  1976 "Sex differences in the games children play." Social Problems 23(4):478-487.
  1978 "Sex differences in the complexity of children's play." American Sociological Review 43(4):471-482.

Levin, J. and A. Kimmel
  1977 "Gossip columns: media small talk." Journal of Communication 27:169-175.
Lewin, K.
  1949 "Cassirer's philosophy of science and the social sciences." Pp. 269-288 in P. Schilpp (ed.), The Philosophy of Ernst Cassirer. New York: Tudor.
  1962 Field Theory in Social Science. New York: Harper.
  1964 Field Theory in Social Science: Selected Theoretical Papers. D. Cartwright (ed.). New York: Harper Torchbooks.
Lewin, K., R. Lippitt and R.K. White
  1939 "Patterns of aggressive behavior in experimentally created social climates." Journal of Social Psychology 10:271-299.
Lewko, J. and M. Ewing
  1980 "Sex differences and parental influence in sport involvement of children." Journal of Sport Psychology 2(1):62-68.
Lieberman, J.N.
  1979 Playfulness: Its Relationship to Imagination and Creativity. New York: Academic Press.
Lindblom, C.
  1980 The Policymaking Process. Englewood-Cliffs, NJ: Prentice-Hall.
Looft, W.
  1973 "Socialization and personality throughout the life span: an examination of contemporary psychological approaches." Pp. 26-52 in P.B. Baltes and K.W. Schaie (eds.), Life Span Developmental Psychology: Personality and Socialization. New York: Academic Press.
Lorenz, K.
  1963 On Aggression. New York: Harcourt, Brace, & Jovanovich.
Loy, J.W.
  1978 An exploratory analysis of the scholarly productivity of North American based sport sociologists. Paper presented at the IX World Congress of Sociology, Uppsala, Sweden.
Loy, J.W. and A. Ingham
  1973 "Play, games, and sport in the psychological development of children and youth." Pp. 257-302 in G.L. Rarick (ed.), Physical Activity: Human Growth and Development. New York: Academic Press.
Loy, J.W. and J.F. McElvogue
  1971 "Racial segregation in American sport." Pp. 113-127 in R. Albonico and K. Pfister-Binz (eds.), Sociology of Sport. Basel: Birkhäuser.

Loy, J.W., G.S. Kenyon, and B.D. McPherson
1980 "The emergence and development of the sociology of sport as an academic speciality." Research Quarterly for Exercise and Sport 51(1):91-109.

Loy, J.W., B. McPherson and G.S. Kenyon
1978a The Sociology of Sport as an Academic Speciality: An Episodic Essay on the Development and Emergence of an Hybrid Subfield in North America. University of Calgary, Canada.

1978b Sport and Social Systems. Reading, MA: Addison-Wesley.

Lueptow, L.
1980 "Social structure, social change and parental influence in adolescent sex-role socialization: 1964-1975." Journal of Marriage and the Family 93:103.

Lüschen, G.
1963 "Soziale Schichtung und Soziale Mobilität bei jungen Sportlern." Kölner Zeitschrift fur Sociologie und Sozialpsychologie 15:74-93. (English version 1969, pp. 258-276 in J.W. Loy and G.S. Kenyon (eds.), Sport, Culture and Society. New York: Macmillan.)

1966a "Leistungsorientierung und ihr Einfluss auf das soziale und personale System." Pp. 209-233 in G. Lüschen (ed.), Kleingruppenforschung und Gruppe im Sport. Köln and Opladen: Westdeutscher Verlag.

1966b Kleingruppenforschung und Gruppe im Sport. Köln and Opladen: Westdeutscher Verlag.

1967 "The interdependence of sport and culture." International Review of Sport Sociology 2:127-139.

1969 "Small group research and the group in sport." Pp. 57-66 in G. Kenyon, Contemporary Sport Sociology. Chicago: Athletic Institute.

1970 "Cooperation, association and contest." Journal of Conflict Resolution 4(1):21-34.

1979 "Organization and policy making in National Olympic Committees." International Review of Sport Sociology 14:5-20.

1980 "Sociology of sport: development, present state, and prospects." Annual Review of Sociology 6:315-347.

Lüschen, G. and G. Sage
1981 Handbook of Social Science of Sport. Champaign, IL: Stipes.

Lynn, L.F. (ed.)
1978 Knowledge and Policy: The Uncertain Connection. Washington, DC: National Academy of Science.

Magill, R.A. and M. Ash
  1979 "Academic, psycho-social, and motor characteristics of participants and nonparticipants in children's sports." Research Quarterly 50(2):230-240.
Magill, R.A., M.J. Ash and F.L. Smoll
  1982 Children in Sport: A Contemporary Anthology (2nd Ed.). Champaign, IL: Stipes.
Malewski, A.
  1964 O zastosowaniach teorii zachowania. Warsaw: PWN (German translation, Tübingen: Mohr (Interaction and Behavior).
Malinowski, B.
  1954 Magic, Science and Religion. New York: Anchor.
Mantel, R. and L. VanderVelden
  1974 "The relationship between the professionalization of attitude toward play of preadolescent boys and participation in sport." Pp. 172-178 in G. Sage (ed.), Sport in American Society. Reading, MA: Addison-Wesley.
Marjoribanks, K. and J. Walberg
  1976 "Family Socialization and adolescent behavior: a canonical analysis." The Alberta Journal of Educational Research 22:334-344.
Marsh, P.
  1975 Understanding Aggro. New Society 32:7-9.
  1978 Aggro: The Illusion of Violence. London: Dent.
Marsh, P. and R. Harré
  1978 "The world of football hooligans." Human Nature 1(10):62-69.
Marsh, P., E. Rosser and R. Harré
  1978 The Rules of Disorder. London: Routledge & Kegan Paul.
Martens, R.
  1975 Social Psychology of Physical Activity. New York: Harper & Row.
  1978 Joy and Sadness in Children's Sports. Champaign, IL: Human Kinetics.
  1981 "Thank heaven for Little League." Woman's Day (April):58-59.
Marx, K. and F. Engels
  1951 "The Communist Manifesto." In Selected Works, Vol. I. Moscow: Foreign Languages Publishing House.
  1963 "Economic and philosophical manuscripts." Pp. 63-219 in T.B. Bottomore (ed.), Karl Marx Early Writings. New York: McGraw-Hill.
Matveyev, L.
  1980 "The formation of the general theory of physical culture." Social Sciences 11(2):26-38.

McBride, E.
  1979 "Intrafamilial interaction patterns." Free Inquiry in Creative Sociology 7(1):28-33.
McCall, G. and J.L. Simmons
  1970 "The stolen base as a social object." Pp. 93-94 in G. Stone and H. Farberman (eds.), Social Psychology Through Symbolic Interaction. Waltham, MA: Xerox.
McCarrey, M. and J. Weisbord-Hemmingsen
  1980 "Impact of ethnicity and sex on personal values and socialization experiences of Canadian Anglophones and Francophones." Journal of Psychology 104:129-138.
McDonald, G.
  1977 "Parental indentification by the adolescent: a social power approach." Journal of Marriage and the Family 39:705-719.
  1978 "A reconsideration of the concept 'sex-role identification' in adolescent and family research." Adolescence 13:215-220.
McGrath, J.E.
  1964 Social Psychology: A Brief Introduction. New York: Holt, Rinehart & Winston.
McGrath, J. and I. Altman
  1966 Small Group Research. New York: Holt, Rinehart & Winston.
McGuire, W.J.
  1973 "The yin and yang of progression social psychology: seven koan." Journal of Personality and Social Psychology 26:446-456.
McMurtry, W.P.
  1974 Investigation and Inquiry into Violence in Amateur Hockey. Toronto: Ontario Government Bookstore.
McPhail, C. and A. Rexroat
  1979 "Mead versus Blumer: the divergent methodological perspectives of social behaviorism and symbolic interactionism." American Sociological Review 44:449-467.
  1980 "Et cathedra Blumer or ex liberis Mead?" American Sociological Review 45:420-430.
McPherson, B.D.
  1978 "Avoiding chaos in the sociology of sport brickyard." Quest 301:72-79.
  1981a "Socialization into and through sport involvement." Pp. 246-273 in G. Lüschen and G. Sage (eds.), Handbook of Social Science of Sport. Champaign, IL: Stipes.
  1981b "Socialization: toward a new wave of scholarly inquiry in a sport context." Paper presented at the meetings of the North American Society for the Sociology of Sport, Fort Worth, TX.

McPherson, B.D. and L. Davidson
  1980 Minor Hockey in Ontario: Toward a Positive Learning Environ-
        ment for Children in the 1980's. Toronto: Ontario Government
        Bookstore.
McPherson, B.D., L. Guppy and J. McKay
  1976 "The social structure of the game and sport milieu." Pp. 161-200
        in J. Albinson and G. Andrew (eds.), Child in Sport and Physical
        Activity. Baltimore: University Park Press.
McPherson, B.D. and C.A. Kozlik
  1980 "Canadian leisure patterns by age: disengagement, continuity
        or ageism?" Pp. 113-122 in V.W. Marshall (ed.), Aging in Canada:
        Social Perspectives. Pickering, Ontario: Fitzhenny and Whiteside.
McPherson, B.D., R.G. Marteniuk, J. Tihanyi and W.J. Clark
  1980b "The social system of age group swimming: the perceptions of
        swimmers, parents and coaches." Canadian Journal of Applied
        Sport Sciences 5:142-145.
McPherson, B.D., R.G. Marteniuk, J. Tihanyi, B. Rushall and W.J. Clark
  1980a "Age group swimming: a multi-disciplinary review of the
        literature." Canadian Journal of Applied Sport Sciences
        5:107-131.
Mead, G.H.
  1934 Mind, Self, and Society. Chicago: University of Chicago Press.
Melnick, M.J.
  1975 "A critical look at sociology of sport." Quest 25:34-47.
  1979 "The nature, scope, and concerns of the academic sub-discipline,
        sport sociology." The Physical Educator 36(1):51-54.
  1981 "Toward an applied sociology of sport." Journal of Sport and
        Social Issues 5:1-12.
  1983 "A selected bibliography of psychological factors related to
        athletic team performance." The Physical Educator 40:92-95.
Melnick, M.J. and M. Chemers
  1974 "Effects of group social structure on the success of basketball
        teams." Research Quarterly 45:1-8.
Mergen, B.
  1980 Play and Playthings of American Children. Westport, CT: Green-
        wood Press.
Merton, R.K.
  1968 Social Theory and Social Structure. New York: Free Press.
Michener, J.A.
  1976 Sports in America. New York: Random House.
Middleton, L.
  1981 "New group pushes bill of rights for athletes." The Chronicle
        of Higher Education (October 7):4.
Millet, K.
  1970 Sexual Politics. New York: Doubleday.

Mills, C.W.
  1956   The Power Elite. New York: Oxford University Press.
Milton, B.G.
  1972   Sport as a Functional Equivalent of Religion. Unpublished master's of science thesis, School of Physical Education, University of Wisconsin, Madison.
Morgan, W.R.
  1975   "Bales' role theory: an attribution theory interpretation." Sociometry 38(4):429-444.
Mortimer, J. and R. Simmons
  1978   "Adult socialization." Annual Review of Sociology 41:421-454.
Mullins, N.C.
  1973   Theories and Theory Group in Contemporary American Sociology. New York: Harper and Row.
Murphy, R.F.
  1971   The Dialects of Social Life. New York: Basic Books.
Myers, A.E. and F.E. Fiedler
  1966   "Theorie und Probleme der Fuhrung." Pp. 92-106 in G. Lüschen (ed.), Kleingruppenforschung und Gruppe im Sport. Opladen: Westdeutscher Verlag.
Nakayama, K.
  1972   "A theory of socialization system: a systems analysis approach." Japanese Sociological Review 22:60-77.
Nash, J.
  1980   "Lying about running: the functions of talk in a scene." Qualitative Sociology 3:83-99.
Noel-Baker, P.
  1964   "Sport and international understanding." Pp. 3-8 in E. Jokl and E. Simon (eds.), International Research in Sport and Physical Education. Springfield, IL: C.C. Thomas.
Nord, W.
  1973   "Adam Smith and contemporary social exchange theory." The American Journal of Economics and Sociology 32:421-436.
Novak, M.
  1975   The Joy of Sports. New York: Basic Books.
O'Connor, M., T. Foch, T. Sherry and R. Plomin
  1980   "A twin study of specific behavioral problems of socialization as viewed by parents." Journal of Abnormal Child Psychology 81:189-199.
Ogilvie, B.C. and T.A. Tutko
  1966   Problem Athletes and How to Handle Them. London: Pelham Books.
Opie I. and P. Opie
  1959   The Lore and Language of Schoolchildren. Oxford: Oxford University Press.

1969   Children's Games in Street and Playground. Oxford: Clarendon Press.

Orlick, T.
1973   "Children's sports—a revolution is coming." Journal of the Canadian Association for Health, Physical Education, and Recreation 39(3):12-14.
1974   "The athletic drop-out: a high price for inefficiency." Journal of the Canadian Association for Health, Physical Education, and Recreation 41(2):21-27.

Orlick, T. and C. Botterill
1975   Every Kid Can Win. Chicago: Nelson-Hall.

Ostler, S.
1981   "Norm Ellenberger: I cheated to win, but. . ." Los Angeles Times (September 15): Part III, 1, 9.

Parenti, M.
1978   Power and the Powerless. New York: St. Martin's.

Parkin, F.
1979   Marxism and Class Theory: A Bourgeois Critique. New York: Columbia University Press.

Parsons, T.
1949   The Structure of Social Action (2nd Ed.). Glencoe, IL: Free Press.
1951   The Social System. Glencoe, IL: Free Press.
1962   "Individual autonomy and social pressure: an answer to Dennis Wrong." Psychoanalytic Review 49:70-79.

Parsons, T., R.F. Bales and E.A. Shils
1953   Working Papers in the Theory of Action. New York: Macmillan.

Pearton, R. and G. Gaskell
1978   "Youth and social conflict." Proceedings—Ninth World Congress of Sociology, Upsala, Sweden.

Pease, D., L.F. Locke and M. Burlingame
1971   "Athletic exclusion: a complex phenomenon." Quest 16:42-46.

Penman, K., D. Hastad and W. Cords
1974   "Success of the authoritarian coach." Journal of Social Psychology 92:155-156.

Piaget, J.
1961   Play, Dreams and Imitation in Childhood. New York: Norton.
1962   The Moral Judgment of the Child. New York: Collier. (Originally published, 1932.)

Pierce, M.
1979   Keep the Kettle Boiling. New York: M.K. Pierce.

Pirtle, W.
1972   The Social Sciences: An Integrated Approach. New York: Random House.

Plessner, H.
  1952 Soziologie des Sports. (Sociology of Sport). Deutsche Univer-
        sitatszfeitung 7:9ff.
Popper, K.R.
  1957 The Poverty of Historicism. London: Routledge and Kegan Paul.
  1959 The Logic of Scientific Discovery. New York: Basic Books.
Reasons, C.E. and W.D. Perdue
  1981 The Ideology of Social Problems. Sherman Oaks, Ca: Alfred.
Redfield, R.
  1960 The Little Community and Peasant Society and Culture. Chicago:
        University of Chicago Press.
Rees, C.R.
  In Press "The child in sport—psychological and sociological aspects." In
        E. Coryllos, M. Gruber, P. Collipps, R., Feingold and D. Bal-
        sam (eds.), The Child in Athletics: A Textbook in Pediatric Sports
        Medicine. Philadelphia: Saunders.
Reichenbach, H.
  1938 Experience and Prediction. Chicago: University of Chicago Press.
Ritzer, G.
  1970 "Toward an integrated sociological perspective." Pp. 25-46 in
        W. Snizek, E. Fuhrman, and M. Miller (eds.), Contemporary
        Issues in Theory. London: Aldwych Press.
  1975 Sociology: A Multiple Paradigm Science. Boston: Allyn and
        Bacon.
  1981 Toward an Integrated Sociological Paradigm. Boston: Allyn and
        Bacon.
Roadburg, A.
  1980 "Factors precipitating fan violence: A comparison of professional
        soccer in Britain and North America." British Journal of Sociology
        31(2):265-276.
Roberts, G., D. Keilber and J. Duda
  1981 "An analysis of motivation in children's sport: the role of per-
        ceived competence in participation." Journal of Sport Psychology
        3(3):206-216.
Rose, P.
  1979 Socialization and the Life-Cycle. New York: St. Martin's Press.
Rosenbaum, J.
  1975 "The stratification of socialization processes." American
        Sociological Review 40:48-54.
Rosenblatt, P. and M. Cunningham
  1976 "Sex differences in cross-cultural perspective." Pp. 71-94 in B.B.
        Lloyd and J. Archer (eds.), Exploring Sex Differences. New York:
        Academic Press.

Rosow, I.
  1974   Socialization to Old Age. Berkeley: University of California Press.
Rossi, P.H.
  1980   "The Presidential address: the challenge and opportunities of applied social research." American Sociological Review 45:889-904.
  1981   "The ASA: a portrait of organizational success and intellectual paralysis." The American Sociologist 16(1):113-115.
Rossi, P.H. and W.F. Whyte
  1983   "The applied side of sociology." Pp. 5-31 in H.E. Freeman, R.R. Dynes, P.H. Rossi & W.F. Whyte (eds.), Applied Sociology: Rules and Activities of Sociologists in Diverse Settings. San Francisco: Jossey-Bass.
Rubin, K., G. Fein and B. Vandenberg
  1983   "Children's play." In P. Mussen (ed.), Handbook of Child Development. New York: John Wiley and Sons.
Russell, G.W.
  1974   "Machiavellianism, locus of control, aggression, performance and precautionary behaviour in ice hockey." Human Relations 27:825-837.
Ruzicka, M.F., A.T. Palisi and N.L. Berven
  1979   "Use of Cattell's three-panel model: remedying problems in small group research." Small Group Behavior 10:40-48.
Ryan, W.
  1976   Blaming the Victim (revised edition). New York: Vintage.
Ryback, D., A. Sanders, J. Lorentz and M. Koestenblast
  1980   "Child-rearing practices reported by students in six cultures." Journal of Social Psychology 110:153-162.
Saal, C.
  1972   "The significance of the family for the transfer of culture." International Journal of Sociology of the Family 21:80-86.
Sage, G.
  1972a "Machiavellianism among college and high school coaches." Pp. 45-60 in National College Physical Education Association for Men, Proceedings. 75th annual meeting, Jan. 9-12, 1972, New Orleans.
  1972b "Value orientations of American college coaches compared to male college students and businessmen." Pp. 174-186 in National College Physical Education Association for Men, Proceedings. 75th annual meeting, Jan. 9-12, 1972, New Orleans.
  1974   "Psychological implications of age-group sports programs. Paper presented at the AAHPER National Convention, Anaheim, CA.
  1979   "Theory and research in physical education and sport sociology: points of convergence and divergence." Review of Sport and Leisure 4(2):50-64.

1980 "Sport sociology, normative and non-normative arguments: playing the same song over and over and. . ." Unpublished paper presented at the First Annual Conference of the North American Society for the Sociology of Sport, Denver.

Scanlon, T. and M. Passer
1978 "Factors related to competitive stress among male youth sport participants." Medicine and Science in Sports 10(12):103-108.
1979 "Sources of competitive stress in young female athletes." Journal of Sport Psychology 1(2):151-159.

Schachtel, E.G.
1959 Metamorphosis: On the Development of Affect, Preception, Attention, and Memory. New York: Basic Books.

Schafer, W.
1966 "Die soziale Struktur von Sportgruppen." Pp. 107-117 in G. Lüschen (ed.), Kleingruppenforschung und Gruppe im Sport. Köln and Opladen: Westdeutscher Verlag.

Scheibe, C.
1979 "Sex roles in TV commercials." Journal of Advertising Research 19(1):23-27.

Schneider, F. and L. Coutts
1979 "Teacher orientations toward masculine and feminine: role of sex of teachers and sex composition of school." Canadian Journal of Behavioral Sciences 11:99-111.

Schulian, J.
1981 "The statistician is the poet of baseball." St. Paul Sunday Pioneer Press (August 9):3.

Schulz, R.
1961 Uber Wesen and Methoden Wissenschaftlicher Soziologie. (Essence and Method of Scientific Sociology.) Theorie und Praxis Der Korperkultur 10(3):108-114.

Schutz, W.
1955 "What makes groups productive?" Human Relations 8:429-465.
1958 Firo: A Three-Dimensional Theory of Interpersonal Behavior. New York: Holt, Rinehart & Winston.

Schwartz, B. and S. Barskey
1977 "The home advantage." Social Forces 55:641-661.

Schwartzman, H.
1978 Transformations. The Anthropology of Children's Play. New York: Plenum.

Scott, J.
1971 The Athletic Revolution: New York: The Free Press.
1972 "Introduction." Pp. ix-xvii in P. Hoch (ed.), Rip Off the Big Game. Garden City, NY: Doubleday.

Scott, M. and S. Lyman
  1968 "Accounts." American Sociological Review 33:46-62.
Scott, R.A. and A.R. Shore
  1979 Why Sociology Does Not Apply. A Study of the Uses of
         Sociology in Public Policy. New York: Elsevier.
Scully, G.
  1974 "Discrimination: the case of baseball." Pp. 221-274 in R. Noll
         (ed.), Government and the Sports Business. Washington, DC:
         Brookings Institute.
Seefeldt, V., D. Blievernicht, R. Bruce and T. Gilliam
  1976 Joint Legistative Study on Youth Sports Programs. Phase 1. State
         of Michigan.
  1978a Joint Legislative Study on Youth Sports Programs. Phase 2. State
         of Michigan.
  1978b Joint Legislative Study on Youth Sports Programs. Phase 3. State
         of Michigan.
Selznick, P.
  1948 "Foundations of the theory of organizations." American
         Sociological Review 13:25-35.
  1959 "The sociology of law." Pp. 115-127 in R.K. Merton, L. Broom
         and L.S. Cottrell (eds.), Sociology Today. New York: Basic Books.
Seppänen, P.
  1981 "Olympic success in a cross-cultural perspective." Pp. 91-106 in
         G. Lüschen and G. Sage (eds.), Handbook of Social Science of
         Sport. Champaign, IL: Stipes.
Sewart, J.J.
  1981 "The rationalization of modern sport: the case of professional
         football." Arena Review 5:45-51.
Shaw, G.
  1972 Meat on the Hoof. New York: St. Martin's Press.
Shaw, M.E.
  1959 "Some effects of individually prominent behavior upon group
         effectiveness and member satisfaction." Journal of Abnormal and
         Social Psychology 59:382-386.
  1981 Group Dynamics: The Psychology of Small Group Behavior.
         New York: McGraw-Hill.
Shepard, C.
  1964 Small Groups: Some Sociological Perspectives. Scranton, PA:
         Chander.
Sherif, C.
  1973 "Intergroup conflict and competition." Sportwissenschaft
         2(3):138-152.

Sherif, C. and G. Rattray
  1976 Psychological development and activity in middle childhood (5-12
        years). Pp. 97-132 in J. Albinson and G. Andrew (eds.), Child
        in Sport and Physical Activity. Baltimore: University Park Press.
Sherif, M. and C. Sherif
  1961 The Robbers Cave Experiment. Norman: University of Oklahoma
        Press.
Shibutani, T.
  1955 "Reference groups as perspectives." American Journal of
        Sociology 60:522-529.
Simmel, G.
  1950 The Sociology of George Simmel (K. Wolff, translator). New
        York: Free Press.
Simon, H.
  1962 "The architecture of complexity." Proceedings of American
        Philosophical Society 106:467-482.
Singer, J. and D. Singer
  1978 Partners in Play. New York: Random House.
Sipes, R.
  1973 "War, sports and aggression: an empirical test of two rival
        theories." American Anthropologist 75 (February):64-80.
Slepicka, P.
  1975 "Interpersonal behavior and sports group effectiveness." Inter-
        national Journal of Sport Psychology 6:14-27.
Sluckin, A.
  1981 Growing Up in the Playground. London: Routledge & Kegan.
Smelser, N.
  1963 Theory of Collective Behavior. New York: Free Press.
Smilansky, S.
  1968 The Effects of Sociodramatic Play on Disadvantaged Preschool
        Children. New York: John Wiley and Sons.
Smith, M.D.
  1973 "Hostile outbursts in sport." Sociology Bulletin 2(1):19-23.
  1977 "Aggression in sport." Sport Sociological Bulletin 6(1).
  1979 "Getting involved in sport: Sex differences." International
        Review of Sport Sociology 14:93-99.
Smoll, F.L. and R.E. Smith (eds.)
  1978 Psychological Perspectives in Youth Sports. Washington, DC:
        Hemisphere Publishing.
Snyder, E.E.
  1972 "Athletic dressing room slogans as folklore: a means of socializa-
        tion." International Review of Sport Sociology 7:89-102.

Snyder, E.E. and E.A. Spreitzer
  1976a "Correlates of sport participation among adolescent girls."
         Research Quarterly 47:804-809.
  1976b "Family influence and involvement in sports." Research Quarter-
         ly 44:249-255.
  1978 Social Aspects of Sport. Englewood Cliffs, NJ: Prentice-Hall.
  1979 "Structural strains in the coaching role and alignment actions."
         Review of Sport and Leisure 4:97-109.
  1980 Dimensions of Attraction to Sport: A Review of Research.
         American Alliance for Health, Physical Education, Recreation and
         Dance. Unpublished paper presented at the National Midwest
         District Convention, Detroit, MI.
Sorokin, P.
  1956 Fads and Foibles in Modern Sociology. Chicago: Henry Regnery.
Sorrentino, R.M. and B. Sheppard
  1978 "Effects of affiliation-related motives on swimmers in individual
         versus group competition: a field experiment." Journal of Per-
         sonality and Social Psychology 36:704-714.
Southard, D.
  1982 "A national survey: sociology of sport within American colleges
         as university physical education professional preparation pro-
         grams." Pp. 365-372 in A.O. Dunleavy, A. Miracle and C.R. Rees
         (eds.), Studies in the Sociology of Sport. Fort Worth, TX: TCU
         Press.
  1983 "Importance of selected competencies and relationship to cor-
         responding coursework in programs of teacher preparation."
         Research Quarterly 54(4):383-388.
Spreitzer, E.A., E.E. Snyder and C. Jordan
  1980 "Reflections on the integration of sport sociology into the larger
         discipline: intimations from a citation analysis." Sociological
         Symposium 30: 1-17.
Staples, C.L.
  1981 "Cumulative and reflective theorizing." Paper presented at the
         Sociological Association Annual Meeting, Toronto.
Stegmüller, W.
  1971 "Das Problem der Induktion." Pp. 13-74 in H. Lenk (ed.), Neue
         Aspekte der Wissenschaftstheorie. Braunschweig: Vieweg
Steiner, I.
  1972 Group Process and Productivity. New York: Academic Press.
Stern, N.
  1979 "The development of an interorganizational control network: the
         case of intercollegiate athletics." Administrative Science Quarter-
         ly 24:252-266.

Stevenson, C.L.
  1974 "Sport as a contemporary social phenomenon: a functional explanation." Gymnasium 11(3):8-13.
  1975 "Socialization effects of participation in sport: a critical review of the literature." Research Quarterly 46:287-301.

Stevenson, C.L. and J.E. Nixon
  1972 "A conceptual scheme of the social functions of sport." Sportwissenschaft 2:119-132.

Stogdill, R.
  1972 "Group productivity, drive, and cohesiveness." Organizational Behavior and Human Performance 8:26-43.

Stokes, R. and J. Hewitt
  1976 "Aligning actions." American Sociological Review 41:838-845.

Stolyarov, V.
  1980 "Methodology of research into sport as a social phenomenon." Social Sciences 11(2):47-59.

Stone, G.P.
  1955 "American sports: play and dis-play." Chicago Review 9:83-100.
  1965 "The play of little children." Quest 4:23-31.
  1966 "Bergiffliche Probleme in der Kleingruppenforschung." Pp. 44-65 in G. Lüschen (ed.), Kleingruppenforschung und Gruppe im Sport. Köln and Opladen: Westdeutscher Verlag.
  1969 "Reaction to Sutton-Smith paper." Pp. 148-155 in G.S. Kenyon (ed.), Aspects of Contemporary Sport Sociology. Chicago: Athletic Institute.
  1972 "Wrestling: the great American passion play." Pp. 301-335 in E. Dunning (ed.), Sport: Readings from a Sociological Perspective. Toronto: University of Toronto Press.

Strauss, A.
  1978a Negotiations: Varieties, Contexts, Processes and Social Order. San Francisco: Jossey-Bass.
  1978b "A social world perspective." Pp. 119-128 in N. Denzin (ed.), Studies in Symbolic Interaction, Vol. 1. Greenwich, CT: Jai Press.

Streib, G.F.
  1983 "Research on aging." Pp. 261-274 in H.E. Freeman, R.R. Dynes, P.H. Rossi, and W.F. Whyte (eds.), Applied Sociology: Roles and Activities of Sociologists in Diverse Settings. San Francisco, CA: Jossey-Bass.

Stryker, S.
  1980 Symbolic Interactionism: A Social Structural Version. Menlo Park, CA: Benjamin/Cummings.

332   *Sport and Social Theory*

Suchman, E.
  1967 Evaluative Research: Principles and Practice in Public Service and
        Social Action Programs. New York: Russell Sage Foundation.
Sugden, J.P.
  1980 "Toward a Marxist sociology of sport." Paper presented at the
        First Annual Conference of the North American Society for the
        Sociology of Sport, Denver.
  1981 "The sociological perspective: the political economy of violence
        in American sport." Arena Review 5:57-62.
Sutton-Smith, B.
  1969 "The two cultures of games." Pp. 135-147 in G.S. Kenyon (ed.),
        Aspects of Contemporary Sport Sociology. Chicago: Athletic
        Institute.
  1979 Die Dialektik des Spiel. Schorndorf, German Federal Republic:
        Hoffman.
  1980 "Review of 'Two Ball Games'." Contemporary Psychology
        25:745-746.
  1981 A History of Children's Play: The New Zealand Playground
        1840-1850. Philadelphia, PA: University of Pennsylvania Press.
In Press "Play theory for the rich and for the poor." In P. Gilmore and
        A. Glatthorn (eds.), Ethnography in Education: 1977 Conference,
        Philadelphia: University of Pennsylvania.
Sutton-Smith, B. and D. Kelly-Byrne
  1984 The Masks of Play. West Point, NY: Leisure Press.
Sutton-Smith, B. and S. Sutton-Smith
  1974 How to Play With Children. New York: Hawthorne.
Szasz, T.S.
  1970 "Involuntary mental hospitalization." Pp. 113-139 in T.S. Szasz
        (ed.), Ideology and Insanity. New York: Doubleday.
Tatano, H.
  1981 "The relevance of systematic general theory in sport sociology."
        Journal of Health Science, Hyushu University 3:23-35.
Taubman, P.
  1978 "Oklahoma football: a powerhouse that Barry built." Esquire
        90:91-95.
Taylor, I.
  1971 "'Football mad'—a speculative sociology of football
        hooliganism." Pp. 352-377 in E. Dunning (ed.), Sport: Readings
        From a Sociological Perspective. Toronto: University of Toronto
        Press.
Tenbruck, F.
  1972 Zur Kritik der planenden Vernunft. Freiburg: Rombach.
Thornton, R. and P. Nardi
  1975 "The dynamics of role acquisition." American Journal of
        Sociology 80:870-885.

Thune, E., R. Manderscheid and S. Silbergeld
  1980 "Personal versus relationship orientation as a dimension of sex-role differentiation." Psychological Reports 46:455-465.
Tilly, C.
  1969 "Collective violence in European perspective." Pp. 4-45 in H.D. Graham and T.R. Gurr (eds.), The History of Violence in America: Historical and Comparative Perspectives. New York: Bantam Books.
Tönnies, F.
  1957 Community and Association. East Lansing, MI: University Press. (Originally published, 1887.)
Triandis, H.
  1977 "Cross-cultural social and personality psychology." Personality and Social Psychology Bulletin 3:143-158.
Tripplett, N.
  1898 "The dynamogenic factors in pacemaking and competition." American Journal of Psychology 9(5):7-33.
Tsukada, G.
  1979 "Sibling interaction: a review of the literature." Smith College Studies in Social Work 49:229-247.
Turk, H.
  1965 "An enquiry into the undersocialized conception of man." Social Forces 43:518-521.
Turner, J.H.
  1982 The Structure of Sociological Theory. Homewood, IL: Dorsey Press.
Turner, V.
  1974 Dramas, Fields and Metaphors. Ithaca, NY: Cornell University.
Turowetz, A. and M. Rosenberg
  1978 "Exaggerating everyday life: the case of professional wrestling." In J. Haas and W. Shaffir (eds.), Shaping Identity in Canadian Society. Scarborough, Ontario: Prentice Hall of Canada.
Underwood, J.
  1980 "The writing is on the wall." Sports Illustrated (May 19):36-72.
  1981a "A game plan for America." Sports Illustrated (February 23): 64-80.
  1981b "To-do over what to do." Sports Illustrated (September 21): 34-39.
Vaillancourt, P.
  1973 "Stability of children's responses." Public Opinion Quarterly 37:373-387.
Vallee, F.G. and D.R. Whyte
  1968 "Canadian society: trends and perspectives." Pp. 833-852 in B.R. Blishen, F.E. Jones, K.D. Naegele, and J. Porter (eds.), Canadian Society: Sociological Perspectives (3rd Ed.). Toronto: Macmillan.

Vandenberg, I.
1964 The Changing Nature of Man. New York: Delta.
van de Vall, M. and C. Bolas
1980 "Applied social discipline research or social policy research: the emergence of a professional paradigm in sociological research." The American Sociologist 15:128-137.
Vanfossen, B.
1977 "Sexual stratification and sex-role socialization." Journal of Marrige and the Family 39:563-574.
Van Gennep, A.L.
1960 The Rites of Passage. Chicago: University of Chicago Press. (Originally published, 1909.)
Vaz, E.
1976 "The culture of young hockey players: some initial observations." P. 212 in A. Yiannakis, T.D. McIntyre, M.J. Melnick and D.P. Hart (eds.), Sport Sociology-Contemporary Theories. Dubuque, IA: Kendall Hunt.
1978 "Institutionalized rule violation and control in professional hockey." Proceedings from the Ninth World Congress of Sociology, Uppsala, Sweden.
Volkamer, M.
1974 "Zur aggressivitat in Konkumenz." Sportweissenschaft 1:68-79.
Wackman, D.
1977 "Learning to be consumers: the role of the family." Journal of Communication 27:138-151.
Walker, H.A. and B.P. Cohen
1981 "In the beginning there was scope: the logical implications of scope statements in formal theory." Paper presented at the Annual Meeting of the American Sociological Association, Toronto.
Wallace, R. and A. Wolf
1980 Contemporary Sociological Theory. Englewood Cliffs, NJ: Prentice-Hall, Inc.
Walsh, J. and A. Carron
1977 "Attributes of volunteer coaches." Paper presented at the Annual Meeting of Canadian Association of Sport Sciences, Winnipeg.
Warshay, L.H.
1975 The Current State of Sociological Theory. New York: David McKay.
Washburn, P.
1977 "Children and Watergate: some neglected considerations." Sociological Focus 10:341-351.
Watson, G.
1974 "Family organization and Little League baseball." International Review of Sport Sociology 9:5-32.

1976 "Reward systems in children's games: the attraction of game interaction in Little League baseball." Review of Sport and Leisure 1:93-117.

1977a "Games, socialization and parental values: social class differences in parental evaluation of Little League baseball." International Review of Sport Sociology 1(13):17-48.

1977b "Social conflict and parental involvement in Little League baseball." Quest, Monograph 27:71-86.

Watson, G. and M.W. Wells
1978 "Social motivation in games: a re-interpretation of the conflict-enculturation hypothesis." Unpublished paper presented at the Ninth World Congress of Sociology, Uppsala, Sweden.

Webb, H.
1969 "Professionalization of attitudes toward play among adolescents." Pp. 161-178 in G. Kenyon (ed.), Aspects of Contemporary Sport Sociology. Chicago: The Athletic Institute.

Weber, M.
1946 "Bureaucracy." Pp. 196-244 in H.H. Gerth and C.W. Mills (eds.), From Max Weber: Essays in Sociology. New York: Oxford University Press.

1956 The Protestant Ethic and the Spirit of Capitalism. London: Allen & Unwin.

Webster, M. and L. Smith
1978 "Justice and revolutionary coalitions: a test of two theories." American Journal of Sociology 84:267-292.

Webster's New Twentieth Century Dictionary
1961 (2nd Ed.). Springfield, MA: Merriam-Webster, Inc.

Weis, K.
1976 "Role models and the learning of violent behavior patterns." Pp. 511-524 in Proceedings of the International Congress of Physical Activity Sciences, Quebec.

Wentworth, W.
1980 Context and Understanding: An Inquiry Into Socialization Theory. New York: Elsevier.

Westkott, M. and J. Coakley
1981 "Women in sport: modalities for feminist social change." Journal of Sport and Social Issues 5(1):32-45.

White, B.L.
1975 The First Three Years of Life. New York: Prentice-Hall.

Whiting, B. and J. Whiting
1975 Children in Six Cultures: A Psycho-Cultural Analysis. Cambridge, MA: Harvard University Press.

Whitlow, S.
1977 "How male and female gatekeepers respond to news stories of women." Journalism Quarterly 54:573-579.

Whitson, D.J.
   1976 "Method in sport sociology: the potential of a phenomenological
         contribution." International Review of Sport Sociology
         11(4):53-68.
Whyte, W.F.
   1943 Street Corner Society. Chicago: University of Chicago Press.
   1980 "Exploring the frontiers of the possible: Social inventions for solv-
         ing human problems." Footnotes 8:1, 5.
   1982 "Social inventions for solving human problems." American
         Sociological Review 47:1-13.
Widmeyer, W.
   1977 When Cohesiveness Predicts Performance Outcome in Sport. Un-
         published doctoral dissertation, University of Illinois,
         Champaign-Urbana.
Widmeyer, W. and D. Gossett
   1978 "Cohesion variability and the cohesion-performance outcome in
         sport." Paper presented at the North American Society for the
         Psychology of Sport and Physical Activity, Monterey, CA.
Widmeyer, W., J. Loy and J. Roberts
   1980 "The relative contributions of action styles and ability to perfor-
         mance outcomes of doubles tennis teams." Pp. 209-218 in C.
         Nadeau, W. Halliwell, K. Newell and G. Roberts (eds.),
         Psychology of Motor Behavior and Sport 1979. Champaign, IL:
         Human Kinetics.
Widmeyer, W. and R. Martens
   1978 "When cohesion predicts performance outcome in sport."
         Research Quarterly 9:372-380.
Williams, R.
   1976 "Social science in America: the first two hundred years." Social
         Science Quarterly 59:77-111.
Willimczik, K.
   1980 "Der Entwicklungsstand der sportwissenschaftlichen
         Wissenschaftstheorie." (The Development of a Scientific Theory
         of Sport Studies—A Cross-Cultural Comparative Analysis.)
         Sportwissenschaft 10(4):337-359.
Wilson, E.K.
   1964 "Conformity revisited." Transaction 2:28-32.
Wohl, A.
   1966 "Conception and range of sport sociology." International
         Review of Sport Sociology 1:5-27.
   1970 "Competitive sport and its social functions." International
         Review of Sport Sociology 5:117-124.

1979 "Sport and social development." International Review of Sport Sociology 3/4:5-18.

Wolf, T.
1975 "Influence of age and sex of model on sex-inapproprate play." Psychological Reports 36:99-105.

Wolfe, A.
1978 The Seamy Side of Democracy: Repression in America. New York: Longman.

Wolff, K.
1950 The Sociology of George Simmel. New York: Free Press.
1959 "The sociology of knowledge and sociological theory." Pp. 567-602 in L. Gross (ed.), Symposium on Sociological Theory. New York: Harper and Row.

Wooden, J.
1972 They Call Me Coach. New York: Bantam Books.

Wrong, D.
1961 "The oversocialized conception of man in modern sociology." American Sociological Review 26:183-193.
1964 "Reply to Wilson." Transaction 2:28-32.

Yaels, W. and D. Karp
1978 "A social psychological critique of 'oversocialization': Dennis Wrong revisited." Sociological Symposium 24:27-39.

Yaffe, M.
1974 "The psychology of soccer." New Society 14:378-380.

Yerles, M.
1980 Similarities and Differences in Modes of Integration and Strategies Among French and Quebec Sport Executives. Unpublished doctoral dissertation, University of Illinois, Champaign—Urbana.

Yiannakis, A., T.D. McIntyre, M.J. Melnick and D.P. Hart (eds.)
1976 Sport Sociology—Contemporary Themes. Dubuque, IA: Kendall Hunt.

Yuchtman-Yaar, E. and M. Semyonov
1979 "Ethnic inequality in Israeli schools and sports: an expectation-status approach." American Journal of Sociology 85:576-590.

Zander, A.
1971 Motives and Goals in Groups. New York: Academic Press.
1974 "Team spirit versus the individual achiever." Psychology Today 8:65, 67, 68.
1978 "Motivation and performance of sports groups." Pp. 96-110 in W. Straub (ed.), Sport Psychology: An Analysis of Athlete Behavior. Ithaca, NY: Movement Publications.

1979   "The psychology of group processes." Annual Review of
        Psychology 30:417-451.
Zeigler, E.F.
    1980   "A systems approach to the development and use of theory and
            research in sport and physical education." Sportwissenschaft
            10(4):404-416.
Zeitlin, I.M.
    1973   Rethinking Sociology: A Critique of Contemporary Theory. New
            York: Appleton-Century-Crofts.

Index